Machine Learning

Machine Learning: Concepts, Techniques and Applications starts at the basic conceptual level of explaining machine learning and goes on to explain the basis of machine learning algorithms. The mathematical foundations required are outlined along with their associations to machine learning. The book then goes on to describe important machine learning algorithms along with appropriate use cases. This approach enables the readers to explore the applicability of each algorithm by understanding the differences between them. A comprehensive account of various aspects of ethical machine learning has been discussed. An outline of deep learning models is also included. The use cases, self-assessments, exercises, activities, numerical problems, and projects associated with each chapter aims to concretize the understanding.

Features

- Concepts of machine learning from basics to algorithms to implementation
- Comparison of different machine learning algorithms—when to use them and why—for Application Developers and Researchers
- Machine learning from an application perspective—general and machine learning for healthcare, education, business, and engineering applications
- Ethics of machine learning including bias, fairness, trust, and responsibility
- Basics of deep learning, important deep learning models, and applications
- Plenty of objective questions, use cases, and activity and project based learning exercises

The book aims to make the thinking of applications and problems in terms of machine learning possible for graduate students, researchers, and professionals so that they can formulate the problems, prepare data, decide features, select appropriate machine learning algorithms, and do appropriate performance evaluation.

Machine Learning

Concepts, Techniques and Applications

T V Geetha
S Sendhilkumar

CRC Press
Taylor & Francis Group
Boca Raton London New York

CRC Press is an imprint of the
Taylor & Francis Group, an **informa** business

A CHAPMAN & HALL BOOK

First edition published 2023
by CRC Press
6000 Broken Sound Parkway NW, Suite 300, Boca Raton, FL 33487-2742

and by CRC Press
4 Park Square, Milton Park, Abingdon, Oxon, OX14 4RN

CRC Press is an imprint of Taylor & Francis Group, LLC

© 2023 T V Geetha and S Sendhilkumar

Library of Congress Cataloging-in-Publication Data
Names: Geetha, T. V., author. | Sendhilkumar, S., author.
Title: Machine learning : concepts, techniques and applications / T.V. Geetha, S. Sendhilkumar.
Description: First edition. | Boca Raton, FL : Chapman & Hall/CRC Press, 2023. |
Includes bibliographical references and index. |
Identifiers: LCCN 2022051414 (print) | LCCN 2022051415 (ebook) | ISBN 9781032268286 (hbk) |
ISBN 9781032268293 (pbk) | ISBN 9781003290100 (ebk)
Subjects: LCSH: Machine learning.
Classification: LCC Q325.5 .G42 2023 (print) | LCC Q325.5 (ebook) | DDC 006.3/1--dc23/eng20230123
LC record available at https://lccn.loc.gov/2022051414LC ebook record available at https://lccn.loc.gov/2022051415

ISBN: 978-1-032-26828-6 (hbk)
ISBN: 978-1-032-26829-3 (pbk)
ISBN: 978-1-003-29010-0 (ebk)

DOI: 10.1201/9781003290100

Typeset in Palatino
by SPi Technologies India Pvt Ltd (Straive)

Contents

Preface

This book aims to explain machine learning from multiple perspectives such as conceptual, mathematical, and algorithmic, as well as focusing on using tools and software. However, the main focus of this book is to make readers think of applications in terms of machine learning so that readers can define their applications in terms of machine learning tasks through appropriate use cases that run throughout the chapters. Moreover, handling of data, selection of algorithms, and evaluation needed for the applications are discussed. The important issues of fairness-aware and interpretable machine learning are also discussed. The book then goes on to discuss deep learning basics and will discuss similar applications for both machine learning and deep learning, highlighting the difference between the two approaches. In addition, this book will have a large number of exercises and activities to enable the reader to understand concepts and apply them. Therefore, this book hopes to address the issue of understanding machine learning and enabling applications using machine learning.

Author Biography

T V Geetha is a retired senior professor of Computer Science and Engineering with over 35 years of teaching experience in the areas of artificial intelligence, machine learning, natural language processing, and information retrieval. Her research interests include semantic, personalized, and deep web search, semi-supervised learning for Indian languages, application of Indian philosophy to knowledge representation and reasoning, machine learning for adaptive e-learning, and application of machine learning and deep learning to biological literature mining and drug discovery. She is a recipient of the Young Women Scientist Award from the Government of Tamilnadu and Women of Excellence Award from the Rotract Club of Chennai. She is a receipt of the BSR Faculty Fellowship for Superannuated Faculty from the University Grants Commission, Government of India for 2020–2023.

S Sendhilkumar is an associate professor in the Department of Information Science and Technology, CEG, Anna University with 18 years of teaching experience in the areas of data mining, machine learning, data science, and social network analytics. His research interests include personalized information retrieval, bibliometrics, and social network mining. He is the recipient of the CTS Best Faculty Award for the year 2018 and was awarded the Visvesvaraya Young Faculty Research Fellowship by the Ministry of Electronics and Information Technology (MeitY), Government of India for 2019–2021.

1

Introduction

1.1 Introduction

The important question that can be asked is "Why is there a sudden interest in machine learning?" For anyone in the computing field, if you know machine learning you have a definite edge. Why is that? One important aspect is the huge availability of data from multiple and varied sources, for example shopping data, social network data, and search engine data becoming available online. The world today is evolving and so are the needs and requirements of people. Furthermore, now there is the fourth industrial revolution of data. In order to derive meaningful insights from this data and learn from the way in which people and the system interface with the data, we need computational algorithms that can churn the data and provide us with results that would benefit us in various ways. Machine learning facilitates several methodologies to make sense of this data. In addition, now the time is ripe to use machine learning due to many basic effective and efficient algorithms becoming available. Finally, large amounts of computational resources are now available, as we know computers are becoming cheaper and cheaper day by day. In other words, higher performance of computers, larger memory in handling the data, and greater computational power has made even online learning possible. These are the reasons why studying and applying machine learning has gained prominence, where machine learning is more about analyzing large amounts of data; the bigger the amount of data, the better the learning ability.

The challenges of the world today, which are vastly different from a few years ago, can be outlined as a largely instrumented and interconnected world with complex organizations, demanding citizens, requirements of compliance with regulations, highly automated adversaries, and diverse, evolving, and sophisticated threats. In addition, the top technology trends of 2021, in the post-COVID era, are digital workplaces, online learning, telehealth, contactless customer experience, and artificial intelligence (AI)-generated content. These challenges and trends have made AI, machine learning, and deep learning the center of the connected world of today.

Finally, we can judge the importance of a topic by the opinions expressed by eminent industrialists and researchers across the spectrum. A few quotes are as follows:

- "A breakthrough in machine learning would be worth ten Microsofts." —Bill Gates, chairman, Microsoft- Bill Gates (Lohr, 2004)
- "Machine learning is the next Internet." —Tony Tether, director, DARPA

DOI: 10.1201/9781003290100-1

- "Web rankings today are mostly a matter of machine learning." —Prabhakar Raghavan, director of Research, Yahoo
- "Machine learning is going to result in a real revolution." —Greg Papadopoulos, CTO, Sun
- "If data is the new oil, machine learning is the refinery of these large datasets." — Toby Walsh, "2062: The World that AI Made"
- "Machine intelligence is the last invention that humanity will ever need to make." —Nick Bostrom
- "Machine Learning will increase productivity throughout the supply chain." — Dave Waters
- "Machine learning is today's discontinuity." —Jerry Yang, CEO, Yahoo
- "Artificial Intelligence, deep learning, machine learning—whatever you're doing if you don't understand it—learn it. Because otherwise you're going to be a dinosaur within 3 years." —Mark Cuban

As you can see, many industries and research organizations realize and predict that machine learning is going to play a bigger and defining role in society as well as in industry.

Some of the important concepts we will be talking about are intelligence, learning, and machine learning.

1.1.1 Intelligence

Before we start off, let us look at what intelligence is. The Merriam-Webster definition of *intelligence* says that "intelligence is the ability to learn, understand or deal with new or trying situations (it is not rote learning) and the ability to apply knowledge to manipulate one's environment or to think abstractly as measured by some objective criteria." (Merriam Webster Online Dictionary 2023). One important perspective is that we should have improved some parameter that describes the learning objective. Another important aspect of intelligence is abstraction, that is the ability to find common patterns—especially true for research and even for many commercial applications. Finally, intelligence involves adaptation or the ability to apply what we have learned to the changing environment of tomorrow, or in other words intelligence requires learning to be dynamic. Some of the tasks that require intelligence include reasoning for solving puzzles and making judgements, planning action sequences, learning, natural language processing, integrating skills, and the ability to sense and act.

1.1.2 Learning

Having looked at the definition of intelligence, let us understand learning. Herbert Simon defines learning thus: "Learning is any process by which a system improves its performance from experience" (Herbert Simon, 1983). Simon explains that learning also entails the ability to perform a task in a situation which has never been encountered before. This definition is important because one important definition of machine learning is based on it. For a machine, experience comes in the form of data. One of the reasons machine learning has become important today is because of the huge amounts of data that have become available. The task we want to do may be, for example, classification, problem solving, planning, or control. The next component in the definition of learning is the improvement in performance. This improvement in performance is measured in terms of an objective which can be expressed as gain (for example, gain in profit) or loss (as loss in error).

Learning is the core of many activities including high-level cognition, performing knowledge-intensive inferences, building adaptive intelligent systems, dealing with messy real-world data, and analyzing data. The purpose of learning could be manifold, including acquiring knowledge, adapting to humans as well other systems, and making decisions.

With these definitions of intelligence and learning, we can proceed to define machine learning. We will talk about many definitions of machine learning, but before we do that, let us look at why we need machine learning.

1.1.3 Informal Introduction to Machine Learning

A machine learning model is the output generated when you train a machine learning algorithm with data. For example, a predictive algorithm will create a predictive model. Then, when you provide the predictive model with data, you will receive a prediction based on the data that trained the model. Machine learning is now essential for creating analytics models.

1.1.4 Artificial Intelligence, Machine Learning, and Deep Learning

Artificial intelligence (AI) is the name of a whole knowledge field, where machine learning is an important subfield. Artificial intelligence is defined in Collins Dictionary as "The study of the modelling of human mental functions by computer programs (Collins Dictionary, 2023)." AI is composed of two words: *artificial* and *intelligence*. Anything which is not natural and created by humans is artificial. *Intelligence* means the ability to understand, reason, plan, and so on. Therefore, any code, technology, or algorithm that enables a machine to mimic human cognition or behavior is called AI. AI uses logic, if–then rules, decision trees, and machine learning, which includes deep learning.

Machine learning is a subset of AI that involves implementing algorithms that are able to learn from the data or previous instances and are able to perform tasks without explicit instructions or programming. The procedure for learning from data involves statistical recognition of patterns and fitting the model so as to evaluate the data more accurately and provide precise results.

Deep learning is a part of machine learning that involves the usage of artificial neural networks where neural networks are one of the types of machine learning approaches. Deep learning involves a modern method of building, training, and using neural networks and performs tasks by exposing multilayered neural networks to enormous amounts of data. Deep learning machine learning algorithms are the most popular choice in many industries due to the ability of neural networks to learn from large data more accurately and provide reliable results to the user (Microsoft 2022).

Figure 1.1 shows a comparison of artificial intelligence, machine learning, and deep learning.

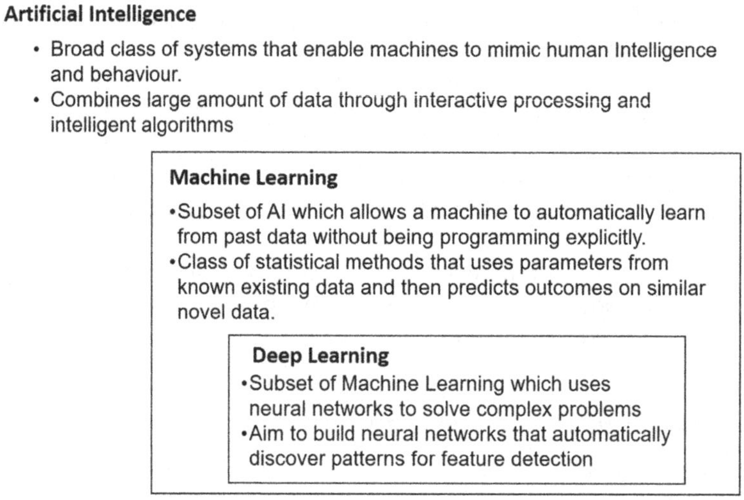

Artificial Intelligence
- Broad class of systems that enable machines to mimic human Intelligence and behaviour.
- Combines large amount of data through interactive processing and intelligent algorithms

Machine Learning
- Subset of AI which allows a machine to automatically learn from past data without being programming explicitly.
- Class of statistical methods that uses parameters from known existing data and then predicts outcomes on similar novel data.

Deep Learning
- Subset of Machine Learning which uses neural networks to solve complex problems
- Aim to build neural networks that automatically discover patterns for feature detection

FIGURE 1.1
Comparison of AI, machine learning and deep learning.

1.2 Need for Machine Learning

1.2.1 Extracting Relevant Information

We need computers to make informed decisions on new and unseen data. In the previous era we had lots of information; we just tried to find patterns from the information, and if we gave similar information we would be able to find the same answer—this is pure pattern matching. Today we are looking at finding answers from new and unseen data. Here we are talking about large volumes of data. Therefore, often it is too difficult to design a set of rules by hand. Machine learning is about automatically extracting relevant information from data and applying it to analyze new unseen data. This particular aspect talks about extracting information; that is, extracting relevant information from data, or in other words we need to cull out information from data. We apply this extracted information to analyze new data.

1.2.2 Why Study Machine Learning?

Now comes the next question—why study machine leaning? Machine learning helps to engineer better computing systems. Machine learning is a subsection of artificial intelligence—now a prominent subsection of artificial intelligence. One of the problems traditionally associated with artificial intelligence is the **knowledge engineering bottleneck**. The knowledge engineering bottleneck is the difficulty associated with acquiring knowledge. Machine learning helps to solve the knowledge engineering bottleneck since it can be used when there is a need to develop systems that are difficult or too expensive to construct manually and to handle large amount of data available (e.g., medical diagnostics). Machine learning is often used when it is difficult to continuously redesign systems by hand and when environments change over time. Thus we require a dynamic changing learning system. These are some of the reasons why instead of going for normal rule-based systems, we use machine learning.

1.2.3 Importance of Machine Learning

Where is machine learning normally used? Machine learning is used to discover new knowledge from large databases (known as data mining). **Data mining can be considered as the trigger for the renewed interest in machine learning today**. Machine learning is used to develop systems that can automatically adapt and customize themselves to individual users—the concept of *personalization*. In today's mobile environment, personalization is an important concept. Initially it started with personalization of search engines, desktops, and so on. Now personalization is becoming an important aspect of commercial products, and so automatically adapting and customizing your products to suit individual users requires the help of machine learning.

Machine learning specifically assumes importance in situations where human expertise does not exist, such as in navigating on Mars. Some tasks cannot be defined well; you have to define the task only through examples. One example is medical diagnosis, and another example is recognition of faces. You cannot define how you will recognize a face; you can only give positive and negative examples, analyze the features, and then decide on the recognition task. Such tasks where you can explain only through examples is another reason to study machine learning. Another important aspect of machine learning is finding relationships and correlations which can be hidden within large amounts of data, where by data we mean not only databases, but all types of data including images, speech, text, video, and so on. In this case, handwritten rules and equations are too complex to define. This is another reason why we should study machine learning and learn general models which are good and useful approximations of the abundant data. Machine learning is also important when humans are unable to explain their expertise such as speech recognition, bicycle riding,. Moreover, machine learning is crucial when solutions are changing over time such as routing in a computer network or financial transactions, or when solutions need to be adaptable to particular cases such as user biometrics. Machine learning is also valuable when the nature of the input and quantity of data keeps changing, such as hospital admissions or healthcare records.

1.3 Machine Learning—Road Map

In order to understand machine learning, it is necessary to study its evolution (IBM Cloud Education, 2020). It is interesting to note that the field of machine learning has a history of approximately only 60 years. Yet today machine learning forms an integral part of most activities of everyday life and all spheres of commercial activity and industry. The evolution of machine learning can be viewed from three perspectives, namely a focus on neural networks, focus on fundamental concepts and algorithms of AI, and focus on applications, competitions, and open source aspects as shown in Figure 1.2.

1.3.1 Early History

Neural networks first came into being in 1943, when neurophysiologist Warren McCulloch and mathematician Walter Pitts created a model of neurons and their working using an electrical circuit. Meanwhile, Arthur Samuel of IBM developed a learning-based computer program for playing checkers in the 1950s. Arthur Samuel first came up with the phrase

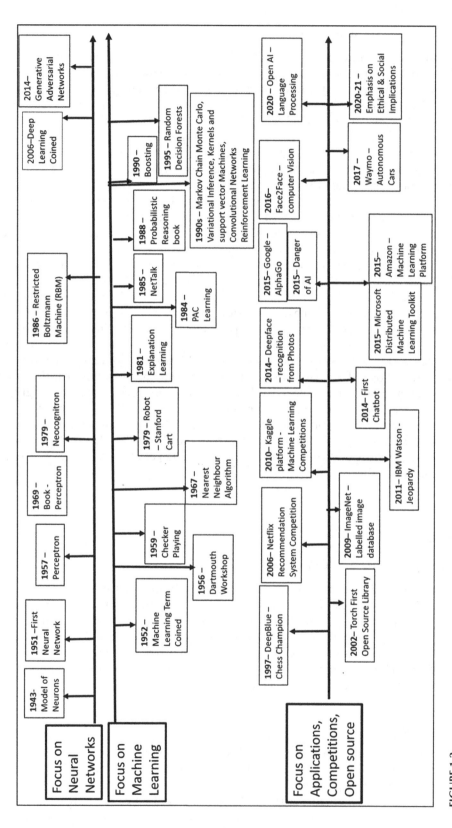

FIGURE 1.2
Machine learning—a roadmap.

"machine learning" in 1952. In 1956, a two-month Dartmouth workshop with prominent researchers of the time brainstormed about AI and machine learning.

1.3.2 Focus on Neural Networks

The first artificial neural network was built in 1951 by Minsky and Edmonds, consisting of 40 interconnected neurons. In 1957, Frank Rosenblatt developed the perceptron, combining Hebb's model of brain cell interaction with Arthur Samuel's concepts of machine learning. Though it was considered as the first successful neuro-computer, the Mark I perceptron could not recognize many kinds of visual patterns. It was only in 1990s that neural network/machine learning research saw a promising resurgence. In the 1960s, it was discovered that providing and using two or more layers in the perceptron offered significantly more processing power. The use of multiple layers led to feed forward neural networks and backpropagation. A book titled *Perceptrons: Limitations of Linear Models* was published in 1969 by Minsky and Papert. Backpropagation, developed in the 1970s, allows a network to adjust its hidden layers of neurons/nodes to adapt to new situations. Backpropagation is now being used to train deep neural networks. In 1979, FukuShima released work on a neocognitron, which was a hierarchical, multilayered type of artificial neural network (ANN) which was used in pattern recognition tasks such as handwritten character recognition. In 1986, cognitive scientist Paul Smolensky developed the restricted Boltzmann machine (RBM), which analysed a set of inputs and learned probability distributions from them.

1.3.3 Discovery of Foundational Ideas of Machine Learning

In 1967, the nearest neighbour algorithm, a basic pattern recognition algorithm, was used for mapping routes and was one of the earliest algorithms used in finding a solution to the travelling salesperson's problem of finding the most efficient route. In the late 1970s and early 1980s, artificial intelligence research had focused on using logical, knowledge-based approaches rather than algorithms. Machine learning was essentially used as a training program for AI. The 1980s was also the period when some foundational ideas were discovered. In 1979, the "Stanford Cart" was developed at Stanford University, which was a robot capable of navigating obstacles within a room. In 1981, Gerald Dejong introduced the concept of explanation-based learning (EBL). In this type of learning, the computer analyses training data and generates a general rule that it can follow by discarding the data that doesn't seem to be important. In 1984, Lee Valiant formalized the problem of learning as "probably approximately correct learning." In 1985 for the first time Terry Sejnowski used artificial neural network to invent the NetTalk program for a human-level cognitive task. This program could learn to pronounce words during the process of language acquisition. The artificial neural network aimed to reconstruct a simplified model that would show the complexity of learning human-level cognitive tasks. In 1988, Judea Pearl's book titled *Probabilistic Reasoning in Intelligent Systems* introduced the concept of Bayesian Networks.

1.3.4 Machine Learning from Knowledge-Driven to Data-Driven

During the 1990s, the work in machine learning shifted from the knowledge-driven approach to the data-driven approach. The focus of machine learning shifted from the approaches inherited from AI research to methods and tactics used in probability theory and statistics. Programs were created that could analyse large amounts of data and draw conclusions from the results. In 1990, Robert Schapire and Yoav Freund introduced boosting for machine learning in order to enhance the predicting power by combining many weak machine learning models and combining them using either averaging or voting. In 1995, Tin Kam Ho introduced the random decision forests that merged multiple decision trees into a forest to improve accuracy. However, in general the 1990s was considered the "AI Winter" period, where funding for AI research was low. However, this was also the golden period for AI research, including research on Markov chain Monte Carlo, variation inference, kernels and support vector machines, boosting, convolutional networks, and reinforcement learning. In addition, there was the development of the IBM Deep Blue computer, which won against the world's chess champion Garry Kasparov in 1997.

1.3.5 Applied Machine Learning—Text and Vision and Machine Learning Competitions

The 2000s was the age for applied machine learning where vision and natural language processing (NLP) adopted machine learning techniques. The term *deep learning* was coined by Geoffrey Hinton in 2006 to explain a brand-new type of algorithm that allows computers to see and distinguish objects or text in images or videos. In 2002, Torch, the first open-source software library for machine learning, was released. In 2006, Netflix launched a competition where the goal was to create a machine learning algorithm which was more accurate than the then current Netflix version for user recommendation. In 2010, Kaggle was launched originally as a platform for machine learning competitions.

1.3.6 Deep Learning—Coming of Age of Neural Nets

In 2009, a massive visual database of labelled images, called ImageNet, was released by Fei-Fei Li, which provided good training data enabling extensive research in deep learning. The 2010s was the deep learning era where systems based on neural nets improved their performance on speech-to-text and object recognition, resulting in increasing adoption of machine learning by the technology industry. In 2011, IBM's Watson managed to beat human competitors at Jeopardy. Moreover, in 2012, Google developed Google Brain equipped with a deep neural network that could learn to discover and categorize objects (in particular, cats). In 2014, a group of scientists developed the generative adversarial networks (GAN) that enable the generation of new data based on the training data.

1.3.7 Industrial Participation and Machine Learning

In 2014, Facebook introduced DeepFace, a special software algorithm able to recognize and verify individuals on photos at the same level as humans. In the same year Google introduced Sibyl, a large-scale machine learning system used for ranking products and pages and measuring user behaviour and for advertising. Again in 2014 the first chatbot that was considered to pass the Turing test, named "Eugene Goostman," was developed by three friends. In 2015, Amazon launched its own machine learning platform, making machine learning more accessible and bringing it to the forefront of software development. Moreover, in 2015, Microsoft created the Distributed Machine Learning Toolkit, which enabled developers to efficiently distribute machine learning problems across multiple machines. During the same year, however, more than three thousand AI and robotics researchers endorsed by figures like Elon Musk, Stephen Hawking, and Steve Wozniak signed an open letter warning about the dangers of autonomous weapons that could select targets without any human intervention.

In 2015, Google's artificial intelligence algorithms managed to beat a professional player at the Chinese board game Go. Go is considered the world's most complex board game. The AlphaGo algorithm developed by Google won five out of five games in the competition, bringing AI again into prominence. In 2017, Waymo started the testing of autonomous cars based on machine learning.

In 2020, Open AI announced a ground-breaking natural language processing algorithm, GPT-3, with a remarkable ability to generate human-like text when given a prompt. Today, GPT-3 is considered the largest and most advanced language model in the world, using 175 billion parameters and Microsoft Azure's AI supercomputer for training. Currently there is a huge focus on ethical and societal implications of machine learning.

1.4 What Is Machine Learning?

In simple terms, machine learning is the most popular technique of predicting the future or classifying information to help people in making necessary decisions. Here again we are explaining the most common type of machine learning, supervised learning. Now let us try to understand how we solve a specific problem. We write a program that encodes a set of rules that are useful to solve the problem. However, in many cases it is very difficult to understand the problem and write specific rules to solve it, such as example how to determine whether a given image is that of a human. A machine learning system is not directly programmed to solve the problem but develops its own program or model based on a large number of examples and on trial-and-error experience on how to solve the problem. Figure 1.3 shows the difference between traditional programming and machine learning. Therefore, machine learning tries to learn an unknown function based on the input–output pairs called training data.

Machine learning algorithms are trained over examples through which they learn from past experiences and also analyze the historical data. In other words, as they train over the examples again and again, machine learning algorithms are able to identify patterns in order to make predictions about the future. There are many definitions of machine learning that have evolved over the years.

The first definition of machine learning was given by Arthur Samuel in 1959: "Machine Learning is the field of study that gives computers the ability to learn without being explicitly programmed." (Samuel, 1959)

In machine learning you are not going to give the program, but you are going to define that this is the data, this is our expected output, and the computer has to model this or program itself such that you get the necessary output when you give the data. The program is the output of machine learning. This is one of the earliest definitions of machine learning which holds good even today because today machine learning is all about learning a model.

Another perspective in the definition of machine learning has to do with learning from data and improving performance. Herbert Simon (1970) defined machine learning as "Any process by which a system improves its performance."

In 1983, Simon again defined machine learning in the same vein as follows: Learning denotes changes in the system that are adaptive in the sense that they enable the system to do the same task (or tasks drawn from a population of similar tasks) more effectively the next time.

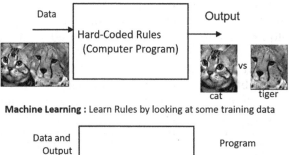

FIGURE 1.3
Traditional programming versus machine learning.

Tom Mitchell (Mitchell, 2017) defined machine learning as a computer program that improves its performance at some task through experience (1997). His definition reads,

> A Computer Program is said to learn from past experience E with respect to some class of tasks T and performance measure P, if its performance at tasks in T, as measured by P, improves with the experience E.

Machine learning is thus the study of algorithms that improve their performance at some task with experience. As an example, in the game playing scenario, the experience or data could be games played by the program against itself, and the performance measure is the winning rate. As another example, let us consider an email program that observes which mails you mark as spam and which you do not and based on these observations learns to filter spam. In this example, classifying emails as spam or not spam is the task T under consideration, observing the labelling of emails as spam and not spam is the experience E, and the fraction of emails correctly classified is the performance criterion P.

In fact, Tom Mitchell was the first person to come out with a book on machine learning. We will be discussing the components of Mitchell's definition later. Later on, Ethem Alpaydin (Alpaydin, 2020), the author of a machine learning book, gave the following definition:

> "Machine learning is programming computers to optimize a performance criterion using example data or past experience."

Here he explains machine learning as a subset of AI which uses statistical methods to enable machines to improve with experience, enables a computer to act and take data driven decisions to carry out a certain task, and uses algorithms designed in such a way that they can learn and improve over time when exposed to new data. This view is reflected in by other authors:

> The goal of machine learning is to develop methods that can automatically detect patterns in data, and then to use the uncovered patterns to predict future data or other outcomes of interest.

(Kevin P. Murphy, 2012)

> The field of pattern recognition is concerned with the automatic discovery of regularities in data through the use of computer algorithms and with the use of these regularities to take actions.
>
> **(Christopher M. Bishop, 2013)**

Another definition was given by Svensson and Söderberg in 2008 (Svensson and Söderberg 2008) where the focus for the first time was on the methods used namely computational and statistical methods. This definition gives emphasis to data mining, because at that time data mining was perhaps the only important aspect of machine learning:

> Machine learning (ML) is concerned with the design and development of algorithms and techniques that allow computers to "learn". The major focus of ML research is to extract information from data automatically, by computational and statistical methods. It is thus closely related to data mining and statistics.

Therefore, in conclusion, we can describe machine learning as a system that learns models (programs) from input data and output that optimize performance for a specified class of tasks using example data or past experience by automatically detecting patterns in data utilizing computational and statistical methods.

1.5 Explaining Machine Learning

The next important question is understanding the magic of machine learning. In this section we will discuss only one type of machine learning, namely supervised machine learning. In simple terms this type of machine learning is based on most definitions of machine learning, namely we give input and output—in other words, labelled data—and during the training phase, learn a model based on this labelled data using an appropriate machine learning algorithm, and then during the prediction phase use this model to obtain or predict output about hitherto unknown input data (Figure 1.4).

Now the learning model actually generalizes over the data and is the main idea of machine learning. Discussing in detail, let us assume we are given a set of data samples (input) having a number of fields, which are known as independent variables or features. Associated with each data sample is the target value or labels or dependent variables. This set of independent and dependent data is called the training Set (Figure 1.5). The learning from this training set is encapsulated as a model. Each model represents a hypothesis, which is essentially the relationship of the independent to dependent variables based on the ability to generalize.

Let us consider some examples explaining the preceding model of machine learning. First let us discuss the case of **text classification**, where given a text file we want it to be classified. The first step in understanding how to use machine learning for text classification is to prepare the input data set or the training data. In our case, the input is a set of documents along with the label or class associated with each document. Another important criterion at this stage is the features used to represent the document. We will look at this issue in detail later on. The training data is used to learn a classifier model. There are different ways to build this model. For the moment we assume that the training data set along with the labels are sufficient to learn the classifier model. Once the model is learned, then a new document is given to it as input, and the model outputs the class of the new document. Now when a new text file is given to this model, it would output the class (Figure 1.6a).

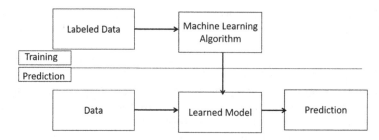

FIGURE 1.4
Training and prediction model of machine learning.

Number of Samples	Values of Independent Variables/Features			
Sample1	Field1 Value	Field2 Value	....	FieldM Value
Sample 2	Field1 Value	Field2 Value	....	FieldM Value
.....	....	....	....	....
......	....	....	....	....
Sample N	Field1 Value	Field2 Value	....	FieldM Value

Number of Samples	Dependent Variables /Target Values
Sample1	Targetvalue1
Sample 2	Targetvalue2
......	....
Sample N	TargetvalueN

FIGURE 1.5
Data samples and target values.

The next slightly different example is the **game playing** example. This is an interesting example because the training data, new samples, and output can be specified in different ways. For example, the input could be specified as a state of the chessboard and the best move for that state, where the new sample would be just a state (hitherto unseen) and the learning would output the best move. On the other hand, the input could be a sequence of moves starting from the initial position leading to a final position with the final position being marked as win or loss. The specification could also be altered where the training data consists of board positions and how many times the particular move from the board position resulted in a win. This explanation is to impress upon you that the same problem can be specified and represented in different ways. The learning involved could be finding a sequence of moves that would result in a win. In Figure 1.6b, the training data consists of the sequence of moves of many games played and whether the game resulted in a win or a loss. The learning model uses this training data to decide the strategy of searching and evaluating whether a move from the current board is likely to end in a win. Based on this evaluation, the model suggests the best move possible from the current board position. The next example we will consider is the case of **disease diagnosis**. Here the input to the training phase is a database of patient medical records, with the target value indicating whether the disease is present or absent. In this case the learned disease classifier when given the new patient's data would indicate the absence or presence of the disease

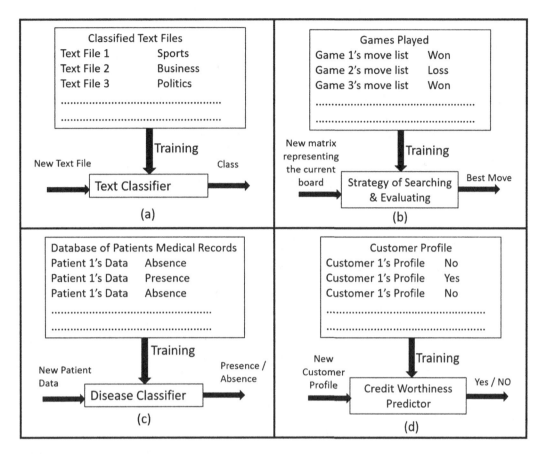

FIGURE 1.6
Examples of machine learning.

(Figure 1.6c). Another example is **checking creditworthiness** of a customer for giving a loan. Here the input would be the previous customer profiles along with labels indicating whether the loan was repaid or not. The model, when given a new customer, will predict whether he or she is creditworthy (Figure 1.6d). We should understand at this early stage that the effectiveness of machine learning depends on the features of the input we use and how we represent it. Depending on the learning task at hand, the features can be different.

Now we will go a little more in detail to two examples of machine learning where we try to understand the features that are used. The first is one where we want to label the mention of all names of organizations in text articles. As human beings, how would we approach the problem? One simple approach would be to use a list or dictionary of organization names. But this comes down to a look-up table approach. Another approach is to look for features that would indicate an organization name like words beginning with capital letters or identifying typical expressions such as *$Organization manufactures* or *$Organization and Sons*. We also need training data where each word is marked as $Organization or $Other. Now we have to fit a model such that we can label words as $Organization in a new article.

1.6 Areas of Influence for Machine Learning

Machine learning is a subfield of computer science that evolved from the study of pattern recognition and computational learning theory in artificial intelligence. Machine learning algorithms for acquiring knowledge are based on artificial intelligence. Statistics plays a very important role in machine learning. Primarily machine learning uses unknown probability distributions to learn. Brain models have been used for modeling the cognitive process by using nonlinear elements with weighted inputs for learning. This is the principle behind artificial neural networks. Machine learning also studies how to model biological evolution to improve the program performance.

1.7 Applications of Machine Learning

Now comes the important question, who is actually using machine learning? In the current scenario, the answer to this question is almost everyone, including you and me in our everyday lives. Most industries working with large amounts of data have recognized the value of machine learning. Some of the successful applications of machine learning include learning to recognize spoken words (SPHINX; Lee 1989), learning to drive an autonomous vehicle (ALVINN; (Pomerleau 1988)), learning to classify celestial objects (Fayyad et al. 1995), Learning to play world-class backgammon (TD-GAMMON; Tesauro 1992), designing the morphology and control structure of electro-mechanical artefacts (GOLEM; Lipton, Pollock 2000).

In general, applications of machine learning include computer vision and robotics including detection, recognition, and categorization of objects; face recognition; tracking objects (rigid and articulated) in video and modeling visual attention; speech recognition; recommendation systems (which products/books to buy); computer security, and so on. Some other applications of machine learning in the real world include machine translation, question answering, social network analysis, weather prediction, autonomous vehicles, and so on (Harrington, 2012).

1.7.1 Applications of Machine Learning Across the Spectrum

By analyzing and obtaining insights from this data in real time, organizations are able to leverage the data, work more efficiently, or gain advantage over their competitors. Now let us look at who uses machine learning in one way or another. Figure 1.7 shows the different application areas of machine learning.

Financial services such as banks and other financial enterprises use machine learning to identify important insights in data and to prevent fraud. The analysis of data can predict the price and market for investment opportunities. Data mining can help to identify clients with high-risk profiles or detect usage patterns to detect fraud.

Government agencies use machine learning to gain insight into multiple sources of data to improve services provided for public safety and utilities. Analyzing sensor data, for example, identifies ways to increase efficiency and save money. Machine learning can identify ways to increase efficiency and save money, and can help to detect fraud and minimize identity theft.

| Financial Services
Fraud Prediction
Price & Market Prediction
Credit Profile | Government Agencies
Minimize Identity Theft
Improve Efficiency
Save Money | Health Care
Medical Diagnosis &
Prognosis
Drug Discovery
Health Monitoring |
|---|---|---|
| Retail
Personalize Shopping
Experience
Targeted Marketing
Price Optimization | Oil and Gas Industry
Discover Energy Sources
Efficient Distribution | Transportation
Optimized Routing
Increase Profitability |
| Web Applications
Information Retrieval
Data Visualization | Social Media
Sentiment Analysis
Spam Filtering
Soacial Network Analysis | Virtual Assistants
Natural Language
Processing & Intelligent
Agents |

FIGURE 1.7
Application areas of machine learning.

Health care is another industry where machine learning is used in a variety of ways. Due to the advent of wearable devices and sensors, patient data can be assessed in real time. Machine learning provides methods, techniques, and tools that can help in solving diagnostic and prognostic problems in a variety of medical domains. It is being used for the analysis of the importance of clinical parameters and of their combinations for prognosis. Machine learning is also being used for data analysis, such as detection of regularities in the data by appropriately dealing with imperfect data, interpretation of continuous data used in the intensive care unit, and for intelligent alarms resulting in effective and efficient monitoring. Machine learning methods can help the integration of computer-based systems in the healthcare environment providing opportunities to facilitate and enhance the work of medical experts and ultimately to improve the efficiency and quality of medical care. Machine learning is also used in biology in medicine for drug discovery and computational genomics (analysis and design).

Retail websites use machine learning to recommend items based on analyzing buying history and to personalize shopping experience, devise a marketing campaign, decide price optimization, plan supply, and gain customer insights.

The **oil and gas industry** uses machine learning to discover new energy sources, analyze minerals in the ground, predict refinery sensor failure, and enable streamlining oil distribution for efficiency and cost effectiveness.

Transportation uses machine learning to analyze data to identify patterns and trends in order to make routes more efficient and predict potential problems to increase profitability. Machine learning also improves the efficiency of delivery companies and public transportation.

Web-based applications of machine learning are discussed next. The web contains lot of data. Tasks with very big datasets often use machine learning, especially if the data is noisy or nonstationary. Web-based applications include spam filtering, fraud detection, information retrieval (finding documents or images with similar content), and data visualization where huge databases are displayed in a revealing way.

Social media is based on machine learning where it is used for sentiment analysis, spam filtering, and social network analysis.

Virtual assistants: natural language processing and intelligent agents are areas where machine learning plays an important part.

1.7.2 Machine Learning in the Big Data Era

The definition of machine learning has changed with the advent of the big data era. Machine learning is now also defined as the science of finding patterns and making predictions from data based on multivariate statistics, data mining, pattern recognition, and predictive analytics. Machine learning is generally effective in situations where deep and predictive insights need to be uncovered from data sets that are large, diverse, and rapidly changing. These data sets possess the characteristics of what we today call big data. In this situation machine learning methods outperform traditional methods on accuracy, scale, and speed. High-performance machine learning enables the analysis of all of a big data set rather than a sample of it. This scalability not only allows predictive solutions based on sophisticated algorithms to be more accurate but also drives the importance of software's speed to interpret the billions of rows and columns in real time and to analyze live streaming data.

1.7.3 Interesting Applications

A number of interesting applications combine the effectiveness of both machine learning and big data processing.

Example 1 Automating employee access granting and revocation

One such application is the automation of employee access granting and revocation. Amazon uses its large data set of employee roles and employee access levels and uses a machine learning algorithm that will predict which employees should be granted access to what resources in an effort to minimize the human involvement required to grant or revoke employee access.

Example 2 Protecting animals

An algorithm was developed by Cornell University to identify whales in the ocean based on audio recordings so that ships can avoid hitting them. Similarly, Oregon State University developed an algorithm to determine which bird species are on a given audio recording collected in field conditions.

Example 3 Identifying heart failure

In this case a machine learning algorithm was developed that combs through physicians' free-form text notes (in the electronic health records) and synthesizes the text using NLP. This task extracts information similar to what a cardiologist can get when reading through another physician's notes.

Example 4 Predicting hospital readmissions

In this case a predictive model based on additive analytics identifies which patients are at high risk of readmission and helps to predict emergency room admissions *before* they happen, thus improving care outcomes and reducing costs.

1.8 Identifying Problems Suitable for Machine Learning

Before we start to apply machine learning, we need to understand the problems that are suited for it. Therefore, identification of problems for Machine Learning is important. We need to **focus on problems that would be difficult to solve with traditional programming**. Let us consider the example of Smart Reply. It was discovered that users spent a lot of time replying to emails and messages; therefore, a product that could predict likely responses could save user time. This is a type of application fit for machine learning. Another example suitable for machine learning was Google Photos, where the task was to find a specific photo by keyword search without manual tagging. Both these problems cannot be solved using traditional programming since there is no clear approach. However, machine learning can solve these problems by discovering patterns from the data and adapting with them.

In order to apply machine learning, we need to know the problem we want to solve before concentrating on collecting data. We should be prepared to have some of our assumptions about the problem and the data challenged. It is also important to note that machine learning requires a large amount of relevant data. The task to **discover the features relevant to the problem** is another important requirement. Problems identified for machine learning should not only be predictive but should also result in decision making.

As discussed earlier, a well-posed learning problem should not only be associated with a well-defined task but should **be clear about the performance measure and the experience we use for gathering data**. As an example, let us consider the handwritten digit classification problem. The task T is to map the image of {0.....,9}, the performance measure P is the percentage of correctly classified images, and experience E is the digits obtained from a postal office.

Some problems are not very interesting learning problems. Examples include learning to sort a given set of numbers, which we can solve without experience by just knowing the definition of sorted lists, or learning the speed of a ball falling from the Leaning Tower of Pisa, which we can solve using a well-defined physical model. Therefore, we can conclude that machine learning is for tasks which cannot efficiently be modeled exactly, but where experience is available.

It is important to note that we could have ill-posed learning problems. Examples of such ill-posed problems include "make something reasonable with my email" where no clear objective is given; is it simply to delete the email? Other examples of ill-posed problems include learning to draw a curve through given points (we are not satisfied with every curve) or to learn an arbitrary binary series (we cannot learn random series). Hence, we can conclude that machine learning is for tasks which are learnable, where structure is available (inductive bias), and for which there is a well-defined target.

1.9 Advantages of Machine Learning

As we have already discussed, use of machine learning has many advantages. Let us summarize some of the main advantages.

- **Alleviating knowledge acquisition bottlenecks**: One of the major problems associated with artificial intelligence, especially a rule-based system, is the *knowledge acquisition bottleneck*. The use of machine learning to a large extent eliminates the need for knowledge engineers, and therefore the construction of knowledge bases becomes scalable.

- **Adaptive nature**: Another important problem of earlier expert systems was the inability to adapt to new domains and changing environments. Machine learning makes it possible to be adaptive to the changing conditions and easy to migrate to new domains.

- **Identification of trends and patterns**: Machine learning can review large volumes of data and discover specific trends and patterns that is not apparent to people. For instance, for e-commerce websites, machine learning understands the browsing behaviours and purchase histories of users in order to help cater to the right products, deals, and reminders relevant to them. The system also uses the results to reveal relevant advertisements to them.

- **Automation**: Machine learning provides the ability for systems to learn, make predictions, and autonomously improve the algorithms. One common example is antivirus software, which learns to filter new threats as they occur.

- **Continuous improvement**: As machine learning algorithms gain experience, they use the data newly collected to enhance the learning model and hence enable them to make better decisions. As an example, a machine learning forecast model can be used to predict weather. As more data is obtained, the algorithm learns to make more accurate predictions faster.

- **Handling multidimensional and multi-variety data**: Machine learning algorithms are capable of handling data that are multidimensional and multi-variety even in dynamic or uncertain environments.

- **Tailoring applications**: It is possible to tailor an application to make it more personalized and targeted to the appropriate users.

1.10 Disadvantages of Machine Learning

With all the advantages to its powerfulness and popularity, machine learning also has some disadvantages. Data acquisition is a major issue. Machine learning requires massive data sets for training, which need to be inclusive/unbiased and of good quality. Machine learning requires sufficient time and resources for it to be effective. Machine learning needs time to allow the algorithms to learn and achieve considerable accuracy and relevancy. Machine learning also needs massive resources of both storage and computing power. Machine learning is autonomous but highly susceptible to errors. Let us assume we train a machine learning algorithm with small and not inclusive data sets. This results in biased predictions based on the biased training set. This circumstance can set off a chain of errors that can go undetected for long periods of time. In addition, on detection it is not easy to recognize the source of the issue, but even more difficult to take corrective action.

1.11 Challenges of Machine Learning

In spite of the numerous advantages of machine learning, there are many challenges to be faced before we build successful machine learning systems. These include for example the difficulty in modeling the difference between two images, where we need to choose an appropriate data representation and difference metric so that the model can depict the difference. The other major challenge is in the learning process itself. We need to design the learning process in such a way that it models well by accurately predicting the seen data and at the same time generalizes well so that it can predict for unseen data.

Another major challenge is the ability to accurately interpret results generated by the algorithms, and there is a need for an appropriate algorithm for the purpose. As an example, when we use a clustering algorithm, it is necessary to interpret or determine what each cluster represents.

Machine learning is often used for anomaly detection. However, the challenge is to decide what constitutes an anomaly. Similarly, machine learning can identify correlations or connections between two or more entities, but it is hard to explain why such a connection happened.

Another important requirement of machine learning is data. When we do not have data to train a model, machine learning does not work, and in such circumstances, it is best to use a heuristic rule-based system.

1.12 Summary

- Outlined the different definitions of machine learning
- Explained the need for machine learning and its importance.
- Explored the history of machine learning from different perspectives
- Explained machine learning
- Discussed different applications of machine learning
- Outlined the advantages, disadvantages, and challenges of machine learning

1.13 Points to Ponder

- Can you give a flowchart on how human beings learn to read?
- Is machine learning needed to perform sorting of numbers?
- Why do you think machine learning is suitable for handwriting recognition?
- What is experience in machine learning terms?
- Can you list the important components of machine learning that evolved over the years?

E.1 Exercises

E.1.1 Suggested Activities

E.1.1.1 Fill the following table for the human learning process (use your imagination). Some of the problems are intuitive, and some can use different criteria; however, you are required to outline as shown:

Problem	Data (Experience) Needed	Features Needed for Learning	Process Used	How Will You Evaluate Quantitatively?
Classifying the furniture in a room				
Grouping vegetables in a basket				
Making a sandwich				
Recognizing a cow				
Understanding a lecture				
Learning to play tennis				

E.1.1.2 Give and describe an example data set with values of data with 10 data samples having five independent variables or features and one dependent variable or target for classifying the students in a class.

E.1.1.3 Develop simple models (as shown in Figure 1.6) for the following problems:
  a. Image classification
  b. Finding the best route to travel
  c. Weather prediction

Self-Assessment Questions

E.1.2 Multiple Choice Questions

Give answers with justification for correct and wrong choices:

E.1.2.1 What is intelligence?
  i   Thinking in detail
  ii Rote learning with large amounts of data
  iii The ability to learn, understand or deal with new or trying situations

E.1.2.2 What is machine learning?
  i   Discovering new knowledge from large databases
  ii Large amounts of data becoming available
  iii When a computer program learning from experience E with respect to some class of tasks T and performance measure P

E.1.2.3 What is the knowledge engineering bottleneck?
    i It is difficult or expensive to acquire data manually to develop learning systems.
    ii It is the bottleneck that prevents learning because there is too much data.
    iii Many basic effective and efficient algorithms are not available.

E.1.2.4 Machine learning is the field of study that gives computers the ability to learn.
    i By being explicitly programmed
    ii By being given lots of data and training a model
    iii By being given a model

E.1.3 Match the Columns

No	Match	
E.1.3.1 Intelligence	**A**	Any process by which a system improves performance from experience.
E.1.3.2 Learning	**B**	The ability to learn or understand or to deal with new or trying situations
E.1.3.3 Machine learning	**C**	The difficulty to acquire large amount of data manually
E.1.3.4 Knowledge bottleneck	**D**	When a computer program learns from experience E with respect to some class of tasks T and performance measure P

E.1.4 Sequencing

Order	Please Arrange in Descending Order (Timeline from Latest to Earliest)
E.1.4.1	A massive visual database of labelled images, ImageNet, was released by Fei-Fei Li.
E.1.4.2	Kaggle was launched originally as a platform for machine learning competitions.
E.1.4.3	An artificial neural network was built by Minsky and Edmonds consisting of 40 interconnected neurons.
E.1.4.4	The nearest neighbour algorithm, a basic pattern recognition algorithm, was used for mapping routes in finding a solution to the travelling salesperson's problem of finding the most efficient route.
E.1.4.5	Groundbreaking natural language processing algorithm GPT-3 was released.
E.1.4.6	The IBM Deep Blue computer won against the world's chess champion Garry Kasparov.
E.1.4.7	"Eugene Goostman" was the first chatbot that was considered to pass the Turing test
E.1.4.8	An artificial neural network was used by the NetTalk program for a human-level cognitive task.
E.1.4.9	AlphaGo was developed for Chinese complex board game Go.
E.1.4.10	Facebook introduced DeepFace, a special software algorithm able to recognize and verify individuals on photos at the same level as humans.

References

Alpaydin, E. (2020). *Introduction to machine learning* (4th Ed.). Adaptive Computation and Machine Learning Series. MIT Press.
Bishop, C. M. (2013). *Pattern recognition and machine learning* (Corr. 2nd Ed.). Springer.
Collins Dictionary. (2023). Artificial intelligence. https://www.collinsdictionary.com/dictionary/english/

Harrington, P. (2012). *Machine learning in action*. Manning.

IBM Cloud Education. (2020, July 15). Machine learning. https://www.ibm.com/uk-en/analytics/machine-learning

Lohr, S. (2004, March 1). Microsoft, amid dwindling interest, talks up computing as a career. *New York Times*. https://www.nytimes.com/2004/03/01/business/microsoft-amid-dwindling-interest-talks-up-computing-as-a-career.html

Merriam Webster Online Dictionary. (2023). Intelligence. https://www.merriam-webster.com/dictionary/

Microsoft. (2022, November 4). Deep learning vs. machine learning in Azure Machine Learning. https://docs.microsoft.com/en-us/azure/machine-learning/concept-deep-learning-vs-machine-learning

Mitchell, Tom. (2017). *Machine learning*. McGraw Hill Education.

Murphy, K. P. (2012). *Machine learning: A probabilistic perspective*. MIT Press.

Pollack, J., & Lipson, Hod. (2000). The GOLEM project: Evolving hardware bodies and brains, Proceedings. The Second NASA/DoD Workshop on Evolvable Hardware.

Pomerleau, D. A. (1988). ALVINN: An Autonomous Land Vehicle in a Neural Network in Advances in Neural Information Processing Systems 1 (NIPS 1988).

Samuel, A. L. (1959). Some studies in machine learning using the game of checkers. *IBM Journal of Research and Development, 3*(3), 210–229.

Simon, H. A. (1970). *Reason in human affairs*. Stanford University Press.

Simon, H. A. (1983). Why should machines learn? In R. Michalski, J. Carbonell, & T. Mitchell (Eds.), *Machine learning—An artificial approach* (pp. 25–37). Tioga.

Svensson, M., & Söderberg, J. (2008). Machine learning technologies in telecommunications. *Ericsson Review, 2008*(3), 29–33.

Tesauro, Gerald. (1992). Practical issues in temporal difference learning. *Machine Learning, 8*, 257277.

Weir, N., Fayyad, U. M., & Djorgovski, S. (1995). Automated star/galaxy classification for digitized poss-II. *Astronomical Journal, 109*, 2401.

2

Understanding Machine Learning

2.1 General Architecture of a Machine Learning System

One perspective of understanding machine learning (ML) is that it consists of three major components, namely representation, evaluation, and optimization. **Representation** indicates the way in which we want to characterize what is being learned. **Evaluation** is the measure of the goodness of what is being learned, and finally **optimization** indicates the optimum representation given the characterization and evaluation.

Another way of understanding machine learning is that the only objective of machine learning is to predict results based on incoming data. All ML tasks can be represented this way. The greater the variety of attributes and volume of samples, the better the performance of the machine learning technique to find relevant patterns and predict the result. Viewed from this angle, machine learning needs the following three components:

- **Data**: The more diverse the data, the better the output of the machine learning system. In case we want to detect spam, we need to provide the system with a large number of samples of both spam and non-spam messages. Similarly, if we want to forecast price of stocks, we need to provide price history; and if we want to find user preferences, we need to provide a large history of user activities.

- **Features**: Features are also known as attributes or variables. Selecting the right set of features is important for the success of machine learning. Features are factors for the machine learning system to consider, such as car mileage, user's gender, stock price, or word frequency in a text. We have to remember that the selection of features depends on the learning task at hand as well as the availability of information. When data is stored in tables, then features are column names. However, data can be in the form of pictures where each pixel can be considered as a feature.

- **Algorithms**: Any problem can be solved using any of the available machine learning algorithms. The method we choose affects the precision, performance, and size of the final model. There is one important aspect—if the data is bad, even the best algorithm won't help.

When we apply machine learning in practice, we first need to understand the domain, the prior knowledge available, and the goals of the problem to be tackled. In addition, even if the data to be considered is available, it needs to be integrated, cleaned, preprocessed, and selected. Feature selection is the next important step because this selection can make or break the success of a machine learning system. Another issue is that some of the features

DOI: 10.1201/9781003290100-2

may be sensitive or protected. The next issue is the choice of the learning model or the type of machine learning that is going to be used. Training the model on a data set and tuning all relevant parameters for optimal performance is the next component. Once we build the system, then evaluating and interpreting the results is important. Finally comes the deployment in an actual scenario. After deployment, the system is looped to fine tune the variables of the machine learning system. These top-level understandings of the machine learning process (Mohri et al. 2012) are given in Figure 2.1.

Consider the following two simple examples given in Table 2.1 to illustrate the procedure shown in Figure 2.1.

Viewed from another perspective, specifically from the supervised learning viewpoint, in machine learning the labelled input data (data with both independent and dependent variables) needs to divided into training and test sets. The training set is used to learn the hypothesis or model. The learning model depends on the type of learning algorithm used. Finally, an important component is the measurement of system performance in terms of gain or loss, which in turn depends on the type of output or goal of the system. It is also important that the system generalizes well to unknown samples.

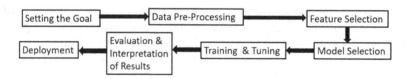

FIGURE 2.1
Applying machine learning in practice.

TABLE 2.1

Examples of the Machine Learning Process

No	Step	Example 1	Example 2
1	Set the goal	Predict heavy traffic on given day	Predict stock price
2	Choosing features	Weather forecast could be a good feature	Previous wear price could be a good feature
3	Collect the data	Collect historical data and weather for each day	Collect price for each year
4	Test the hypothesis	Train a model using this data	Train a model using this data
5	Analyse results	Is this model performing satisfactorily?	Is this model performing satisfactorily?
6	Reach a conclusion	Reason why this model is not good	Reason why this model is not good
7	Refine hypothesis	Time of year alternative feature	Average price of previous week

2.2 Machine Learning Terminology

Before proceeding further, let us clarify some terminology (Google, 2023) generally used in machine learning (Figure 2.2).

- **Examples/samples**: Items or instances for learning or evaluation.
- **Data set**: A collection of examples.
- **Features/attributes/independent variables**: Set of attributes represented as a vector associated with an example.
- **Categorical data**: In this case the features take on values from a discrete set of values. For example, consider a categorical feature such as size of a garment, which has a discrete set of five possible values: XXL, XL, L, M, and S. By representing size as categorical data, the learning model can learn the separate availability of each size.
- **Labels**: Values or categories assigned to examples. In the case of classification or clustering, these labels are categories, whereas in regression they are real numbers.
- **Numerical data**: Numerical data, also called quantitative data, are features represented as integers or real-valued numbers. For example, in a rainfall prediction model, the amount of rainfall would be represented as numerical data. Features represented as numerical data indicate that they can have a *mathematical* relationship to each other and maybe to the label.
- **Target/dependent variable**: The correct label for a training sample needed in the case of supervised learning.
- **Feature vector**: The list of feature values representing the example passed into a model.
- **Class**: One of a set of enumerated target values for a label. For example, in a binary classification model that detects spam, the two classes are *spam* and *not spam*.
- **Model**: Information that the machine learning algorithm learns after training. This model is used for predicting the output labels of new, unseen examples.

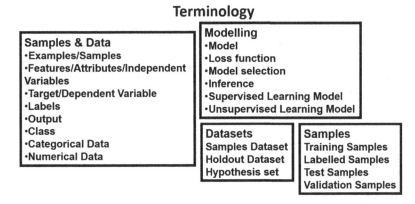

FIGURE 2.2
Machine learning terminology.

- **Output**: Prediction label obtained from input set of samples using a machine learning algorithm.
- **Training samples**: Examples used to train a machine learning algorithm.
- **Labelled samples**: Examples that contain features and a label. In supervised training, models learn from labelled examples.
- **Test samples**: Examples used to evaluate the performance of a learning algorithm. The test sample is separate from the training and validation data and is not made available during the learning stage.
- **Validation samples**: Examples used to tune parameters of a learning algorithm.
- **Loss function**: This is a function that measures the difference/loss between a predicted label using the learnt model and the true label (actual label). The aim of the learning algorithms is to minimize the error (cumulative loss across all training examples).
- **Holdout data set**: Examples intentionally not used ("held out") during training. The validation data set and the test data set are examples of holdout data. Holdout data helps evaluate a model's ability to generalize to data other than the data it was trained on. The loss on the holdout set provides a better estimate of the loss on an unseen data set than does the loss on the training set.
- **Hypothesis set**: A set of mapping functions that maps features (feature vectors) to the set of labels. The learning algorithm chooses one function among those in the hypothesis set as a result of training. In general, we pick a class of functions (e.g., linear functions) parameterized by a set of free parameters (e.g., coefficients of the linear function) and pinpoint the final hypothesis by identifying the parameters that minimize the error.
- **Model selection**: Process for selecting the free parameters of the algorithm (actually of the function in the hypothesis set).
- **Inference**: Inference refers to the process of applying trained machine learning models to hitherto unseen data to make predictions. In statistics, inference refers to the process of drawing conclusions about some parameters of a distribution obtained from observed data.
- **Supervised learning model**: Here the model trains from input data that is also associated with the corresponding outputs. This learning is similar to a student learning a subject by studying a set of questions and their corresponding answers. After studying the mapping between questions and answers, the student can possibly provide answers to new, hitherto unseen questions on the same topic.
- **Unsupervised learning model**: Training a model to find patterns in a dataset, typically an unlabelled dataset.

2.3 Types of Machine Learning Tasks

In this section we will discuss some typical types of machine learning tasks (Kumar, 2022). Please note that many of the applications can be modelled as more than one type of task. The different types of machine learning tasks are as follows Figure 2.3):

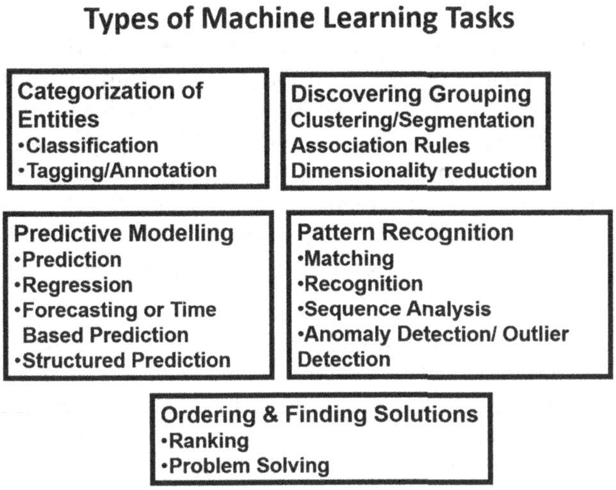

Types of Machine Learning Tasks

Categorization of Entities •Classification •Tagging/Annotation	Discovering Grouping Clustering/Segmentation Association Rules Dimensionality reduction
Predictive Modelling •Prediction •Regression •Forecasting or Time Based Prediction •Structured Prediction	**Pattern Recognition** •Matching •Recognition •Sequence Analysis •Anomaly Detection/ Outlier Detection

Ordering & Finding Solutions
•Ranking
•Problem Solving

FIGURE 2.3
Types of machine learning tasks.

- **Classification:** This is the task that is intuitive and easy to understand. This type of machine learning task distinguishes among two or more discrete classes; that is, it specifies which among a set of given categories the input belongs to. There are basically two types of classification. Binary classification distinguishes between two classes, for example whether an email is spam or not, whether a person is diagnosed with a disease or not, or whether a loan can be sanctioned to a person or not. On the other hand, multiclass classification distinguishes between more than two classes. For example, an image processing classification could determine whether an input image is a flower, a tree, or an automobile, or a student result classification system could distinguish between performance grades as excellent, very good, good, average, and poor. Note that this student result system could also be considered as a binary classification task, with the student result being pass or fail. Another variation in classification is multi-label classification, where one sample can belong to more than one class. An example would be classifying people according to their job where a cricketer, for example, can also be a businessman. Yet another variation is hierarchical classification, where a sport can be classified as cricket, tennis, football, and so on, where again within the cricket class we can have test cricket, one-day cricket, and T20 cricket. The performance of classification is often evaluated using accuracy, that is, how many unknown samples were classified correctly among all the unknown samples.

- **Regression:** This task outputs continuous (typically, floating-point) values. Examples include prediction of stock value, prediction of amount of rainfall, prediction of cost of house, and prediction of marks of a student. Again, note here that a student performance problem can also be considered as a regression task. The performance of regression is often evaluated using squared loss, which will be explained later.

- **Clustering/segmentation:** Clustering involves automatically discovering natural groupings in data. This task can be described as grouping or partitioning items into homogeneous groups by finding similarities between them. In other words,

clustering can be described as grouping a given set of samples based on the similarity and dissimilarity between them. One of the most important real-world examples of clustering is customer segmentation, or understanding different customer groups around which to build marketing or other business strategies. Another example of clustering is identifying cancerous data sets from a mix of data consisting of both cancerous and noncancerous data. The performance of clustering is often evaluated using purity, which is a measure of the extent to which clusters contain a single class based on labelled samples available. Since the evaluation uses samples that are labelled, it is considered as the external evaluation criterion of cluster quality.

- **Predictive modelling**: This is the task of indicating something in advance based on previous data available. Predictive modelling is a form of artificial intelligence that uses data mining and probability to forecast or estimate granular, specific outcomes. For example, predictive modelling could help identify customers who are likely to purchase a particular product over the next 90 days. Thus, given a desired outcome (a purchase of the product), the system identifies traits in customer data that have previously indicated they are ready to make a purchase soon. Predictive modelling would run the data and establish which factors actually contributed to the sale.

- **Ranking**: In the task of ranking, given a set of objects, the system orders them in such a way that the most interesting one comes first and then the next most interesting one, and so on; in other words, it orders examples by preferences which are represented as scores. For example, a ranking system could rank a student's performance for admission. Another important example is the ranking of web pages in the case of a search engine. The performance is measured based on the minimum number of swapped pairs required to get the correct ranking.

- **Problem solving**: This task uses using generic or *ad hoc* methods, in an orderly manner, for finding solutions to problems. Problem solving requires acquiring multiple forms of knowledge, and then problem solving is viewed as a search of a state-space formulation of the problem. With this formalism, operators are applied to states to transit from the initial state to the goal state. The learning task is to acquire knowledge of the state-space to guide search. Examples of problem-solving include mathematical problems, game playing, and solving puzzles. Performance is measured in terms of correctness.

- **Matching**: This task is about finding if one entity is like another in one or more specified qualities or characteristics. The main tasks in many applications can be formalized as matching between heterogeneous objects, including search, recommendation, question answering, paraphrasing, and image retrieval. For example, search can be viewed as a problem of matching between a query and a document, and image retrieval can be viewed as a problem of matching between a text query and an image. Matching two potentially identical individuals is known as "entity resolution." The performance measure used here is again accuracy.

- **Tagging/annotation**: This task is a part of classification that may be defined as the automatic assignment of labels or tokens for identification or analysis. Here the descriptor is called a tag, which may represent the part of speech, semantic information, image name, and so on. Text tagging adds tags or annotation to various components of unstructured data. In Facebook and Instagram, tagging notifies the recipient and hyperlinks to the tagged profile. A label is assigned for identification. The performance measure used here is again accuracy.

- **Recognition**: This task refers to the identification of patterns in data. Pattern recognition indicates the use of powerful algorithms for identifying the regularities in the given data. Pattern recognition is widely used in domains like computer vision, speech recognition, face recognition, and handwriting recognition. Performance is measured in terms of efficiency.

- **Forecasting or time-based prediction**: This task is often used when dealing with time series data and refers to forecasting the likelihood of a particular outcome, such as whether or not a customer will churn in 30 days, where the model learning is based on past data and then applied to new data. It works by analysing current and historical data and projecting what it learns on a model generated to forecast likely outcomes. Examples where forecasting can be used include weather prediction, a customer's next purchase, credit risks, employee sentiment, and corporate earnings.

- **Structured prediction**: This machine learning task deals with outputs that have structure and are associated with complex labels. Although this task can be divided into sequential steps, each decision depends on all the previous decisions. Examples include parsing—mapping a sentence into a tree—and pixel-wise segmentation, where every group of pixels is assigned a category.

- **Sequence analysis**: This task involves predicting the class of an unknown sequence. An example would be, given a sequence of network packets, to label the session as intrusion or normal. The task can also be defined as the process of analyzing sequences; in the context of bioinformatics, given protein or DNA sequences, seeks to understand their features, function, structure, and evolution. The performance measure is generally accuracy.

- **Anomaly detection/outlier detection**: This task involves analysing a set of objects or events to discover any of them as being unusual or atypical. Examples include credit card fraud detection, intrusion detection, and medical diagnosis.

- **Association rules**: This task identifies hidden correlations in databases by applying some measure of interestingness to generate an association rule for new searches. This involves finding frequent or interesting patterns, connections, correlations, or causal structures among sets of items or elements in databases or other information repositories. Examples include store design and product pricing in business and associations between diagnosis and patient characteristics or symptoms and illnesses in health care. The performance measure is generally accuracy.

- **Dimensionality reduction**: This task involves transforming an input data set (reducing the number of input variables in a data set) into a lower-dimensional representation while preserving some important properties. Dimensionality reduction aims to map the data from the original dimension space to a lower dimension space while minimizing information loss. Examples could include preprocessing images, text, and genomic data.

Although this section outlines the basics of different machine learning tasks, any application problem can be modelled based on more than one type. However, understanding the type of machine learning task associated with the problem we want to solve is the first step in the machine learning process.

2.4 Design of a Simple Machine Learning System

The steps in the design of a learning system can be listed as follows:

- Choose the training experience (the set X), and how to represent it.
- Choose exactly what is to be learnt, i.e., the *target function C*.
- Choose how to represent the target function C.
- Choose a learning algorithm to infer the target function from the experience.
- Find an evaluation procedure and a metric to test the learned function.

The design cycle (Pykes, 2021) is shown in Figure 2.4. The first step is the collection of data. The next step is the selection of features. This is an important step that can affect the overall learning effectiveness. In most cases, prior knowledge about the input data and what is to be learned is used in selecting appropriate features. The third step is model selection, which is essentially selection of a model that will fit the data. Again here prior knowledge about the data can be used to select the model. Once the model is selected, the learning step fine tunes the model by selecting parameters to generalize it. Finally, the evaluation and testing step evaluates the learning system using unseen data. The steps are explained in detail as follows.

1 **Collection of data**: As already explained, the first step is the collection of the data $D = \{d_1, d_2,...d_m,...d_n\}$, where each data point represents the input data and corresponding output (Figure 2.5). Here for simplicity we assume input **x** is one dimensional.

As a simple example, let us consider the case where we want to find the expected weight of a person given the height. Here we need to collect the data of each weight–height combination, where each point in the one-dimensional graph represents a data point. However, in all machine learning examples, the number of features or attributes considered and the number of data points are both large. The weight–height example is purely for understanding. Here note each data point d_1 can be associated with many attributes or features, say m attributes, and

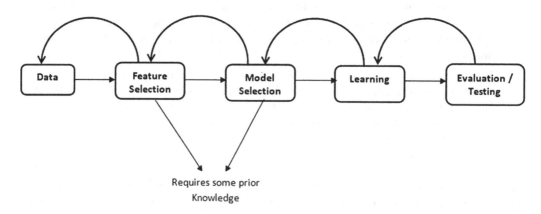

FIGURE 2.4
Design cycle.

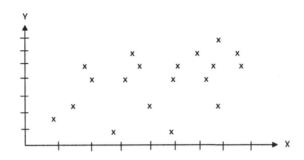

FIGURE 2.5
The collected data.

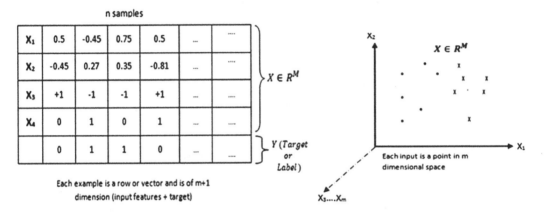

FIGURE 2.6
Visualization of a higher dimensional example.

so each data point can be m-dimensional. When dimensions are higher, the data set can be imagined as a point cloud in high-dimensional vector space. A higher dimension example can be visualized as shown in Figure 2.6.

2 **Feature selection**: Feature selection is essentially the process of selecting relevant features for use in model construction. The selection of features depends on the learning problem as given in Example 2.1.

Example 2.1 Feature Selection

The students of a class have different attributes associated with them. Examples of such attributes include marks, native place, height, and so on. If the learning required is to find the association between native place and height, the marks feature should not be selected.

Feature selection could be carried out in two ways; one is by reducing the number of attributes considered for each data point. This type of feature selection is called dimensionality reduction as shown in Figure 2.7. The second method is to reduce the number of data points considered, where the original $D = \{d_1, d_2, \ldots d_m, \ldots d_n\}$ is reduced to $D = \{d_1 \ldots d_m\}$, where $m < n$ (Figure 2.8).

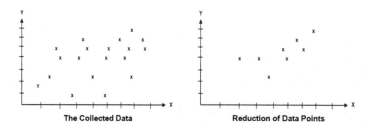

FIGURE 2.7
Reduction of attributes.

The Collected Data	**Reduction of Data Points**

FIGURE 2.8
Reduction of data points.

3 **Model selection**: The model is learnt from the training data. The next step is the model selection, where we select a model or set of models that would most likely fit the data points. Note that the model is selected manually. Associated with the selected model (or function), we need to select the parameters. We assume a very simple linear model (Equation 2.1),

$$\varepsilon = N(0, \sigma) \tag{2.1}$$

and learning is associated with fitting this model to the training data given, which in this simple example involves learning the parameters slope a and intercept b (Figure 2.9).

Here this line can help us to make prediction. Our main goal is to reduce the distance between estimated value and actual value, i.e., the error. In order to achieve this, we will draw a straight line which fits through all the points.

When the number of dimensions increases, the model can be represented as

$$y = a_m x_m + a_{m-1} x_{m-1} + \ldots \ldots a_2 x_2 + a_1 x + b + \varepsilon \tag{2.2}$$

This equation (Equation 2.2) represents the linear regression model and will be explained in detail in the chapter on linear regression. The role of error ε will now be explained. Here error is an important aspect and is defined as the difference between the output obtained from the model and the expected outputs from the training data. An error function ε needs to be optimized. A simple example of an error function is the mean squared error given subsequently, which describes the difference between the true and predicted values of output y (Equation 2.3):

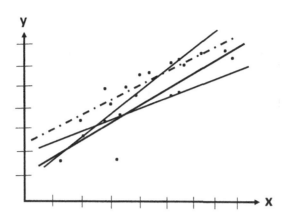

FIGURE 2.9
Choosing a model.

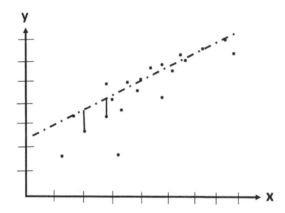

FIGURE 2.10
The error function.

$$\frac{1}{n}\sum_{i=1}^{n}\left(y_i - f\left(x_i\right)\right)^2 \qquad (2.3)$$

In this function n is the number of data points, y_i is the true value of y from the training data, and $f(X_i)$ gives the predicted value of y obtained by applying the function learnt (Figure 2.10).

4 **Learning**: The learning step involves finding the set of parameters that optimizes the error function, that is, the model and parameters with the smallest error. Our main goal is to minimize the errors and make them as small as possible. Decreasing the error between actual and estimated value improves the performance of the model, and in addition the more data points we collect, the better our model will become. Therefore, when we feed new data, the system will predict the output value.

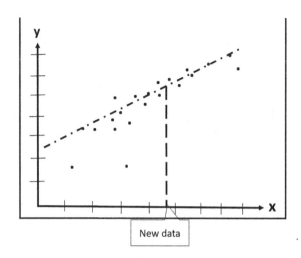

FIGURE 2.11
Testing the system.

5 **Testing and evaluation**: The final step is the application of the learnt model for
   evaluation to predict outputs y for hitherto unseen inputs x using learned function $f(x)$ (Figure 2.11).

Here we have a first look at evaluation. In the succeeding chapters we will discuss other
methods of evaluation. One method of evaluation is the simple holdout method where
the available experience (data) is divided into training and testing data. While we design
the model using only the training data, we test it using the test data. When we want to
compare the prediction performance of a regression or classification problem using two
different learning methods, we need to compare the error results on the test data set. In
the context of the discussion in this chapter, the learning method with smaller testing error
would work better.

2.4.1 Important Aspects in the Design of a Learning System

Before we discuss other interesting examples, let us discuss some of the choices we need
to make and consider the learning task of playing checkers as an illustrative example to
explain the concepts. The following are the aspects to be considered (Huyen, 2022):

*   **Choose the training experience**: The choice of training experience depends on
    the learning paradigm that is chosen, such as supervised learning, unsupervised
    learning, reinforcement learning, and so on. In this chapter we will be considering
    the context of supervised learning. These learning paradigms will be discussed in
    detail in Chapter 4. In addition, this choice also depends on the availability of data
    and whether we are considering online or offline examples.

    In addition, we need to know training experience will provide *direct* or *indirect*
    feedback. In the case of direct feedback, the system learns from examples of indi-
    vidual checkerboard states and the correct move for each. On the other hand, in
    the case of indirect feedback the move sequences and final outcomes of various
    games played are made available and credit assignment must be calculated where
    the value of early states must be inferred from the outcome.

We also need to understand the degree to which the learner controls the sequence of training examples. In some cases, the teacher selects appropriate informative boards and gives the correct move. In other cases the learner requests the teacher to provide correct moves for some board states which they find confusing. Finally, the learner controls the board states as well as the training classifications.

It is also important that the training experience represents the distribution of examples over which the final system performance P will be measured. In the case of training the checkers program, if we consider only experiences played against itself, then crucial board states that are likely to be played by the human checkers champion will never be encountered. Most machine learning systems assume that the distribution of training examples is identical to the distribution of test examples.

- **Choose the target function**: The choice of the target function is possibly one of the most important aspects of the design. The model we choose must be as simple as possible. This is in keeping with the principle of Occam's razor, which states that we need to prefer a simpler hypothesis that best fits the data. However, we need to ensure that all the prior information is considered and integrated, and we learn only the aspect that is the goal of the learning task.

- **Choose a representation**: The representation of the input data should integrate all the relevant features only and not include what is not affecting the learning. If too many features are chosen, then we will encounter the curse of dimensionality, which we will discuss later. The other aspect is the representation of the target function and model to be used. There are different types of function such as classification, regression, density estimation, novelty detection, and visualization, which to a large extent depends on how we look at the machine learning task. Then we need to decide on the model that is to be used, whether symbolic, such as logical rules, decision trees, and so on, or sub-symbolic, such as neural networks or a number of other models which we will discuss in detail in other chapters.

- **Choose the parameter fitting algorithm**: This is the step where we estimate the parameters to optimize some error or objective on the given data. There are many such parameter estimation techniques such as linear/quadratic optimization and gradient descent greedy algorithm, which also will be discussed later.

- **Evaluation**: Evaluation needs to determine whether the system behaves well in practice and whether the system works for data that is not used for training; that is, whether generalization occurs. In other words, the system finds the underlying regularity and does not work only for the given data.

2.4.2 Illustrative Examples of the Process of Design

Before we proceed, let us understand the meaning of learning in this context. We will explain learning using the examples of handwriting recognition (Nkengsa, 2018) and checkers learning problems.

2.4.2.1 Recognition of Handwritten Characters

We can define the handwriting recognition problem as:

Task *T*: Recognizing handwritten characters
Performance measure *P*: Percentage of characters correctly classified
Training experience *E*: A database of handwritten characters with given correct labels

This example will now be used to explain the design steps. We use handwriting character recognition (Figure 2.12) as an illustrative example to explain the design issues and approaches.

We explain learning to perform a task from experience. Therefore, let us understand the meaning of the task. The task can often be expressed through a mathematical function. In this case input can be x, output y, and w the parameters that are learned. In case of classification, output y will be discrete, such as class membership, posterior probability, and so on. For regression, y will be continuous. For the character recognition, the output y will be as shown in Figure 2.13.

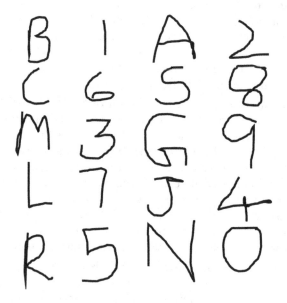

FIGURE 2.12
Set of handwritten characters.

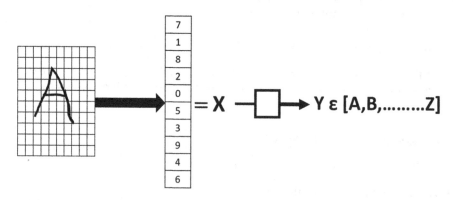

FIGURE 2.13
Character recognition task.

The following are the steps in the design process for character recognition.

Step 0: Let us treat the learning system as a black box (Figure 2.14).

Step 1: Next we collect training examples (experience). Without examples, our system will not learn as we are learning from examples (Figure 2.15).

Step 2: Representing experience
The next step is to choose a scheme for representing the experience/examples. In our example the sensor input can represented by an n-dimensional vector, called the feature vector, $X = (x_1, x_2, x_3, ..., x_n)$. We can assume a 64-dimensional vector to represent the 8×8 matrix of pixels (Figure 2.16).

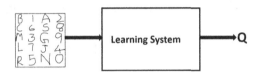

FIGURE 2.14
Learning system as a black box.

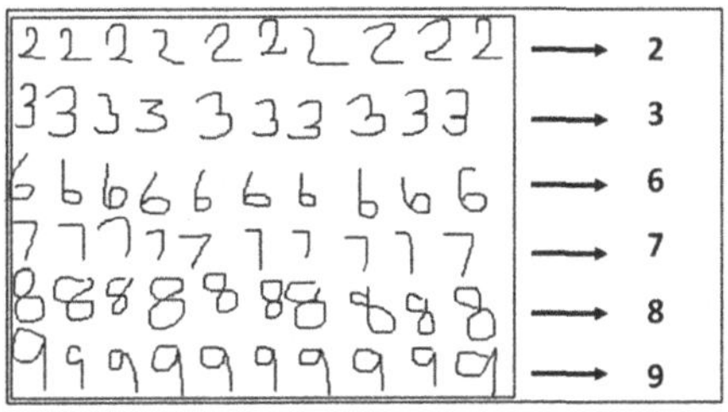

FIGURE 2.15
Collection of training data.

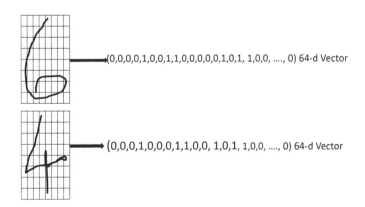

FIGURE 2.16
Representation of data.

In order to represent the experience, we need to know what X is. Therefore, we need a corresponding vector D, which will record our knowledge (experience) about X. The experience E is a pair of vectors $E = (X, D)$. Now the question is how to represent D. Assuming our system is to recognise 10 digits only, then D can be a 10-dimensional binary vector, with each dimension corresponding to one of the digits (Figure 2.17).

Step 3: Choosing a representation for the black box
The next step is the choice of a representation for the black box. Here we need to choose a function F to approximate the black box, and for a given X, the value of F would give the classification of X (Figure 2.18).

Step 4: Learning/adjusting the weights
We need a learning algorithm to adjust the weights such that the experience/prior knowledge from the training data can be incorporated into the system, where experience E is represented in terms of input X and expected output D. The function $F(X)$ would be modified with weights W to obtain the learned output L as given in Figure 2.19.

Step 5: Testing and evaluation
After learning is completed, all parameters are fixed and an unknown input X can be presented to the system for which the system computes its answer according to the function $F(W,X)$ (Figure 2.20).

D= (do,d1,d2,d3,d4,d5,d6,d7,d8,d9)
If X is digit 6, then d5=1: all others 0
If X is digit 4, then d4=1: all others 0

FIGURE 2.17
10-dimensional binary vector.

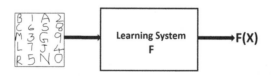

FIGURE 2.18
Choosing function *F*.

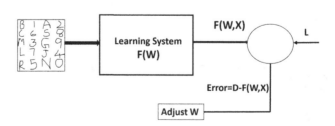

FIGURE 2.19
Adjusting weights.

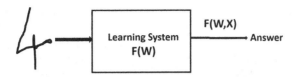

FIGURE 2.20
Testing.

2.4.2.2 Checkers Learning

A checkers learning problem can be defined as:

Task *T*: Playing checkers

Performance measure *P*: Percent of games won in the world tournament

Training experience *E*: Games played against itself

Let us assume that we can determine all legal moves. Then the system needs to learn the best move from among legal moves; this is defined as a large search space known a priori. Then we can define the target function as (Equation 2.4):

$$\text{target function}: \text{Choose Move}: B \to M \tag{2.4}$$

However, "choose move" is difficult to learn when we are given only indirect training. An alternative target function can be defined. Let us assume that we have an evaluation function that assigns a numerical score to any given board state (Equation 2.5).

$$V: B \to \Re \left(\text{where } \Re \text{ is the set of real numbers} \right) \tag{2.5}$$

Let $V(b)$ be an arbitrary board state b in B. Let us give values for $V(b)$ for games that are won, lost, or drawn. If b is a final board state that is won, then $V(b) = 100$; if b is a final board state that is lost, then $V(b) = -100$; if b is a final board state that is drawn, then $V(b) = 0$. However, if b is not a final state, then $V(b) = V(b')$, where b' is the best final board state that can be achieved starting from b and playing optimally until the end of the game. $V(b)$ gives a recursive definition for board state b but is not usable because the function cannot be determined efficiently except for the first three trivial cases discussed previously. Therefore, the goal of learning is to discover an operational description of V, in other words learning the target function as a function approximation problem.

Now we need to choose the representation of the target function. The choice of representations involves trade-offs, where the choice can be of a very expressive representation to allow close approximation to the ideal target function V; however, the more expressive the representation, the more training data is required to choose among alternative hypotheses. One option is the use of a linear combination of the following six board features.: x1 is the number of black pieces on the board, x2 is the number of red pieces on the board, x3 is the number of black kings on the board, x4 is the number of red kings on the board, x5 is the number of black pieces threatened by red, and x6 is the number of red pieces threatened by black. The target function representation for the target function V: Board $\to \Re$ is given in Equation (2.6):

$$\hat{V}(b) - w_0 + w_1 x_1 + w_2 x_2 + w_3 x_3 + w_4 x_4 + w_5 x_5 + w_6 x_6 \tag{2.6}$$

Here the weights are to be determined to obtain the target function. Choose the weights w_i to best fit the set of training examples in such a way that error E between the training values and the values predicted by the hypothesis is minimized. One algorithm that can be used is the least mean squares (LMS) algorithm where the weights are refined as new training examples become available and will be robust to errors in these estimated training values (Equation 2.7):

$$E \equiv \sum_{\langle b, V_{\text{train}}(b) \rangle \in \text{training examples}} \left(V_{\text{train}}(b) - \hat{V}(b) \right)^2 \tag{2.7}$$

As can be seen, the concept used is similar to the simple example we have discussed in the previous section.

In order to learn the function, we require a set of training examples describing the board b and the training value $V_{\text{train}}(b)$; that is, we need the ordered pair $<b, V_{\text{train}}(b)>$. For example, a winning state may be presented by the ordered pair given in Equation (2.8):

$$\left\langle \langle x1 = 3, x2 = 0, x3 = 1, x4 = 0, x5 = 0, x6 = 0 \rangle, +100 \right\rangle \tag{2.8}$$

In the preceding example we need to estimate training values; that is, there is a need to assign specific scores to intermediate board states. Here we approximate intermediate board state b using the approximation of the next board state following b given as (Equation 2.9)

$$V_{\text{train}}(b) \leftarrow \hat{V}(\text{Successor}(b)) \tag{2.9}$$

The simple approach given here can be used in any game playing or problem solving scenario. The final design of this game playing scenario is given in Figure 2.21.

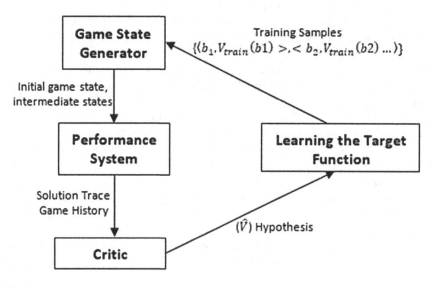

FIGURE 2.21
Final design flow of playing checkers.

Therefore, in the example of playing checkers, the following choices were made during the design. While determining type of training experience, what was considered was games played against self rather than games against experts or a table of correct moves. While choosing the target function, we chose Board $\rightarrow$ (Real value) rather than Board $\rightarrow$ Move. Again, for the representation of the learnt function, we chose a linear function of six features, and finally we chose gradient descent as the learning algorithm.

2.5 Summary

In this chapter the following topics were discussed:

- Outlined the different terms associated with machine learning
- Explored the different types of machine learning tasks
- Discussed the general architecture of a machine learning system
- Explained the basic steps in the design of a learning system
- Outlined how a function is chosen to fit the data and the parameters are tuned to minimize the error
- Explained the design process using two illustrative examples.

2.6 Points to Ponder

- Machine learning is not suitable for finding the speed of a vehicle using an equation but the same problem is modelled based on machine learning to predict the speed of a vehicle?
- Many machine learning applications can be modelled using more than one type of machine learning task.

E.2 Exercises

E.2.1 Suggested Activities

E.2.1.1 Can you think of experience as described in this chapter for predicting credit risk?

E.2.1.2 Can you list some other terms commonly associated with machine learning?

E.2.1.3 By searching the web, find at least five common terms encountered but not already mentioned in the chapter and give a suitable explanation of each term.

S.No	Term	Explanation
1.		
2.		
3.		
4.		
5.		

E.2.1.4 Fill the following table with a statement on an example, explained in one or two sentences, to fit the particular machine learning task (do not give examples already mentioned in the chapter):

S.No	Type of Machine Learning Task	Example
1.	Classification	
2.	Clustering	
3.	Regression	
4.	Ranking	
5.	Prediction	
6.	Forecasting	
7.	Outlier detection	
8.	Tagging	
9.	Sequence analysis	
10.	Association rules	

E.2.1.5 Take any three applications, and formulate each application using any three machine learning tasks, with examples.

S.No	Application	Machine Learning Task Type—Examples
1.	1.	
	2.	
	3.	
2.	1.	
	2.	
	3.	
3.	1.	
	2.	
	3.	

E.2.1.6 Develop a simple design (as shown in illustrative examples) for the following problems:
   a. Weather prediction
   b. Medical diagnosis
   c. Sentiment classification

Self-Assessment Questions

E.2.2 Multiple Choice Questions

Give answers with justification for correct and wrong choices.

E.2.2.1 What is representation?
    i Indicates the way in which what is being learnt is characterized.
    ii Indicates the way in which input is represented
    iii Indicates the way the algorithm is represented

E.2.2.2 Features are also known as
    i Dependent variables
    ii Target variables
    iii Independent variables

E.2.2.3 Labelled samples consist of
    i Features only
    ii Features and labels
    iii Labels only

E.2.2.4 Model selection involves
    i Selecting the model
    ii Selecting the learning algorithm
    iii Selecting the free parameters of the algorithm

E.2.2.5 Validation samples are
    i Used to tune parameters of the model
    ii Used to test the model
    iii Used to train the model

E.2.2.6 The Occam's razor principle is to
    i Prefer a complex hypothesis that exactly fits the data
    ii Prefer a simpler hypothesis that best fits the data
    iii Prefer a simpler hypothesis that does not fit the data

E.2.2.7 The learning step involves
    i Finding the set of parameters that optimizes the error function
    ii Finding the model that fits the data
    iii Finding the test data

E.2.3 Match the Columns

No	Match	
E.2.3.1 Classification	A	Outputs continuous values
E.2.3.2 Ranking	B	Indicating something in advance based on previous data available
E.2.3.3 Regression	C	Search of a state-space formulation of the problem
E.2.3.4 Tagging	D	One among a set of given categories the input belongs to

No	Match	
E.2.3.5 Predictive modelling	E	Finding if one entity is like another in one or more specified qualities or characteristics
E.2.3.6 Anomaly detection	F	Grouping items into homogeneous groups by finding similarities between them
E.2.3.7 Dimensionality detection	G	Reducing number of input variables in a data set
E.2.3.8 Matching	H	Analysing a set of objects or events to discover any of them as being unusual or atypical
E.2.3.9 Problem solving	I	Automatic assignment of labels or tokens for identification or analysis
E.2.3.10 Clustering	J	Ordering of entities of a class from highest to lowest

E.2.4 Short Questions

E.2.4.1   What are the three important components of machine learning?

E.2.4.2   What is meant by the hypothesis set?

E.2.4.3   What is inference in the context of machine learning?

E.2.4.4   Why is loss function important in machine learning?

E.2.4.5   What is the difference between classification and regression?

E.2.4.6   What is the difference between classification and clustering?

E.2.4.7   Describe association rule mining as a machine learning task.

E.2.4.8   Give the steps in the design of a machine learning task assuming the input has three features.

E.2.4.9   Why is feature selection important in machine learning?

E.2.4.10   Assume you have a student database. Give two machine learning tasks you want to learn, outlining different features needed for each task.

References

Google. (2023). Machine learning glossary. https://developers.google.com/machine-learning/glossary

Huyen, C. (2022). Design a machine learning system. https://huyenchip.com/machine-learning-systems-design/design-a-machine-learning-system.html

Kumar, A. (2022, December 4). Most common machine learning tasks. *Data analytics.* https://vitalflux.com/7-common-machine-learning-tasks-related-methods/

Mohri, M., Rostamizadeh, A., & Talwalkar, A. (2012). *Foundations of machine learning.* MIT Press.

Nkengsa, B. (2018, October 26). Applying machine learning to recognize handwritten characters. *Medium.* https://medium.com/the-andela-way/applying-machine-learning-to-recognize-handwritten-characters-babcd4b8d705

Pykes, K. (2021, September 5). How to design a machine learning system. *Medium.* https://medium.com/geekculture/how-to-design-a-machine-learning-system-89d806ff3d3b

3

Mathematical Foundations and Machine Learning

3.1 Introduction

In Table 3.1 we list the context in which mathematical concepts are used.

The applications mentioned in the table will be discussed in the succeeding chapters.

TABLE 3.1

Mathematical Concepts Used in Machine Learning

Linear Algebra for Machine Learning

- Data representation and data preprocessing—attributes of input, image, audio, text
- Operations on or between vectors and matrices for finding patterns in data
- Linear equations to model the data
- Linear transformation to map input and output
- Cosine similarity between vectors
- Eigen vectors, principal components, and dimensionality reduction

Probability Theory for Machine Learning

- Classification models generally predict a probability of class membership.
- Many iterative machine learning techniques like maximum likelihood estimation (MLE) are based on probability theory. MLE is used for training in models like linear regression, logistic regression, and artificial neural networks.
- Many machine learning frameworks based on the Bayes theorem are called in general Bayesian learning (e.g., naive Bayes, Bayesian networks).
- Learning algorithms make decisions using probability (e.g., information gain).
- Algorithms are trained under probability frameworks (e.g., maximum likelihood).
- Models are fitted using probabilistic loss functions (e.g., log loss and cross entropy).
- Model hyper-parameters are configured with probability (e.g., Bayesian optimization).
- Probabilistic measures are used to evaluate model skill (e.g., brier score, receiver operator characteristic (ROC)).

Information Theory for Machine Learning

- Entropy is the basis for information gain and mutual information used in decision tree learning—ID3 algorithm.
- Cross-entropy is used as a loss function that measures the performance of a classification model.
- Kullback–Liebler (KL) divergence measures are used in deep learning.
- KL divergence is also used in dimensionality reduction technique—*t*-distributed stochastic neighbour embedding (tSNE). Entropy can be used to calculate target class imbalances.

DOI: 10.1201/9781003290100-3

3.2 What Is Linear Algebra?

Linear algebra is a branch of mathematics that can be called the mathematics of data. It deals with linear equations and linear functions, which are represented through matrices and vectors. It enables the understanding of geometric concepts such as planes in higher dimensions, and the performing of mathematical operations on them. It is in fact an extension of algebra into an arbitrary number of dimensions, and therefore, instead of working with scalars, we work with matrices and vectors.

3.2.1 Linear Algebra and Machine Learning

Machine learning is effective only when trained with large data sets ranging from hundreds to millions of data. The data can be represented in the form of linear equations, which in turn can be represented as matrices and vectors. Operations on or between vectors and matrices are used for finding patterns in data in an efficient way. Mathematical functions used include coordinate transformations, dimensionality reduction, linear regression, and solutions of linear systems of equations.

Let us first explore the connection between linear algebra and data sets. In machine learning, we fit a model to the data set. Data representation and data preprocessing associated with machine learning are based on linear algebra. This is because the large number of features associated with data representation in machine learning lead to high dimensional spaces. Vectors and matrices allow us to describe and manipulate high dimensional feature spaces in a compact manner.

The most common form of data set organization for machine learning is a 2D array, where *rows* represent examples or observations (records, items, data points) and *columns* represent attributes or characteristic of the observation (features, variables). It is a natural way to think of each sample as a *vector* of attributes, and the set of examples as a whole array represented as a *matrix* (Figure 3.1).

Figure 3.1 shows an example where the attributes are pattern, size, colour, and texture and the Boolean output class we need is whether a discount can be given or not. Each vector or row has the same length, that is, the same number of columns; therefore we can say that the data is vectorized where rows can be provided to a model one at a time or in a batch and the model can be preconfigured to expect rows of a fixed width.

Generally, a table is created to represent the variable with one column for each category and a row for each example in the data set. A one-value is added in the column for the categorical value for a given row, and a zero-value is added to all other columns. The 10-dimensional binary vector discussed in Chapter 2 is an example of this type of encoding (Figure 3.2). Each row is encoded as a binary vector, a vector with zero or one values, which is an example of sparse representation, a whole subfield of linear algebra.

Let us consider the linear equation (Equation 3.1):

$$a_1 x_1 + a_2 x_2 + \ldots\ldots\ldots a_n x_n = b \tag{3.1}$$

In vector notation this equation is represented as $a^T x = b$ and is called the linear transformation of x. Therefore, linear algebra is essential to understanding machine learning algorithms, where often input vectors $(x_1, x_2, \ldots x_n)$ are converted into outputs by a series of linear transformations. Linear regression is often used in machine learning to simplify numerical values as simpler regression problems. Linear equations often represent the

Shirts	Pattern	Size	Colour	Texture	Discount
Product1	Full Sleeve	XL	Green	Cotton	Y
Product2	Sleeveless	S	White	Rayon	N
Product3	Full Sleeve	XL	Green	Cotton	Y
Product4	Half Sleeve	M	White	Rayon	Y
Product5	Half Sleeve	L	Black	Cotton	N
Product6	Full Sleeve	M	Red	Silk	Y

Vector

Matrix

FIGURE 3.1
Example data showing vector and matrix representation.

D=(d0,d1,d2,d3,d4,d5,d6,d7,d8,d9)
If X is digit 6, then d6=1: all others 0
If X is digit 4, then d4=1: all others 0

FIGURE 3.2
10-dimensional binary vector.

linear regression, which uses linear algebra notation: $y = A \cdot b$ where y is the output variable, A is the data set, and b is the model coefficients.

Modelling data with many features is challenging, and models built from data that include irrelevant features are often less effective than models trained from the more relevant data. Methods for automatically reducing the number of columns of a data set are called dimensionality reduction, and these methods are used in machine learning to create projections of high-dimensional data for both visualizations and training models.

Linear algebra accomplishes tasks such as graphical transformations for applications such as face morphing, object detection and tracking, audio and image compression, edge detection, signal processing, and many others.

Therefore, concepts such as vectors and matrices, products, norms, vector spaces, and linear transformations are used in machine learning.

3.2.2 Matrix and Matrix Operations

A matrix is a set of elements organized into rows and columns. We just list and illustrate matrix operations without discussing the details. Addition, subtraction, and multiplication by a scalar are the simplest of matrix operations (Figure 3.3).

Other important matrix operations include an n by m matrix A and its m by n transpose A^T (Figure 3.4). Matrix product AB is defined only if the number of columns of A is equal to the number of rows of B, and even if defined, in general $AB \neq BA$ (Figure 3.5).

The rank of a matrix is also another important aspect. The rank of a matrix is the number of linearly independent rows (or equivalently columns). A square matrix is nonsingular if its rank is equal to the number of rows. If its rank is less than the number of rows, then it

$$\text{Add elements} \quad \begin{bmatrix} a & b \\ c & d \end{bmatrix} + \begin{bmatrix} e & f \\ g & h \end{bmatrix} = \begin{bmatrix} a+e & b+f \\ c+g & d+h \end{bmatrix}$$

$$\text{Subtract elements} \quad \begin{bmatrix} a & b \\ c & d \end{bmatrix} - \begin{bmatrix} e & f \\ g & h \end{bmatrix} = \begin{bmatrix} a-e & b-f \\ c-g & d-h \end{bmatrix}$$

$$\begin{matrix} \text{Multiply every} \\ \text{element by a scalar} \end{matrix} \quad \alpha \cdot \begin{bmatrix} a & b \\ c & d \end{bmatrix} = \begin{bmatrix} \alpha \cdot a & \alpha \cdot b \\ \alpha \cdot c & \alpha \cdot d \end{bmatrix}$$

FIGURE 3.3
Matrix operations with scalar.

$$A = \begin{bmatrix} x_{11} & x_{12} & \cdots & x_{1m} \\ x_{21} & x_{22} & \cdots & x_{2m} \\ \vdots & \vdots & \cdots & \vdots \\ x_{n1} & x_{n2} & \cdots & x_{nm} \end{bmatrix} \quad A^T = \begin{bmatrix} x_{11} & x_{21} & \cdots & x_{n1} \\ x_{12} & x_{22} & \cdots & x_{n2} \\ \vdots & \vdots & \cdots & \vdots \\ x_{1m} & x_{2m} & \cdots & x_{nm} \end{bmatrix}$$

FIGURE 3.4
Transpose of a matrix.

$$AB = \begin{bmatrix} a_{11} & a_{12} & a_{13} & \cdots & a_{1d} \\ \vdots & \vdots & \vdots & \vdots & \vdots \\ a_{n1} & a_{n2} & a_{n3} & \cdots & a_{nd} \end{bmatrix} \begin{bmatrix} b_{11} & \cdots & b_{1m} \\ b_{21} & \cdots & b_{2m} \\ b_{31} & \cdots & b_{3m} \\ \vdots & \cdots & \vdots \\ b_{d1} & \cdots & b_{dm} \end{bmatrix} = \begin{bmatrix} & & \\ & c_{ij} & \\ & & \end{bmatrix}$$

$c_{ij} = \langle a^i, b_j \rangle$	• # of columns of A = # of rows of B
a^i is row *i* of **A**	• even if defined, in general AB ≠ BA
b_j is column *j* of **B**	

FIGURE 3.5
Product of a matrix.

$$I = \begin{bmatrix} 1 & 0 & \cdots & 0 \\ 0 & 1 & \cdots & 0 \\ 0 & 0 & \ddots & \vdots \\ 0 & 0 & \cdots & 1 \end{bmatrix} \quad \begin{bmatrix} 1 & 2 & 9 & 5 \\ 2 & 7 & 4 & 8 \\ 9 & 4 & 3 & 6 \\ 5 & 8 & 6 & 4 \end{bmatrix}$$

FIGURE 3.6
Identity matrix and symmetric matrix.

is singular. The identity matrix and symmetric matrices are important special cases of a matrix (Figure 3.6).

The inverse of a matrix is defined only for a square matrix. To calculate the inverse, one has to find the determinant and adjoint of that given matrix. The adjoint is given by the transpose of the cofactor of the particular matrix. The equation (Equation 3.2) to find out the inverse of a matrix is given as,

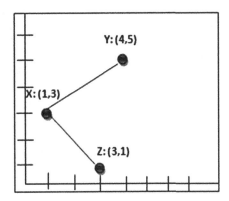

FIGURE 3.7
Vector in 2D Euclidean space.

$$A^{-1} = \frac{\mathrm{adj}(A)}{|A|}; |A| \neq 0 \tag{3.2}$$

Next let us discuss vector and vector operations.

3.2.2.1 Vector and Vector Operations

A vector is an ordered collection of numbers and represents a point in some Euclidean space.

Example 3.1

x: $(1, 3)$, y: $(4, 5)$, z: $(3, 1)$ and $y - x = (4 - 1, 5 - 3) = (3, 2)$, $x - z = (1 - 3, 3 - 1) = (-2, 2)$.

In general, the vector is defined as an n-tuple of values (usually real numbers) where n is the *dimension* of the vector. The dimension n can be any positive integer from 1 to infinity. The vector can be written in column form or row form; however, it is conventional to use the column form. In the column form the vector elements are referenced by using subscripts.

$$v = \begin{bmatrix} x_1 \\ x_2 \end{bmatrix}$$

We can think of a vector as a point in space *or* as a directed line segment with a magnitude and direction as shown in Figure 3.8.

3.2.2.2 Operations with Vectors

The operations of transpose, addition, scalar multiplication, dot product, Euclidean distance or norm of a point, and the angle between two vectors are discussed in this section. The first operation we illustrate (Figure 3.9) is the transpose of a vector (the elements are denoted by subscripts) where an n dimensional column vector is transposed to form a row

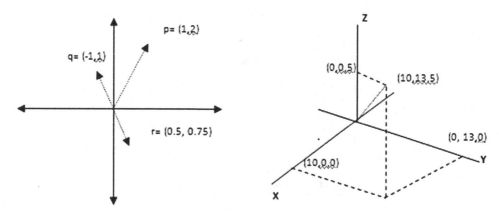

FIGURE 3.8
Vector as directed line segment in 2D and 3D space.

$$X = \begin{pmatrix} x_1 \\ \vdots \\ x_n \end{pmatrix}$$

$$X^T = (x_1 \dots x_n) \; means \; "transpose"$$

$$X^T = \begin{bmatrix} x_1 \\ x_2 \\ \vdots \\ \vdots \\ x_n \end{bmatrix}^T$$

FIGURE 3.9
Transpose of a row vector.

vector. Similarly, an n dimensional row vector could be transformed to the corresponding column vector.

Next we discuss the operations of vector arithmetic. The first is the addition of two vectors where the corresponding elements are added and the result is a vector (Equation 3.3).

$$z = x + y = \left(x_1 + y_1 + \dots x_n + y_n \right)^T \tag{3.3}$$

Figure 3.10 shows the vector representation, vector addition, and vector addition graphically.

The next operation is the scalar multiplication of a vector where each element of the vector is multiplied by a scalar (Equation 3.4).

$$y = ax = \left(ax_1 \dots \dots ax_n \right)^T \tag{3.4}$$

To obtain the dot product (scalar product or inner product) of two vectors, we multiply the corresponding elements and add products, resulting in a scalar (Equation 3.5).

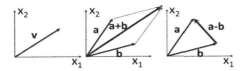

FIGURE 3.10
Graphical representation vector operations.

$$a = \mathbf{x} \cdot \mathbf{y} = \|\mathbf{x}\|\|\mathbf{y}\|\cos(\theta)$$

FIGURE 3.11
Graphical representation of dot product of two vectors.

The alternative form of the dot product is shown graphically in Figure 3.11. The dot product and magnitude are defined on vectors only.

$$a = x.y = \sum_{i=1}^{n} x_i y_i \tag{3.5}$$

where $\langle x, y \rangle = x. \, y = x^T y = x_1 y_1 + x_2 y_2 + \cdots . + x_n y_n = \Sigma_{i=1\ldots n} x_i y_i.$

The Euclidean norm or length of a vector in Euclidean space is defined as given by Equation (3.6), where n is the dimension of each point. If the Euclidean norm or length of a vector $||x|| = 1$, we say x is the *normalized* or *unit* length.

$$\|x\| = \sqrt{\langle x, x \rangle} = \sum_{i=1..n} x_i^2 \tag{3.6}$$

In Example 3.1 given in Figure 3.8, the Euclidean distance of a point x is given by Equation (3.7):

$$\|X\| = \sqrt{\sum_{i=0}^{d-1} (x_i)^2} = \|X\| = \sqrt{1^2 + 3^2} = \sqrt{10} \tag{3.7}$$

The Euclidean distance between vectors x and y is given by Figure 3.12. For Example 3.1, the length of $y - x = (2, 3) = \sqrt{3^2 + 2^2} = \sqrt{13}$.

$$\|x - y\| = \sqrt{\sum_{i=1..n} (x_i - y_i)^2}$$

FIGURE 3.12
Euclidean distance between vectors.

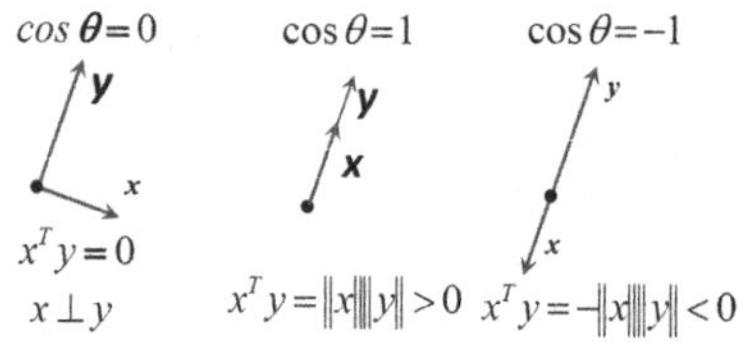

FIGURE 3.13
Angle between two vectors.

Vectors x and y are orthonormal if they are orthogonal and $\|x\| = \|y\| = 1$.

The angle θ between vectors x and y is given by defining the cosine of the angle θ (Equation 3.8) between them (Figure 3.13). This cosine of the angle is used extensively in machine learning to find similarity between vectors. We will discuss this in detail in subsequent chapters.

$$\cos\theta = \frac{x^T y}{\|x\|\|y\|} \tag{3.8}$$

3.2.2.3 Linear Dependence and Independence

Vectors $x_1, x_2,..., x_n$ are linearly **dependent** if there exist constants $\alpha_1, \alpha_2,..., \alpha_n$ $\alpha_1 x_1 + \alpha_2 x_2 +...+ \alpha_n x_n = 0$ and $\alpha_i \neq 0$ for at least one i. Vectors $x_1, x_2,..., x_n$ are linearly **independent** if $\alpha_1 x_1 + \alpha_2 x_2 +...+ \alpha_n x_n = 0 \Rightarrow \alpha_1 = \alpha_2 =...= \alpha_n = 0$. The set of all n-dimensional vectors is called a vector space V. A set of vectors $\{u_1, u_2,..., u_n\}$ are called a basis for vector space if any v in V can be written as $v = \alpha_1 u_1 + \alpha_2 u_2 +...+ \alpha_n u_n$. $u_1, u_2,..., u_n$ are independent implies they form a basis, and vice versa. $u_1, u_2,..., u_n$ gives an orthonormal basis if the conditions specified by Equations (3.9) and (3.10) hold.

$$\|u_i\| = 1 \quad \forall i \tag{3.9}$$

$$u_i \perp u_j \quad \forall i \neq j \tag{3.10}$$

Example 3.2:   Example of Orthonormal Basis

$x = \begin{bmatrix} 1 & 0 & 0 \end{bmatrix}^T$ $x \cdot y = 0$

$x = \begin{bmatrix} 0 & 1 & 0 \end{bmatrix}^T$ $x \cdot z = 0$

$x = \begin{bmatrix} 0 & 0 & 1 \end{bmatrix}^T$ $y \cdot z = 0$

3.2.2.3.1 Vector Projection

Orthogonal projection of y onto x can take place in any space of dimensionality ≥ 2. Unit vector in direction of x is $x / \|x\|$. Length of projection of y in direction of x is $\|y\|$ $\cos(\theta)$ (Figure 3.14). Orthogonal projection of y onto x is the vector $\mathbf{proj}_x(y) = \dfrac{x\|y\|\cos(\theta)}{\|x\|}$ or $\dfrac{x.y}{\|x\|}$ (using dot product alternative form).

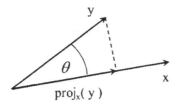

FIGURE 3.14
Orthogonal projection of y on x.

In this section we discussed the role of linear algebra in machine learning.

3.3 Probability Theory

As already discussed, data and analysis of data play a very important role in machine learning, and here we discuss approaches based on probability and the Bayes theorem. Probability theory is a mathematical framework for representing uncertain statements and provides a means of quantifying uncertainty and axioms for deriving new uncertain statements.

3.3.1 Machine Learning and Probability Theory

Machine learning needs to always deal with uncertain quantities and also with uncertain nondeterministic or stochastic quantities. Machine learning has to deal with uncertainty basically from three sources: uncertain inputs such as missing or noisy data; uncertain knowledge such as incomplete modelling of conditions, effects, or causality of the machine learning task; and uncertain outputs due to the inferencing process.

3.3.2 Basics of Probability

When we talk about probability, there are basically two aspects that we consider. One is the classical interpretation, where we describe the frequency of outcomes in random experiments. The other is the Bayesian viewpoint or subjective interpretation of probability, where we describe the degree of belief about a particular event.

Before we go further let us first discuss about a **random variable**. A random variable takes values subject to chance. In probability, the set of outcomes from an experiment is known as an **event**. In other words, an event in probability is the subset of the respective sample space. The entire possible set of outcomes of a random experiment is the **sample space** or the individual space of that experiment. The likelihood of occurrence of an event is known as **probability**. The probability of occurrence of any event lies between 0 and 1. **Probability quantifies the likelihood of an event**. Specifically, it quantifies how likely a specific outcome is for a random variable, such as the flip of a coin, the roll of a die, or the drawing a playing card from a deck. For example, A is the result of an uncertain event such as a coin toss, with nonnumeric values Heads and Tails. It can be denoted as a random variable A, which has values 1 and 0, and each value of A is associated with a probability. In informal terms, probability gives a measure of how likely it is for something to happen. There are three approaches to assessing the probability of an uncertain event.

```
┌─────────────────────────────────────────────────┐
│ Three Axioms of Probability                     │
│ 1. All probabilities are between 0 and 1        │
│      0 ≤ P(A) ≤ 1                                │
│ 2. Valid propositions have probability 1, and   │
│    unsatisfiable propositions have probability 0.│
│    P(true)=1, P(false)=0                         │
│ 3. Probability of a disjunction is given by     │
│    P(A ∨ B) = P (A) + P (B) – P(A ∧B)            │
└─────────────────────────────────────────────────┘
```

FIGURE 3.15
Axioms of probability.

There are three basic axioms of probability as shown in Figure 3.15.

Random variables can be discrete or continuous. A **discrete random variable** has a **countable number of possible values**. The probability of each value of a discrete random variable is between 0 and 1, and the sum of all the probabilities is equal to 1. A **continuous random variable** is one which takes an **infinite number of possible values**. Continuous random variables are usually measurements. Examples include height, weight, the amount of sugar in an orange, and the time required to run a mile. A mathematical function can also describe the possible values of a continuous random variable and their associated probability values, and this mathematical function is called a **probability distribution**.

3.3.3 Three Approaches to Probability

A priori classical probability: Prior knowledge of the process involved determines the probability (Equation 3.11).

$$\text{Probability of Occurence} = \frac{X}{T} = \frac{\text{number of ways the event can occur}}{\text{total number of possible outcomes}} \qquad (3.11)$$

┌───┐
│ **Example 3.3:   Priori classical probability**   │
│   │
│ Find the probability of selecting a face card (Jack, Queen, or King) from a standard deck of 52 cards. │
│   │
│ $$\text{Probability of face card} = \frac{\text{number of face cards}}{\text{total number of cards}}$$ │
│   │
│ $$\frac{X}{T} = \frac{12 \text{ face cards}}{52 \text{ total cards}} = \frac{1}{13}$$ │
└───┘

Empirical classical probability is the probability of an event based on **observed data**. Here it is assumed that all outcomes are equally likely (Equation 3.12).

$$\text{Probability of Occurence} = \frac{\text{number of favorable outcomes observed}}{\text{total number of outcomes observed}} \qquad (3.12)$$

Subjective probability: Here the probability of an event is **determined by an individual**. This **probability** is based on an individual's personal judgment about whether an event is likely to occur. This probability is not based on any formal calculations but reflects the opinion of an individual based on past experience.

Example 3.4: Empirical classical probability

Find the probability of selecting a male taking statistics from the population described in the following table:

	Taking Stats	Not Taking Stats	Total
Male	84	145	229
Female	76	134	210
Total	160	279	439

$$\text{Probability of Male Taking Stats} = \frac{\text{number of males taking stats}}{\text{total number of people}} = \frac{84}{439} = 0.191$$

3.3.4 Types of Events in Probability

Simple events are events that consist of a single point in the sample space. For example, if the sample space S = {Monday, Tuesday, Wednesday, Thursday, Friday, Saturday, Sunday} and event E = {Wednesday}, then E is a simple event.

Joint events involve two or more characteristics simultaneously, such as drawing an ace that is also red from a deck of cards. In other words, the simultaneous occurrence of two events is called a joint event. The probability of a joint event $P(A \text{ and } B)$ is called a **joint probability**. Considering the same example if the sample space S = {Monday, Tuesday, Wednesday, Thursday, Friday, Saturday, Sunday} and event E = {Wednesday, Friday}, then E is a joint event.

Independent and dependent events: If the occurrence of any event is completely unaffected by the occurrence of any other event, such events are known as **independent events** in probability and the events which are affected by other events are known as **dependent events**.

Mutually exclusive events: If the occurrence of one event excludes the occurrence of another event, such events are mutually **exclusive events**, that is, two events that don't have any common point. For example, if sample space S = {Monday, Tuesday, Wednesday, Thursday, Friday, Saturday, Sunday} and E_1, E_2 are two events such that E_1 = {Monday, Tuesday} and E_2 = {Saturday, Sunday}, then E_1 and E_2 are mutually exclusive.

Exhaustive events: A set of events is called **exhaustive** if all the events together consume the entire sample space.

Complementary events: For any event E_1 there exists another event E_1' which represents the remaining elements of the sample space S. $E_1 = S - E_1'$. In the sample space S = {Monday, Tuesday, Wednesday, Thursday, Friday, Saturday, Sunday} if E_1 = {Monday, Tuesday, Wednesday}, then E_1' = {Thursday, Friday, Saturday, Sunday}.

Collectively exhaustive event: A set of events is said to be collectively exhaustive if it is mandatory that at least one of the events must occur. For example, when rolling a six-sided die, the outcomes 1, 2, 3, 4, 5, and 6 are collectively exhaustive, because they encompass the entire range of possible outcomes. Another way to describe collectively exhaustive events is that their union must cover all the events in the entire sample space. For example, two events A and B are collectively exhaustive if and only if $A \cup B = S$ where S is the sample space.

Example 3.5:   Collectively exhaustive

A = aces; B = black cards; C = diamonds; D = hearts
Events A, B, C, and D are **collectively exhaustive** (but not mutually exclusive).
Events B, C, and D are **collectively exhaustive** and also mutually exclusive.

3.3.4.1 Visualizing Events in Sample Space

There are basically two ways in which events can be visualized in the sample space, namely contingency tables and tree diagrams.

Figure 3.16a and 3.16b show an example of black and red aces as events in a sample space which is a pack of 52 cards represented as a contingency table and tree diagram, respectively.

3.3.5 Probability of Multiple Random Variables

In machine learning, we are likely to work with many random variables. We will discuss probability associated with two random variables (A, B), although the principles generalize to multiple variables. Key concepts associated with probability with two variables are marginal probability, joint probability, and conditional probability.

3.3.5.1 Simple Versus Joint Probability

Simple (marginal) probability refers to the probability of a simple event. It is an unconditional probability that is it is not conditioned on the occurrence of any other event.

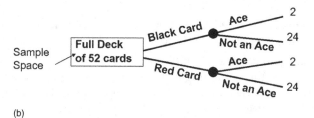

	Ace	Not Ace	Total
Black	2	24	26
Red	2	24	26
Total	4	48	52

(a)   (b)

FIGURE 3.16
(a) Contingency table, (b) tree diagram.

Example 3.6: Simple probability

Suppose that out of a total of 500 customers, 200 are new customers; then the probability of new customers is given as (Equation 3.11):

$$P(\text{new customers}) = \frac{\text{Number of new customers}}{500} = \frac{200}{500}$$

$$= 0.4$$

Joint probability refers to the probability of the simultaneous occurrence of two or more events or **the probability of the intersection of two or more events**. In a pack of cards, for example, P (King and Spade) is as follows (Equation 3.13):

$$P(A \text{ and } B) = \frac{\text{Number of outcomes satisfying } A \text{ and } B}{\text{total number of elementary outcomes}} \tag{3.13}$$

The contingency table for joint probability is given in Figure 3.17. In this figure we have taken the example of two sets of events A_1, A_2 and B_1, B_2. When events A and B occur together, we have joint probability, but the total is the marginal probability of events A and B.

3.3.6 Marginalization

Let us now explain the concept of marginalization. Marginal probability is defined as the probability of an event irrespective of the outcome of another variable. Consider the probability of X irrespective of Y (Equation 3.14):

$$P(X = x_j) = \frac{c_j}{N} \tag{3.14}$$

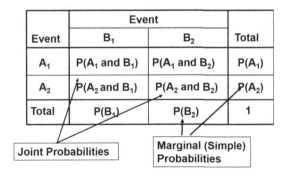

FIGURE 3.17
Contingency table for joint probability.

The number of instances in column j is the sum of instances in each cell of that column and is as follows (Equation 3.15):

$$c_j = \sum_{i=1}^{L} n_{ij}$$ (3.15)

Therefore, we can **marginalize** or "sum over" Y (Equation 3.16):

$$p\left(X = x_j\right) = \sum_{j=1}^{L} p\left(X = x_j, Y = y_i\right)$$ (3.16)

Sum and Product Rules

Before we discuss probability distribution, let us discuss the concept of a random variable. The random variable is a variable that assumes numerical values associated with the random outcome of an experiment, where one (and only one) numerical value is assigned to each sample point. There are two types of random variables. A discrete random variable can assume a countable number of values. An example is the number of students in a class. On the other hand, a continuous random variable can assume any value along a given interval of a number line. An example is the time spent studying for an exam. Normally the values that a continuous random variable can take are defined using a distribution.

In general, we'll refer to a distribution over a random variable as $p(X)$ and a distribution evaluated at a particular value as $p(x)$. Two important rules of probability are sum and product rules, shown in Equations (3.17) and (3.18).

$$\text{Sum Rule } p\left(X\right) = \sum_{y} p\left(x, y\right)$$ (3.17)

$$\text{Product Rule } p\left(X, Y\right) = p(Y \mid X) P\left(X\right)$$ (3.18)

3.3.7 Conditional Probability and Bayes Theorem

Another important concept that we need to understand is the concept of conditional probability. Conditional probability is defined as the probability of one event occurring along with another event. The conditional probability of A given B is the probability that an event, A, will occur given that another event, B, has occurred.

A conditional probability is the probability of one event given that another event has occurred, as follows (Equation 3.19):

$$P(A \mid B) = \frac{P\left(A \text{ and } B\right)}{P\left(B\right)} \quad \text{The conditional probability of A given that B has occurred} \quad (3.19)$$

The conditional probability can also be with respect to B given A and is as follows (Equation 3.20):

$$P(B \mid A) = \frac{P\left(A \text{ and } B\right)}{P\left(A\right)} \quad \text{The conditional probability of B given that A has occurred} \quad (3.20)$$

In these definitions.

$P(A \text{ and } B)$ = joint probability of A and B

$P(A)$ = marginal probability of A

$P(B)$ = marginal probability of B

Based on the concept of conditional probability, we go on to discuss an important probability theorem which is used extensively in machine learning.

3.3.7.1 Bayes Theorem

Bayes theorem is used to revise previously calculated probabilities based on new information. This theorem was developed by Thomas Bayes in the eighteenth century. This theorem has become one of the most important underlying concepts of many machine learning approaches. Let us first discuss the Bayes theorem for two variables A and B. It is an extension of conditional probability and is given by (Equation 3.21):

$$P(B|A) = \frac{P(A|B).P(B)}{P(A|B).P(B) + P(A|\sim B).P(\sim B)} \tag{3.21}$$

Now we can extend this to the general case as follows (Equation 3.22):

$$P(B_i|A) = \frac{P(A|B_i).P(B_i)}{P(A|B_1).P(B_1) + P(A|B_2).P(B_2) + \ldots + P(A|B_k).P(B_k)} \tag{3.22}$$

Where

B_i = ith event of k mutually exclusive and collectively exhaustive events

A = new event that might impact $P(B_i)$.

3.3.7.2 Example 3.7 Bayes Theorem

A drilling company has estimated a 40% chance of striking oil for their new well. A detailed test has been scheduled for more information. Historically, 60% of successful wells have had detailed tests, and 20% of unsuccessful wells have had detailed tests. Given that this well has been scheduled for a detailed test, what is the probability that the well will be successful?

- Let S = successful well and U = unsuccessful well
- $P(S) = .4$, $P(U) = .6$ (prior probabilities)
- Define the detailed test event as D.
- Conditional probabilities: $P(D|S) = 0.6$, $P(D|U) = 0.2$

Goal: To find $P(S \mid D)$ using Bayes theorem

$$P(S \mid D) = \frac{P(D \mid S)P(S)}{P(D \mid S)P(S) + P(D \mid U)P(U)}$$

$$= \frac{(0.6)(0.4)}{(0.6)(0.4) + (0.2)(0.6)}$$

$$= \frac{0.24}{0.24 + 0.12} = 0.667$$

Given the detailed test, the revised probability of a successful well has risen to .667 from the original estimate of .4. The given probabilities can be represented using a contingency table (Figure 3.18):

3.3.7.3 Example 3.8 Bayes Theorem

A video surveillance system is designed such that the probability of detecting the presence of a fraudulent activity is 98%. However, if no such activity is present it still reports (falsely) that there is fraudulent activity with a probability of 6%. At any time, the probability that a fraudulent activity happens is 8%.

(a) What is the probability that no fraudulent activity happened given that it was detected by the system?

(b) What is the probability that fraudulent activity actually happened given that a fraudulent activity was detected?

(c) What is the probability that fraudulent activity happened given that no fraudulent activity was detected?

(d) What is the probability that fraudulent activity happened given that no fraudulent activity was detected?

First let us list all the probabilities available. Let the happening of the fraudulent activity be denoted as event **F** and the complement of this event, that is, no fraudulent activity happening, as **F^**. Let the event of fraudulent activity being detected be denoted by **D** and it not being detected as **D^**. Here we present probability as a percentage.

The probabilities of fraudulent activity happening and not happening are as follows:

$$P(F) = 8\% \text{ and therefore } P(F^{\wedge}) = 100 - 8 = 92\%$$

Event	Prior Prob.	Condition al Prob.	Joint Prob.	Revised Prob.
S (successful)	0.4	0.6	0.4*0.6 = 0.24	0.24/0.36 = 0.667
U (unsuccessful)	0.6	0.2	0.6*0.2 = 0.12	0.12/0.36 = 0.333

FIGURE 3.18
Contingency table for Example 3.7.

Similarly, the probability that the system detects the fraudulent activity happening and that the system does not detect the fraudulent activity happening are as follows:

$$P(D) = 98\% \text{ and therefore } P(D\wedge) = 100 - 8 = 2\%$$

Now the conditional probability that a fraudulent activity happening is detected given that it has happened is:

$$P(D|F) = 98\% \text{ and therefore } P(D|F\wedge) = 6\%$$

1. With these probabilities we can use the Bayes theorem to calculate the probability that no fraudulent activity happened even if the system detected that it had happened (Equation 3.22):

$$P(F\wedge|D) = \frac{P(D|F\wedge)P(F\wedge)}{P(D|F\wedge)P(F\wedge) + P(D|F)P(F)}$$
$$= \frac{2\% \times 92\%}{2\% \times 92\% + 98\% \times 8\%}$$
$$= 0.1901$$

2. Now we use the Bayes theorem to calculate the probability that a fraudulent activity actually happened when the system detects it has happened (Equation 3.23):

$$P(F|D) = \frac{P(D|F)P(F)}{P(D|F)P(F) + P(D|F\wedge)P(F\wedge)}$$
$$= \frac{98\% \times 8\%}{98\% \times 8\% + 2\% \times 92\%}$$
$$= 0.8099$$

3. We will first calculate the following probabilities:
$P(D\wedge|F) = 100\% - 98\% = 2\%$
$P(D\wedge|F\wedge) = 100\% - 6\% = 94\%$

Now we use the Bayes theorem again to calculate the probability that a fraudulent activity happened but it was not detected by the system (Equation 3.24):

$$P(F|D\wedge) = \frac{P(D\wedge|F)P(F)}{P(D\wedge|F)P(F) + P(D\wedge|F\wedge)P(F\wedge)}$$
$$= \frac{2\% \times 8\%}{2\% \times 8\% + 94\% \times 92\%}$$
$$= 0.0018$$

4. Now we again use the Bayes theorem to calculate the probability that a fraudulent activity did not happen and it was correctly not detected by the system (Equation 3.25).

$$P(F \wedge | D \wedge) = \frac{P(D \wedge | F \wedge) P(F \wedge)}{P(D \wedge | F \wedge) P(F \wedge) + P(D \wedge | F) P(F)}$$

$$= \frac{94\% \times 92\%}{94\% \times 92\% + 2\% \times 8\%}$$

$$= \mathbf{0.9982}$$

3.3.8 Bayes Theorem and Machine Learning

The Bayes theorem gives a mathematical formula for determining conditional probability. The Bayes theorem is very widely used in machine learning. Fitting a model to training data is important in machine learning because based on this model built from data and associated target values, we predict target values for unknown hitherto unseen data. Some of the important criteria when we fit a model are the choice of weights and thresholds. In some cases, we need to incorporate prior knowledge, and in other cases we need to merge multiple sources of information. Another important factor is the modelling of uncertainty. Bayesian reasoning provides solutions to these issues. Bayesian reasoning is associated with probability, statistics, and data fitting. The Bayes theorem is used for probabilistically fitting a model to a training data set, and hence developing models for classification and predictive modelling problems.

3.3.9 Probability of Continuous Variables for Modelling the World

Now let consider the case of probability of continuous variables. The probability function that accompanies a continuous random variable is a continuous mathematical function that integrates to 1. Let x be a real number. Then we need to describe beliefs over x where x may be joint angles, price of stock, and so on.

Let $x - R^N$: How do we describe beliefs over x? e.g., x is a face, joint angles

In the case of continuous variables, we describe the data in terms of a probability distribution function (PDF). One common distribution that is used to describe the data is the Gaussian or normal distribution. This distribution can be defined by the parameters mean μ and standard deviation σ (Figure 3.19). This is a bell-shaped curve with different centers and spreads depending on μ and σ.

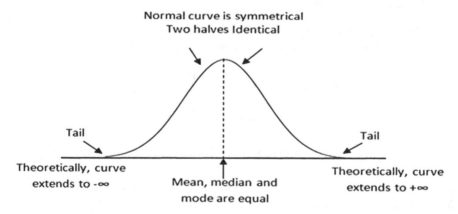

FIGURE 3.19
Normal or Gaussian distribution.

Now the question is, why do we use a Gaussian distribution? This is due to the fact that it has convenient analytic properties; it is governed by the central limit theorem and works reasonably well for most real data. Though it does not suit all types of data, it acts as a good building block. The values of the data point x is given by the function (Equation 3.23)

$$f(x) = \frac{1}{\sqrt{2\pi}\sigma} e^{-(x-\mu)^2/2\sigma^2}$$

(3.23)

where m = mean, s = standard deviation, π = 3.14159, and e = 2.71828.

3.3.9.1 Characteristics of a Normal Probability Distribution

A normal probability distribution is bell-shaped with a single peak at the center of the distribution, and

1. It is **symmetrical** about the mean.
2. It is **asymptotic**: The curve gets closer and closer to the x-axis but never actually touches it. To put it another way, the tails of the curve extend indefinitely in both directions.
3. The location of a normal distribution is determined by the mean, m, and the dispersion or spread of the distribution is determined by the standard deviation, σ.
4. The arithmetic **mean, median**, and **mode are equal**.
5. The total **area under the curve is 1.00**; half the area under the normal curve is to the right of this center point, and the other half to the left of it.
6. If two independent random variables follow a Gaussian distribution, then the sum of the two random variables also follows the Gaussian distribution.

3.3.9.2 Standard Normal Probability Distribution

- A random variable that has a normal distribution with a **mean of zero and a standard deviation of one** is said to have a **standard normal probability distribution**.
- The letter z is commonly used to designate this normal random variable.
- The following expression (Equation 3.24) converts any normal distribution into the standard normal distribution:

$$z = \frac{x - \mu}{\sigma}$$

(3.24)

In this section we discussed the basics of probability theory, which is an important mathematical basis for many machine learning techniques.

3.3.10 Use Case—Bayes Theorem—Diagnostic Test Scenario

We consider a typical medical diagnosis scenario.

Scenario: Consider a human population that may have the COVID-19 disease (COVID-19 is True or False) and a medical test that returns positive or negative for COVID-19 detection (test is Positive or Negative).

Problem: *What is the probability that the patient has COVID-19 given that the test comes back positive?*

Given values:

A patient can have COVID-19, but the test may not detect it. This capability of the test to detect COVID-19 is referred to as the **sensitivity**, or the true positive rate. In this case, we assume a sensitivity value of 85%. In other words

$$\text{Sensitivity} = P(\text{Test} = +ve | \text{COVID} - 19 = \text{True}) = 0.90$$

Now, we can assume the probability of COVID-19 given that infection rate is low and it is (0.0001); 0.01% have COVID-19.

$$\text{Infection rate} = P(\text{COVID} - 19 = \text{True}) = 0.01\% = 0.0001$$

We also assume that is the probability of a negative test result (Test=-ve) given a person has no COVID-19 (COVID-19 = False). This is called as the true negative rate or the **specificity**.

$$\text{Specificity} = P(\text{Test} = -ve | \text{COVID} - 19 = \text{False}) = 0.98$$

Using the Bayes Theorem

The probability of a patient having COVID-19 given a positive test result can be calculated using the Bayes theorem.

$$P(\text{COVID} - 19 = \text{True} | \text{Test} = +ve) - \text{Posterior probability}$$

Let's map our scenario onto the Bayes theorem rule:

$$P(A|B) = \frac{P(B|A)P(A)}{P(B)}$$

The Bayes rule for the problem:

$$P(\text{COVID} - 19 = \text{True} | \text{Test} = +ve)$$
$$= \frac{P(\text{Test} = +ve | \text{COVID} - 19 = \text{True})P(\text{COVID} - 19 = \text{True})}{P(\text{Test} = +ve)}$$

In this mapping we have the following given values only:

$$\text{Sensitivity} = P(\text{Test} = +ve | \text{COVID} - 19 = \text{True}) = 0.90 \left(\text{Likelihood} \right)$$

$$\text{Infection Rate} = P(\text{COVID} - 19 = \text{True}) = 0.0001$$

Now we have to calculate $P(\text{Test} = +ve)$

Calculation of $P(\text{Test} = +ve)$

However, we are not given $P(\text{Test} = +ve)$, but we will estimate this value.

$$P(B) = P(B|A) * P(A) + P(B| \sim A) * P(\sim A)$$

$$P(\text{Test} = +\text{ve}) = P(\text{Test} = +\text{ve}|\text{COVID} - 19 = \text{True}) * P(\text{COVID} - 19 = \text{True})$$
$$+ P(\text{Test} = +\text{ve}|\text{COVID} - 19 = \text{False}) * P(\text{COVID} - 19 = \text{False})$$

Step1a: Calculation of *P*(COVID-19 = False)
First, we can calculate

$$P(\text{COVID} - 19 = \text{False}) = P(\text{COVID} - 19 = \text{False}) = 1 - P(\text{COVID} - 19 = \text{True})$$
$$= 1 - 0.0001$$
$$= 0.9999$$

Step 1b: Calculation of False Positive Rate
The false positive or false alarm rate can be calculated given specificity value *P*(Test = −*ve* | COVID-19 = False)= 0.98

$$P(\text{Test} = +\text{ve} | \text{COVID} - 19 = \text{False}) = 1 - P(\text{Test} = -\text{ve} | \text{COVID} - 19 = \text{False})$$
$$= 1 - 0.98$$
$$= 0.02$$

Now we can plug this false alarm rate into our calculation of $P(\text{Test} = +ve)$

$$P(\text{Test} = +\text{ve}) = P(\text{Test} = +\text{ve} |\text{COVID} - 19 = \text{True}) * P(\text{COVID} - 19 = \text{True})$$
$$+ P(\text{Test} = +\text{ve} |\text{COVID} - 19 = \text{False}) * P(\text{COVID} - 19 = \text{False})$$
$$= 0.90^* 0.0001 + 0.02^* 0.9999$$
$$= 0.020088$$

In other words, irrespective of the person suffering from COVID-19 or not, the probability of the test returning a positive result is about 2%.
Calculation After Plugging into Bayes Theorem
With information available, we can estimate the probability of a randomly selected person having COVID-19 if they get a positive test result using the Bayes theorem.

$$P(\text{COVID} - 19 = \text{True} \| \text{Test} = +\text{ve}) = \frac{P(\text{Test} = +\text{ve} | \text{COVID} - 19 = \text{True}) \; P(\text{COVID} - 19 = \text{True})}{P(\text{Test} = +\text{ve})}$$
$$= \frac{0.90^* 0.0001}{0.020088}$$
$$= 0.00448$$

This shows that even if a patient tests positive with this test, the probability that they have COVID-19 is only 0.44%. In a diagnostic setup, considerable information such as sensitivity, infection rate, and specificity is needed for the determination of conditional probability.

3.4 Information Theory

Information theory is about the analysis of a communication system and is concerned with data compression and transmission, and it builds upon probability and supports machine learning. Information provides a way to quantify the amount of surprise for an event measured in bits. Quantifying information essentially means measuring how much surprise there is in an event. Those events that are rare have low probability and are more surprising, and therefore have more information than those events that are common and have high probability. Information theory quantifies how much information there is in a message, and in general, it can be used to quantify the information in an event and a random variable. This is called entropy and is calculated using probability.

Calculating information and entropy is used in machine learning and forms the basis for techniques such as feature selection, building decision trees, and in general for fitting classification models.

Claude Shannon came up with the mathematical theory of communication which was published in the *Bell System Technical Journal* in 1948 (Shannon 1948) and marked the beginning of the area of information theory. Shannon's theory remains the guiding foundation for the most modern, faster, more energy efficient, and more robust communication systems.

3.4.1 Shannon's Fundamental Theorems

Data compression (entropy) and the transmission rate (channel capacity) can be the basis for maximizing the amount of information that can be transmitted over an imperfect communication channel. Shannon stated an important coding theorem: "Source coding and channel coding can be optimized *independently*, where *binary symbols* can be used as intermediate format assuming that the delays are arbitrarily long."

3.4.1.1 Information Source

The characteristics of any information source can be specified in terms of the number of symbols n, say $S1$, $S2$,....,Sn and the probability of occurrence of each of these symbols, $P(S_1)$, $P(S_2)$, ..., $P(S_n)$; the correlation between a stream of successive symbols (called a message) can specify the characteristics of an information source.

3.4.1.2 Stochastic Sources

Assume that a source outputs symbols $X1$, $X2$, ... which take their values from an alphabet $A = (a1, a2, ...)$. The model $P(X1,...,XN)$ will be a sequence consisting of all combinations. For such stochastic sources, there are two special cases:

- The **memoryless source** where the value of each symbol is independent of the value of the previous symbols in the sequence.

  $P(S1, S2, ..., Sn) = P(S1) . P(S2) . .... .P(Sn)$

- The **Markov source** where the value of each symbol depends only on the value of the previous one in the sequence.

  $P(S1, S2, ..., Sn) = P(S1) . P(S2 | S1) . P(S3 | S2) . .... . P(Sn | Sn-1)$

3.4.2 Self Information

Before we discuss entropy associated with information, let us understand how to measure the amount of information contained in a message from the sender to the receiver. We can calculate the amount of information there is in an event using the probability of the event. This is called "Shannon information," "self-information," or simply the information.

Shannon associated self information in order to find the amount of information conveyed by a symbol a_i of a memoryless source with alphabet $A = (a_1, ..., a_n)$ and symbol probabilities $(p_1, ..., p_n)$, knowing that the next symbol is a_i. The negative of the algorithm is taken to indicate that with decreasing probabilities the information conveyed increases (Equation 3.25).

$$I(a_i) = \log \frac{1}{p_i} = -\log(p_i) \tag{3.25}$$

where log() is the base-2 logarithm and $p(x)$ is the probability of the event x.

The choice of the base-2 logarithm means that the unit of the information measure is in bits (binary digits). This can be directly interpreted in the information processing sense as the number of bits required to represent the event.

Example 3.10:   Self Information—Result of a Student

Let us find the amount of information obtained during the result of an examination where the student gets a pass. If the result is fair, i.e., $P(\text{pass}) = P(\text{fail}) = 0.5$, the amount of information obtained is 1 bit. However, if we already have the information that the result is pass, i.e., $P(\text{pass}) = 1$, then the amount of information obtained is zero. The amount of information is greater than 0 and less than 1 if we have an unfair result.

$$p_i = 0.5 = I(0.5) = \log_2 \frac{1}{0.5} = 1\,[bit]$$

$$p_i = 1 = I(1) = \log_2 \frac{1}{1} = 0$$

Assume two independent events A and B, with probabilities $P(A) = p_A$ and $P(B) = p_B$. When both the events happen, the probability is $p_A \cdot p_B$. The amount of information is as follows (Equation 3.26):

$$I(P_A . P_B) = I(P_A) + I(P_B) \tag{3.26}$$

3.4.3 Entropy

Entropy provides a measure of the average amount of information needed to represent an event drawn from a probability distribution of a random variable. Information about the symbols in a sequence is given by *averaging over the probability of all the symbols*, given as (Equation 3.27):

$$H = \sum_{1}^{N} p_i a_i \tag{3.27}$$

$H(X)$ is the degree of *uncertainty* about the succeeding symbol and hence is called the first-order *entropy* of the source.

Source entropy is defined as the minimum average number of binary digits needed to specify a source output uniquely. Entropy is the average length of the message needed to transmit an outcome using the optimal code.

For a memoryless source,

$$p = P(X_k = 1), q = P(X_k = 0) = 1 - p$$

Then entropy is as given in Equation (3.28):

$$H = p \log \frac{1}{p} + (1-p) \log \frac{1}{1-p} \tag{3.28}$$

where H is often denoted as $h(p)$. The uncertainty (information) is greatest when $p = q = \frac{1}{2}$.

Entropy H is a measurement of information. Its value lies between 0 and log N. The maximum value occurs when all symbols are equiprobable.

3.4.4 Entropy for Memory and Markov Sources

Entropy for Memory Source

Assuming a block of source symbols $(X_1, \ldots, X_n)$, we can define the *block entropy* in Equation (3.29):

$$H(X_1, \ldots, X_n) = \sum_{1}^{Nn} P(X_1, \ldots, X_n) \log \frac{1}{P(X_1, \ldots, X_n)} \tag{3.29}$$

Assuming that the block length approaches infinity, we can divide by n to get the number of bits per symbol. Thus the entropy for a memory source is defined as follows (Equation 3.30):

$$H_\infty = \lim_{n \to \infty} \frac{1}{n} H(X_1, \ldots, X_n) \tag{3.30}$$

Entropy for a Markov Source

The entropy for a state S_k can be expressed as follows (Equation 3.31):

$$H(S_k) = \sum_{i=1}^{r} P_{kl} \log \frac{1}{P_{kl}} \tag{3.31}$$

In this case P_{kl} is the transition probability from state k to state l in a sequence. Averaging over all states, we get the entropy for the Markov source as follows (Equation 3.32):

$$H_M = \sum_{k=1}^{r} P(S_k) H(S_k)$$

(3.32)

where summation lower index $k = 1$.

3.4.4.1 The Source Coding Theorem

Shannon shows that source coding algorithms exist that have a unique average representation length that approaches the entropy of the source, and we cannot reduce beyond this length. A *long* sequence from a binary memoryless source with $P(1) = p$, with approximately $w = n \cdot p$ ones is assumed; then the number of bits per symbol we need to code any typical sequence is $H(X)$ and the entropy is given by Equation (3.33):

$$H(X) = h(p) = -p \log p - (1-p) \log (1-p)$$

(3.33)

Entropy can be used as a measure to determine the quality of our models and as a measure the difference between two probability distributions. We will discuss these aspects later.

3.4.5 Cross Entropy

Cross-entropy is a measure from the field of information theory, building upon entropy and generally calculating the difference between two probability distributions. Cross-entropy can be used as a loss function when optimizing classification models like logistic regression and artificial neural networks. Cross entropy is a concept very similar to relative entropy. Relative entropy is when a random variable compares the true distribution p with how the approximated distribution q differs from p at each sample point (divergence or difference). On the other hand, cross-entropy directly compares true distribution p with approximated distribution q. Cross-entropy is heavily used in the field of deep learning. It is used as a loss function that measures the performance of a classification model whose output is a probability value between 0 and 1. Cross-entropy loss increases as the predicted probability diverges from the actual label.

3.4.6 Kullback–Leibler Divergence or Relative Entropy

Relative entropy, also called KL divergence (Kullback–Leiber divergence), is **the measurement of the distance of two probability distributions**. The relative entropy or Kullback–Leibler divergence score, or KL divergence score, quantifies how much one probability distribution differs from another probability distribution (over the same event space). The *KL* divergence between two distributions Q and P is often stated using the following notation:

KL($P \parallel Q$), where the " $\parallel$ " operator indicates "divergence" or *P*s divergence from Q.

KL divergence can be calculated as the positive sum of probability of each event in P multiplied by the log of the probability of the event in P over the probability of the event in Q (e.g., the terms in the fraction are flipped). This is the more common implementation used in practice (Equation 3.34):

$$KL(P \| Q) = \text{sum x in } X\, P(x) * \log\big(P(x)/Q(x)\big) \tag{3.34}$$

The KL divergence between p and q can also be seen as the average number of bits that are wasted by encoding events from a distribution p with a code based on a not-quite-right distribution q. The intuition for the KL divergence score is that when the probability for an event from P is large, but the probability for the same event in Q is small, there is a large divergence. It can be used to measure the divergence between discrete and continuous probability distributions, where in the latter case the integral of the events is calculated instead of the sum of the probabilities of the discrete events.

In this section we discussed information theory which will be used in decision trees in general machine learning evaluation.

3.5 Summary

- Discussed the basics of linear algebra and the need for linear algebra in machine learning.
- Outlined the definitions of basics of probability for machine learning and its role in machine learning.
- Explained the concept of the Bayes theorem and the concepts of Bayesian learning to understand the normal probability distribution.
- Discussed the principles and practice of information theory.
- Outlined the role of the preceding mathematical concepts in machine learning.

3.6 Points to Ponder

- Most data is represented with vectors or matrices.
- Probability plays a major role in machine learning.
- Entropy for information gained in your professional degree is an interesting concept.

E.3 Exercises

E.3.1 Suggested Activities

Case study

E.3.1.1 Take an example of university results and formulate it as a Bayes method. Clearly state any assumptions made.

E.3.1.2 Use Case—Bayes Theorem—Bayesian Spam Filtering

- Assume that we want to use the Bayes theorem to carry out spam filtering given some words. We assume the Event A is that the message is spam. We have a Test X that records that the message contains certain words.
- Given:
  i. The probability of Test X being true given that the message is spam = 0.85%.
  ii. The probability that a message is generally spam is 30%.
  iii. The probability that the message is not spam although Test X is true = 2%.
- We need to find the probability of the message being spam given that the test is true, that is, it contains certain words.

Self-Assessment Questions

E.3.2 Multiple Choice Questions

Give answers with justification for correct and wrong choices.

E.3.2.1 The most common data organization for machine learning is a
    i Graph
    ii Array
    iii String

E.3.2.2 For a matrix A, the inverse of the matrix does exist if and only if the
    i Matrix is singular and square
    ii Matrix is nonsingular and square
    iii Matrix is singular and rectangular

E.3.2.3 The rank of a matrix if the number of linearly independent rows (or equivalently columns)
    i Is the number of linearly independent rows
    ii Is the number of rows
    iii Is the product of rows and columns

E.3.2.4 Two variables are independent
    i If their rank is zero
    ii If their covariance equals one
    iii if their covariance equals zero

$$\begin{pmatrix} 1 & 1 & 0 & 0 \\ 2 & 2 & 0 & 0 \\ 0 & 0 & 3 & 0 \\ 0 & 0 & 5 & 5 \end{pmatrix}$$

E.3.2.5 The number of linearly independent eigen vectors is
    i 1
    ii 3
    iii 4

E.3.2.6 $A^2 - A = 0$, where A is a 9×9 matrix. Then
    i A must be a zero matrix
    ii A is an identity matrix
    iii A is diagonalizable

E.3.2.7 A is 5×5 matrix, all of whose entries are 1, then
    i A is not diagonalizable
    ii A is idempotent
    iii The minimal polynomial and the characteristics polynomial of A are not equal.

E.3.2.8 The sample space is
    i All events in the space
    ii Variables that fit the distribution
    iii Values that variables take

E.3.2.9 What is conditional probability?
    i Probability of two event occurring together
    ii Probability of one event, given that another event has occurred
    iii Probability of two events not occurring together

E.3.2.10 There are only crayons in a pencil case, and the crayons are either orange, purple, or brown. The table shows the probability of taking at random a brown crayon from the pencil case.

Colour	orange	purple	brown
Probability			0.4

    The number of orange crayons in the pencil case is the same as the number of purple crayons. Complete the table.
    i 0.2, 0.2
    ii 0.3, 0.3
    iii 0.4, 0.2

E.3.2.11 What will be the probability of getting odd numbers if a die is thrown?
    i 2
    ii ½
    iii ¼

E.3.2.12 The probability of getting two tails when two coins are tossed is
    i ¼
    ii 1/3
    iii 1/6

E.3.2.13 In a box, there are 8 orange, 7 white, and 6 blue balls. If a ball is picked up randomly, what is the probability that it is neither orange nor blue?
    i 1/21
    ii 5/21
    iii 1/3

E.3.2.14 In 30 balls, a batsman hits the boundaries 6 times. What will be the probability that he did not hit the boundaries?
    i 1/5
    ii 4/5
    iii 3/5

E.3.2.15 A card is drawn from a well shuffled pack of 52 cards. Find the probability that the card is neither a heart nor a red king.
    i 27/52
    ii 25/52
    iii 38/52

E.3.2.16 The conditional probability $P(Ei\,|\,A)$ is called a _____ probability of the hypothesis Ei.
    i Bayes
    ii Posteriori
    iii Hypothesis

E.3.2.17 The normal distribution is used
    i To determine the probability distribution used when we have to find the probability that at least 1 outlier is detected while clustering is done for the documents in the PUBMED corpus.
    ii To determine whether a researcher is an expert in an area.
    iii To determine the probability distribution used when we have to find the probability that at least 4 out of 10 sentences have two articles (*a, an, the*) in them.

E.3.2.18 The shape of a normal distribution is
    i Bell shaped
    ii Circular
    iii Spiked

E.3.2.19 Suppose you could take all samples of size 64 from a population with a mean of 12 and a standard deviation of 3.2. What would be the standard deviation of the sample means?
    i 3.2
    ii 0.2
    iii 0.4

E.3.2.20 For M equally likely messages, the average amount of information H is
    i $H = \log_{10}M$
    ii $H = \log_2 M$
    iii $H = \log_{10}M^2$

E.3.2.21 The entropy for a fair coin toss is exactly
     i   5 bits
    ii   2 bits
  iii   1 bit

E.3.3 Match the Columns

No		Match
E.3.3.1 Linear algebra	**A**	Dimensionality reduction
E.3.3.2 Bayesian optimization	**B**	Dimensionality reduction technique—tSNE
E.3.3.3 Entropy	**C**	Decision tree learning
E.3.3.4 Probability theory	**D**	Calculate target class imbalances
E.3.3.5 Vectors	**E**	Data representation of attributes of input, image, audio, text
E.3.3.6 KL divergence	**F**	Map input and output
E.3.3.7 Information gain	**G**	Cosine similarity
E.3.3.8 Linear transformation	**H**	Maximum likelihood estimation (MLE)
E.3.3.9 Eigen vectors	**I**	Classification models generally predict extent of class membership.
E.3.3.10 Probability value	**J**	Model hyper-parameters are configured with probability

E.3.4 Problems

E.3.4.1 A coin is thrown three times. What is the probability that at least one head is obtained?

E.3.4.2 Find the probability of getting a numbered card when a card is drawn from the pack of 52 cards.

E.3.4.3 A problem is given to three students, Ram, Tom, and Hari, whose chances of solving it are $2/7, 4/7, 4/9$ respectively. What is the probability that the problem is solved?

E.3.4.4 A vessel contains 5 red balls, 5 green balls, 10 blue balls, and 10 white balls. If four balls are drawn from the vessel at random, what is the probability that the first ball is red, the second ball is green, the third ball is blue, and finally the fourth ball is white?

E.3.4.5 Suppose you were interviewed for a technical role. 50% of the people who sat for the first interview received the call for a second interview. 95% of the people who got a call for the second interview felt good about their first interview. 75% of people who did not receive a second call also felt good about their first interview. If you felt good after your first interview, what is the probability that you will receive a second interview call?

E.3.4.6 Suppose we send 40% of our dresses to shop A and 60% of our dresses to shop B. Shop A reports that 4% of our dresses are defective, and shop B reports that 3% of our dresses are defective. (Use a tree diagram)
  a. Find the probability that a dress is sent to shop A and it is defective.
  b. Find the probability that a dress is sent to shop A and it is not defective.
  c. Find the probability that a dress is sent to shop B and it is defective.
  d. Find the probability that a dress is sent to shop B and it is not defective.

E.3.4.7 Assume you sell sandwiches. 60% people choose vegetable, and the rest choose cheese. What is the probability of selling two vegetable sandwiches to the next three customers?

E.3.4.8 One of two boxes contains 5 red balls and 4 green balls, and the second box contains 2 green and 3 red balls. By design, the probabilities of selecting box 1 or box 2 at random are 1/4 for box 1 and 3/4 for box 2. A box is selected at random, and a ball is selected at random from it.
   a. Given that the ball selected is red, what is the probability it was selected from the first box?
   b. Given that the ball selected is red, what is the probability it was selected from the second box?

E.3.4.9 0.5% of a population have a certain disease and the remaining 99.5% are free from this disease. A test is used to detect this disease. This test is positive in 95% of the people with the disease and is also (falsely) positive in 5% of the people free from the disease. If a person, selected at random from this population, has tested positive, what is the probability that they do not have the disease?

E.3.4.10 Three factories produce air conditioners to supply to the market. Factory A produces 30%, factory B produces 50%, and factory produces 20%. 2% of the air conditioners produced in factory A, 2% produced in factory B, and 1% produced in factory C are defective. An air conditioner selected at random from the market was found to be defective. What is the probability that this air conditioner was produced by factory B?

E.3.5 Short Questions

E.3.5.1   What is the importance of vectors in machine learning? Explain.

E.3.5.2   Differentiate between linear dependence and linear independence.

E.3.5.3   Discuss covariance between two variables.

E.3.5.4   What are the three fundamental axioms of probability?

E.3.5.5   What are the three approaches to probability? Discuss.

E.3.5.6   Explain collectively exhaustive events with an example.

E.3.5.7   Differentiate between marginal, joint, and conditional probabilities.

E.3.5.8   What is the Bayes theorem? Explain with an example

E.3.5.9   Describe the characteristics of a normal probability distribution.

E.3.5.10   Discuss self-information.

E.3.5.11   Differentiate between entropy, cross-entropy, and relative entropy.

E.3.5.12   Differentiate between entropy of a memory source and a Markov source.

4

Foundations and Categories of Machine Learning Techniques

4.1 Introduction

Data refers to distinct pieces of information, usually formatted and stored in such a way that it can be used for a specific purpose. The basic aspect of machine learning is data and how it is collected and represented, how features specific to the objective of the learning process and their representation are described, and the types of machine learning algorithms used. In this chapter we will discuss these aspects. We will also discuss the underlying concepts of machine learning algorithms.

4.1.1 Data and Its Importance

The basic goal of machine learning is to predict results based on data. All machine learning tasks can be represented this way. The greater variety in the samples you have, the easier it is to find relevant patterns and predict the result. Therefore, one of the important components of a machine learning problem is the data used. The more diverse the data, the better the result. Tens of thousands of samples are the bare minimum needed for proper learning. The data is collected from databases, online platforms, documents, sensors, industrial processes, and so on; it can be in many forms and formats such as structured, unstructured, and so on; and it can be clean or messy. In machine learning, data is viewed as a list of examples. Ideally, we need many examples of the same nature. Each example is often represented as a vector of numbers (if it is not, we convert it into such vectors). Figure 4.1 shows an example of image labelling of fruits. Please notice how the image has been converted into a feature vector of dimension d after appropriate preprocessing.

4.1.2 Problem Dimensions

When we talk of a machine learning problem we talk of problem dimensions, the number of samples n (often very large), input dimensionality d that is the number of input features or attributes characterizing each sample (often 100 to 1000 or even more), and target dimensionality m, for example the number of classes (often small). The data suitable for machine learning will often be organized as a matrix having dimension $n \times (d + 1)$ if the target dimension is 1 as is true in many applications (as in Figure 4.1) or $n \times (d + m)$ if the target dimension is m. The data set shown in Figure 4.1 can be visualized as a point cloud in a high-dimensional vector space as shown in Figure 4.2.

DOI: 10.1201/9781003290100-4

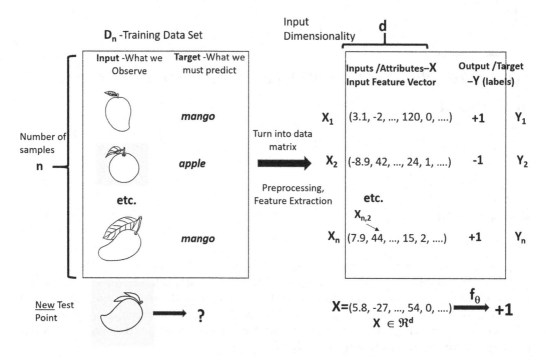

FIGURE 4.1
Data representation for binary classification of images.

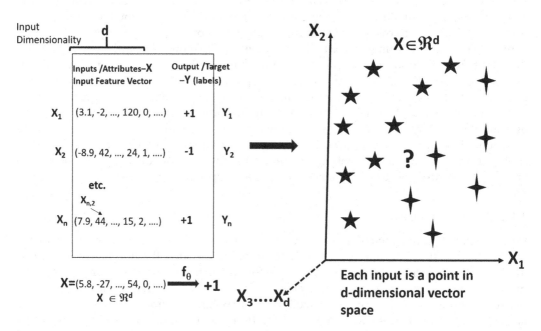

FIGURE 4.2
Data set as a point cloud in high-dimensional vector space.

Cell sample images from tumours in breast cancer patients before surgery. Follow-up of patients were carried out to determine whether the cancer recurred and time until reoccurrence or disease free					
Tumor Size	**Texture**	**Perimeter**	....	**Outcome**	**Time**
18.62	25.67	118,50		N	34
17.50	12,35	125.62		N	67
19.58	15.67	138.90		R	28
....	....	....		....	....
....	....	....		....	....
We assume thirty real valued features per tumour. Two variables can be predicted • Outcome (R-Recurred & N – Non-Reoccurrence) – Binary Classification • Time (until reoccurrence for R and time healthy for N) - Regression					

FIGURE 4.3
Example of data set with two target variables.

As we will discuss later, in the case of classification the labels will be discrete; in the care of regression they will be continuous; and in case of structured prediction these labels may be more complex. In the example in Figure 4.1, we assumed one target variable, but there can be more than one target variable. Such an example is shown in Figure 4.3 where two variables are predicted; one is binary classification and the other is a regression problem, the details of which will be discussed later.

4.2 Data and Data Representation

In the previous examples the input variables shown were real valued. However, data can be of many types. In addition, there are other aspects of data that need to be understood.

4.2.1 Types of Data

The following are the common types of data that can be used to represent features:

- **Discrete data**: A set of data having a finite number of values or data points is called discrete data. In other words, discrete data only include integer values. "Count" data, derived by counting the number of events or animals of interest, are types of discrete data. Other examples of discrete data include marks, number of registered cars, number of children in a family, and number of students in a class.

- **Ordinal data**: Ordinal data are inherently categorical in nature but have an intrinsic order to them. A set of data is said to be ordinal if the values or observations belonging to it can be ranked or have an attached rating scale. Examples include academic grades (i.e., O, A+, A, B+), clothing size, and positions in an organization.

- **Continuous or real valued data**: Continuous data can take any of a range of values, and the possible number of different values which the data can take is infinite. Examples of types of continuous data are weight, height, and the infectious period of a pathogen. Age may be classified as either discrete (as it is commonly measured in whole years) or continuous (as the concept of a fraction of a year is possible).

- **Structural, temporal, and spatio-temporal data**: In addition, structural, temporal, spatial, and spatio-temporal models can also be used as input data to represent features. Examples of structural data include library catalogues (date, author, place, subject, etc.) and census records (birth, income, employment, place, etc.). Temporal data examples include showing the time stamp of the change in percentage of forest land worldwide from 1990 to 2020. This is also an example of a spatio-temporal model.

4.2.2 Data Dependencies

Another important aspect to be considered when talking about input data is the data dependencies between the different features.

- **Independent and identically identified (IID)**: In many cases of machine learning a simplifying assumption is made regarding data dependency. This assumption is the so-called independent and identically identified (IID) and refers to sequences of random variables. "Independent and identically distributed" implies an element in the sequence is independent of the random variables that came before it.

- **Linear and nonlinear dependencies**: The dependencies between different input data can sometimes be represented by linear functions or may be complex, in which case the dependencies can be represented only by a nonlinear function.

- **Observable versus latent variables**: Another important concept about the data is whether the variables are observable or latent. Observable variables can be directly measured. Latent variables or hidden variables are not directly observable but are inferred from observable variables. One advantage of using latent variables is that it reduces the dimensionality of data. Examples include abstract concepts, like categories, quality of life, or mental states.

- **Availability of prior knowledge**: Another important aspect of the input data is the presence or absence of prior knowledge. A majority of learning systems do not have prior knowledge while statistical learning systems use prior knowledge.

- **Presence of missing data**: There may a number of reasons why missing data occur, including human errors during data entry, incorrect sensor readings, missing pixels of camera, censored data, and software bugs in the data processing pipeline. There are many ways of dealing with such data, which will be discussed in subsequent chapters.

4.2.3 Data Representation

The way the input is represented by a model is also important for the machine learning process. Vectors and matrices are the most common representations used in machine learning. Vectors are collections of features, examples being height, weight, blood pressure, age, and so forth. Categorical variables can also be mapped to vectors. Matrices are often used to represent documents, images, multispectral satellite data, and so on. In addition, graphs provide a richer representation. Examples include recommendation systems with graph databases which enable learning the paths customers take when buying a product, and when another new customer is halfway through that path, we recommend where they may want to go.

The representations may be the instances themselves but may also include decision trees, graphical models, sets of rules or logic programs, neural networks, and so on. These representations are usually based on some mathematical concepts. Decision trees are based on propositional logic, Bayesian networks are based on probabilistic descriptions, and neural networks are based on linear weighted polynomials.

4.2.4 Processing Data

The data given to the learning system may require a lot of cleaning. Cleaning involves getting rid of errors and noise and removal of redundancies.

Data preprocessing: Real-world data generally contains noises; is missing values; can be incomplete, inconsistent, or inaccurate (contains errors or outliers); and often lacks specific attribute values or trends and hence cannot be directly used for machine learning models. Data preprocessing helps to clean, format, and organize the raw data and make the data ready to be used by machine learning models in order to achieve effective learning. The first step is the acquiring of the data set, which comprises data gathered from multiple and disparate sources which are then combined in a proper format to form a data set. Data set formats differ according to use cases. For instance, a business data set will contain relevant industry and business data while a medical data set will include healthcare-related data. **Data cleaning** is one of the most important steps of preprocessing and is the process of adding missing data and correcting, repairing, or removing incorrect or irrelevant data from a data set.

Preprocessing techniques include renaming, rescaling, discretizing, abstracting, aggregating, and introducing new attributes. Renaming or relabeling is the conversion of categorical values to numbers. However, this conversion may be inappropriate when used with some learning methods. Such an example is shown in Figure 4.3 where numbers impose an order to the values that is not warranted.

Some types of preprocessing are discussed subsequently. Rescaling, also called normalization, is the transferring of continuous values to some range, typically [–1, 1] or [0, 1]. Discretization or binning involves the conversion of continuous values to a finite set of discrete values. Another technique is abstraction, where categorical values are merged together. In aggregation, actual values are replaced by values obtained with summary or aggregation operations, such as minimum value, maximum value, average, and so on. Finally, sometimes new attributes that define a relationship with existing attributes are introduced. An example is replacing weight and height attributes by a new attribute, obesity factor, which is calculated as weight/height. These preprocessing techniques are used only when the learning is not affected due to such preprocessing.

4.2.5 Data Biases

It is important to watch out for data biases. For this we need to understand the data source. It is very easy to derive unexpected results when data used for analysis and learning are biased (preselected). The results or conclusions derived for preselected data do not hold for general cases.

4.2.6 Features and Feature Selection

4.2.6.1 Why Feature Selection?

Features are the basic building blocks of data sets. The quality of the features in our data set has a major impact on the quality of the learning we achieve when using that data set for machine learning. The selection of features also depends on the particular machine learning task. The first task is feature extraction; that is, the task of obtaining meaningful and accurate features. For example, if music tempo is required to determine emotion in music, then music tempo needs to be a feature for the task.

Sometimes the size (dimension) of a sample collection can be enormous. First, we need to remove redundant or irrelevant features. It is not true that the greater the number of features, the better the machine learning model. The selection of features requires prior knowledge about the characteristics of the input data. Whether we retain selected features or conceive new features, we are alleviating the problem of the so-called "curse of dimensionality" (discussed in detail in a later chapter) which states that as the number of features increases, the volume of the feature space increases exponentially, adversely affecting the process of machine learning.

4.2.6.2 Approaches to Feature Selection

Feature selection is the problem of selecting some subset of a learning algorithm's input variables upon which it should focus attention, while ignoring the rest. Mathematically speaking, given a set of features $F = \{f1,..., fi ,..., fn\}$ the feature selection aims to find a subset F' that maximizes the learner's ability to classify patterns. One method used for reducing features in a data set is called dimensionality reduction. Though feature selection and dimensionality reduction have the same goals of reducing features, feature selection retains a feature or removes it completely from the data set while dimensionality reduction reduces the number of features by creating new features as combinations of existing ones.

Feature subset selection reduces dimensionality of data without creating new features. This is carried out by removing the following types of features: redundant features, where highly correlated features contain duplicate information; irrelevant features, which have no information; and noisy features where the signal-to-noise ratio is too low, each being useless for discriminating outcome. Some of the approaches to feature subset selection include filter approaches, wrapper approaches, and embedded approaches. In filter approaches, features are selected before the machine learning algorithm is run, while in wrapper approaches, the machine learning algorithm is used as a black box to find the best subset of features. In the embedded method, feature selection occurs naturally as part of the machine learning algorithm.

4.2.6.3 Feature Extraction

In some cases, instead of only reducing existing features, well-conceived new features can capture the important information in a data set much more effectively than the existing original features. In this context, three general methodologies are used, namely feature extraction, which can be domain specific and typically results in significant reduction in dimensionality; mapping existing features to a new space using an appropriate mapping function; and feature construction, where existing features are combined. One method of dimensionality reduction is to extract relevant inputs using a measure such as a mutual

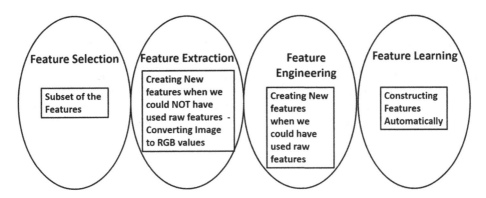

FIGURE 4.4
Perspectives of feature processing.

information measure. Another method of dimensionality reduction which can be explained with the example of document classification is the grouping or clustering of similar words using a suitable similarity measure and replacing the group of words with group label. The differences between feature selection, feature extraction, feature engineering, and feature learning can be explained by Figure 4.4. Feature learning is generally associated with deep learning, which we will discuss in subsequent chapters.

Benefits of reducing the feature set include alleviation of the curse of dimensionality, enhancing generalization, speeding up the learning process, and in some cases improving model interpretability.

4.3 Basis of Machine Learning

4.3.1 Inductive Learning

The basis of machine learning is inductive learning. Inductive reasoning moves from specific observations to broader generalizations and theories, or in other words is based on the bottom-up approach. This is different from deduction, which works in the opposite manner and seeks to learn specific concepts from general rules. In inductive reasoning, we begin with specific observations (the data), then go on to detect patterns and regularities, formulate some tentative hypotheses that we can explore, and finally end up developing a general model. This is the same process as that of a supervised learning model.

In inductive learning, given examples of a function $(X, F(X))$, we are required to predict function $F(X)$ for new examples X. The function $F(X)$ can be:

- Discrete $F(X)$: Classification—classification (discrete labels)—for example, predicting whether e-mail is spam or not
- Continuous $F(X)$: Regression—regression (real values)—for example, predicting tomorrow's temperature
- $F(X) = \text{Probability}(X)$: Probability estimation

4.3.2 Generalization

The central concept of machine learning is the generalization from data by finding patterns in data. Machine learning attempts to generalize beyond the input examples given at the time of learning the model by applying the model and making predictions about hitherto unseen examples during test time. Generalization decides how well a model performs on new data. Now the big question is how to get good generalization with a limited number of examples. The intuitive idea is based on the concept of Occam's razor, which advises favoring simpler hypothesis when we select among a set of possible hypothesis. For example, a simpler decision boundary may not fit ideally to the training data but tends to generalize better to new data.

4.3.3 Bias and Variance

A good machine learning model generalizes input training data and the model to make predictions on hitherto unseen data. Now let us understand the following two components of generalization error in association with the modelling of the data:

- **Bias** indicates the extent to which the average model over all training sets differs from the true model. Bias is affected by the assumptions or simplifications made by a model to make a function easier to learn or caused because the model cannot represent the concept. High bias results in a weaker modelling process having a simple fixed size model with small feature set.
- **Variance** indicates the extent to which models estimated from different training sets differ from each other. In other words, if the model is trained using a data set and a very low error value is obtained, but when the data set is changed using the same model, a high error value is obtained, then variance is said to occur. This may be because the learning algorithm overreacts to small changes (noise) in the training data. High variance results in a complex scalable model of a higher order polynomial with a large feature set.

When we are finding a model to fit the data, there needs to be a trade-off between bias and variance since they measure two different sources of error of the model. As discussed, bias measures the expected deviation from the true value of the function or parameter of the model while variance provides a measure of the expected deviation that any particular sampling of the data is likely to cause.

4.3.4 Overfitting and Underfitting

In order to check how well our machine learning model learns and generalizes to the new data, we must understand the concepts of overfitting and underfitting, which mainly decide the performance of machine learning algorithms. The data fitting leading to underfitting, appropriate fitting, and overfitting is shown in Figure 4.5.

4.3.4.1 Overfitting

Overfitting occurs when the model fits the training data including the details and therefore does not generalize so it performs badly on the test data. This can happen if a model fits more data than needed and starts fitting the noisy data and inaccurate values in the data. Overfitting is often a result of an excessively complicated model which even fits irrelevant

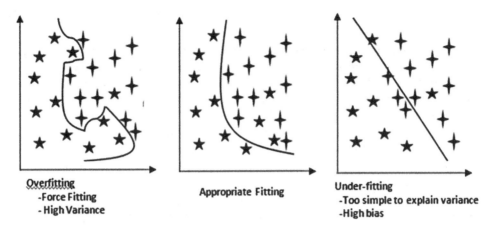

FIGURE 4.5
Overfitting and underfitting.

characteristics such as noise and can lead to poor performance on unseen data. This means that the noise or random fluctuations in the training data are picked up and learned as concepts by the model. The problem is that these learnt concepts do not apply to new data, hence impacting the generalization of the model. Thus overfitting occurs when there is high variance and low bias.

Overfitting is more likely with flexible nonparametric and nonlinear models; many such algorithms often constrain the amount of detail learnt. For example, decision trees are a nonparametric machine learning algorithm that is very flexible and is subject to overfitting training data. Methods to address these issues will be discussed in the respective chapters. A simple solution to avoid overfitting is using a linear algorithm if we have linear data.

The evaluation of machine learning algorithms carried out on training data is different than the evaluation that is actually required on unseen data, resulting in overfitting becoming a problem.

4.3.4.1.1 Methods to Avoid Overfitting

Here we discuss several techniques used in general to avoid overfitting in machine learning.

- **Hold-out method** is a technique where we hold some data out of the training set and train or fit the model on the remaining training set (without data held out) and finally use the held out data for fine tuning the model.

- **Cross validation** is one of the most powerful techniques to avoid or prevent overfitting. The initial training data is used to generate mini train–test splits, and then these splits are used to tune the model. In a standard k-fold validation, the data is partitioned into k subsets also known as folds. After this, the algorithm is trained iteratively on $k - 1$ folds while using the remaining folds as the test set, also known as the holdout fold. In cross-validation, only the original training set is used to tune the hyper-parameters, that is, parameters whose values control the learning process. Cross-validation basically keeps the test set separate as a true unseen data set for selecting the final model. This helps to avoid overfitting altogether.

- **Training with more data**: One method to avoid overfitting is to ensure that there are sufficient numbers of samples in the training set. However, in some cases the increased data can also mean feeding more noise to the model. Therefore, when we are training the model with more data, it is necessary to make sure the data is clean and free from randomness and inconsistencies.

- **Removing features**: There are some machine learning algorithms which incorporate the automatic selection of features. Otherwise, a few irrelevant features can be removed from the input features to improve the generalization. This can be carried out by deriving how a feature fits into the model. A few feature selection heuristics can be used as a good starting point.

- **Early stopping**: In the course of training the model, the performance of the model can be measured after each iteration. The model can be trained until the iterations do not improve the performance of the model. It can be assumed that after this point model overfitting happens as the generalization weakens.

- **Regularization**: Another important mathematical technique is the use of the concept of regularization, which is the process of introducing additional information in order to prevent overfitting. This information is usually in the form of a penalty for complexity. A model should be selected based on the Occam's razor principle (proposed by William of Ockham), which states that the explanation of any phenomenon should make as few assumptions as possible, eliminating the observable predictions of the explanatory hypothesis or theory choosing complex ones. In other words, the simplest hypothesis (model) that fits almost all the data is the best compared to more complex ones; therefore, there is explicit preference toward simple models.

Other methods to tackle overfitting are specific to the machine learning techniques used and will be discussed in the corresponding chapters.

4.3.4.2 Underfitting

In order to avoid overfitting, training may stop at an earlier stage, which however may lead to the model not being able to learn enough from training data and may not capture the dominant trend. This is known as underfitting. The result is the same as overfitting: inefficiency in predicting outcomes. In other words, underfitting occurs when the model does not properly fit the training data. Underfitting is often a result of an excessively simple model that fails to represent all the relevant data characteristics. Thus underfitting occurs when there is high bias and low variance.

Underfitting usually happens when we have less data to build an accurate model or when we try to build a linear model with nonlinear data. In such cases the machine learning model will probably make a lot of wrong predictions. Underfitting can be essentially avoided by using more data. Techniques to reduce underfitting include increasing model complexity, performing feature engineering, removing noise from the data, and increasing the number of epochs or increasing the duration of training to get better results.

Both overfitting and underfitting lead to poor predictions on new data sets; that is, they result in poor generalization.

4.4 Issues in Building Machine Learning Models

The basic issues in building machine learning models are the type of tasks that the system can learn and the best way for the system to represent the knowledge. The first question to be answered is the list of algorithms available for learning, which in turn depends on the availability of the data and its characteristics. The next issue is the performance of these algorithms. The amount of training data that is sufficient to learn with high confidence is the next question to be answered. Then comes the question whether prior knowledge will be useful in getting better performance of the algorithm. Another interesting question is whether some training samples can be more useful than others.

4.5 Offline and Online Machine Learning

In general, machine learning enables models to train on data sets and discover patterns before being deployed. After a model has been trained, these machine learning models can be used in real time to learn from new data. Offline machine learning models are based on machine learning algorithms and, once deployed, do not change. On the other hand, online machine learning models continuously adapt as new data is ingested. This iterative process of online models leads to an improvement in the types of associations that are made between data elements. In addition, when using online algorithms, complex algorithms can be automatically adjusted based on rapid changes in variables, such as sensor data, time, weather data, and customer sentiment metrics. For example, inferences can be made from a machine learning model—if the weather changes quickly, a weather predicting model can predict a tornado and a warning siren can be triggered. In conclusion, online machine learning algorithms continuously refine the models by continuously processing new data in near real time and training the system to adapt to changing patterns and associations in the data.

4.6 Underlying Concepts of Machine Learning Algorithms— Parametric and Nonparametric Algorithms

Machine learning algorithms estimate the target function (f) to predict the output variable (Y) given input variables (X).

$$Y = f(x).$$

The method in which this mapping function is modelled differentiates parametric and nonparametric methods.

4.6.1 Parametric Learning Versus Nonparametric

Parametric machine learning algorithms simplify the function that is to be learnt to a known form, and the set of parameters of the learnt function is of fixed size irrespective of the number of training samples. Parametric algorithms consist of two steps, namely selecting the form of the function and then learning the coefficients of the function from the training data. In Chapter 2, for example, we assumed that the mapping function is a line as is the case with linear regression. Nonparametric algorithms do not make strong assumptions about the form of the mapping function but attempt to learn a functional form from the training data.

The difference between parametric and nonparametric learning is shown in Table 4.1.

TABLE 4.1

Parametric and Nonparametric Learning

Description	Parametric Method	Nonparametric Method
Assumption	Simplify the function that is to be learnt to a known form, and the set of parameters of the learnt function is of fixed size irrespective of the number of training samples.	No strong assumptions about the form of the mapping function, and hence learn any functional form from the training data.
Learning	Learns the coefficients of the selected function from the training data	Seeks to best fit the training data to a mapping function from a large number of functional forms.
Usage	Prior information about the problem is available	Large amount of data is available, and there is no prior knowledge
Example methods	Logistic regression, linear discriminant analysis, perceptron, and naïve Bayes methods.	k-nearest neighbors (KNN), decision trees, support vector machines (SVMs)
Advantages	Simplicity; learn faster with the training data and require less training data Works even if the function does not perfectly fit the data.	Flexibility due to fitting with a large number of functional forms Powerful since no assumptions are made about the underlying function Better performance models for prediction
Disadvantages	Form of the function is predetermined. Suited to solve simpler problems. Unlikely match of the mapping function to the actual training data.	Requirement of a large amount of training data to estimate the mapping function Comparatively slower to train as more parameters need to be trained Risk of overfitting Harder to explain why specific predictions are made.
Probabilistic methods	General form (model) of prior probabilities, likelihood, and evidence with several unknown parameters is selected, and these parameters are estimated for the given data.	Assume an infinite dimensional function can capture the distribution about the input data Flexibility, since function can improve as the amount of data increases

4.7 Approaches to Machine Learning Algorithms

In the previous chapters and sections, we have discussed that the input data samples are represented as a sample space or instance space. This space needs to be segmented in such a way that all possible samples are covered but at the same time results in mutually exhaustive segments. Most machine learning algorithms used for this segmentation are based on three approaches, namely the **logical model**, **geometric model**, and **probabilistic model**. Logical models use logical expressions to define the homogeneous segments. In the case of classifications, the logical expression needs to ensure that all examples belonging to same class fall into the same segment. Rule-based and tree-based methods fall into this category. These models are nonparametric since the expressions are formed to fit the examples and are not fixed beforehand. In geometric models, the features are considered as points in the instance space, and similarity between examples is based on geometry. There are two types of geometric models, namely linear models and distance-based models. In linear models, a function defines a line or a plane to separate the instances. Linear models are parametric since the function has a fixed form and only the parameters of the function are learnt from the instance space. The linear models need to learn only a few parameters and hence are less likely to overfit. In the distance-based geometric models, the concept of distance between instances is used to represent similarity. The most common distance metrics used are **Euclidean**, **Minkowski**, **Manhattan**, and **Mahalanobis distances**. These distances will be described in detail in a succeeding chapter. Examples of distance-based models include the **nearest-neighbour** models for classification, which use the training data as exemplars, while the *k*-**means clustering** algorithm uses exemplars to create clusters of similar instances.

The third class of machine learning algorithms is the probabilistic models. Probabilistic models use the idea of probability and represent features and target variables as random variables. The process of modelling represents and manipulates the level of uncertainty with respect to these variables. The Bayes rule (inverse probability) allows us to infer unknown quantities, adapt our models, make predictions, and learn from data (Figure 4.6). Bayes rules allow us to carry out inference about the hypothesis from the input data.

These models can further be classified as **generative and discriminative methods** where the difference lies in determining the posterior probability. In Bayes rules terms, in generative methods, the likelihood, prior, and evidence probabilities are modelled, using which the posterior probability is determined. In discriminative methods, the posterior probability is determined directly, thus focusing the computational resources on the task at hand directly.

This section discussed the basis of machine learning algorithms, and as can be seen from Figure 4.7, many machine learning algorithms fall into more than one category. Understanding this basis will help us when we discuss the types of machine learning algorithms in the following section as well as when we outline the details of the various machine learning algorithms.

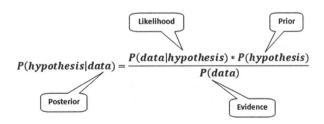

FIGURE 4.6
Bayes rule.

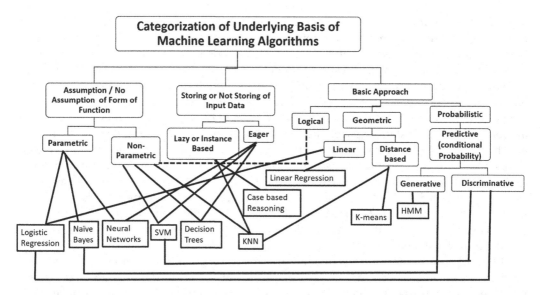

FIGURE 4.7
Categorization of underlying basis of machine learning algorithms.

4.8 Types of Machine Learning Algorithms

Types of machine learning algorithms can be classified as classical machine learning, reinforcement learning, and those based on neural networks and deep learning. We will first discuss types of so-called classical machine learning algorithms. This categorization depends on the extent of feedback given to the machine learning algorithm, where we have two main types of machine learning algorithms, namely supervised learning and unsupervised learning. There are basically two categories of supervised machine learning, namely classification and regression. Unsupervised learning can be further categorized as clustering, association rule mining, and dimensionality reduction (Figure 4.8).

In the classical category we also discuss semi-supervised machine learning, where training data includes some of the desired outputs. Note that most of the concepts we discussed in Chapter 2 were based on supervised learning. The details of all the machine learning algorithms will be discussed in subsequent chapters. In the following sections we will give a broad overview of the preceding techniques.

4.8.1 Supervised Learning

Supervised learning is the most well understood category of machine learning algorithms. Here the training data given to the algorithm is composed of both the input and the corresponding desired outputs or targets. Supervised learning aims to learn a function from examples and map its inputs to the outputs. Therefore, the algorithm learns to predict the output when given a new input vector. Learning decision trees is a form of supervised learning. The advantages of supervised learning are that it can learn complex patterns and in general give good performance. However, these algorithms require large amount of output labeled data.

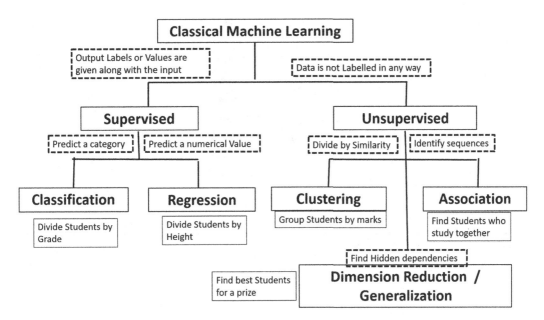

FIGURE 4.8
Categorization of classical machine learning.

Supervised learning is also called a predictive model, which means they predict a target *y* from a given new input *x* once it has learnt the model. In classification, *y* represents a category or "class," while in regression, *y* is a real valued number. Classification can be described as grouping of entities or information based on similarities. Supervised methods take in two kinds of training data: a set of objects for which we have input data (e.g., images, or features) and a set of associated labels for those objects. The labels could be things like "dog," "cat," or "horse," and these are considered to be ground truths, or feedback provided by an expert. The labels need not necessarily have discrete classifications; they can be continuous variables, like the length of a dog or the amount of food the dog eats per day. Now let us consider an example of classification (Figure 4.9). This example has as input two words and output labels that classify the set of words as having positive or negative sentiment. The machine is trained to associate input data with their labels.

4.8.1.1 Workflow of a Supervised Learning System

The overall working of a supervised learning system is shown in Figure 4.10. The training phase consists of the machine learning algorithm, which uses the feature vectors obtained from the input data and the labels indicating the output.

The supervised machine learning learns the predictive model or hypothesis that maps the input to the output labels. Thus the training phase involves feature extraction from the raw data to form the feature vector *x*. In Figure 4.10, the feature vector matrix of *I*1, *I*2, ... in training samples each associated with *m* features is shown. Each row in the matrix corresponds to *x*. Then learning involves fitting the training data (*x*, *y*) to a hypothesis *h*.

During the testing phase, a hitherto unknown input is converted to a feature vector and given to the prediction model, which then outputs the label for the input. Here again, the unseen raw data is converted to the **feature vector** *x*, and then we apply the function *h* to *x* as *h*(*x*) and then evaluate error.

(good, healthy)	✚
(bad, frowning)	▬
(good, smiling)	✚
(healthy, dancing)	✚
(ugly, angry)	▬
(smiling, dancing)	✚
(bad, angry)	▬
(ugly, frowning)	▬

FIGURE 4.9
Example of classification.

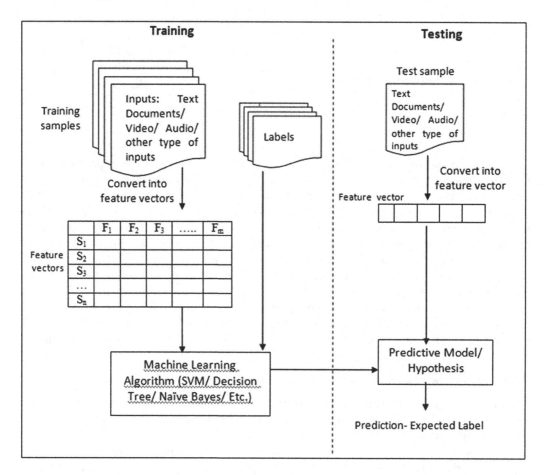

FIGURE 4.10
Workflow of a supervised learning system.

4.8.1.2 Classification and Regression

As shown in Figure 4.8, supervised learning can be further categorized into classification and regression. As both are examples of supervised learning, the input along with output label needs to be given. In the case of classification, a category is predicted, while in regression a numerical output value is predicted based on the training data. Therefore, in classification, the output type is discrete; we try to find a boundary between categories; and the evaluation normally used is accuracy. In regression, the output type is continuous; we try to best fit a line, that is, find a linear or polynomial function to fit the data; and the evaluation is done using the sum of squared errors (which will be discussed later). It is to be noted that the same problem can be modelled as either classification or regression. An example would be prediction of temperature, where in classification we predict whether the temperature is hot or cold tomorrow, while in regression we predict the actual temperature tomorrow.

4.8.1.3 Examples of Supervised Learning

Here we describe some examples of supervised learning (Table 4.2) and also indicate the type of supervised learning.

4.8.2 Unsupervised Learning

Unsupervised machine learning is described as learning without a teacher, where the desired output is not given. In unsupervised learning, also called descriptive modelling, no explicit output label is given. The learning task involves discovering underlying structures in the data or modelling the probability distribution of the input data. Here the machine is trained to understand which data points in the instance space are similar. When a new unseen input is given, it determines which group this data point is most similar to. In other words, the goal of unsupervised learning is to discover useful representations of the data, such as finding clusters, reduced space using dimensionality reduction, or modelling the data density.

TABLE 4.2

Examples of Supervised Learning

Sl. No.	Example	Instance Space X	$h(x)$	Type
1.	Face recognition	Raw intensity of face images x	Name of the person	Classification
2.	Loan approval	Properties of customers (age, income, liability, job, …)	Approval of loan or not	Classification
3.	Predicting student height	Properties of Students (age, weight, height)	Height	Regression
4.	Classifying cars	Features of cars (engine power, price)	Family car or otherwise	Classification
5.	Predicting rainfall	Features (year, month, amount of rainfall)	Amount of rainfall	Regression
6.	Classifying documents	Words in documents	Classify as sports, news, politics, etc.	Classification
7.	Predicting share price	Market information up to time t	Share price	Regression
8.	Classification of cells	Properties of cells	Anemic cell or healthy cell	Classification

4.8.2.1 Workflow of Unsupervised Learning System

The overall working of an unsupervised learning system is shown in Figure 4.11. The training phase consists of the machine learning algorithm, which uses the feature vectors obtained from the input data and groups them based on similarity. Note that here we do not provide labels or the expected output. During the testing phase, a hitherto unknown input is converted to a feature vector and given to the prediction model, which then finds the best similarity match for this input to groups already formed and accordingly outputs the group or cluster ID.

4.8.2.2 Clustering, Association Rule Mining, and Dimensionality Reduction

Clustering, association rule mining, and dimensionality reduction are important categories of unsupervised learning (Figure 4.8). In **clustering**, we group entities by similarity and hence find a set of prototypes representing the data. In other words, we partition the data into groups (clusters) that satisfy the two constraints; namely, points in the same cluster should be similar and points in different clusters should be dissimilar.

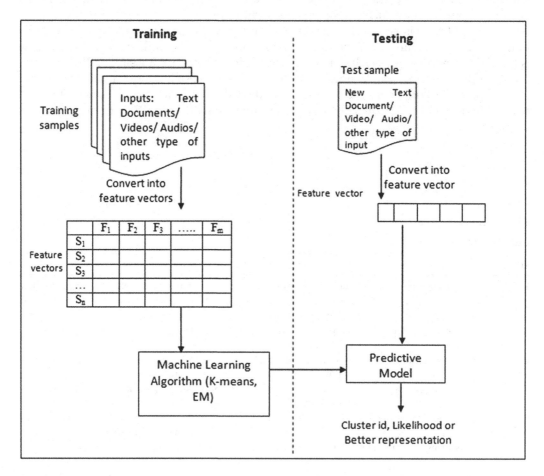

FIGURE 4.11
Workflow of unsupervised learning system.

In **association rule mining** we discover interesting relations between variables. Association rule mining is a procedure which aims to observe frequently occurring patterns, correlations, or associations from data sets found in various kinds of databases such as relational databases, transactional databases, and other forms of data collections.

Most machine learning algorithms may not be effective for high-dimensional data, basically called the curse of dimensionality. The goal of dimensionality reduction is to summarize the data in a reduced number of dimensions, that is, using a reduced number of variables. Dimensionality reduction is often used to facilitate visualization of the data, as well as a preprocessing method before supervised learning. There are generally two strategies for dimensionality reduction, namely one that transforms data into spaces of smaller dimension that capture global properties of a data set X, and the second method that embeds data into lower dimensional spaces that retain local properties of a data set X (which will be discussed in detail in later chapters).

4.8.3 Semi-supervised Learning

In semi-supervised machine learning the training data includes some of the desired outputs but not completely, as is the case with supervised learning. In many applications, while unlabeled training samples are readily available, obtaining labelled samples is expensive, and therefore semi-supervised learning assumes importance. In semi-supervised learning we use the unlabeled data to augment a small set of labelled samples to improve learning. In order to make any use of unlabeled data, semi-supervised learning must assume some structure to the underlying distribution of data. These algorithms make use of following three assumptions, namely the **smoothness assumption**, that is, if two points $x1$, $x2$ are close, then so should be the corresponding outputs $y1$, $y2$; the **cluster assumption**, that is, if points are in the same cluster, they are likely to be of the same class; and finally the **manifold assumption**, that is, the (high-dimensional) data lie (roughly) on a low-dimensional manifold. Some of the common types of semi-supervised learning techniques include co-training, transductive SVM, and graph-based methods.

4.8.4 Reinforcement Learning

Supervised (inductive) learning is the simplest and most studied type of machine learning. Now we need to question how an agent can learn behaviors when it doesn't have a teacher to tell it how to perform as is the case of supervised learning. In reinforcement learning, the agent takes actions to perform a task. The agent obtains feedback about its performance of the task. The agent then performs the same task repeatedly depending on the feedback. This situation is called reinforcement learning. The agent gets *positive reinforcement* for tasks done well and gets *negative reinforcement* for tasks done poorly. This method is inspired by behavioral psychology. The goal is to get the agent to act in the world so as to maximize its rewards. For example, consider teaching a monkey a new trick: you cannot instruct the monkey what is to be done, but you can reward (with a banana) or punish (scold) it depending on whether it does the right or wrong thing. Here the monkey needs to learn the action that resulted in reward or punishment, which is known in reinforcement learning contexts as the **credit assignment problem**. Reinforcement learning consists of the agent and the environment. The agent performs the action under the policy being followed, and the environment is everything else other than the agent. Learning takes place as a result of interaction between an agent and the world. In other words, the percept received by an agent should be used not only for understanding, interpreting, or prediction, as in the machine learning tasks we have discussed so far, but also for acting. Reinforcement learning is more general than supervised and unsupervised learning and involves learning from interaction with the environment to achieve a goal and getting an agent to act in the world so as to maximize its rewards. Reinforcement learning approaches can be used to train computers to do many tasks such as playing backgammon and chess and controlling robot limbs.

The major difference between reinforcement learning and supervised and unsupervised learning is shown in Table 4.3.

4.8.5 Neural Networks and Deep Learning

Neural networks are a biologically inspired programming paradigm which enables a computer to learn from observed data and attempts to understand natural biological systems through computational modelling. The massive parallelism allows for computational efficiency, and the distributed nature of neural computation allows robustness and graceful degradation. In other words, intelligent behaviour is modelled as an emergent property of a large number of simple units rather than from explicitly encoded symbolic rules and algorithms.

In general, neural networks are a supervised classification machine learning model where the learned classification model is an algebraic function (or a set of functions), rather than a Boolean function. The function can be linear as is the case for the perceptron algorithm, or nonlinear, as is the case for the backpropagation algorithm. In neural network models, the features as well as the output class are allowed to be real valued.

However, one of the issues of neural network models for large-scale real problems was that the fundamental core of the algorithms, that is, the weight-learning algorithms, did not work well on multilayer architectures. Then came deep learning, which is a powerful set of techniques for learning in multilayer neural network architectures. Deep network training used greedy layer-wise training with a small final trained step for fine-tuning to learn the weights of multilayer architectures. This allowed abstraction to develop naturally from one layer to another and helped the network initialize with good parameters. The details of both neural network and deep learning models will be discussed in subsequent chapters.

TABLE 4.3

Supervised, Unsupervised, and Reinforcement Learning

Type of Learning	Difference
Supervised learning	The training information consists of the input and desired output pairs of the function to be learned. The learning system needs to predict the output by minimizing some loss.
Unsupervised learning	Training data contains the features only, and the learning system needs to find "similar" points in high-dimensional space.
Reinforcement learning	The agent receives some evaluation ("rewards" or "penalties") of the output, that is, the action of the agent, but is not told which action is the correct one to achieve its goal. The learning system needs to develop an optimal policy so as to maximize its long-term reward.

4.9 Summary

- Explained the importance of data, types of data, representation, and processing of data.
- Discussed features and their extraction and selection.
- Explained the different aspects of the basics of machine learning including inductive learning, generalization, bias and variance, and overfitting and underfitting.
- Discussed the underlying concepts of machine learning algorithms.
- Explored the basic concepts of major types of machine learning algorithms.

4.10 Points to Ponder

- Problem dimensions depend on the number of samples, number of input features, and target dimensionality.
- The same data (for example images) can be represented in different ways.
- Data cleaning is the process of adding missing data and correcting, repairing, or removing incorrect or irrelevant data from a data set.
- Generalization is needed in all application areas of machine learning.
- Concept learning can be defined as discovering rules by observing examples.
- Parametric learning need not produce a good prediction model.
- Supervised learning aims to learn a function from examples that map its inputs to the outputs.
- In unsupervised learning, no explicit output label is given.

E.4 Exercises

E.4.1 Suggested Activities

Use Case

E.4.1.1 Take two examples from the business scenario and formulate the same examples as a classification, clustering, associative rule mining, and reinforcement learning problem. Clearly state any assumptions made.

Thinking Exercise

E.4.1.2 Give an everyday mathematical example of overfitting.

E.4.1.3 Can you give an example data set with three target variables?

E.4.1.4 Can you think of examples of generalization in education and industry?

Self-Assessment Questions

E.4.2 Multiple Choice Questions

Give answers with justification for correct and wrong choices.

E.4.2.1 When is overfitting observed?
      When a model is simple, overfitting is normally observed.
      i   When a model is excessively complex, overfitting is normally observed.
      ii When a model is fits a large amount of data, overfitting is normally observed.

E.4.2.2 What is model selection in machine learning?
      i   The process of selecting any model which is used to describe the data set.
      ii The process of selecting binary models which are used to describe the different data sets.
      iii The process of selecting models among different mathematical models, and selecting the appropriate parameters for the model.

E.4.2.3 Give an example of regression.
      ii Finding categories of users based on their behavior
      ii Finding groups of students based on their profile
      iii Finding height of a plant based on soil condition

E.4.2.4 What is independent and identically identified dependency?
      i   An element in a sequence is independent of the random variables that came before it/
      ii Identification of an element in a sequence is dependent on the variables that preceded it.
      iii Identification of an element in a sequence is dependent on the variables that succeed it.

E.4.2.5 What is supervised learning?
      i   System memorizes the training samples to predict the new ones.
      ii A model is trained to predict the new data through a training process with unlabelled examples.
      iii A model is trained to predict the new data through a training process with labelled examples.

E.4.2.6 What is the disadvantage of supervised learning?
      i   Requires a large amount of output labeled data
      ii Good performance
      iii Learns a function from examples of its inputs alone

E.4.2.7 Ordinal data is
      i   A set of data having a finite number of values or data points
      ii A set of data having values that can be ranked
      iii A set of data that can take any of a range of values

E.4.2.8 Latent variables are variables that are
    i Not directly observable
    ii Directly observable
    iii Missing

E.4.2.9 Rescaling is the
    i Renaming of variables
    ii Aggregation of variables
    iii Transferring of continuous values to a range

E.4.2.10 The curse of dimensionality describes that as the number of features
    i Increases, the volume of feature space increases exponentially.
    ii Increases, the volume of feature space decreases exponentially.
    iii Decreases, the volume of feature space increases exponentially.

E.4.2.11 Inductive learning
    i Moves from broader generalizations to specific observations
    ii Is a top-down approach
    iii Moves from specific observations to broader generalizations

E.4.2.12 The goal of a good machine learning model is to
    i Generalize from the data to fit any sample from the training data
    ii Generalize well from the training data to any data from the problem domain
    iii Specialize for the training data

E.4.2.13 Bias indicates
    i The extent to which models estimated from different training sets differ from each other.
    ii When the model is trained using a data set and a very low error is obtained but when the data set is changed, a high error is obtained
    iii The extent to which the average model over all training sets differs from the true model.

E.4.2.14 Variance indicates
    i The extent to which models estimated from different training sets differ from each other.
    ii When the model is trained using a data set and a very low error is obtained but when the data set is changed, a high error is obtained
    iii The extent to which the average model over all training sets differs from the true model.

E.4.2.15 Overfitting occurs
    i When there is low variance and low bias.
    ii When there is high variance and low bias.
    iii When there is high variance and high bias.

E.4.2.16 Parametric algorithms
    i Simplify the function that is to be learnt to a known form
    ii Are free to learn any functional form from the training data
    iii Store the training data instead of learning an explicit description of the target function

E.4.2.17 Eager learning
    i Is free to learn any functional form from the training data
    ii Stores the training data instead of learning an explicit description of the target function
    iii Constructs a model based on the complete training data before receiving new test data for prediction

E.4.2.18 Linear models
    i Are nonparametric models
    ii Represent the function as a linear combination of its inputs
    iii Are more likely to overfit

E.4.2.19 In generative methods,
    i The likelihood, prior, and evidence probabilities are modelled, using which the posterior probability is determined
    ii The posterior probability is determined directly
    iii Only prior and evidence probabilities are determined

E.4.2.20 The smoothness assumption, cluster assumption, and manifold assumption are associated with
    i Unsupervised learning
    ii Semi-supervised learning
    iii Reinforcement learning

E.4.3 Match the Columns

No	Match	
E.4.3.1 Overfitting	A	Artificial neural network
E.4.3.2 Model selection	B	Grouping similar instances
E.4.3.3 Evaluation	C	Transductive support vector machine
E.4.3.4 Testing	D	Model is excessively complex
E.4.3.5 Supervised learning	E	Reducing the number of features under consideration
E.4.3.6 Unsupervised learning	F	Hold-out set
E.4.3.7 Semi-supervised learning	G	Different hypotheses for a given learning problem
E.4.3.8 Reinforcement learning	H	Expectation-maximization algorithm
E.4.3.9 Dimensionality reduction	I	Trial and error learning paradigm
E.4.3.10 Clustering	J	Given data, finding a function with its parameters.

E.4.4 Short Questions

E.4.4.1   Give a data representation (as in Figure 4.1) for multiple classifications (three classes) of documents.

E.4.4.2   Assume that the number of samples is 1000, the number of input features is 30, and the number of target classes is 1. Find the problem dimension. If the target class increases to 5, find the problem dimension.

E.4.4.3   What are data dependencies? Discuss.

E.4.4.4   What is data bias? Give an example from the education domain.

E.4.4.5   Why do we need feature selection?

E.4.4.6   What is inductive learning? Discuss in terms of classification, regression, and probability estimation.

E.4.4.7   Why is generalization considered the core concept of machine learning?

E.4.4.8   Distinguish between bias and variance. Use an illustrative diagram.

E.4.4.9   Distinguish between overfitting and underfitting. Use an illustrative diagram.

E.4.4.10   Discuss any three methods that are used to handle overfitting.

E.4.4.11   Compare and contrast offline and online machine learning.

E.4.4.12   Compare and contrast parametric and nonparametric learning.

E.4.4.13   Why are lazy methods also called instance-based methods? Discuss.

E.4.4.14   What are the three basic approaches to machine learning? Discuss.

E.4.4.15   Distinguish between linear models and distance-based models.

E.4.4.16   Use another running example from the business domain for categorization of classical machine learning (Figure 4.8).

E.4.4.17   Distinguish the components in the workflow of supervised and unsupervised machine learning systems. Discuss.

E.4.4.18   Why are clustering, association rule mining, and dimensionality reduction considered as unsupervised machine learning? Discuss.

E.4.4.19   What is the concept of reinforcement learning?

E.4.4.20   How does deep learning help neural network models?

5

Machine Learning: Tools and Software

5.1 Weka Tool

Weka is an open-source software that provides a collection of machine learning algorithms developed at the University of Waikato. Weka stands for Waikato Environment for Knowledge Analysis and is also a bird.

There are two ways in which these algorithms can be used: the data can be given directly to the algorithms or they can be called as part of Java code. Weka is a collection of tools for tasks needed for data mining such as data preprocessing, regression, association, classification, and clustering.

5.1.1 Features of Weka

Weka includes all aspects needed to create and apply data mining models. It covers all important data mining tasks including tools needed for preprocessing and visualization. The features of Weka are listed in Figure 5.1 and include platform independence, free and open-source software, ease of use, data-preprocessing facility, availability of different machine learning algorithms, flexibility, and a good graphical interface.

5.1.2 Installation of Weka

In order to download Weka, you need to go the official website, http://www.cs.waikato.ac.nz/ml/weka/. You need to download and install by choosing a stable version to download, not the developer version. You also need to be sure that you choose the Windows, Mac OS, or Linux version as appropriate for your machine The following commands can be executed at the command prompt to set the Weka environment variable for Java:

```
setenv WEKAHOME /usr/local/weka/weka-3-0-2
setenv CLASSPATH $WEKAHOME/weka.jar:$CLASSPATH
```

Once the download is completed, the *exe* file is run, and initially the default setup can be chosen.

DOI: 10.1201/9781003290100-5

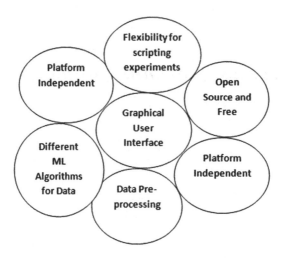

FIGURE 5.1
Features of Weka.

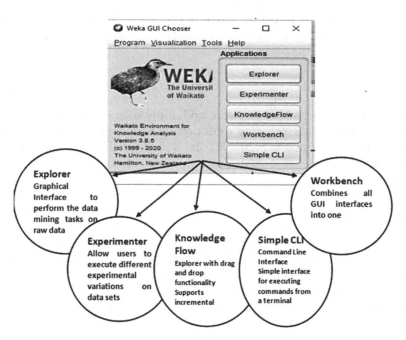

FIGURE 5.2
Application interfaces of Weka.

5.1.3 Weka Application Interfaces

On opening Weka, it will open the Weka GUI Chooser screen, which will let you open one of the Weka application interfaces. The Weka GUI screen and the five available application interfaces are seen in Figure 5.2. The various application interfaces of Weka are as follows.

Explorer is WEKA's main application interface, which provides an environment for exploring data. It is a graphical interface that performs data mining tasks such as preprocessing, attribute selection, learning, and visualization on raw data.

Experimenter allows users to test and evaluate machine learning algorithms by executing different experimental variations on data sets and conducting statistical tests between learning schemes.

Knowledge Flow, a Java-Beans–based interface, is similar to the Explorer but here each step is represented as a node in a graph, so flow can be explicitly represented. It provides drag and drop facility so that each step is a node that you drop onto the workspace, and you can connect nodes to create a process flow. Hence it supports multiple process flows, and paths can be designed with steps to preprocess data and so on, and then branch to build different classifiers. It also supports incremental learning from previous results.

Simple CLI provides a command line interface for typing commands from a terminal and allows direct execution of Weka commands. Shell scripts can be used to control experiments where each command is a function.

Workbench combines all graphical user interfaces into one.

5.1.4 Data Formats of Weka

By default, the Attribute Relation File Format (ARFF) is used by Weka for data analysis. However, Weka supports the following formats for importing data:

- CSV
- ARFF
- Database using ODBC

Attribute Relation File Format (ARFF)

Files are "flat files," usually comma separated. ARFF consists of two sections:

1. The header section, which allows specification of features and defines the relation (data set) name, attribute name, and the type.
2. The actual data section lists the data instances.

An ARFF file requires the declaration of the relation, attribute, and data.
An example of an ARFF file is shown in Figure 5.3.

- *@relation*: Written in the header section, this is the first line in any ARFF file. This is followed by the relation/data set name. The relation name must be a string, and in case there are spaces, then the relation name must be enclosed within quotes.

- *@attribute*: This part is also included in the header section, and the attributes are declared with their names and the type or range. The following attribute data types are supported by Weka"

- Numeric
- <nominal-specification>
- String

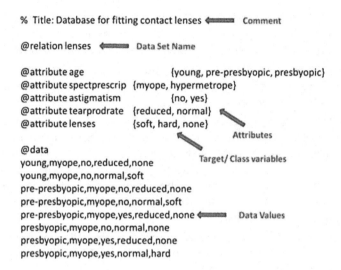

FIGURE 5.3
Example of an ARFF file.

- date
- @data is defined in the Data section, and the list of all data segments follows @data

5.1.5 Weka Explorer

The Weka Explorer is illustrated in Figure 5.4 and contains a total of six tabs.
The tabs are as follows.

1. **Preprocess**: This tab allows choosing the data file.
2. **Classify**: This tab allows the application and experimentation with different algorithms using preprocessed data files as input.
3. **Cluster**: This tab allows the identification of clusters within the data using different clustering tools.
4. **Association**: This tab allows the identification of associations within the data by applying association rules.
5. **Select attributes**: The inclusion and exclusion of attributes from the experiment and the associated changes can be viewed using this tab.
6. **Visualize**: The visualization of the data set in a 2D format using scatter plot and bar graph output is allowed by this tab.

The user cannot move between the different tabs until the initial preprocessing of the data set has been completed.

5.1.6 Data Preprocessing

The data that is collected from the field contains many unwanted things that lead to wrong analysis. For example, the data may contain null fields, it may contain columns that are

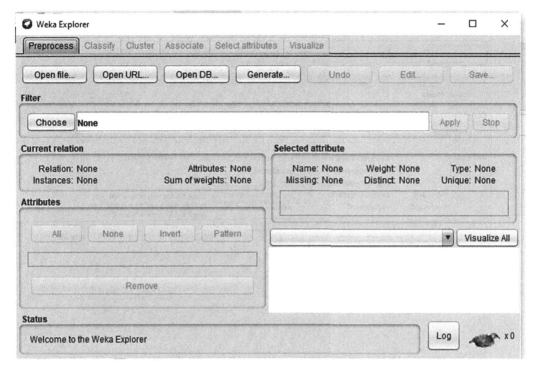

FIGURE 5.4
Weka Explorer.

irrelevant to the current analysis, and so on. Thus, the data must be preprocessed to meet the requirements of the type of analysis you are seeking. This is the done in the preprocessing module.

To demonstrate the available features in preprocessing, we will use the **Weather** database that is provided in the installation (Figure 5.5).

Using the **Open file** … option under the **Preprocess** tag, select the **weather-nominal. arff** file.

When you open the file, your screen looks as shown here (Figure 5.6).

This screen tells us several things about the loaded data, which are discussed further in this chapter.

5.1.7 Understanding Data

Let us first look at the highlighted **Current relation** sub-window. It shows the name of the database that is currently loaded. You can infer two points from this sub-window:

- There are 14 instances—the number of rows in the table.
- The table contains five attributes—the fields, which are discussed in the upcoming sections.

On the left side, notice the **Attributes** sub-window that displays the various fields in the database (Figure 5.7).

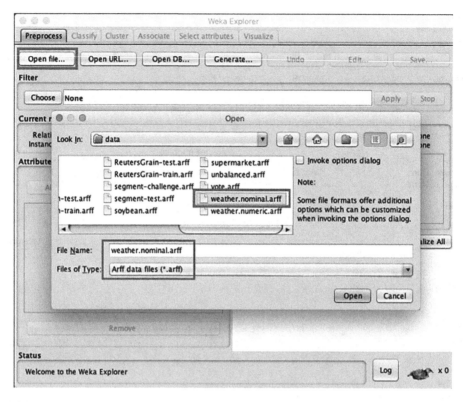

FIGURE 5.5
Demonstration with sample dataset.

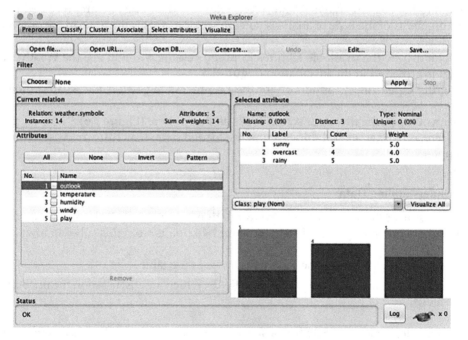

FIGURE 5.6
Snapshot of loading the data.

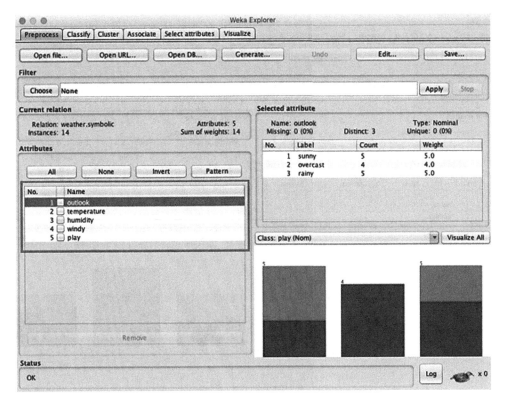

FIGURE 5.7
Snapshot of understanding the data.

The **weather** database contains five fields: outlook, temperature, humidity, windy, and play. When you select an attribute from this list by clicking on it, further details on the attribute itself are displayed on the right-hand side.

Let us select the temperature attribute first. When you click on it, you would see the following screen (Figure 5.8).

5.1.7.1 Selecting Attributes

In the **Selected Attribute** sub-window, you can observe the following:

- The name and the type of the attribute are displayed.
- The type for the **temperature** attribute is **Nominal**.
- The number of **Missing** values is zero.
- There are three distinct values with no unique value.
- The table underneath this information shows the nominal values for this field as hot, mild, and cold.
- It also shows the count and weight in terms of a percentage for each nominal value.

At the bottom of the window, you see the visual representation of the **class** values.

If you click on the **Visualize All** button, you will be able to see all features in one single window as shown here (Figure 5.9).

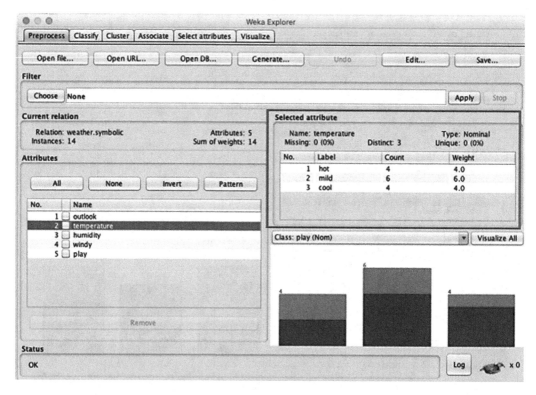

FIGURE 5.8
Snapshot of viewing single attribute ("temperature").

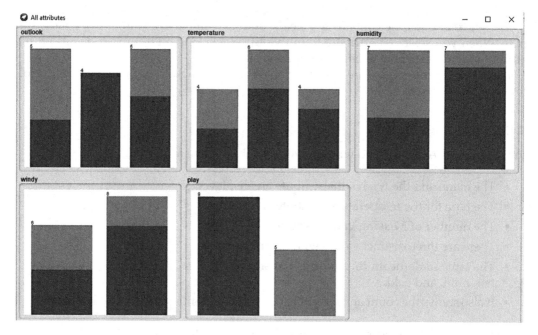

FIGURE 5.9
Visualization of all attributes.

5.1.7.2 Removing Attributes

Many times, the data that you want to use for model building comes with many irrelevant fields. For example, the customer database may contain customers' mobile number, which is irrelevant in analyzing their credit rating (Figure 5.10).

To remove attributes, select them and click on the **Remove** button at the bottom. The selected attributes are removed from the database. After you fully preprocess the data, you can save it for model building.

Next, you will learn to preprocess the data by applying filters on this data.

5.1.7.3 Applying Filters

Some of the machine learning techniques such as association rule mining require categorical data. To illustrate the use of filters, we will use the weather-numeric.arff database that contains two **numeric** attributes—temperature and humidity. We will convert these to **nominal** by applying a filter on our raw data. Click on the Choose button in the Filter sub-window and select the following filter (Figure 5.11):

weka→filters→supervised→attribute→Discretize

Click on the Apply button and examine the temperature and/or humidity attribute. You will notice that these have changed from numeric to nominal types.

Let us look into another filter now (Figure 5.12). Suppose you want to select the best attributes for deciding the **play**. Select and apply the following filter:

weka→filters→supervised→attribute→AttributeSelection

You will notice that it removes the temperature and humidity attributes from the database (Figure 5.13).

After you are satisfied with the preprocessing of your data, save the data by clicking the Save … button. You will use this saved file for model building.

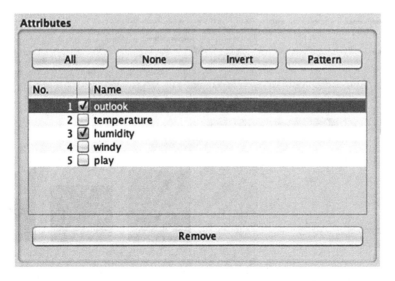

FIGURE 5.10
Snapshot of removing attributes.

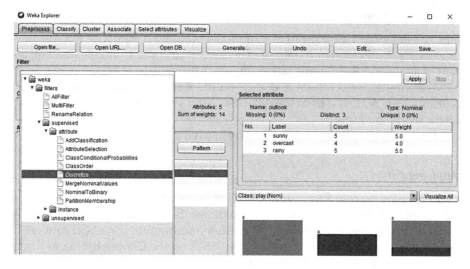

FIGURE 5.11
Sub-window of filter.

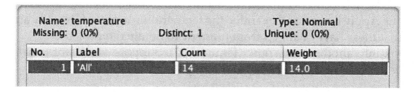

FIGURE 5.12
Snapshot another filter example.

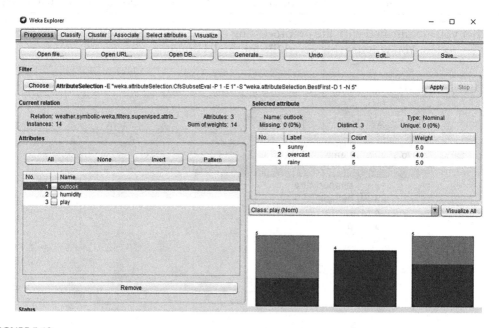

FIGURE 5.13
After removing attributes (temperature and humidity).

5.2 Introduction to Machine Learning Support in R

The R language was basically developed by statisticians to help other statisticians and developers work faster and more efficiently with the data. By now, we know that machine learning is basically working with a large amount of data and statistics as a part of data science, so the use of the R language is always recommended. Therefore the R language is becoming handy for those working with machine learning, making tasks easier, faster, and more innovative. Here are some top advantages of the R language to implement a machine learning algorithm in R programming.

5.2.1 Advantages to Implement Machine Learning Using R Language

- It provides good explanatory code. For example, if you are at the early stage of working with a machine learning project and you need to explain the work you do, it becomes easy to work with R language in comparison to Python language as it provides the proper statistical method to work with data with fewer lines of code.
- R language is perfect for data visualization. R language provides the best prototype to work with machine learning models.
- R language has the best tools and library packages to work with machine learning projects. Developers can use these packages to create the best pre-model, model, and post-model of the machine learning projects. Also, the packages for R are more advanced and extensive than for Python language, which makes it the first choice to work with machine learning projects.

5.2.2 Popular R Language Packages

- **lattice**: The lattice package supports the creation of graphs displaying the variable or relations between multiple variables with conditions.
- **DataExplorer**: This R package focuses on automating the data visualization and data handling so that the user can pay attention to data insights of the project.
- **Dalex (Descriptive Machine Learning Explanations)**: This package helps to provide various explanations for the relation between the input variable and its output. It helps to understand the complex models of machine learning
- **dplyr**: This R package is used to summarize the tabular data of machine learning with rows and columns. It applies the "split–apply–combine" approach.
- **Esquisse**: This R package is used to explore the data quickly to get the information it holds. It also allows to plot bar graphs, histograms, curves, and scatter plots.
- **caret**: This R package attempts to streamline the process for creating predictive models.
- **janitor**: This R package has functions for examining and cleaning dirty data. It is basically built for the purpose of user-friendliness for beginners and intermediate users.
- **rpart**: This R package helps to create the classification and regression models using two-stage procedures. The resulting models are represented as binary trees.

5.2.3 Application of R in Machine Learning

There are many top companies like Google, Facebook, Uber, and so on using the R language for applications of machine learning. The applications are:

- Social network analytics
- Analyzing trends and patterns
- Getting insights for behaviour of users
- Finding the relationships between the users
- Developing analytical solutions
- Accessing charting components
- Embedding interactive visual graphics

5.2.4 Examples of Machine Learning Problems

- **Web search like Siri, Alexa, Google, Cortona**: Recognize the user's voice and fulfill the request made
- **Social media service**: Help people to connect all over the world and also show the recommendations of the people we may know
- **Online customer support**: Provide high convenience for customers and efficiency of support agent
- **Intelligent gaming**: Use high-level responsive and adaptive nonplayer characters similar to human intelligence
- **Product recommendation**: A software tool used to recommend products that you might like to purchase or engage with
- **Virtual personal assistance**: Software which can perform tasks according to the instructions provided
- **Traffic alerts**: Help to switch the traffic alerts according to the situation provided
- **Online fraud detection**: Check unusual functions performed by the user and detect fraud
- **Healthcare**: Manage a large amount of data beyond the imagination of normal human beings and help to identify the illness of the patient according to symptoms
- **Real-world example**: When you search for some kind of cooking recipe on YouTube, you will see the recommendations below with the title "You May Also Like This." This is a common use of machine learning.

5.2.5 Types of Machine Learning Problems

An overview of typical machine learning tasks solved using R language is as follows:

- **Regression**: The regression technique helps the machine learning approach to predict continuous values, for example, the price of a house.
- **Classification**: The input is divided into one or more classes or categories for the learner to produce a model to assign unseen modules. For example, in the case of email fraud, we can divide the emails into two classes, namely "spam" and "not spam."

- **Clustering**: This technique follows the summarization, finding a group of similar entities. For example, we can gather and take readings of the patients in the hospital.

- **Association**: This technique finds co-occurring events or items, for example, a market basket.

- **Anomaly detection**: This technique works by discovering abnormal cases or behavior, for example, credit card fraud detection.

- **Sequence mining**: This technique predicts the next stream event, for example, a click-stream event.

- **Recommendation**: This technique recommends an item, for example, songs or movies according to the celebrity in them.

5.2.6 Setting Up Environment for Machine Learning with R Programming Using Anaconda

In R programming, the environment for machine learning can be set easily through RStudio.

Step 1: Install Anaconda (Linux, Windows) and launch the navigator.

Step 2: Open Anaconda Navigator and click the **Install** button for RStudio (Figure 5.14).

Step 3: After installation, create a new environment (Figure 5.15). Anaconda will then send a prompt asking to enter a name for the new environment and launch RStudio.

5.2.7 Running R Commands

Method 1: R commands can run from the console provided in RStudio (Figure 5.16). After opening RStudio, simply type R commands to the console.

Method 2: R commands can be stored in a file and can be executed in an Anaconda prompt (Figure 5.17). This can be achieved by the following steps.

1. Open an Anaconda prompt.
2. Go to the directory where the R file is located.
3. Activate the Anaconda environment by using the command:

   conda activate <ENVIRONMENT_NAME>

4. Run the file by using the command:

   Rscript <FILE_NAME>.R

5.2.8 Installing Machine Learning Packages in R

Packages help make code easier to write as they contain a set of predefined functions that perform various tasks. The most used machine learning packages are **data.table, nnet, dplyr, ggplot2, caret, e1071, rpart, kernlab, xgboost,** and **randomForest**. There are two methods that can be used to install these packages for your R program.

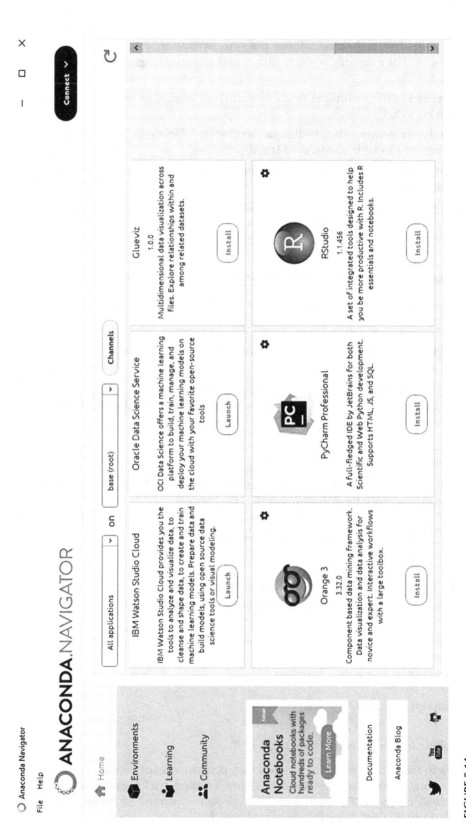

FIGURE 5.14
Anaconda Navigator.

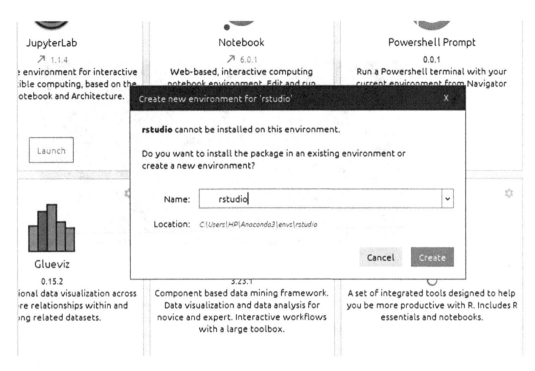

FIGURE 5.15
Creating new environments.

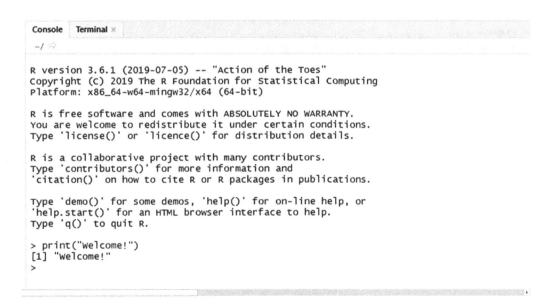

FIGURE 5.16
Running R Command—Method 1.

FIGURE 5.17
Running R Command—Method 2.

Method 1: Installing Packages Through RStudio

1. Open RStudio and click the **Install Packages** option under **Tools**, which is present in the menu bar (Figure 5.18).
2. Enter the names of all the packages you want to install, separated by spaces or commas, and then click Install (Figure 5.19).

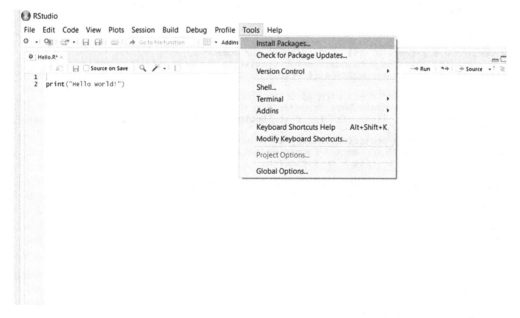

FIGURE 5.18
Step 1: Installing packages through RStudio.

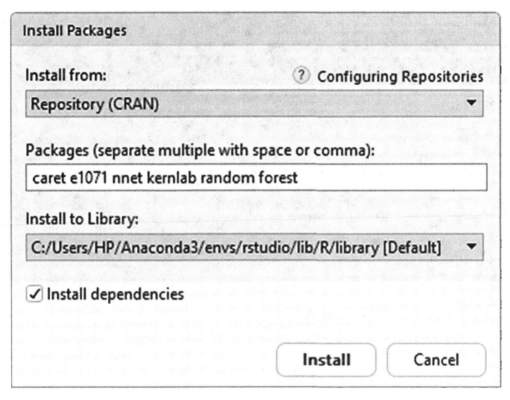

FIGURE 5.19
Step 2: Installing the packages by giving name of the package.

Method 2: Installing Packages Through Anaconda Prompt/RStudio Console

1. Open an Anaconda prompt.
2. Switch the environment to the environment you used for RStudio using the command:

   conda activate <ENVIRONMENT_NAME>

3. Enter the command **r** to open the R console (Figure 5.20).
4. Install the required packages using the command:

   install.packages(c("<PACKAGE_1>", "<PACKAGE_2>", ..., "<PACKAGE_N>"))

While downloading the packages, you might be prompted to choose a **CRAN** mirror. It is recommended to choose the location closest to you for a faster download.

5.2.9 Specific Machine Learning Packages in R

There are many R libraries that contain a host of functions, tools, and methods to manage and analyze data. Each of these libraries has a particular focus, with some libraries managing image and textual data, data manipulation, data visualization, web crawling, machine

```
R is a collaborative project with many contributors.
Type 'contributors()' for more information and
'citation()' on how to cite R or R packages in publications.

Type 'demo()' for some demos, 'help()' for on-line help, or
'help.start()' for an HTML browser interface to help.
Type 'q()' to quit R.

> install.packages(c("caret", "e1071", "nnet", "kernlab", "random forest"))
--- Please select a CRAN mirror for use in this session ---
trying URL 'https://cloud.r-project.org/bin/windows/contrib/3.6/caret_6.0-86.zip'
Content type 'application/zip' length 6259100 bytes (6.0 MB)
downloaded 6.0 MB

trying URL 'https://cloud.r-project.org/bin/windows/contrib/3.6/e1071_1.7-3.zip'
Content type 'application/zip' length 1022788 bytes (998 KB)
downloaded 998 KB

trying URL 'https://cloud.r-project.org/bin/windows/contrib/3.6/nnet_7.3-14.zip'
Content type 'application/zip' length 138022 bytes (134 KB)
downloaded 134 KB

trying URL 'https://cloud.r-project.org/bin/windows/contrib/3.6/kernlab_0.9-29.zip'
Content type 'application/zip' length 2641401 bytes (2.5 MB)
downloaded 2.5 MB

package 'caret' successfully unpacked and MD5 sums checked
package 'e1071' successfully unpacked and MD5 sums checked
package 'nnet' successfully unpacked and MD5 sums checked
package 'kernlab' successfully unpacked and MD5 sums checked
```

FIGURE 5.20
Installing the packages through R console or terminal.

learning, and so on. Here let's discuss some of the important machine learning packages by demonstrating an example.

- **Preparing the data set**: Before using these packages, first of all import the data set into RStudio, clean the data set, and split the data into train and test data sets.
- **CARET**: Caret stands for classification and regression training. The CARET package is used for performing classification and regression tasks. It consists of many other built-in packages.
- **ggplot2**: R is most famous for its visualization library ggplot2. It provides an aesthetic set of graphics that are also interactive. The ggplot2 package is used for creating plots and for visualizing data.
- **randomForest**: The randomForest package allows us to use the random forest algorithm easily.
- **nnet**: The nnet package uses neural networks in deep learning to create layers which help in training and predicting models. The loss (the difference between the actual value and predicted value) decreases after every iteration of training.
- **e1071**: The e1071 package is used to implement the support vector machines, naive Bayes algorithm, and many other algorithms.
- **rpart**: The rpart package is used to partition data. It is used for classification and regression tasks. The resultant model is in the form of a binary tree.
- **dplyr**: Like rpart, the dplyr package is also a data manipulation package. It helps manipulate data by using functions such as filter, select, and arrange.

5.2.10 Supervised Learning Using R

In supervised learning, labelled data is provided to train the machine to learn a model which will then be used to predict the labels of hitherto unseen data. Supervised learning is classified into two categories of algorithms:

- **Classification**: A classification problem identifies the correct label or category of new observations based on training data. Categories could be "rainy" or "sunny" and "fraud" or "not fraud."
- **Regression**: A regression problem identifies the relationship between independent variables and dependent or real-valued output variables such as "stock price" or "amount of rainfall."

Types
- Regression
- Logistic regression
- Classification
- Naïve Bayes classifiers
- Decision trees
- Support vector machines

Implementation in R

Let's implement one of the very popular supervised learning algorithms, namely simple linear regression, in R programming. Simple linear regression is a statistical method that allows us to summarize and study relationships between two continuous (quantitative) variables. One variable, denoted x, is regarded as an independent variable, and the other one, denoted y, is regarded as a dependent variable. It is assumed that the two variables are linearly related. Hence, we try to find a linear function that predicts the response value (y) as accurately as possible as a function of the feature or independent variable (x). The basic syntax for regression analysis in R is as follows:

Syntax:

lm(Y ~ model)
where
Y is the object containing the dependent variable to be predicted and model is the formula for the chosen mathematical model.

The command **lm()** provides the model's coefficients but no further statistical information. The following R code is used to implement simple linear regression.

5.2.11 Unsupervised Learning Using R

Unsupervised learning analyzes and discover hidden patterns, similarities, and differences without any labelled data, that is, any prior training. Unsupervised learning is classified into two categories of algorithms:

- **Clustering**: Clustering is the task of discovering the inherent groupings in the data where members within the same group are similar to each other and dissimilar to members of other groups. Examples including grouping students based on their interests or grouping customers based on their purchasing behaviour.

- **Association**: An association rule learning problem is where you want to discover interesting hidden relationships and associations from large databases. Examples include rules like if A buys milk and ghee, A is likely to buy sugar.

Types

Clustering:

1. Exclusive (partitioning)
2. Agglomerative
3. Overlapping
4. Probabilistic

Clustering Types:

1. Hierarchical clustering
2. K-means clustering
3. KNN (*k* nearest neighbors)
4. Principal component analysis
5. Singular value decomposition
6. Independent component analysis

5.2.11.1 Implementing k-Means Clustering in R

Let's implement one of the very popular unsupervised learning algorithms, namely *k*-means clustering, in R programming. *k*-means clustering in R programming is an unsupervised nonlinear algorithm that clusters data based on similarity or similar groups. It seeks to partition the observations into a prespecified number of clusters. Segmentation of data takes place to assign each training example to a segment called a cluster. In the unsupervised algorithm, high reliance on raw data is given with large expenditure on manual review for relevance. It is used in a variety of fields like b, health care, retail, media, and so on.

Syntax: *kmeans(x, centers = 3, nstart = 10)*
where:

- *x is numeric data*
- *centers is the predefined number of clusters*
- *the k-means algorithm has a random component and can be repeated nstart times to improve the returned model*

The tools and software described in this chapter can be used for implementation of the programming assignments given in subsequent chapters.

5.3 Summary

- Introduced the features of Weka.
- Described the application interfaces available in Weka.
- Outlined the installation of the Weka tool.
- Discussed the tabs of Weka Explorer used for data preprocessing, selection of attributes, removing attributes, and visualization.
- Outlined the use of R programming for supervised as well as unsupervised machine learning.
- Listed some advantages of using R programming.

5.4 Points to Ponder

- Weka is a free, open-source tool having a collection of machine learning algorithms.
- The Weka tool provides the facility to upload a data set, choose from among available machine learning algorithms, and analyze the results.
- The R language is a convenient method to carry out programming for machine learning as it provides several powerful packages to carry out the task.

E.5 Exercises

E.5.1. Suggested Activities

E.5.1.1 Configure a machine learning experiment with the iris flower data set and three algorithms ZeroR, OneR, and J48 available in Weka. Explain the data set and algorithms used. You are required to analyze the results from an experiment and understand the importance of statistical significance when interpreting results.

E.5.1.2 Use the air quality data set and carry out data visualization using a histogram, box plot, and scatter plot with R programming.

Self-Assessment Questions

E.5.2 Multiple Choice Questions

E.5.2.1 Which one of the following options is used to start the **weka** application from command line?
- i java -jar weka.jar
- ii java jar weka.jar
- iii java weka.jar

E.5.2.2 Which one of the following tab does not exist in the Weka Explorer options?
  i Associate
  ii Cleaning
  iii Visualize

E.5.2.3 The data file format which is not supported by the Weka tool is
  i .arff
  ii .tsv
  iii .txt

E.5.2.4 Which one of the following options contains the j48 algorithm?
  i Cluster
  ii Classify
  iii Associate

E.5.2.5 The "split–apply–combine" approach is used by the _____ package.
  i rpart
  ii dplyr
  iii lattice

E.5.2.6 How does one activate the Anaconda Navigator from the command line?
  i anaconda activate <ENVIRONMENT_NAME>
  ii activate conda <ENVIRONMENT_NAME>
  iii conda activate <ENVIRONMENT_NAME>

E.5.2.7 How do we install packages in RStudio using the menu bar?
  i Tools
  ii Debug
  iii Build

E.5.2.8 The package used to implement a support vector machine in the R programming language is
  i rpart
  ii dplyr
  iii e1071

E.5.2.9 The command to run the R programming via console is
  i Rscript <FILE_NAME>.R
  ii <FILE_NAME>.R Rscript
  iii Rscript -<FILE_NAME>.R

E.5.2.10 Which of the following can be used to impute data sets based only on information in the training set?
  i Postprocess
  ii Preprocess
  iii Process

E.5.3 Match the Columns

No	Match	
E.5.3.1 Weka	A	Graphical interface to perform the data mining tasks on raw data
E.5.3.2 Supervised learning	B	Used to see the possible visualization produced on the data as scatter plot or bar graph output
E.5.3.3 Explorer	C	Building a decision model from labelled training data
E.5.3.4 .libpaths()	D	Used to view all installed packages
E.5.3.5 Visualize	E	Used for seeing currently active libraries
E.5.3.6 library	F	Has functions for examining and cleaning dirty data
E.5.3.7 getOption(defaultPackages)	G	"Recommended" package in R
E.5.3.8 janitor	H	Explorer with drag and drop functionality that supports incremental learning
E.5.3.9 Spatial	I	Data mining tool
E.5.3.10 Knowledge flow	J	Shows the default packages in R

E.5.4 Short Questions

E.5.4.1 Discuss features of Weka.

E.5.4.2 Explain the ARFF file format.

E.5.4.3 Describe the different packages used to implement machine learning algorithms.

E.5.4.4 Explain the steps for setting up the environment for machine learning with R programming.

E.5.4.5 Describe the application interfaces of Weka.

6

Classification Algorithms

6.1 Introduction

Classification is the process of assigning any unknown data X with a known class label C_i from set $C = \{C_1, C_2, \ldots, C_n\}$, where $C_i \; \mathcal{E} \; C$. Classification algorithms help you divide your data into different classes. A classification algorithm helps you in classifying data like how books are sorted in a library under various topics.

Classification is a machine learning technique which identifies any particular data to be of one target label or another. Figure 6.1 shows two classes, class A and class B. The items of the same class are similar to each other while items of different classes are dissimilar to each other.

For any classification model, there is going to be two phases: training and testing. During the training phase, the model is said to be built by learning using a supplied data set. Hence, all we require is a training data set that has many instances with appropriate attributes with corresponding output labels using which learning of the model is carried out. Having trained, next the model has to be tested for how well the model has learnt. We need a testing data set which is similar to the training data. The model is tested with the test data set for how accurately the model predicts a class label for the test data and hence its accuracy.

The most basic example for classification can be how incoming emails are segregated in our mail box as either "spam" or "not spam." As another example, suppose we want to

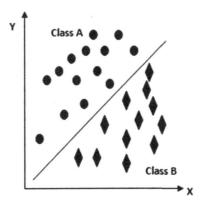

FIGURE 6.1
Two class problem.

DOI: 10.1201/9781003290100-6

predict whether our customers would buy a particular product or not according to the customer data we have. In this case, the target classes would be either "Yes" or "No."

On the other hand, we might want to classify vegetables according to their weight, size, or color. In this scenario, the available target classes might be spinach, tomato, onion, potato, and cabbage. We might perform gender classification as well, where the target classes would be female and male.

Classification can be of three types, such as **binary classification**, when we have only two possible classes; **multi-class classification**, when we are dealing with more than two classes where every sample is assigned only a single target label; and **multi-label classification**, when each sample can have more than one target label assigned to it.

6.1.1 Basic Concepts of Classification

Features: A feature is an individual measurable property of a particular phenomenon we observe at a time.

Classifiers: A classifier is an algorithm that maps the input data of a model to a particular category/class label.

Classification models: Classification models have to conclude the input values we give to the model during training. These models predict the categories (class labels) for the new data we provide to them.

6.1.2 Binary Classification

A binary classification classifies examples into one of two classes. Examples include emails classified as spam and not spam, customer retention where customers are classified as not churned and churned, customers' product purchase classified as bought an item and not bought an item, and cancer detection classified as no cancer detected and cancer detected.

Generally, we use binary values where the normal state is assigned a value of 0 and the abnormal state a value of 1. Some of the most popular algorithms used for binary classification are as follows:

- k-nearest neighbors
- Logistic regression
- Support vector machine
- Decision trees
- Naive Bayes

6.1.3 Multi-Class Classification

Multi-class types of classification problems can deal with more than two classes. An example is a face recognition system, which uses a huge number of labels for predicting a picture as to how closely it might belong to one of tens of thousands of faces. Some of the common algorithms used for multi-class classification are as follows:

- k-nearest neighbours
- Naive Bayes
- Decision trees

- Gradient boosting
- Random forest

We can also use the algorithms for binary classification for multi-class classification by classifying one-versus-rest or one-versus-one where we define a binary model for every pair of classes.

6.1.4 Multi-Label Classification for Machine Learning

When a single example is assigned two or more classes, it is known as multi-label classification. For example, we need to classify a single image of a photo as tree, sea, human and so on since the image contains multiple objects. Multi-label classification requires modification to traditional classification algorithms in order to incorporate the assigning of multiple classes.

6.2 Decision Based Methods—Nonlinear Instance-Based Methods— *k*-Nearest Neighbor

6.2.1 Introduction

k-nearest neighbors (KNN) also known as k-NN, a type of supervised learning algorithm, is used for both regression and classification. KNN is used to make predictions on the test data set based on the characteristics of the current training data points. This is done by calculating the distance between the test data and training data, assuming that similar data items exist within close proximity.

The algorithm will have stored learned data, making it more effective at predicting and categorizing new data points. When a new data point is inputted, the KNN algorithm will learn its characteristics and features. It will then place the new data point at closer proximity to the current training data points that share the same characteristics or features. Because it does not create a model of the data set beforehand, the *k*-nearest-neighbor technique is an example of a "lazy learner." It only performs calculations when prompted to poll the data point's neighbors. This makes KNN a breeze to use in data mining.

To understand KNN, you can take a look at a real-life example. Suppose you want to befriend a person about whom you don't have much information. To get to know them better, you'd first talk to their friends and colleagues to get an idea of what they're like. This is how the KNN algorithm works. While using the *k*-nearest neighbor algorithm, ensure that you normalize the variables, as higher range variables can develop a bias. Moreover, KNN algorithms are quite expensive, computationally.

The "K" in KNN decides the number of nearest neighbors considered. *k* is a positive integer and is typically small in value and is recommended to be an odd number.

In layman's terms, the *k*-value creates an environment for the data points. This makes it easier to assign which data point belongs to which category.

6.2.2 Need for KNN

Assume there are two categories, category A and category B, and we receive a new data point x1. Which of these categories will this data point fall into? A KNN algorithm is required to address this type of problem. We can simply determine the category or class of a data set with the help of KNN.

Because it delivers highly precise predictions, the KNN algorithm can compete with the most accurate models. As a result, the KNN algorithm can be used in applications that require high accuracy but don't require a human-readable model.

The distance measure affects the accuracy of the predictions. As a result, the KNN method is appropriate for applications with significant domain knowledge. This understanding aids in the selection of an acceptable metric.

6.2.3 Working of KNN

The following example is explained using Figures 6.2–6.4. In Figure 6.2, the "initial data" is a graph where data points are plotted and clustered into classes, and a new example to classify is present. In Figure 6.3, the "calculate distance" graph, the distance from the new example data point to the closest trained data points is calculated. However, this still does not categorize the new example data point. Therefore, using a *k*-value essentially created a neighbourhood where we can classify the new example data point.

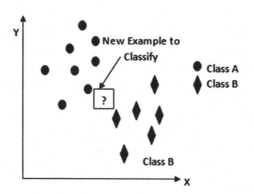

FIGURE 6.2
Initial data.

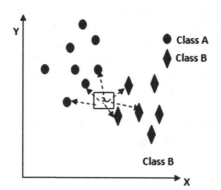

FIGURE 6.3
Calculate distance.

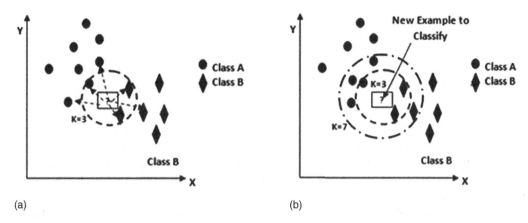

FIGURE 6.4
Finding neighbors and voting for labels.

Figure 6.4 shows different value of k. We would say that $k = 3$ and the new data point will belong to class B as there are more trained class B data points with similar characteristics to the new data point in comparison to class A. If we increase the k-value to 7, we will see that the new data point will belong to class A, as there are more trained class A data points with similar characteristics to the new data point in comparison to class B.

A figure shows the initial data points, where data points are plotted.

6.2.4 Calculating the Distance

KNN calculates the distance between data points in order to classify new data points. The most common methods used to calculate this distance in KNN are Euclidian, Manhattan, and Minkowski.

Euclidean distance is the distance between two points using the length of a line between the two points. The formula for Euclidean distance is the square root of the sum of the squared differences between a new data point (x) and an existing trained data point (y) (Equation 6.1).

Manhattan distance is calculated as the sum of the absolute difference of the Cartesian coordinates of two points. The formula for Manhattan distance is the sum of the lengths between a new data point (x) and an existing trained data point (y) using a line segment on the coordinate axes (Equation 6.2).

Minkowski distance is the distance between two points in the normed vector space and is a generalization of the Euclidean distance and the Manhattan distance (Equation 6.3). In the formula for Minkowski distance when $p = 2$, we get the Euclidian distance, also known as L2 distance. When $p = 1$ we get the Manhattan distance, also known as L1 distance, city-block distance, and LASSO. The distance functions as follows:

$$\text{Euclidean Distance} = \sqrt{\sum_{i=1}^{k} (x_i - y_i)^2} \tag{6.1}$$

$$\text{Manhattan Distance} = \sum_{i=1}^{k} |x_i - y_i| \tag{6.2}$$

$$\text{Minkowski Distance} = \left(\sum_{i=1}^{k} \left(|x_i - y_i| \right)^q \right)^{1/q} \qquad (6.3)$$

Figure 6.5 explains the difference between the three distance functions.

6.2.5 Two Parameters of KNN

Although the KNN algorithm is nonparametric, there are two parameters we usually use to build the model: k (the number of neighbours that will vote) and the **distance metric**.

There are no strict rules around the selection of k. It really depends on the data set as well as your experience when it comes to choosing an optimal k. When k is small, the prediction would be easily impacted by noise. When k is getting larger, although it reduces the impact of outliers, it will introduce more bias. (Think about when we increase k to n, the number of data points in the data set. The prediction will be the majority class in the data set).

The selection of the other parameter, **distance metric**, also varies on different cases. By default, people use Euclidean distance (L2 norm). However, Manhattan distance and Minkowski distance might also be great choices in certain scenarios.

The two parameters that are used to assess different k-values are the training error rate and the validation error rate. Figure 6.6 shows the plot of the training error rate for varying values of k.

At $k = 1$ the error is always zero and the prediction is always accurate. However, the validation error curve shows a different picture. Figure 6.7 shows the validation error curve for varying value of k.

At $k = 1$, the boundaries are overfitted. The error rate initially decreases and reaches a minimum, after which it increases with increasing k. To get the optimal value of k, we can segregate the training and validation data sets and then plot the validation error curve to get the optimal value of k. This value of k should be used for all predictions.

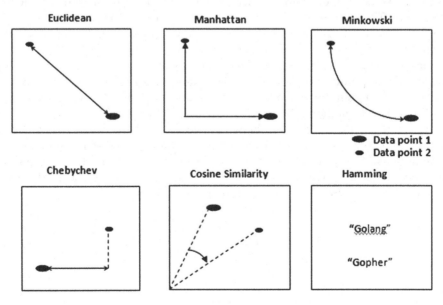

FIGURE 6.5
Distance functions.

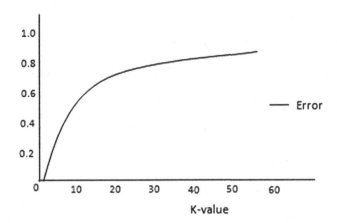

FIGURE 6.6
Training error rate.

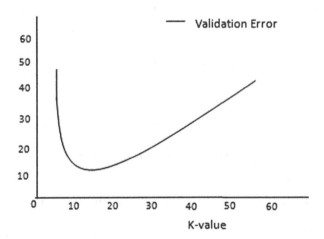

FIGURE 6.7
Validation error curve.

6.2.6 KNN Algorithm

- Store all input data in the training set.
- Initialize the value of k.
- For each sample in the test set,
  - Search for the k nearest samples to the input sample using a Euclidean distance measure. (other distances such as Hamming or Manhattan, or metrics such as Chebyshev, cosine, etc. can also be used.)
- For classification, compute the confidence for each class as
  - C_i/k (where C_i is the number of samples among the k nearest neighbors belonging to class i).
  - The classification for the input sample is the class with the highest confidence.

6.2.7 Pros and Cons of KNN

There are multiple advantages of using KNN:

1. It is a simple machine learning model. It is also very easy to implement and interpret.
2. There is no training phase of the model.
3. There are no prior assumptions on the distribution of the data. This is especially helpful when we have ill-tempered data.
4. KNN has a relatively high accuracy.

Of course, there are disadvantages of the model:

1. High requirements on memory. We need to store all the data in memory in order to run the model.
2. Computationally expensive. Recall that the model works in the way that it selects the k nearest neighbors. This means that we need to compute the distance between the new data point to all the existing data points, which is quite expensive in computation.
3. Sensitive to noise. Imagine we pick a really small k; the prediction result will be highly impacted by the noise if there is any.

6.3 Decision Based Methods—Decision Tree Algorithm

6.3.1 Decision Tree Based Algorithm

Decision trees, an induction learning technique, are essentially if-then rules and can be easily interpreted by humans. Decision trees are used to predict the relationship between input variables and the desired target (output) variable based on a series of Boolean tests.

The decision tree algorithm can be used for solving both **regression and classification problems**. The decision tree creates a training model by **learning simple decision rules** inferred from prior data (training data). This model is then used to predict the class of the unknown data. Instances are classified by decision trees starting at the root of the tree and, depending on the value of the attribute associated with the example, choosing the appropriate sub-tree at each decision node until a leaf node is reached.

Decision trees can be classified depending on whether the target variable is categorical or continuous as a **categorical variable decision tree** and **continuous variable decision tree**, respectively.

6.3.2 Terminology Associated with Decision Trees

Figure 6.8 shows the components of a decision tree:

1. **Root node:** This is the initial node of the decision tree and represents the entire population. A decision tree is grown by starting at the root node and dividing or splitting the sample space into homogeneous sets.

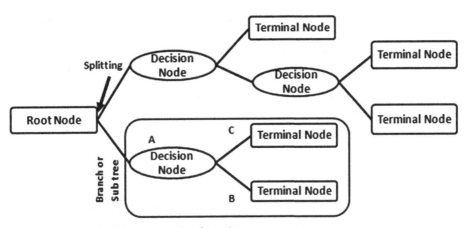

FIGURE 6.8
Components of decision trees.

2. **Splitting**: Starting from the root node and dividing a node into two or more subnodes is called splitting. There exist several methods to split a decision tree, involving different metrics (e.g., information gain, Gini impurity).

3. **Decision node**: The internal node of a decision tree which can be split into subnodes is called the decision node.

4. **Leaf/terminal node**: This represents a final node and cannot be further split.

5. **Pruning**: By removing sections that are not critical, in other words removing some sub-nodes of a decision node, we reduce the size of the decision tree. This pruning process enables better generalization and less overfitting, leading to better predictive accuracy

6. **Branch**: A subtree rooted at the root or any of the decision nodes is called a branch.

7. **Parent and child node**: A parent node is divided into sub-nodes or children of the node.

Decision trees are created by the process of splitting the input space or the examples into several distinct, nonoverlapping sub-spaces. Each internal node in the tree is tested for the attribute, and based on all features and threshold values we find the optimal split. On finding the best split, we continue to grow the decision tree recursively until stopping criteria such as maximum depth are reached. This process is called recursive binary splitting.

6.3.3 Assumptions While Creating Decision Tree

Some of the assumptions made when we create a decision tree are s follows.

- Initially, while starting the training, the complete training set is taken to be the **root**.
- Decision trees work based on categorical feature values. If we are dealing with continuous values, they need to be discretized prior to building the model.
- The recursive distribution of the samples is based on attribute values.
- The placing of attributes as root or internal nodes is decided by using some informatation theoretic measures.

The decision trees are a disjunctive normal form of the attribute set. Thus the form of a decision rule is limited to conjunctions or adding of terms and allows disjunction (or-ing) over a set of rules. The attribute to be tested at each nonterminal node is identified by the model. The attributes are split into mutually exclusive disjoint sets until a leaf node is reached.

An important aspect of decision trees is the identification of the attribute to be considered as root as well as attribute at each level, or in other words, how do we decide the best attribute? The best choice of attribute will result in the smallest decision tree. Now the basic heuristic is to choose the attribute that produces the "purest."

6.3.4 How Do Decision Trees Work?

Strategic splits decide the accuracy of the decision tree. Different strategies are used by decision trees to split a node into two or more sub-nodes. Nodes of all available variables are split by the decision tree, and then the split that results in most homogeneous sub-nodes is selected.

Some popular algorithms used in decision trees include the following:

- **ID3** → (extension of D3)
- **C4.5** → (successor of ID3)
- **CART** → (Classification And Regression Tree)

6.3.5 Steps in ID3 Algorithm

1. It begins with the original data set as the root node.
2. On each iteration of the algorithm, the **Entropy (*H*)** and **Information gain (IG)** of each attribute of the data set are calculated.
3. Then the attribute which has the smallest entropy or largest information gain is selected.
4. The data set is then split based on the selected attribute to produce subsets of the data set.
5. The algorithm is repeated for each subset till the stopping criterion is reached.

6.3.6 Attribute Selection Measures

If the data set consists of **N** attributes, then deciding which attribute to place at the root or at different levels of the tree as internal nodes is a complicated step. For solving this attribute selection problem, some criteria, like entropy, information gain, Gini index, gain ratio, reduction in variance, chi-square, and so on have been used. These criteria will calculate values for every attribute, and the attribute with a high value (in the case of information gain) is placed at the root.

6.3.6.1 Entropy

Entropy is a measure of the purity or the degree of uncertainty of a random variable. The distribution is called pure when all the items are of the same class (Equation 6.4).

$$\text{Entropy} = \sum_{i=1}^{c} -p_i \log_2(p_i) \tag{6.4}$$

The value of entropy normally ranges from 0 to 1.

6.3.6.2 Gini Impurity

If all elements are accurately split into different classes, the division is called pure (an ideal scenario). In order to predict the likelihood of a randomly chosen example being incorrectly classified, we use the Gini impurity wherein impurity indicates how the model departs from a simple division and ranges from 0 to1. A Gini impurity of 1 suggests that all items are scattered randomly across various classes, whereas a value of 0.5 shows that the elements are distributed uniformly across some classes (Equation 6.5).

$$\text{Gini} = 1 - \sum_{i=1}^{n} (p_i)^2 \tag{6.5}$$

The Gini coefficients are calculated for the sub-nodes, and then the impurity of each node is calculated using a weighted Gini score.

6.3.6.3 Information Gain

When it comes to measuring information gain, the concept of entropy is key. Information gain is based on information theory and identifies the most important attributes that convey the most information about a class. Information gain is the difference in entropy before and after splitting, which describes in turn the impurity of in-class items (Equation 6.6).

$$\text{Information Gain} = 1 - \text{Entropy} \tag{6.6}$$

For the calculation of information gain, we first calculate for each split the entropy of each child node independently. Then we calculate the entropy of each split using the weighted average entropy of child nodes. Then we choose the split with the lowest entropy or the greatest gain in information. We repeat these steps until we obtain homogeneous split nodes.

6.3.6.3.1 Information Gain—An Example

Consider the following sample data for calculating information gain. There are two features a and b and also five objects, two of which are labeled as "positive" and the rest are labeled as "negative."

$$S: \begin{bmatrix} a & b & \text{class} \\ \hline 0 & 0 & \text{positive} \\ 0 & 1 & \text{positive} \\ 1 & 0 & \text{negative} \\ 1 & 1 & \text{positive} \\ 0 & 0 & \text{negative} \end{bmatrix}$$

The information gain helps us to decide which feature should we test first and add a new node. It's the expected amount of information we get by inspecting the feature. Intuitively, the feature with the largest expected amount is the best choice. That's because it will reduce our uncertainty the most on average.

6.3.6.4 Calculation of the Entropies

In our example, the entropy before adding a new node is:

$$H(S) = -\frac{2}{5}\log_2\frac{2}{5} - \frac{3}{5}\log_2\frac{3}{5} = 0.971$$

That's the measure of our uncertainty in a random object's class (assuming the previous checks got it to this point in the tree). If we choose a as the new node's test feature, we'll get two sub-trees covering two subsets of S:

$$S|a=0: \begin{bmatrix} 2 & \text{positive objects} \\ 1 & \text{negative object} \end{bmatrix} S|a=1: \begin{bmatrix} 1 & \text{positive object} \\ 1 & \text{negative object} \end{bmatrix}$$

Their entropies are:

$$H(S|a=0) = H\left(\frac{2}{3},\frac{1}{3}\right) = 0.918$$

$$H(S|a=1) = H\left(\frac{1}{2},\frac{1}{2}\right) = 1$$

6.3.6.5 Computing the Gain

The information gain **IG(a)** is the expected amount of information we get by checking feature 'a':

$$\begin{aligned} IG(a) &= P(a=0).AI(a=0) + P(a=1).AI(a=1) \\ &= P(a=0)\big(H(S)-H(S|a=0)\big) + P(a=1)\big(H(S)-H(S|a=1)\big) \\ &= \big(P(a=0)+P(a=1)\big)H(S) - P(a=0)H(S|a=0 - P(a=1)H(S|a=1) \\ &= H(S) - P(a=0)H(S|a=0) - P(a=1)H(S|a=1) \\ &= 0.971 - 0.6^*0.918 - 0.4^*1 \\ &= 0.0202 \end{aligned}$$

We define $P(a = 0)$ and $P(a = 1)$ to be the frequencies of $a = 0$ and $a = 1$ in S, respectively. The same calculation for b shows that its gain is:

$$\begin{aligned} IG(a) &= H(S) - P(b=0)H(S|b=0) - P(b=1)H(S|b=1) \\ &= 0.971 - 0.6^*0.918 - 0.4^*0 \\ &= 0.4202 \end{aligned}$$

Since IG(*b*) > IG(*a*), we choose *b* to create a new node.

As we see, IG favors the splits that maximize the purity of the subsets so that each has its majority class's fraction as high as possible.

The calculation of IG shows us **the formula for the gain in the general case**. Let *S* denote the data set to be split by creating a new node. Let's suppose that the attribute *a* can take *m* values: {$a_1, a_2, \ldots a_m$}, and that p_i is the fraction of the objects in *a* with $a = a_i$. Then, **the information gain of *a* is Equation (6.7)**:

$$IG(a) = H(S) - \sum_{i=1}^{m} p_i H(S|a = a_i) \tag{6.7}$$

The gain cannot be negative even though individual pieces of information can have a negative contribution.

6.3.6.6 *Information Gain Versus Gini Impurity*

- While using information gain prefers splits with small partitions with a wide range of values, Gini impurity prefers larger partitions.
- Information gain uses log(base = 2) of the class probability to weigh probability of class. Squared proportion of classes is used by Gini impurity.
- Information gain is the entropy of the parent node minus the entropy of the child nodes and hence a smaller value of entropy is better while a variable split with low Gini index is preferred.

6.4 Linear Models—Support Vector Machines

The support vector machine (SVM) is mainly used for classification. Each data item is represented as a point in *n*-dimensional space assuming *n* is a number of features associated with each item. Then, classification is carried out by finding the hyper-plane that best differentiates the two classes.

Considering an example where we have two classes, *circles* and *diamonds*, and our data have two features: *x* and *y*. We want a classifier that, given a pair of (*x, y*) coordinates, outputs its classification. The labelled training data is plotted as shown in Figure 6.9.

A support vector machine plots these data points and outputs the hyperplane (which in two dimensions is simply a line) that best separates the classes. This line is the **decision boundary**: anything that falls to one side of it we will classify as *circle*, and anything that falls to the other as *diamond*.

For SVM, we need to find the best hyperplane that is the one that maximizes the margins from both classes. In other words, we want the hyperplane whose distance to the nearest element of each class is the largest (Figure 6.10).

6.4.1 Nonlinear Data

Now this example was easy, since clearly the data was linearly separable—we could draw a straight line to separate circles and diamonds. Consider the example shown in Figure 6.11a.

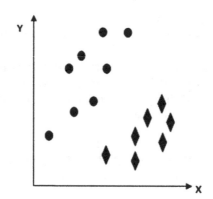

FIGURE 6.9
Sample labelled data.

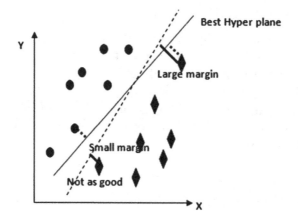

FIGURE 6.10
Not all hyperplanes are created equal.

Here there is no linear decision boundary that separates both classes. However, the vectors are very clearly segregated. To tackle this example, we need to add a third dimension. We create a new z dimension, and we rule that it be calculated a certain way that is convenient for us: $z = x^2 + y^2$ (that is the equation for a circle). This will give us a three-dimensional space as shown in Figure 6.11b. Note that since we are in three dimensions now, the 3D hyperplane is a plane parallel to the x axis at a certain z (let's say $z = 1$) as shown in Figure 6.11c. Finally, we can visualize the separation as in Figure 6.11d.

6.4.2 Working of SVM

Step 1: SVM algorithm takes data points and classifies them into two classes as either 1 or –1, or SVM discovers the hyperplane or decision boundary that best separates the classes.

Step 2: Machine learning algorithms in general represent the problem to be solved as a mathematical equation with unknown parameters, which are then found by formalizing the problem as an optimization problem. In the case of the SVM classifier, the optimization aims at adjusting the parameters. A hinge loss function is used to find the maximum margin (Equation 6.8). This hinge loss not

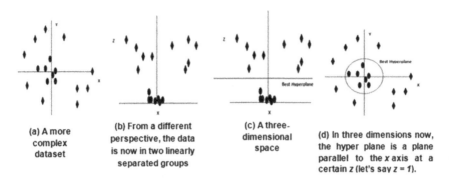

(a) A more complex dataset

(b) From a different perspective, the data is now in two linearly separated groups

(c) A three-dimensional space

(d) In three dimensions now, the hyper plane is a plane parallel to the *x* axis at a certain *z* (let's say *z* = 1).

FIGURE 6.11
Nonlinear hyperplane.

only penalizes misclassified samples but also correctly classified ones that fall within a defined margin from the decision boundary.

Hinge Loss Function

$$c(x,y,f(x)) = \begin{cases} 0, & \text{if } y^*f(x) \geq 1 \\ 1 - y^*f(x), & \text{else} \end{cases} \tag{6.8}$$

Step 3: The hinge loss function is a special type of cost function whose value is zero when all classes are correctly predicted, else the error/loss (Equation 6.9) needs to be calculated. Therefore, there needs to be a trade-off between maximizing margin and the loss generated, and in this context, a regularization parameter is introduced which decides the extent of misclassification allowed by SVM optimization. Large values of the regularization parameter will allow the optimization to choose a smaller-margin hyperplane in case the hyperplane results in all training points being classified correctly. However, for small values of the regularization parameter, the optimization will choose a larger-margin separating hyperplane, in spite of more misclassification.

Loss Function for SVM

$$\min \lambda \|w\|^2 + \sum_{i=1}^{n} \left(1 - y_i \langle x_i, w \rangle\right) \tag{6.9}$$

Step 4: A general method of minimizing an optimization function is to start with an initial guess for w, say $w0$, and iterate till convergence. In SVM, one method is computing the gradient at each iteration, updating w by taking a step in the opposite direction of the gradient as shown in Equations (6.10) and (6.11).

Gradients

$$\frac{\delta}{\delta w_k} \lambda \|w\|^2 = 2\lambda w_k \tag{6.10}$$

$$\frac{\delta}{\delta w_k} \left(1 - y_i \langle x_i, w \rangle\right) = \begin{cases} 0 & \text{if } y_i \langle x_i, w \rangle \geq 1 \\ -y_i x_{ik}, & \text{else} \end{cases} \tag{6.11}$$

Step 5: Only the regularization parameter is used to update the gradient when there is no error in the classification (Equation 6.12) while in addition, the loss function is also used when there is misclassification (Equation 6.13).

Updating of gradients when there is no misclassification:

$$w = w - \alpha^* \left(2\lambda w\right) \tag{6.12}$$

Updating of gradients when there is misclassification:

$$w = w - \alpha^* \left(2\lambda w\right) * \left(y_i^* x_i - 2\lambda w\right) \tag{6.13}$$

6.4.3 Important Concepts in SVM

Now we discuss a few phenomena and concepts that must be understood before we start applying SVM (Figure 6.12).

6.4.3.1 Support Vectors

Support vectors are those data points based on which the margins are calculated and maximized. One of the hyper-parameters to be tuned is the number of support vectors.

6.4.3.2 Hard Margin

A hard margin enforces the condition that all the data points be classified correctly and there is no training error (Figure 6.13a). While this allows the SVM classifier to have no error, the margins shrink, thus reducing generalization.

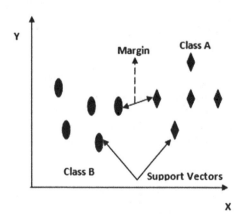

FIGURE 6.12
Concepts of SVM.

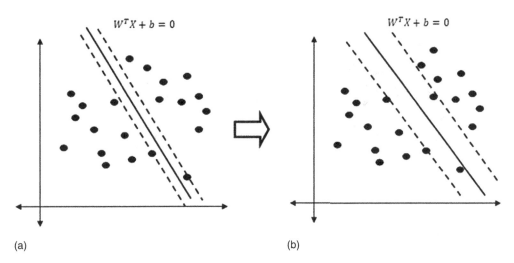

(a)   (b)

FIGURE 6.13
(a) Hard margin classification, (b) soft margin classification.

6.4.3.3 Soft Margin

Soft margins are used when we need to allow some misclassification to increase general-ization of the classification and avoid overfitting. Soft margins are also used when training set is not linearly separable or we have a data set with noise. A soft margin allows a certain number of errors and at the same time keeps margin as large as possible so that other points can still be classified correctly. This can be done simply by modifying the objective of the SVM (Figure 6.13b). Slack variables or a soft margin are introduced, which allows misclas-sification of difficult or noisy examples. In other words, we allow some errors and let some points be moved to where they actually belong, but at a cost. We thus add slack variables to allow misclassification of difficult or noisy examples, resulting in a soft margin.

6.4.3.4 Different Kernels

In general, working in high-dimensional feature space will be computationally expen-sive since while constructing the maximal margin hyperplane, we need to evaluate high-dimensional inner products. Moreover, there are problems which are nonlinear in mature. Now the "kernel trick" comes to the rescue. The use of kernels makes the SVM algorithm a powerful machine learning algorithm. For many mappings from a low-dimensional space to a high-dimensional space, there is a simple operation on two vectors in the low-dimensional space that can be used to compute the scalar product of their two images in the high-dimensional space (Figure 6.14).

Depending on the problem, you can use differnt types of kernel functions: linear, polyno-mial, radial basis function, Gaussian, Laplace, and so on. Choosing the right kernel function is important for building the classifier, and another hyperparameter is used to select kernels.

6.4.4 Tuning Parameters

The most important parameters used for tuning the SVM classifier are as follows:

- **Kernel**: We have already discussed how important kernel functions are. Depending on the nature of the problem, the right kernel function has to be chosen as the kernel-function defines the hyperplane chosen for the problem.

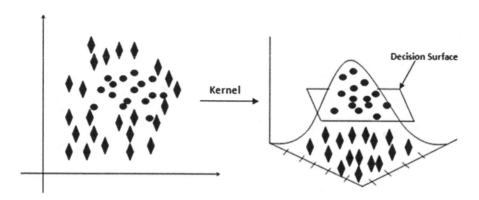

FIGURE 6.14
SVM kernel functions.

- **Regularization**: In SVM, to avoid overfitting, we choose a soft margin instead of a hard one; that is, we let some data points enter our margin intentionally (but we still penalize it) so that our classifier doesn't overfit our training sample. Here we use an important parameter: gamma (γ), which controls overfitting in SVM. The higher the gamma, the more closely the hyperplane tries to match the training data. Therefore, choosing an optimal gamma to avoid overfitting as well as under fitting is the key.

- **Error penalty**: Parameter C represents the error penalty for misclassification for SVM. It maintains the trade-off between a smoother hyperplane and misclassifications. As mentioned earlier, we do allow some misclassifications to avoid overfitting our classifier.

6.4.5 Advantages and Disadvantages of SVM

Now we will discuss the advantages and disadvantages of the SVM algorithm.

Advantages

- SVM being a mathematically sound algorithm makes it one the most accurate machine learning algorithms.
- SVM can handle a range of problems, including linear and nonlinear problems, and binary, binomial, and multi-class classification problems whether they are classification or regression problems.
- SVM is based on the concept of maximizing margins between classes and hence differentiates the classes well.
- The SVM model is designed to reduce overfitting, thus making the model highly stable.
- Due to the use of kernels, SVM handles high-dimensional data.
- SVM is computation fast and allows good memory management.

Disadvantages

- While SVM is fast and can work with high-dimensional data, it is less efficient when compared with the naive Bayes method. Moreover, the training time is relatively long.
- The performance of SVM is sensitive to the kernel chosen.
- SVM algorithms are not highly interpretable, specifically when kernels are used to handle nonlinear separated data. In other words, it is not possible to understand how the independent variable affects the target variable.
- Computational cost is high in tuning the hyper-parameters, especially when dealing with a huge data set.

SVM is a widely used algorithm in areas such as handwriting recognition, image classification, anomaly detection, intrusion detection, text classification, time series analysis, and many other application areas where machine learning is used.

6.5 Use Cases

Decision trees are very easily interpretable and hence are used in a wide range of industries and disciplines, as follows

6.5.1 Healthcare Industries

In healthcare industries, a decision tree can be used to classify whether a patient is suffering from a disease or not based on attributes such as age, weight, sex, and other factors. Decision trees can be used to predict the effect of the medicine on patients based on factors

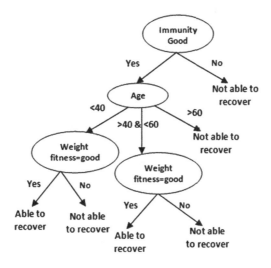

FIGURE 6.15
Decision tree—disease recovery.

such as composition, period of manufacture, and so on. In addition, decision trees can be used in diagnosis of medical reports.

Figure 6.15 represents a decision tree predicting whether a patient will be able to recover from a disease or not.

6.5.2 Banking Sectors

A decision tree can be used to decide the eligibility of a person for a loan based on attributes such as financial status, family members, and salary. Credit card frauds, bank schemes and offers, loan defaults, and so on can also be predicted using decision trees.

Figure 6.16 represents a decision tree about loan eligibility.

6.5.3 Educational Sectors

Decision trees can be used for short listing of a student based on their merit scores, attendance, overall score, and so on. A decision tree can also to be used decide the overall promotional strategy of faculty in the universities.

Figure 6.17 shows a decision tree showing whether a student will like the class or not based on their prior programming interest.

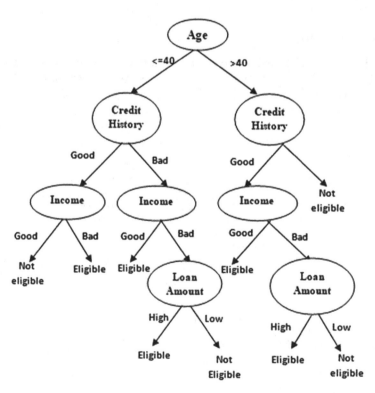

FIGURE 6.16
Decision tree—loan eligibility.

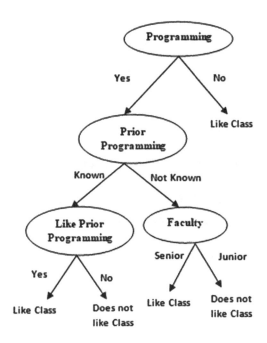

FIGURE 6.17
Decision tree—student likes class or not.

6.6 Summary

- Classification is a machine learning technique which assigns a label value to unknown data.
- When the classification is between two classes, it is termed as binary classification.
- Multi-class types of classification problems have more than two classes.
- Multi-label classification is where two or more specific class labels may be assigned to each example.
- *k*-nearest neighbors (KNN) is a type of supervised learning machine learning algorithm and is used for both regression and classification tasks.
- The most common methods used to calculate this distance in KNN are Euclidian, Manhattan, and Minkowski.
- Decision tree algorithms can be used for both regression and classification.
- Support vector machines (SVMs) are mainly used for classification.

6.7 Points to Ponder

- Classification can be of three types, namely binary classification, multi-class classification, and multi-label classification.

- The "K" in KNN decides the number of nearest neighbors considered. k is a positive integer and is typically small in value and is recommended to be an odd number.

- The two parameters associated with KNN are k (the number of neighbors that will vote) and the distance metric.

- The Minkowski distance is the distance between two points in the normed vector space and is a generalization of the Euclidean distance and the Manhattan distance.

- The internal node of a decision tree which can be split into sub-nodes is called the decision node.

- Entropy is a measure of purity or the degree of uncertainty of a random variable.

- Support vectors are those data points based on which the margins are calculated and maximized.

- The use of kernels makes the SVM algorithm a powerful machine learning algorithm.

E.6 Exercises

E.6.1 Suggested Activities

E.6.1.1 Teacher can list down various real-time tasks and ask the students to identify whether it is a classification task or not.

E.6.1.2 Readers can identify various news events from social media, newspapers, and so on pertaining to classification tasks and justify why each is classification.

E.6.2 Self-Assessment Questions

E.6.2.1 Projects:

Readers are requested to download data sets from the UCI repository and try performing various types of classification tasks mentioned in this chapter.

E.6.3 Multiple Choice Questions

Give answers with justification for correct and wrong choices.

E.6.3.1 What is classification?
  i   Assigning any unknown data X with an unknown class label C
  ii Assigning any unknown data X with a known class label C
  iii Assigning any known data X with a known class label C

E.6.3.2 The following is not an example of classification:
  i   Assigning students marks
  ii Segregating mail as spam and not spam
  iii Tagging vegetables as tomato, onion, and potato

E.6.3.3 Classifying Sachin as both a batsman and a businessman is
    i Binary classification
    ii Multi-class classification
    iii Multi-label classification

E.6.3.4 The KNN algorithm is an example of $a(n)$
    i Eager learner
    ii Lazy learner
    iii One shot learner

E.6.3.5 The distance between two points that is the sum of the absolute difference of their Cartesian coordinates is called the
    i Manhattan distance
    ii Euclidean distance
    iii Minkowski distance

E.6.3.6 The KNN algorithm uses two parameters to build the model, k and the distance metric, and hence KNN is a
    i Parametric model
    ii Probabilistic model
    iii Nonparametric model

E.6.3.7 For KNN classification, the confidence of each class is
    i C_i/k where C_i is the number of samples among the k nearest neighbors belonging to class i
    ii k/C_i where C_i is the number of samples among the k nearest neighbors belonging to class i
    iii C_i where C_i is the number of samples

E.6.3.8 In KNN
    i There are prior assumptions on the distribution of the data
    ii There are no prior assumptions on the distribution of the data
    iii The data samples are normally distributed

E.6.3.9 When using decision trees, we have a predictive model based on
    i An equal distribution of data points
    ii Parallel application of Boolean tests
    iii A series of Boolean tests

E.6.3.10 Pruning in decision trees
    i Reduces overfitting
    ii Improves overfitting
    iii Reduces generalization

E.6.3.11 The decision trees are the _____ of the attribute set.
    i Conjunctive normal form
    ii Disjunctive normal form
    iii Addition of values

E.6.3.12 Entropy is used for
     i Attribute selection
    ii Deciding size of decision tree
   iii Deciding path from root to leaf

E.6.3.13 In SVM, the hyperplane that best separates the classes is called the
     i Hyper boundary
    ii SVM boundary
   iii Decision boundary

E.6.3.14 A hinge loss function
     i Penalizes misclassified samples
    ii Penalizes misclassified samples and correctly classified ones that fall within a defined margin from the decision boundary.
   iii Penalizes correctly classified samples that fall within a defined margin from the decision boundary.

E.6.4 Match the Columns

No	Match	
E.6.4.1 Multi-label classification	A	Distance between two points using the length of a line between the two points
E.6.4.2 *k*-nearest neighbors	B	Starting from the root node and dividing a node into two or more sub-nodes.
E.6.4.3 Lazy learner	C	Distance between two points in the normed vector space
E.6.4.4 Euclidean distance	D	Decide the recursive distribution of the samples
E.6.4.5 Pure distribution	E	When a single example is assigned two or more classes
E.6.4.6 A Gini impurity of 0.5	F	When all the items are of the same class
E.6.4.7 Regularization parameter	G	Shows that the elements are distributed uniformly across some classes
E.6.4.8 Attribute values	H	Assuming that similar data items exist within close proximity
E.6.4.9 Minkowski distance	I	Decides the extent of misclassification allowed by optimization
E.6.4.10 Splitting	J	Because it does not create a model of the data set beforehand

E.6.5 Short Questions

E.6.5.1 Describe classification.

E.6.5.2 Differentiate between the three types of classification using illustrative examples.

E.6.5.3 What are the two parameters associated with the KNN algorithm? Discuss.

E.6.5.4 Describe the KNN algorithm in detail.

E.6.5.5 Discuss the pros and cons of the KNN algorithm.

E.6.5.6 What are the assumptions we make when constructing a decision tree?

E.6.5.7 Differentiate between linear and nonlinear SVM.

E.6.5.8 Discuss the steps of the ID3 algorithm.

E.6.5.9 Discuss the various attribute selection metrics used by decision trees.

E.6.5.10   What is the concept used by SVM? Discuss.

E.6.5.11   Discuss in detail the working of SVM. Describe association rule mining as a machine learning task.

E.6.5.12   What is meant by hard margin and soft margin in connection with SVM?

E.6.5.13   Why and how are kernels used in SVM?

E.6.5.14   List advantages and disadvantages of SVM.

7

Probabilistic and Regression Based Approaches

7.1 Probabilistic Methods

7.1.1 Introduction—Bayes Learning

Bayes learning needs to be understood in the context of fitting a model to data and then predicting target values for unknown hitherto unseen data which we discussed in Chapters 2–4. While in Chapters 2 and 4 we discussed data and fitting models to the training data, in Chapter 3 we discussed the fundamentals of probability, the Bayes theorem, and applications of the Bayes theorem. Some of the important criteria when we fit a model are the choice of weights and thresholds. In some cases, we need to incorporate prior knowledge, and in other cases we need to merge multiple sources of information. Another important factor is the modelling of uncertainty. Bayesian reasoning provides solutions to these above issues. Bayesian reasoning is associated with probability, statistics, and data fitting.

7.1.2 Bayesian Learning

The Bayesian framework allows us to combine observed data and prior knowledge and provide practical learning algorithms. Given a model, we can derive any probability where we describe a model of the world and then compute the probabilities of the unknowns using Bayes' rule. **Bayesian learning** uses probability to model data and quantifies uncertainty of predictions. Moreover, Bayesian learning is a generative (model based) approach where any kind of object (e.g., time series, trees, etc.) can be classified, based on a probabilistic model. Some of the assumptions are that the quantities of interest are governed by probability distribution. The optimal decisions are based on reasoning about probabilities and observations. This provides a quantitative approach to weighing how evidence supports alternative hypotheses. The first step in Bayesian learning is parameter estimation. Here we are given lots of data, and using this data we need to determine unknown parameters. The various estimators used to determine these parameters include maximum a posteriori (MAP) and maximum likelihood estimators. We will discuss these estimators later.

7.1.3 Interpretation of Bayes Rule

Viewed from another perspective a machine learning model is a hypothesis about the relationship between input (X) and output (y). The practice of applied machine learning is the testing and analysis of different hypotheses (models) on a given dataset. Now the Bayes theorem provides a probabilistic model to describe the relationship between data (D) and a

DOI: 10.1201/9781003290100-7

153

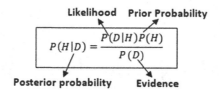

P(H|D) - Posterior probability of hypothesis H holding for observed data D

P(D|H) - Probability of observing data D given hypothesis H

P(H) - Prior Probability of hypothesis H regardless of data D

P(D) - Probability of observing data D regardless of hypothesis H

FIGURE 7.1
Probabilistic model describing relationship between data and hypothesis.

hypothesis (H) as shown in Figure 7.1. Probability is estimated for the different hypotheses being true given the observed data.

Given some model space (set of hypotheses h_i) and evidence (data d), the Bayesian framework works with the following:

Prior probability of h, P(h) reflects any background knowledge or evidence we have about the chance that h is a correct hypothesis. A prior distribution $P(h)$ is essentially prior belief; that is, the probability of the hypothesis h before seeing any data. However, the usage of prior knowledge alone may not be effective.

Likelihood $P(d\,|\,h)$ or conditional probability of observation d, $P(d\,|\,h)$ which denotes the probability of observing data d given some world in which hypothesis h holds. When we observe some data d, we combine our prior distribution with a likelihood term $P(d\,|\,h)$, which is essentially the probability of the data if the hypothesis h is true. The likelihood term takes into account how probable the observed data is given the parameters of the model, and here we assume the observations are independent of each other.

Marginal probability of the data $P(d)$ Moreover, we can also consider data evidence $P(d)$; that is, the marginal probability of the data.

Posterior probability of h, P($h\,|\,d$) which represents the probability that h holds given the observed training data d. It reflects our confidence that h holds after we have seen the training data d, and it is the quantity that machine learning researchers are interested in. This is the unknown probability we want to find; that is, the posterior probability $P(h\,|\,d)$ is the probability of the hypothesis h (hypothesis of a future observation) after having seen the data d.

The framework favors parameter settings that make the data likely. Prior knowledge can be combined with observed data to determine the final probability of a hypothesis. We now have a probabilistic approach to inference where the basic assumptions are that the quantities of interest are governed by probability distributions and the optimal decisions can be made by reasoning about these probabilities together with observed training data.

7.1.4 Benefits of Bayesian Learning

The following are some of the benefits of the general Bayesian approach:

- It defines a unified, conceptually straightforward and modular model for learning and synthesis where essentially all parameters can be learnt and it is possible to get reasonably good results from simple models.
- It provides easy model comparison and selection.
- It defines a rational process for model building and adding domain knowledge and allows the revision of probabilities based on new evidence.
- This model provides straightforward approaches to handle missing and hidden data.
- Bayes learning provides practical learning algorithms such as naïve Bayes learning, and Bayesian belief network learning. The naïve Bayes classifier is one among the most common and practical algorithms of machine learning.

7.1.5 Problems with Bayesian Learning

In spite of the many advantages, the following are some of the problems associated with Bayesian learning:

- These methods are often subjective.
- It is not easy to come up with priors, and often the assumptions made are wrong.
- The learning method follows the closed world assumption where there is a need to consider all possible hypotheses for the data before observing the data.
- The best solutions are usually intractable and often are computationally demanding.
- It is advisable to understand the real problem, and then choose approximations carefully, but sometimes the use of approximations weakens the coherence argument.

7.2 Algorithms Based on Bayes Framework

Bayesian decision theory came long before version spaces, decision tree learning, and neural networks. It was studied in the field of statistical theory and more specifically, in the field of **pattern recognition**. Bayesian decision theory is at the basis of important learning schemes such as the **naïve Bayes classifier, Bayesian belief networks**, and the **expectation maximization (EM) algorithm**. Bayesian decision theory is also useful as it provides a framework within which many non-Bayesian classifiers can be studied.

7.2.1 Choosing Hypotheses

The **Bayes theorem** allows us to find the most probable hypothesis h from a set of candidate hypotheses H given the observed data d, that is, $P(h \mid d)$. We will discuss two common methods, namely **maximum a posteriori (MAP)** and **maximum likelihood (ML)**.

Maximum a posteriori (MAP) hypothesis: Choose the hypothesis with the highest a posteriori probability, given the data. In the MAP method we need to find the hypothesis h among the set of hypothesis H that maximizes the posterior probability $P(h \mid D)$. Now by applying the Bayes theorem, we need to find the hypothesis h that maximizes the likelihood of the data d for a given h and the prior probability of h. The prior probability of the data d does not affect the maximization for finding h, so that is not considered. Hence, we have the MAP hypothesis as follows (Equation 7.1):

$$\text{MAP Hypothesis, } h_{\text{MAP}} = \arg \max_{h \in H} P(h \mid d)$$

$$= \arg \max_{h \in H} \frac{P(d \mid h)P(h)}{P(d)} \tag{7.1}$$

$$= \arg \max_{h \in H} P(d \mid h)P(h)$$

Maximum likelihood estimate (ML): Assume that all hypotheses are equally likely a priori; then the best hypothesis is just the one that maximizes the likelihood (i.e., the probability of the data given the hypothesis). If every hypothesis in H is equally probable a priori, we only need to consider the likelihood of the data D given h, $P(D \mid h)$. This gives rise to h_{ML} or the maximum likelihood, as follows (Equation 7.2):

$$h_{ML} = \text{argmax}_{h \in H} P(D \mid h) \tag{7.2}$$

Example 7.1:   Maximum A Priori

A patient takes a lab test, and the result comes back positive. The test returns a correct positive result (+) in only 98% of the cases in which the disease is actually present, and a correct negative result (–) in only 97% of the cases in which the disease is not present.

Furthermore, 0.008 of the entire population have this cancer. We need to find out whether the patient has cancer.

Here hypotheses are having cancer and not having cancer. We know the prior probabilities of these two hypotheses:

$$P(\text{cancer}) = 0.008 \; P(\neg\text{cancer}) = 1{-}008 = 0.992$$

We know the likelihood of + result given cancer and – result given cancer, and similarly we know the likelihood of + result given ¬cancer and – result given ¬cancer:

$$P(+ \mid \text{cancer}) = 0.98, \; P(- \mid \text{cancer}) = 1{-}0.98 = 0.02$$
$$P(+ \mid \neg\text{cancer}) = 1{-}0.97 = 0.03, \; P(- \mid \neg\text{cancer}) = 0.97$$

We are given that a positive result is returned, that is, $d = +$. We need to find the hypothesis that has the maximum a posteriori probability (MAP); given d is + we need to find h that gives maximum value to $P(+ \mid h)$

$$h_{\text{MAP}} = \text{argmax} \, P(h \mid +) = P(+ \mid h)$$

$P(h)$ that is we need to find whether the hypothesis $h \in (\text{cancer}, \text{cancer})$

is cancer or not cancer.

$P(\text{cancer} \mid +) = P(+ \mid \text{cancer}).P(\text{cancer}) = 0.98.0.008 = 0.0078$
$P(\text{cancer} \mid +) = P(+ \mid \text{cancer}).P(\text{cancer}) = 0.03.0.992 = 0.0298$

Now the hypothesis that gives maximum value when the data (positive test) is positive is cancer.

Therefore, the patient does not have cancer.

7.2.2 Bayesian Classification

Classification predicts the value of a class c given the value of an input feature vector x. From a probabilistic perspective, the goal is to find the conditional distribution $p(c \mid x)$ using the Bayes theorem. Despite its conceptual simplicity, Bayes classification works well. The Bayesian classification rule states that given a set of classes and the respective posterior probabilities, it classifies an unknown feature vector according to when the posterior probability is maximum. There are two types of probabilistic models of classification, the discriminative model and the generative model.

7.2.2.1 Discriminative Model

The most common approach to probabilistic classification is to represent the conditional distribution using a parametric model, and then to determine the parameters using a training set consisting of pairs $<x_n, c_n>$ of input vectors along with their corresponding target output vectors. In other words, in the discriminative approach, the conditional distribution discriminates directly between the different values of c; that is, posterior $p(c \mid x)$ is directly used to make predictions of c for new values of x (Figure 7.2). Here for example the classes can be C_1 = benign mole or C_2 = cancer, which can be modelled given the respective data points.

7.2.2.2 Generative Model

Generative models are used for modelling data directly; that is, modelling observations drawn from a probability density function. This approach to probabilistic classification finds the joint distribution $p(x, c)$, expressed for instance as a parametric model, and then subsequently uses this joint distribution to evaluate the conditional $p(c \mid x)$ in order to make predictions of c for new values of x by application of the Bayes theorem. This is known as

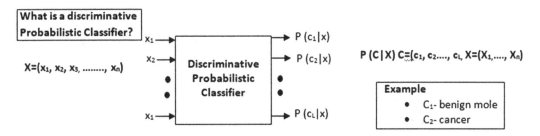

FIGURE 7.2
Discriminative model.

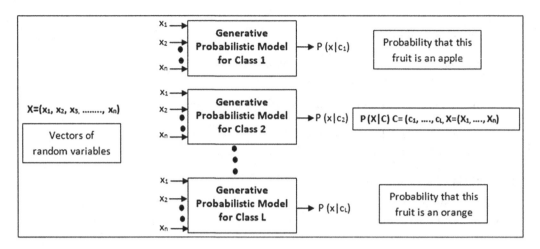

FIGURE 7.3
Generative model.

a generative approach since by sampling from the joint distribution it is possible to generate synthetic examples of the feature vector x (Figure 7.3). Here for the vector of random variables we learn the probability for each class c given the input. In practice, the generalization performance of generative models is often found to be poorer than that of discriminative models due to differences between the model and the true distribution of the data.

7.3 Naïve Bayes Classifier

Naïve Bayes is a very popular classification model and is a type of generative model (Mitchell, 2017). Here we try to determine the conditional probability $P(C \mid X)$, that is, the probability of a class C given a set of features X (Equation 7.3). This probability can be determined by finding the likelihood of the input features given the class and the prior probability of the class. Here the difficulty lies in learning the joint probability of the features given the class.

$$P(C \mid X) \propto P(X \mid C)P(C) = P(X_1, \ldots, X_n \mid C)P(C) \tag{7.3}$$

Naïve Bayes is one of the most practical Bayes learning methods. The naïve Bayes classifier applies to learning tasks where each instance x is described by a conjunction of attribute values and where the target function $f(x)$ can take on any value from some finite set. Some successful applications of the naïve Bayes method are medical diagnosis and classifying text documents.

7.3.1 Naïve Bayes Classifier: Assumptions

As already discussed, for the naïve Bayes classifier we need to determine two probabilities, that is, prior probability of the class and the likelihood of the data with respect to the class.

$$P(X_1, X_2, \ldots, X_n | C) = P(X_1, X_2, \ldots, X_n, C) P(X_2, \ldots, X_n | C)$$

$$= P(X_1 | C) P(P(X_2, \ldots, X_n | C)) \quad \textbf{Product of individual}$$
$$\textbf{probabilities}$$
$$= P(X_1 | C) P(X_2 | C) \ldots P(X_n | C)$$

$$X = (x_1, x_2, \ldots, x_n)$$

FIGURE 7.4
Naïve Bayes assumption.

However, the likelihood or the joint probability of the features of the input data given the class $P(x_1, x_2, \ldots, x_n | c_j)$ is of the order of $O(|X|^n \bullet |C|)$ and can only be estimated if a very, very large number of training examples is available. This is where the naïveté of the naïve Bayes method comes into the picture, that is, the **conditional independence assumption** where we assume that the probability of observing the conjunction of attributes is equal to the product of the individual probabilities. In other words, we assume that the joint probability can be found by finding the individual probability of each feature given the class (Figure 7.4).

Let us first formulate Bayesian learning. Let each instance x of a training set D be a conjunction of n attribute values $<a_1, a_2, \ldots, a_n>$ and let $f(x)$, the target function, be such that $f(x) \in V$, a finite set. According to the Bayesian approach using MAP, we can specify this as follows (Equation 7.4):

$$V_{MAP} = \operatorname{argmax}_{v_j \in V} P(v_j | a_1, a_2, \ldots, a_n)$$

$$= \operatorname{argmax}_{v_j \in V} \left[\frac{P(a_1, a_2, \ldots, a_n | v_j) P(v_j)}{P(a_1, a_2, \ldots, a_n)} \right] \tag{7.4}$$

$$= \operatorname{argmax}_{v_j \in V} \left[P(a_1, a_2, \ldots, a_n | v_j) P(v_j) \right]$$

Here we try to find a value v_j that maximizes the probability given the attribute values. Applying Bayes Theorem this is finding the v_j that maximizes the product of the likelihood $P(a_1, a_2, \ldots, a_n | v_j)$ and the prior probability $P(v_j)$.

Now according to the naïve Bayesian approach, we assume that the attribute values are conditionally independent so that $P(a_1, a_2, \ldots, a_n | v_j) = \prod_i P(a_1 | v_j)$.

Therefore, *naïve Bayes classifier*: $v_{NB} = \operatorname{argmax}_{vj} \in {}_V P(v_j) \Pi_i P(a_i | v_j)$

Now if the i-th attribute is categorical, then $P(x_i | C)$ is estimated as the relative frequency of samples having value x_i. However, if the ith attribute is continuous, then $P(x_i | C)$ is estimated through a Gaussian density function. It is computationally simple in both cases.

7.3.2 Naïve Bayes Algorithm

The naïve Bayes algorithm (considering discrete input attributes) has two phases:

1. **Learning phase**: Given a training set S,

For each target value of c_i $(c_i = c_1, \cdots, c_L)$ $\quad \hat{P}(C = c_i) \leftarrow$ estimate $P(C = c_i)$ with examples in S; $\quad$ For every attribute value x_{jk} of each attribute X_j $(j = 1, \cdots, n; k = 1, \cdots, N_j)$ $\qquad \hat{P}(X_j = x_{jk} \mid C = c_i) \leftarrow$ estimate $P(X_j = x_{jk} \mid C = c_i)$ with examples in S;	Learning is easy, just create probability tables.

2. **Test phase**: Given an unknown instance $X_j, N_j \, X \, L$

Given an unknown instance $X_j, N_j \times L$ Look up tables to assign the label c^* to $\mathbf{X}'$ if $\mathbf{X}' = (a_1', \cdots, a_n')$	Classification is easy, just multiply probabilities
$[\hat{P}(a_1' \mid c^*) \cdots \hat{P}(a_n' \mid c^*)] \hat{P}(c^*) > [\hat{P}(a_1' \mid c) \cdots \hat{P}(a_n' \mid c)] \hat{P}(c), \quad c \neq c^*, c = c_1, \cdots, c_L$	

7.3.3 Characteristics of Naïve Bayes

Therefore, the naïve Bayes classifier only requires the estimation of the prior probabilities $P(C_K)$ (where k is the given number of classes), and p (where p is the number of attributes) conditional probabilities for each class. Empirical evidence shows that naïve Bayes classifiers work remarkable well.

7.3.4 Naïve Bayes Classification—Example 1—Corona Dataset

Given a training set (Figure 7.5), we can compute probabilities from the data.

S.No	Symptoms	Body Temperature	Vaccinated	Lockdown Status	Going out
1	Cough	Normal	False	Full	Yes
2	Cough	Mild	True	Free	Yes
3	Cough	Normal	True	Free	Yes
4	SoreThroat	Normal	True	Free	Yes
5	SoreThroat	High	False	Free	No
6	Fever	Mild	True	Partial	No
7	Fever	Mild	True	Free	Yes
8	Fever	High	False	Free	No
9	Fever	High	True	Free	Yes
10	Cough	High	False	Full	No
11	Cough	High	False	Partial	No
12	SoreThroat	Mild	True	Partial	Yes
13	SoreThroat	High	True	Free	No
14	Cough	Normal	True	Full	No
15	SoreThroat	High	True	Free	Yes

FIGURE 7.5
Corona training dataset.

Training Phase: First we compute the probabilities of going out (positive) and not going out (negative) as $P(p)$ and $P(n)$, respectively (Figure 7.6).

Probabilities of each of the attributes are then calculated as follows.

We need to estimate $P(x_i \mid C)$, where x_i is each value for each attribute given C, which is either positive (p) or negative (n) class for going out. For example, consider the attribute symptom has the value fever for 2 of the 8 positive samples (2/8) and for 2 of the 7 negative samples (2/7). We calculate such probabilities for every other attribute value for attribute symptom and similarly for each value of each of the other attributes body temperature, vaccinated, and lockdown (Figure 7.7).

Test Phase: Given a new instance x' of variable values, we need to calculate the probability of either going out or not going out. Now assume we are given the values of the four attributes as follows:

x = (Symptom = *Sore throat*, Body Temperature = *Normal*, Vaccinated = *false*, Lockdown = *Partial*)

Here we consider the probability of a symptom being sore throat and look up the probability of going out and not going out. Similarly, we look up the probabilities for body temperature = normal, vaccinated = false, and lockdown = partial. Now we can calculate the probability of going out and not going out given the new instance x' by finding the product of each of the probabilities obtained for the value of each variable. Now we find that $P(\text{Yes}/x') = 0.00117$ and $P(\text{No}/x') = 0.003$. Since $P(\text{No}/x')$ is greater, we can conclude that the new instance x' will be labelled as No as shown in Figure 7.8.

$P(p) = 8/15$	$P(n) = 7/15$

FIGURE 7.6
Probability of going out and not going out.

Symptom	
$P(\text{cough}|p) = 3/8$	$P(\text{cough}|n) = 3/7$
$P(\text{sorethroat}|p) = 3/8$	$P(\text{sorethroat}|n) = 2/7$
$P(\text{fever}|p) = 2/8$	$P(\text{fever}|n) = 2/7$
Body Temperature	
$P(\text{normal}/p) = 3/8$	$P(\text{normal}/n) = 1/7$
$P(\text{mild}|p) = 3/8$	$P(\text{mild}|n) = 1/7$
$P(\text{high}|p) = 2/8$	$P(\text{high}|n) = 5/7$
Vaccinated	
$P(\text{true}|p) = 7/8$	$P(\text{true}|n) = 3/7$
$P(\text{false}|p) = 1/8$	$P(\text{false}|n) = 4/7$
Lockdown Status	
$P(\text{full}|p) = 1/8$	$P(\text{full}|n) = 2/7$
$P(\text{free}|p) = 6/8$	$P(\text{free}|n) = 3/7$
$P(\text{partial}|p) = 1/8$	$P(\text{partial}|n) = 2/7$

FIGURE 7.7
Conditional probabilities of each attribute.

P(Symptom= Sore throat |Go out= Yes)=3/8	P(Symptom= Sore throat |Go out= No)=3/8
P(Body Temperature= Normal| Go out=Yes)= 3/8	P(Body Temperature= Normal| Go out=No)= 3/8
P(Vaccinated=False |Go out=Yes)=1/8	P(Vaccinated=False |Go out=No)=1/8
P(Lockdown=Partial |Go out=Yes)=1/8	P(Lockdown=Partial |Go out=No)=1/8
P(Go out=Yes)=8/15	P(Go out=No)= 8/15

Use the MAP rule to calculate Yes or No

P(Yes \|x'):[P(Sore throat \|Yes)P(Normal\| Yes)P(False \| Yes)P(Partial \|Yes)P(Play=Yes)
=3/8*3/8*1/8*1/8*8/15=0.00117

P(No \|x'):[P(Sore throat \|No)P(Normal\| No)P(False \| No)P(Partial \|No)P(Play=No)
=2/7*1/7*4/7*2/7*7/15=0.003

Given the fact P(Yes \|x')<P(No \|x'), we label x' to "No"

FIGURE 7.8
Calculating whether going out is true given the new instance.

7.4 Bayesian Networks

Bayesian networks (BNs) are different from other knowledge-based system tools because uncertainty is handled in a mathematically rigorous yet efficient and simple way. BN is a graphical model that efficiently encodes the joint probability distribution for a large set of variables. While naïve Bayes is based on an assumption of conditional independence, Bayesian networks provide a tractable method for specifying dependencies among variables. BNs have been used for intelligent decision aids, data fusion, intelligent diagnostic aids, automated free text understanding, data mining, and so on, in areas such as medicine, bio-informatics, business, trouble shooting, speech recognition, and text classification.

We need to understand BNs because they effectively combine domain expert knowledge with data. The representation as well as the inference methodology is efficient. It is possible to perform incremental learning using BNs. BNs are useful for handling missing data and for learning causal relationships.

7.4.1 Foundations of Bayesian Network

A Bayesian network is also known as a Bayesian belief network, belief network, probabilistic network, or causal network. Each node of the graph represents a random variable, and each arc represents a direct dependence between two variables. The Bayesian network consists of a qualitative part, encoding the existence of probabilistic influences among a domain's variables in a directed graph, and a quantitative part, encoding the joint probability distribution over these variables (Pearl and Russell 2000). From the viewpoint of machine learning, graphs that reflect the causal structure of the domain are convenient since they normally encode the understanding of the domain and are readily extendible when new information becomes available.

7.4.2 Bayesian Network Perspectives

Bayesian networks (Russell et al. 2022) are powerful enough to be used for many types of learning tasks. The basic Bayesian network is shown in Figure 7.9. The network can be viewed as consisting of nodes indicating causes and those indicating symptoms.

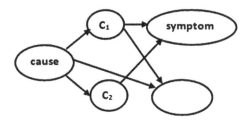

FIGURE 7.9
Basic Bayesian network.

- **Diagnosis**: $P(\text{cause} \mid \text{symptom}) = ?$

  Now a diagnostic problem is defined as the probability of the cause given the symptom.

- **Prediction**: $P(\text{symptom} \mid \text{cause}) = ?$

  On the other hand, a prediction problem is defined as the probability of the symptom given the cause.

- **Classification: max** $P(\text{class} \mid \text{data})$

  In this context, classification is decided by the class that results in maximum probability given the data.

- **Decision-making** (given a cost function)

  Decision making on the other hand is finding any of the previous but with an associated cost function.

7.4.3 Bayesian Network—Probability Fundamentals

A Bayesian network provides a way to describe the joint probability distribution in a compact and structured manner. A set of random variables makes up the nodes of the network. A set of directed links or arrows connects pairs of nodes. The intuitive meaning of an arrow from X to Y is that X has a direct influence on Y—direct dependence. Bayesian network assumes that the graph is acyclic so that there are no directed cycles (DAG). Each node has a conditional probability table that quantifies the effects that the parents have on the node. The parents of a node are all those nodes that have arrows pointing to it. Therefore, the two components of a Bayesian network are the graph structure (conditional independence assumptions) and the numerical probabilities associated with each variable given its parents. A Bayesian belief network describes the probability distribution over a set of random variables $Y_1, Y_2, \ldots Y_n$. Each variable Y_i can take on the set of values $V(Y_i)$. The **joint space** of the set of variables Y is the cross product (Equation 7.5)

$$V(Y_1) \times V(Y_2) \times \ldots \times V(Y_n) \tag{7.5}$$

Joint probability distribution: specifies the probabilities of the items in the joint space. Due to the Markov condition, we can compute the joint probability distribution over all the variables $X_1, \ldots, X_n$ in the Bayesian net using the formula.

$$P(X_1 = x_1, ..., X_n = x_n) = \prod_{i=1}^{n} P(X_i = x_i \mid Parents(X_i))$$

The full joint distribution   graph-structured approximation

Parents (X_i) means the values of the Parents of the node X_i with respect to the graph

In the Figure 7.10 we define the joint probability $p(x_1, x_2, x_3, x_4, x_5, x_6)$ as the product of probability of x_1, probability of x_2 given its parent, probability of x_3 given its parent, probability of x_4 given both its parents x_2 and x_3, and so on.

An important concept we need to define in the context of Bayesian networks is **conditional independence**. Conditional independencemeans that if X and Y are conditionally independent given Z, equivalently if we know Z, then knowing Y does not change predictions of X. That is, $P(X \mid Y, Z) = P(X \mid Z)$, and the usual notation used is Ind($X;Y \mid Z$) or ($X{\perp}Y \mid Z$). Another important aspect is the **Markov condition**, which states that given its parents (P_1, P_2), a random variable X is conditionally independent of its non-descendants (ND_1, ND_2) (Figure 7.11).

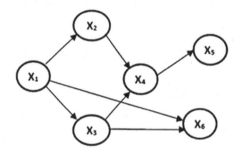

$$P(X, X_2, X_3, X_4, X_5, X_6) = P(X_6 \mid X_1, X_3)P(X_5 \mid X_4)(X_4 \mid X_2, X_3)P(X_3 \mid X_1)P(X_2 \mid X_1)P(X_1)$$

FIGURE 7.10
Example of joint probability.

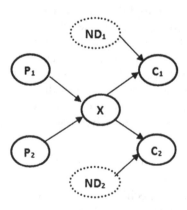

FIGURE 7.11
Markov condition.

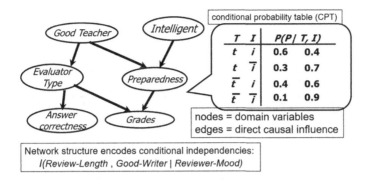

FIGURE 7.12
Example of a Bayesian network.

7.4.4 Semantics of Bayesian Networks

An example explaining the components of the Bayesian network is shown in Figure 7.12. In this example we have six nodes or domain variables.

The edges correspond to direct causal influence. Associated with each child node is a conditional probability table (CPT). In Figure 7.12 the CPT of the child node Preparedness is given for each value of each of its parents—here Good Teacher and Intelligent. Two probability values are associated with each variable, indicating the probability for the variable to be true and for it to be false. The size of the CPT of a node depends on the number of parents it has. Therefore, the conditional dependencies defined by the directional edges in the Bayesian network along with node associated CPTs defines the full joint distribution over the domain. The network is a compact and natural representation, and when nodes have $\leq k$ parents the number of parameters is $O(2^k n)$. The network structure encodes conditional independencies. Here Answer Correctness and Good Teacher are independent given Evaluator Type.

Again for the example given in Figure 7.12, the full joint distribution answers any query that is $P(event \mid evidence)$. It also allows combination of different types of reasoning:

- **Causal**: $P(Evaluator\ Type \mid Good\ Teacher)$
- **Evidential**: $P(Evaluator\ Type \mid not\ good\ Grades)$
- **Intercausal**: $P(Evaluator\ Type \mid not\ good\ Grades, Preparedness)$

Now let us consider a simple Bayesian network given in Figure 7.13. Now the conditional probability distribution for B given A is specified in B's CPT. For a given combination of values of the parents (B in this example), the entries for $P(C = true \mid B)$ and $P(C = false \mid B)$ must add up to 1 (Figure 7.13). For example, $P(C = true \mid B = false) + P(C = false \mid B = false) = 1$. If we have a Boolean variable with k Boolean parents, this table has 2^{k+1} probabilities (but only 2^k need to be stored).

The network given above can be used to calculate

$P(A = true, B = true, C = true, D = true)$ ← * This is from the graph structure

$= P(A = true) * P(B = true \mid A = true) *P(C = true \mid B = true)*P(D = true \mid B = true)$

$= (0.4)*(0.3)*(0.1)*(0.95)$ These numbers are from the conditional probability tables

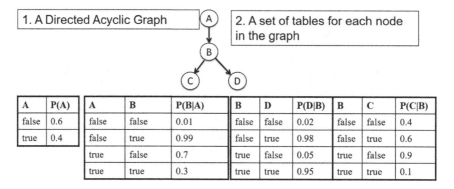

FIGURE 7.13
Example showing CPTs of each node.

7.4.5 Bayesian Network—Putting It All Together

The Bayesian network can be used to compute and infer probabilities where inferences are of the following form:

$$P(X \mid E)$$

X = The query variable(s)   E = The evidence variable(s)

7.4.5.1 Independence

Let us explain the concept of independence using Figure 7.14. *Difficulty* and *Intelligence* are two random variables that are not connected by an edge, so they are independent. This means $P(D,I) = P(I)P(D)$ and the independence is represented as $P(D \mid I) = P(D)D \wedge I$ and $P(I \mid D) = P(I)I \wedge D$. Hence $P(D, I) = P(I \mid D)P(D) = P(I)P(D)$ and $P(D, I) = P(D \mid I)P(I) = P(D)P(I)$.

Letter is independent of Difficulty and Intelligence given Grade, and this is represented as $P(C \mid A,G,S) = P(C \mid S)$ $C \perp A,G \mid S$. However, Difficulty is **dependent** on Intelligence, given Grade. Similarly Grade and SAT are dependent; however, given Intelligence, Grade is independent of SAT, that is $P(S \mid G,I) = P(S \mid I)$.

7.4.5.2 Putting It Together

Figure 7.15 emphasizes what we have been discussing so far.

The network topology and the conditional probability tables give a compact representation of joint distribution. These networks are generally easy for domain experts to construct.

7.4.6 Limitations of Bayesian Networks

Bayesian networks typically require initial knowledge of many probabilities. Quality and extent of prior knowledge play a very important role in Bayesian networks. Significant computational cost (NP hard task) is involved. Unanticipated probability of an event is not taken care of when using Bayesian networks.

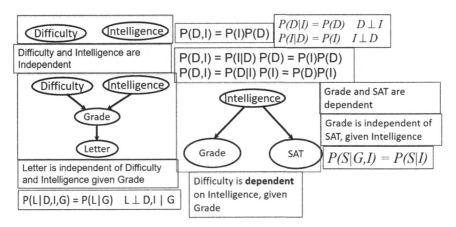

FIGURE 7.14
Explaining independence.

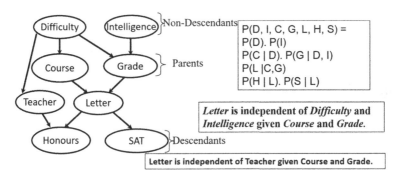

FIGURE 7.15
Putting all the components together.

7.4.7 Constructing Bayesian Networks

Let us now discuss the construction of a Bayesian network. Let us assume that the problem can be defined in terms of n random variables. The steps in the construction are as follows.

1. Choose an ordering of variables $X_1, \ldots, X_n$
2. For $i = 1$ to n

    add X_i to the network
    select parents from $X_1, \ldots, X_{i-1}$ such that
    $P(X_i \mid \text{Parents}(X_i)) = P(X_i \mid X_1, \ldots X_{i-1})$

7.4.8 Bayesian Networks—Eating Habits

Let us consider the simple example given in Figure 7.16. The example shows Obesity having Eating as parent where each can take three values. Probability of eating being each of the three values—that is, Probability of eating being eating well, Probability of eating moderately well, and Probability of eating junk food—are given.

The conditional probability table (CPT) of each of the three values of Obesity (namely no, moderate, high) given the different values of eating is given (Figure 7.16). The product rule for the example is shown in Figure 7.17. Here the conditional probability $P(O|E)$ is multiplied by probability of $P(E)$ to obtain joint probability $P(O,E)$. This table can be used for marginalization as shown in Figure 7.18. The total of the columns gives us $P(O)$—the marginalized value of O. Now using the values calculated we get $P(E|O) = P(O|E).P(E)/P(O)$ $= P(O,E)/P(O)$ as shown in Figure 7.19. Therefore, we can infer the probability of the state of Eating knowing the state of Obesity.

7.4.9 Causes and Bayes' Rule

Let us consider a simple example of Studying well resulting in Good grades (Figure 7.20). We are given that the probability of Study well $P(S)$ is 0.4, which also means that the probability of not Study well is 0.6. In addition, we are given the CPT of the Good Grades under the conditions of Study well and Not Study well. Now how do we proceed to carry out diagnostic inference, that is, Knowing that the Grade is good, what is the probability that Study well is the cause?

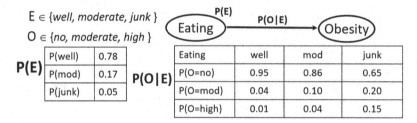

$E \in \{well, moderate, junk\}$

$O \in \{no, moderate, high\}$

Eating — $P(E)$ → Obesity $P(O|E)$

P(E)	
P(well)	0.78
P(mod)	0.17
P(junk)	0.05

P(O|E)	well	mod	junk
P(O=no)	0.95	0.86	0.65
P(O=mod)	0.04	0.10	0.20
P(O=high)	0.01	0.04	0.15

FIGURE 7.16
Example of Bayesian network.

$P(O,E) = P(O|E).P(E)$

E ⇓ ⇒ O	no	mod	high
well	0.7410	0.0312	0.0078
mod	0.1462	0.0068	0.0068
junk	0.0325	0.01	0.0075

FIGURE 7.17
Product rule.

$P(O,E) = P(O|E).P(E)$

E ⇓ ⇒ O	no	mod	high	Total	
well	0.7410	0.0312	0.0078	0.7800	P(Eating) - Given
mod	0.1462	0.0068	0.0068	0.1598	
junk	0.0325	0.01	0.0075	0.0500	
Total	0.9197	0.0480	0.0221		

P(Obesity)

FIGURE 7.18
Marginalization.

P(E|O)=P(O|E).P(E)/P(O) = P(O,E)/P(O)

E⇓ ⇒O	no	mod	high
well	0.7410/0.9197	0.0312/0.0480	0.0078/0.0221
mod	0.1462/0.9197	0.0068/0.0480	0.0068/0.0221
junk	0.0325/0.9197	0.01/0.0480	0.0075/0.0221
Obesity	no	mod	high
P(E=well)	0.8057	0.650	0.3529
P(E=mod)	0.1589	0.4167	0.3076
P(E=junk)	0.0353	0.208	0.3393

FIGURE 7.19
Inferred values using marginalization.

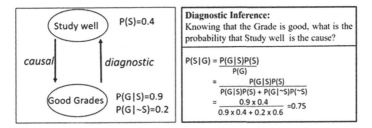

FIGURE 7.20
Causal and diagnostic inference.

Now using the Bayes theorem, we know that $P(S|G)$ can be deduced from $P(G|S) * P(S)$ divided by $P(G)$. Now probability of Good Grades $P(G)$ is the summation of $P(G|S)*P(S) + P(G|\sim S)*P(\sim S)$, that is, the probability of Good Grades is based on the probabilities of the states of its cause (Study well), which in this case has only two states, S and $\sim S$.

7.4.10 Conditional Independence in BNs

Normally edges between the nodes of a Bayesian network represent conditional dependencies. Nodes that are not connected, that is, where there is no path from a node to another in the Bayesian network, represent variables that are said to be conditionally independent of each other. There are three types of conditional independences associated with Bayesian networks, namely serial, diverging, and converging (Figure 7.21).

- **Serial case**: For the serial case, given the condition that F is known, T and C are conditionally independent. Conditional independence is due to the fact that the intermediate cause F is known.

- **Diverging case**: For the diverging case, E, the common cause for two nodes O and B, is known; that is, the two nodes are connected through the common cause E and hence O and B are conditionally independent. Conditional independence is due to the fact that the common cause is known.

- **Converging case**: For the converging case, we have two nodes O and B, both being causes for the node H, which in turn is the cause for the node R. Now given the condition that H, the common effect of O and B is not known, and neither is the

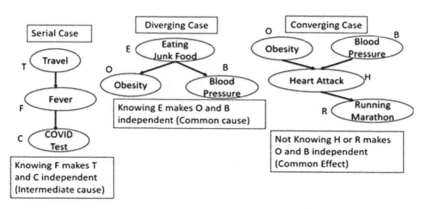

FIGURE 7.21
Conditional independence.

effect R of that common effect H known, then O and B are conditionally independent. Conditional independence is due to the fact that the common effect and in turn its effect are not known.

7.4.11 Bayesian Networks—Alarm (from Judea Pearl)— Example 2

The alarm example given by Judea Pearl is a good example to explain many aspects of Bayesian networks and is therefore a very popular example. Here we use the example to explain the steps in the construction of a Bayesian network. The problem statement is given in Figure 7.22. The steps in the construction are as follows:

Step 1: First we determine what the propositional (random) variables should be. Then we determine causal (or another type of influence) relationships and develop the topology of the network.

Variables are identified as *Burglary, Earthquake, Alarm, JohnCalls, MaryCalls*

- You have a new burglar alarm installed at home. It is fairly reliable at detecting a burglary, but also responds on occasion to minor earthquakes.
- You also have two neighbors, John and Mary, who have promised to call at work when they hear the alarm.
- John always calls when he hears the alarm, but sometimes confuses the telephone ringing with the alarm and calls then, too.
- Mary, on the other hand, likes rather load music and sometimes misses the alarm together.
- Given the evidence of who has or has not called, we would like to estimate the probability of a burglary.

FIGURE 7.22
Bayesian network—alarm example.

The network topology reflecting the "causal" knowledge is as follows:

– A burglar can set the alarm off.
– An earthquake can set the alarm off.
– The alarm can cause Mary to call.
– The alarm can cause John to call.

The resulting topology of the Bayesian network is shown in Figure 7.23.

Step 2: Next, we need to specify a *conditional probability table* or CPT for each node. This can be done through observations or using heuristics. Each row in the table contains the conditional probability of each node value for a conditioning case (possible combinations of values for parent nodes). In the example, the possible values for each node are true/false. The sum of the probabilities for each value of a node given a particular conditioning case is 1. The CPT for alarm node indicates the probability of Alarm given Burglar and Earthquake. Now both Burglar and Earthquake can each take values of T/F. Hence this CPT has four rows. The value of both T and F values of $P(A\,|\,B,E)$ for given T and F values of B and E is indicated in the CPT. Similarly, the CPT for each of the other nodes can be indicated. Please note that the nodes Burglar and Earthquake are independent, and hence independent probability is associated with these nodes (Figure 7.24).

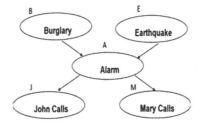

FIGURE 7.23
Topology of the network.

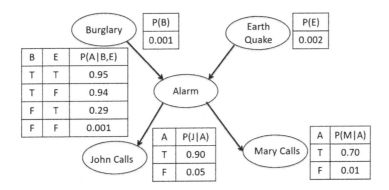

FIGURE 7.24
Bayesian network with CPTs of all nodes for alarm example.

7.4.11.1 Semantics of Bayesian Networks—Alarm Network

There are two views of a Bayesian network. View 1 says that a belief network is a representation of the joint probability distribution ("joint") of a domain. A generic entry in the joint probability distribution is the probability of a conjunction of particular assignments to each variable, such as Equation (7.6):

$$P(x_1,\ldots,x_n) = \prod_{i=1}^{n} P\big(x_i|\text{Parents}(X_i)\big) \tag{7.6}$$

We can see that each entry in the joint probability is represented by the product of appropriate elements of the CPTs in the belief network.

For the alarm example we can calculate the probability of the event that the alarm has sounded but neither a burglary nor an earthquake has occurred, and both John and Mary call as follows:

$$P(J \wedge M \wedge A \wedge \sim B \wedge \sim E) = P(J|A)P(M|A)P(A|\sim B,\sim E)P(\sim B)P(\sim E)$$
$$= 0.90^{*} 0.70^{*} 0.01^{*} 0.999^{*} 0.998$$
$$= 0.0062$$

The second view is that the Bayesian network is an encoding of a collection of conditional independence statements. For the alarm example,

> **JohnCalls is conditionally independent of other variables in the network given the value of Alarm.**

This view is useful for understanding inference procedures for the networks.

7.4.11.2 Inferences in Bayesian Networks—Alarm Network

We have discussed the two types of inferences associated with Bayesian networks, namely causal inferences and diagnostic inferences.

Causal Inference
Causal inference is basically inference from cause to effect. In Figure 7.25, given Burglary (that is, the probability of burglary ($P(B) = 1$)), we can find the probability of John calling ($P(J|B)$). Note that this is indirect inference since Burglary causes Alarm, which in turn causes John to call. Therefore, we first need the probability of Alarm ringing given that Burglary has occurred ($P(A|B)$).

Step 1: Calculating $P(A|B)$
$P(A|B)$ is calculated by considering the probability of Alarm ringing based on both occurrence of Burglary (probability 1 since this is given) and occurrence of Earthquake (which may or may not occur). Therefore, for $P(A|B)$ we consider the two rows from the CPT of the Alarm node where Burglary is True and calculate $P(A|B)$ as the sum of these two terms with associated probabilities as given in Figure 7.25.

Step 2: Calculating $P(J | B)$

In the next step we need to calculate the probability of John calling given the probability of Burglary. Here we have that either the Alarm rings when Burglary occurs $P(A)$, which we calculated in Step 1 or does not ring, which is $1 - P(A)$. Now we associate the probability of $P(J)$ given A from the CPT of J as given in Figure 7.25. Using these two probability values, we can calculate the probability of John calling given Burglary occurred (Figure 7.25).

Diagnostic Inference

Diagnostic inference is basically inference from effect to cause. In Figure 7.26 given that John calls, we can find the probability of Burglary occurring ($P(B | J)$). Note that this is indirect inference since John calling was caused by Alarm ringing $P(J | A)$ which in turn was caused by a Burglary ($P(B | A)$).

Now we first apply Bayes theorem to find $P(B | J)$ as given in Figure 7.26. Now this shows that we need to know the probability of John calling that is $P(J)$. However for finding probability of $P(J)$ we need to know probability of Alarm ringing that is $P(A)$.

Step 1: Calculating $P(A)$

For calculating $P(A)$, we do not have any information of whether Burglary occurred or Earthquake occurred. Hence we consider the four rows of the CPT of the Alarm node with probability of truth values of Burglary and Earthquake from their respective probability tables (Figure 7.25).

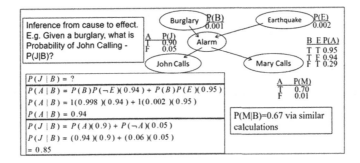

FIGURE 7.25
Causal inference.

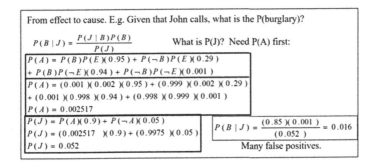

FIGURE 7.26
Diagnostic inference.

Step 2: Calculating $P(J)$

We use the value of $P(A)$ calculated in step 1 for the calculation of the probability of John calling, that is, $P(J)$. Here we consider the probability that Alarm rang and did not ring $(1 - P(A))$ for the calculation of $P(J)$ from its CPT.

Step 3: Calculating $P(B \mid J)$

Now we can calculate the probability of Burglary given John called using the Bayes theorem. We first need the value of $P(J \mid B)$ which we can calculate as shown in the previous section. The probability value of occurrence of Burglary $P(B)$ can be obtained from its probability table, and $P(J)$ has been calculated as explained.

7.5 Regression Methods

Regression is a type of supervised learning which predicts real valued labels or vectors (Pardoe, 2022). For example, it can predict the delay in minutes of a flight route, the price of real estate or stocks, and so on. Another example from health care is, given features such as age, sex, body mass index, average blood pressure, and blood serum measurements, in the case of regression the target can be predicted as quantitative measure of disease progression. Therefore, the goal of regression is to make quantitative, that is, real-valued predictions on the basis of a vector of features or attributes. Here we need to specify the class of functions, decide how to measure prediction loss, and solve the resulting minimization problem. When constructing the predictor $f: X \rightarrow Y$ to minimize an error measure $\text{err}(f)$, the error measure $\text{err}(f)$ is often the mean squared error $\text{err}(f) = E[(f(X) - Y)^2]$.

7.5.1 Linear Regression Models

We have already discussed this model informally in Chapter 2 where we discussed curve fitting. However, in this chapter we will discuss the linear regression models more in detail. Here the goal is to learn the real valued mapping (Equation 7.7).

$$f : \mathfrak{R}^d \rightarrow \mathfrak{R}. (i.e) f\left(x; w\right) = w_0 + w_1 x_1 + \ldots, w_d x_d \tag{7.7}$$

where $\mathbf{w} = [w_0 + w_1 x_1 + \ldots, w_d x_d]^T$ are parameters we need to set.

If we have only one feature, then $y = wx + b$ where $w, x, b \in \mathfrak{R}$ and y is linear in x.

If we have D features, then $y = w^T + b$ where $\mathbf{w}, \mathbf{x} \in \mathfrak{R}^D$ and $b \in \mathfrak{R}$; here again y is linear in x. Therefore, in linear regression, we use a linear function of the features $x = (x_1 + x_2 + \ldots + x_d) \in \mathfrak{R}^d$ to make predictions of y of the target value $t \in \mathfrak{R}$, that is (Equation 7.8):

$$y = f\left(x\right) = \sum_j w_j x_j + b \tag{7.8}$$

where y is the prediction, w is the weights, and b is the bias or intercept. Here w and b are the parameters. We wish that the prediction is close to the target, that is, $y \cong t$.

7.5.1.1 Steps in Learning a Linear Regression Model

There are basically four steps in building the linear model.

7.5.1.1.1 Choosing the Model

We first need to choose a linear model describing relationships between variables of interest. The degree of the polynomial we use is important. If we choose the model with degree of polynomial $M = 0$, the model is too simple and does not fit the training data (underfitting) while if we choose a higher degree polynomial (for example $M = 9$), it is too complex but fits the training data perfectly, leading to overfitting. Generally, $M = 3$ gives a good model which results in small test error but at the same time generalizes well.

7.5.1.1.2 Defining Loss Function

Once we have chosen a model, then we need to define a **loss function** quantifying how bad the fit is for some data x, where the algorithm predicts y, however the target is actually t. Normally the squared error loss function is used and is given by Equation (7.9):

$$(y,t) = \frac{1}{2}(y-t)^2 \tag{7.9}$$

where $y - t$ is the residual which we want to make as small as possible.

Now we average this loss function over all training data to obtain the cost function or overall loss function y^i:

$$(w,b) = \frac{1}{2N}\sum_{i}^{N}(y_i - t_i) = \frac{1}{2N}\sum_{i}^{N}(w^T x_j - t_j) \tag{7.10}$$

Therefore given a data set $D = (x_1,y_1,\ldots,(x_n,y_n)$ we need to find the optimal weight vector (Equation 7.11):

$$W = \text{argmin}_w \sum_{j=1}^{n}(w^T x_j - t_j)^2 \tag{7.11}$$

7.5.1.1.3 Controlling Model Complexity and Overfitting

Next we need to choose a regularizer to control model complexity and overfitting. In linear regression, in addition to learning the data, the model also learns the noise present in it. Hence learning the training points a bit too perfectly results in overfitting. We want to improve the linear regression model by replacing the least square fitting with some alternative fitting procedure, that is, the values that minimize the mean square error (MSE). There are two issues associated with using the ordinary least squares estimates, namely prediction accuracy and model interpretability. The least squares estimates have relatively low bias and low variance, especially when the relationship between target value y and input x is linear and the number of observations n is much greater than the number of predictors p. As we have already discussed, high bias results in underfitting while high variance results in overfitting. However, the least squares fit can have high variance and may result in overfitting, which in turn affects the prediction accuracy of unseen observations. When we have a large number of input variables x in the model there will generally be many of these variables that will have little or no effect on target y. Having these variables in the model makes it harder to see the effect of the "important variables" that actually effect y and hence reduces model interpretability. One method to handle these issues is the subset selection method, where a subset of all p predictors that we believe to be related to the response y are identified and then the model is fitted using this subset.

Shrinkage or Regularization
The subset selection methods involve using least squares to fit a linear model that contains a subset of the predictors. We can also fit a model containing all p predictors using a technique that constrains or regularizes the coefficient estimates, or equivalently, that shrinks the coefficient estimates towards zero. In regression analysis, a fitted relationship appears to perform less well on a new data set than on the data set used for fitting, and we use shrinkage to regularize ill-posed inference problems. Regularization constrains the machine learning algorithm to improve out-of-sample error, especially when noise is present. The model would be easier to interpret by removing (i.e., setting the coefficients to zero) the unimportant variables. Shrinkage regularization methods fit a model containing all p predictors using a technique that constrains or *regularizes* the coefficient estimates (i.e., *shrinks* the coefficient estimates towards zero).

Shrinkage or regularization methods apply a penalty term to the loss function used in the model. Minimizing the loss function is equal to maximizing the accuracy. Recall that linear regression minimizes the squared difference between the actual and predicted values to draw the best possible regression curve for the best prediction accuracy. Shrinking the coefficient estimates significantly reduces their variance. The need for shrinkage method arises due to the issues of underfitting or overfitting the data. When we want to minimize the mean error (MSE in case of linear regression), we need to optimize the bias–variance trade-off.

Ridge Regression
As we know, linear regression estimates the coefficients using the values that minimize the following Equation (7.12):

$$\text{RSS} = \sum_{i=1}^{n}\left(y_i - \beta_0 - \sum_{j=1}^{p}\beta_j x_{ij}\right)^2 \tag{7.12}$$

In other words, the idea of **regularization** modifies the loss function by adding a regularization term that penalizes some specified properties of the model parameters (Equation 7.13). Ridge regression adds a penalty term to this, lambda, to shrink the coefficients to 0:

$$\sum_{i=1}^{n}\left(y_i - \beta_0 - \sum_{j=1}^{p}\beta_j x_{ij}\right)^2 + \lambda\sum_{j=1}^{p}\beta_j^2 = \text{RSS} + \lambda\sum_{j=1}^{p}\beta_j^2 \tag{7.13}$$

Here λ is a scalar that gives the weight (or importance) of the regularization term. Shrinkage penalty $\lambda \geq 0$ is a tuning parameter.

Ridge regression's advantage over linear regression is that it capitalizes on the bias–variance trade-off. As λ increases, the coefficients shrink more towards 0. Ridge regression (also called L1 regularization) has the effect of "shrinking" large values towards zero. It turns out that such a constraint should improve the fit, because shrinking the coefficients can significantly reduce their variance. Ridge regression has a major disadvantage that it includes all p predictors in the output model regardless of the value of their coefficients, which can be challenging for a model with a huge number of features.

Lasso Regression

The disadvantage of ridge regression is overcome by lasso regression, which performs variable selection. Lasso regression uses L–1 penalty as compared to ridge regression's L–2 penalty, which instead of squaring the coefficient, takes its absolute value as shown in Equation (7.14):

$$\sum_{i=1}^{n} \left(y_i - \beta_0 - \sum_{j=1}^{p} \beta_j x_{ij} \right)^2 + \lambda \sum_{j=1}^{p} |\beta_j| = \text{RSS} + \lambda \sum_{j=1}^{p} |\beta_j| \tag{7.14}$$

Ridge regression brings the value of coefficients close to 0 whereas lasso regression forces some of the coefficient values to be exactly equal to 0. It is important to optimize the value of λ in lasso regression as well to reduce the MSE error. The lasso has a major advantage over ridge regression, in that it produces simpler and more interpretable models that involve only a subset of predictors. Lasso leads to qualitatively similar behavior to ridge regression, in that as λ increases, the variance decreases and the bias increases and can generate more accurate predictions compared to ridge regression. In order to avoid ad hoc choices, we should select λ using cross-validation.

7.5.1.1.4 Fitting or Optimizing the Model—Gradient Descent

In simplest terms we can describe linear regression using the equation $y = mx + c$, where y: dependent variable, x: independent variable, m: slope of the line, and c: y intercept. The cost is the error in our predicted value. Usually, we use the mean squared error function to calculate the cost (Equations 7.15 and 7.16).

$$\text{Cost Function (MSE)} = \frac{1}{n} \sum_{i=0}^{n} \left(y_i - y_{i\,\text{pred}} \right)^2 \tag{7.15}$$

Replace $y_{i\text{pred}}$ with $mx_i + c$

$$\text{Cost Function (MSE)} = \frac{1}{n} \sum_{i=0}^{n} \left(y_i - (mx_i + c) \right)^2 \tag{7.16}$$

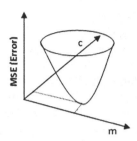

FIGURE 7.27
Bell shape of MSE (error).

Our goal is to minimize the cost as much as possible in order to find the best fit line, and for this purpose we can use the gradient descent algorithm. Gradient descent is an algorithm that finds the best-fit line for a given training data set in a smaller number of iterations. If we plot m and c against MSE, it will acquire a bowl shape as follows (Figure 7.27).

For some combination of m and c, we will get the least error (MSE), which will give us our best fit line. The algorithm starts with some value of m and c (usually starts with $m = 0$, $c = 0$) for the calculation of MSE (cost). Let us assume that the MSE (cost) at $m = 0$, $c = 0$ is 100. Then we reduce the value of m and c by some amount (learning step). We will notice a decrease in MSE (cost). We will continue doing the same until our loss function is a very small value or ideally 0 (which means 0 error or 100% accuracy).

Step by Step Algorithm

1. Let $m = 0$ and $c = 0$. Let L be our learning rate. It could be a small value like 0.01 for good accuracy. Learning rate gives the rate at which the gradient moves during gradient descent. Setting it too high would make our path instable; too low would make convergence slow.

2. Calculate the partial derivative of the Cost function with respect to m. Let the partial derivative of the Cost function with respect to m be D_m (how much the Cost function changes with little change in m). Similarly, let's find the partial derivative with respect to c. Let the partial derivative of the Cost function with respect to c be D_c (how much the Cost function changes with little change in c) (Equations 7.17 and 7.18).

$$D_m = \frac{\partial (\text{cost function})}{\partial m} = \frac{\partial}{\partial m}\left(\frac{1}{n}\sum_{i=0}^{n}\left(y_i - y_{i\,\text{pred}}\right)^2 = \frac{-2}{n}\sum_{i=0}^{n}x_i\left(y_i - y_{i\,\text{pred}}\right)\right) \quad (7.17)$$

$$D_c = \frac{\partial (\text{cost function})}{\partial c} = \frac{\partial}{\partial c}\left(\frac{1}{n}\sum_{i=0}^{n}\left(y_i - y_{i\,\text{pred}}\right)^2 = \frac{-2}{n}\sum_{i=0}^{n}x_i\left(y_i - y_{i\,\text{pred}}\right)\right) \quad (7.18)$$

Now update the current values of m and c using the following Equations (7.19) and (7.20). We will repeat this process until our Cost function is very small (ideally 0).

$$m = m - LD_m \quad (7.19)$$

$$c = c - LD_c \quad (7.20)$$

Gradient descent algorithm gives optimum values of m and c of the linear regression equation. With these values of m and c, we will get the equation of the best-fit line and then we can make predictions.

7.5.2 Logistic Regression

Let us assume that we want to predict what soft drink customers prefer to buy, Fanta or Sprite. The target variable y is categorical: 0 or 1; however, linear regression gives us a value between 0 and 1 which specifies how much the customers are loyal to Fanta. Let us now try to predict the probability that a customer buys Fanta ($P(Y = 1)$). Thus, we can model $P(Y = 1)$ using a function that gives outputs between 0 and 1 where we can use a logistic function based on odds ratio, $P(Y-1)/1-P(Y = 1)$. This is exactly logistic regression.

Logistic regression, despite its name, is a simple and efficient classification model compared to the linear regression model (Sharma, 2021). Logistic regression is a type of classification algorithm based on linear regression to evaluate output and to minimize error. It uses the logit function to evaluate the outputs. **Logistic regression** models a relationship between predictor variables and a categorical response variable. Logistic regression models are classification models; specifically, binary classification models, that is, they can be used to distinguish between two different categories, such as if a person is obese or not given their weight, or if a house is big or small given its size. This means that our data has two kinds of observations (Category 1 and Category 2 observations). Considering another example, we could use logistic regression to model the relationship between various measurements of a manufactured specimen (such as dimensions and chemical composition) to predict if a crack greater than 10 mils will occur (a binary variable: either yes or no). Logistic regression helps us estimate a probability of falling into a certain level of the categorical response given a set of predictors.

The basic idea is to work with a smooth differentiable approximation to the 0/1 loss function. In the logistic model we model the probability of a target label y to be equal, that is, $y \in (-1, 1)$ given data points $x \in R^n$. Given $y_i \in \{0, 1\}$, we want the output to be also in the range $\{0, 1\}$. Then we use the logistic (sigmoid) or S-shaped function (Equation 7.21; Figure 7.28):

$$\sigma(z) = \frac{1}{1+e^{-z}} \tag{7.21}$$

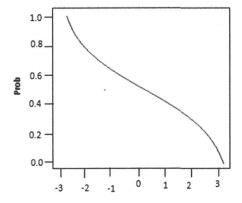

FIGURE 7.28
The sigmoid function.

hence the name logistic regression. In logistic regression, we do not fit a straight line to our data like in linear regression, but instead, we fit an S shaped curve, called **sigmoid**, to our observations. Used in this way, σ is called an activation function, and z is called the logit. This logistic function is a simple strategy to map the linear combination z where $z = w^T x + b$, lying in the $(-\text{inf}, \text{inf})$ range to the probability interval of $[0, 1]$ (in the context of logistic regression, this z will be called the log(odd) or logit or $\log(p/1-p)$). Consequently, logistic regression is a type of regression where the range of mapping is confined to $[0, 1]$, unlike simple linear regression models where the domain and range could take any real value. The Y-axis goes from 0 to 1. This is because the *sigmoid* function always takes as maximum and minimum these two values, and this fits very well our goal of classifying samples into two different categories. By computing the *sigmoid* function of X (that is a weighted sum of the input features, just like in linear regression), we get a probability (between 0 and 1) of an observation belonging to one of the two categories.

7.6 Summary

- Reviewed probabilistic methods, modelling of the world, Bayesian learning, and basics of the Bayesian framework.
- Explained the algorithms based on the Bayesian framework.
- Discussed the principles of Bayesian classification and the naïve Bayes classifier.
- Explained in detail the Bayesian network.
- Discussed the various aspects of linear regression and logistic regression models.

7.7 Points to Ponder

- A part of speech tagging application can be defined using the Bayesian rule.
- How do you think the issues associated with Bayesian learning can be tackled?

E.7 Exercise

E.7.1 Suggested Activities

E.7.1.1 Use the Weka tool for spam filtering using the naïve Bayes classifier. Use the spam base data set, which can be obtained from the UCI machine learning repository.

E.7.1.2 Design a business application using the Bayesian framework. Outline the assumptions made.

E.7.1.3 Take an example of university results and formulate at least five aspects using the naïve classifier. Clearly state any assumptions made.

E.7.1.4 Design a business application using the Bayesian network having at least seven nodes and seven edges. Outline the assumptions made.

E.7.1.5 Design a healthcare application using the Bayesian network having at least seven nodes and seven edges. Outline the assumptions made (including CPTs) and all inferences possible. Implement the application using Python.

Self-Assessment Questions

E.7.2 Multiple Choice Questions

Give answers with justification for correct and wrong choices:

E.7.2.1 Gaussian distribution is associated with a
    i S shaped curve
    ii Q shaped curve
    iii Bell shaped curve

E.7.2.2 _____ uses probability to model data and quantify uncertainty of predictions.
    i Linear regression
    ii Bayesian learning
    iii SVM

E.7.2.3 _____ of a hypothesis reflects any background knowledge or evidence we have about the chance that h is a correct hypothesis.
    i Prior probability
    ii Post probability
    iii Marginal probability

E.7.2.4 Likelihood is the
    i Marginal probability of data
    ii Conditional probability of an observation
    iii Posterior probability of a hypothesis

E.7.2.5 Bayesian decision theory is the basis of
    i SVM
    ii Logistic regression
    iii Expectation maximization algorithm

E.7.2.6 Finding the hypothesis h that maximizes the likelihood of the data d for a given hypothesis h and the prior probability of h is called
    i Maximum a posteriori (MAP)
    ii Maximum likelihood (ML)
    iii Maximum prior (MP)

E.7.2.7 The method by which the posterior p(class | data) directly which is then used to make predictions of class for new values of x is called a
    i Generative model
    ii Probabilistic model
    iii Discriminative model

E.7.2.8 An important assumption that the naïve Bayes method makes is that
    i All input attributes are conditionally independent
    ii All input attributes are conditionally independent
    iii All input attributes are conditionally dependent

E.7.2.9 A Bayesian network is a graphical model that efficiently encodes
    i The conditional probability distribution for a large set of variables
    ii The joint probability distribution for a large set of variables
    iii The prior probability distribution for a large set of variables

E.7.2.10 If the problem is defined as the probability of the cause given the symptom, it is called
    i Prediction
    ii Classification
    iii Diagnosis

E.7.2.11 The conditional probability table (CPT) of a node
    i Is given for each value of each of its parents
    ii Is given for each value of each of its children
    iii Is given for each value of each of its siblings

E.7.2.12 Given the following figure,

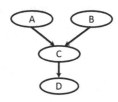

    i C is independent of D given A and B
    ii D is independent of A and B given C
    iii D is independent of C given A and B

E.7.2.13 Given the following figure,

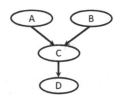

    i A is dependent on B given C
    ii A is dependent on B given D
    iii A is independent of B given C

E.7.2.14 Given the figure,

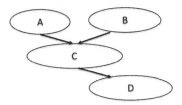

    i Knowing C or D makes A and B independent
   ii Not knowing C or D makes A and B independent
  iii Not knowing C or D makes A and B dependent

E.7.2.15 Fitting a model containing all p predictors using a technique that constrains or regularizes the coefficient estimates towards zero is called
    i Convergence
   ii Shrinkage
  iii Gradient descent

E.7.2.16 The logistic regression uses a
    i Bell shaped function
   ii S shaped function
  iii Spiked function

E.7.3 Match the Columns

No		Match
E.7.3.1 Posterior probability	A	States that given its parents, a random variable X is conditionally independent of its nondescendants
E.7.3.2 Maximum likelihood estimate	B	Choosing a higher degree polynomial as a model
E.7.3.3 Generative models are used for	C	Require initial knowledge of many probabilities
E.7.3.4 Naïve Bayes	D	Bayesian learning
E.7.3.5 Text classification based on naïve Bayes	E	The probability of the symptom given the cause
E.7.3.6 Prediction is defined as finding	F	Assume that all hypotheses are equally likely a priori
E.7.3.7 Bayesian network is associated with Markov condition	G	Probability of observing the conjunction of attributes is equal to the product of the individual probabilities
E.7.3.8 Bayesian networks	H	Vector space representation to represent documents
E.7.3.9 Lead to overfitting.	I	Is a classification model
E.7.3.10 Logistic regression	J	Modelling observations drawn from a probability density function

E.7.4 Problems

E.7.4.1 Ram is a CS 6310 student; recently his mood has been highly influenced by three factors: the weather (W), his study habits (S), and whether his friend talks to him (F). Predict his happiness (H) based on these factors, given observations in the table shown.

Weather (W)	Study (S)	Friend (F)	Happiness (H)
Bad	Fail	Talk	No
Good	Fail	No	No
Good	Fail	No	No
Good	Fail	No	No
Bad	Pass	Talk	No
Bad	Pass	Talk	Yes
Bad	Pass	Talk	Yes
Good	Pass	No	Yes

On a new day when weather is Good, S = Pass, and F = No talk, predict the student's happiness using a naïve Bayes classifier. Show all calculations.

E.7.4.2 Given the following table, find if the car will be stolen if it is yellow in colour, is a sports car, and is of domestic origin. Show all calculations.

Colour	Type	Origin	Stolen
Red	Sports	Domestic	Yes
Red	Sports	Domestic	No
Red	Sports	Domestic	Yes
Yellow	Sports	Domestic	No
Yellow	Sports	Imported	Yes
Yellow	SUV	Imported	No
Yellow	SUV	Imported	Yes
Yellow	SUV	Domestic	No
Red	SUV	Imported	No
Red	Sports	Imported	Yes

E.7.4.3 Given the following table,

WEATHER	WEEKEND	HOUSING	COMPANY	BARBEQUE
Winter	Yes	Bungalow	Family	Yes
Summer	Yes	Villa	Friends	No
Winter	No	Flat	Co-worker	Yes
Autumn	Yes	Bungalow	Co-worker	No
Winter	Yes	Bungalow	Friends	Yes
Autumn	No	Villa	Family	Yes
Summer	No	Flat	Friends	Yes
Spring	No	Villa	Co-worker	No
Spring	Yes	Bungalow	Family	Yes
Winter	Yes	Flat	Friends	No
Summer	No	Villa	Family	Yes
Autumn	Yes	Flat	Co-worker	Yes

Given New Sample X' = {Weather = Winter, Housing = Bungalow, Company = Friend, Weekend = Yes), find whether Barbeque is yes or no.

E.7.4.4 In a medical study, 100 patients all fell into one of three classes: Pneumonia, Flu, or Healthy. The following database indicates how many patients in each class had fever and headache. Consider a patient with a fever but no headache.

Pneumonia

Fever	Headache	Count
T	T	5
T	T	0
F	T	4
F	F	1
	Total	10

Flu

Fever	Headache	Count
T	T	9
T	T	6
F	T	3
F	F	2
	Total	10

Healthy

Fever	Headache	Count
T	T	2
T	T	3
F	T	7
F	F	58
	Total	70

(a) What values would a Bayes optimal classifier assign to the three diagnoses? (A Bayes optimal classifier does not make any independence assumptions about the evidence variables.) Again, your answers for this question need not sum to 1.

(b) What values would a naïve Bayes classifier assign to the three possible diagnoses? Show your work. (For this question, the three values need not sum to 1. Recall that the naïve Bayes classifier drops the denominator because it is the same for all three classes.)

(c) What probability would a Bayes optimal classifier assign to the proposition that a patient has pneumonia? Show your work. (For this question, the three values should sum to 1.)

(d) What probability would a naïve Bayes classifier assign to the proposition that a patient has pneumonia? Show your work. (For this question, the three values should sum to 1.)

E.7.4.5 A naïve Bayes text classifier has to decide whether the document "Chennai Hyderabad" is about India (class India) or about England (class England).

Doc. No.	Document	Class
1	Chennai Mumbai	India
2	Delhi London Hyderabad	England
3	Chennai Kolkata	India
4	Delhi Hyderabad Pune	India
5	London Bristol Chennai	England

(a) Estimate the probabilities that are needed for this decision from the following document collection using maximum likelihood estimation (no smoothing).

(b) Based on the estimated probabilities, which class does the classifier predict? Explain. Show that you have understood the naïve Bayes classification rule.

E.7.4.6 Given the following Bayesian network,

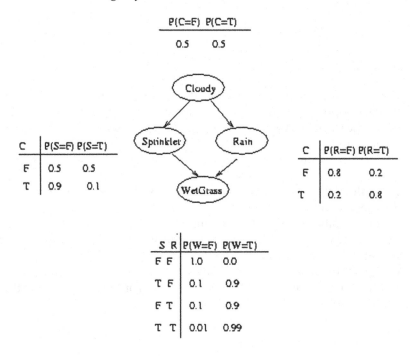

P(C=F)	P(C=T)
0.5	0.5

C	P(S=F)	P(S=T)
F	0.5	0.5
T	0.9	0.1

C	P(R=F)	P(R=T)
F	0.8	0.2
T	0.2	0.8

S	R	P(W=F)	P(W=T)
F	F	1.0	0.0
T	F	0.1	0.9
F	T	0.1	0.9
T	T	0.01	0.99

(a) Given Wet Grass is True, what is probability that it was Cloudy?

(b) Given Sprinkler, what is the probability that it was Cloudy?

E.7.4.7 Given the following Bayesian network,

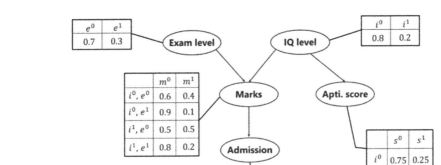

(a) Calculate the probability that in spite of the exam level being difficult, the student having a low IQ level and a low aptitude score manages to pass the exam and secure admission to the university.

(b) In another case, calculate the probability that the student has a high IQ level and aptitude score, with the exam being easy, yet fails to pass and does not secure admission to the university.

(c) Given the fact that a student gets admission, what is the probability that they have a high IQ level?

E.7.4.8 Given the following Bayesian network,

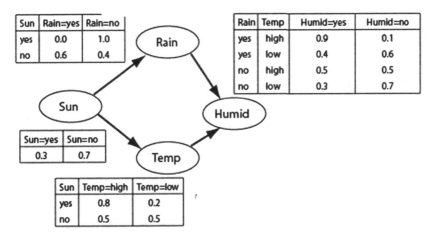

(a) Find $P(S = T, \text{Rain} = \text{Yes}, \text{Temp} = \text{low}, \text{Humid} = \text{Yes})$

(b) Given $(\text{Sun} = T)$ find $P(\text{Humid} = \text{Yes})$

(c) Given $(\text{Humid} = F)$ find $P(\text{Sun})$

(d) Given $(\text{Humid} = T)$ find $P(\text{Rain} = \text{NO})$

E.7.4.9 Given the following Bayesian network,

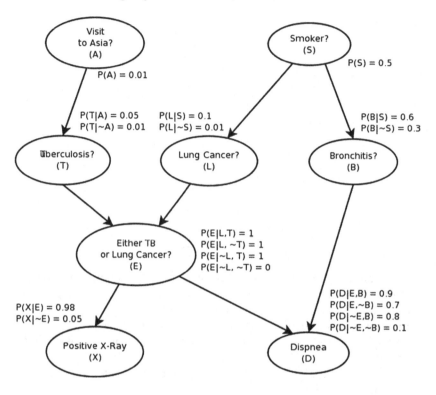

(a) Find the probability of Positive X-Ray given the person has visited Asia and is a smoker.
(b) Find the probability of *D* given the person has not visited Asia but is a smoker.
(c) Given not (Positive X-Ray), find the probability that the person has visited Asia.
(d) Given that the person does not have TB or lung cancer, find the probability that they are a smoker.

E.7.4.10 The number of disk I/Os and processor times of seven programs are measured as

S. No.	Disk I/Os	Processor Time
1.	14	2
2.	16	5
3.	27	7
4.	42	9
5.	39	10
6.	50	13
7.	83	20

    (a) Find the parameters of the Linear regression model for this data set.
    (b) Explain the interpretation of the model.
    (c) Find the mean squared error.
    (d) Find the coefficient of determination.

E.7.5 Short Questions

E.7.5.1   Explain the use of Gaussian distribution in probabilistic learning.

E.7.5.2   Discuss in detail the Bayes theorem from the viewpoint of Bayesian learning.

E.7.5.3   Explain the various methods of choosing a hypothesis in the case of Bayesian learning.

E.7.5.4   Differentiate between discriminative and generative probabilistic models using an illustrative example.

E.7.5.5   Explain the difference between a Bayesian optimal classifier and naïve Bayes classifier.

E.7.5.6   What are the four types of problems that can be solved using a Bayesian network? Illustrate with an example.

E.7.5.7   Explain the probability fundamentals associated with a Bayesian network.

E.7.5.8   Illustrate with diagrams the three types of conditional independence in Bayesian networks.

E.7.5.9   Explain the four steps in learning a linear regression model.

E.7.5.10   Differentiate between ridge regression and lasso regression.

E.7.5.11   Discuss logistic regression.

E.7.5.12   What are the three types of logistic regression? Illustrate with example applications.

E.7.5.13   Differentiate between linear and logistic regression.

E.7.5.14   What are the issues in the wide adoption of Bayesian networks?

E.7.5.15   Why is logistic regression better than linear regression for binary classification?

References

Agrawal, S. K. (2022, December 2). Metrics to evaluate your classification model to take the right decisions. *Analytics Vidhya*. https://www.analyticsvidhya.com/blog/2021/07/metrics-to-evaluate-your-classification-model-to-take-the-right-decisions/

Apple. (n.d.). Classification metrics. https://apple.github.io/turicreate/docs/userguide/evaluation/classification.html

Beheshti, N. (2022, February 10). Guide to confusion matrices & classification performance metrics: Accuracy, precision, recall, & F1 score. *Towards Data Science*. https://towardsdatascience.com/guide-to-confusion-matrices-classification-performance-metrics-a0ebfc08408e

Dharmasaputro, A. A., Fauzan, N. M., et al. (2021). Handling missing and imbalanced data to improve generalization performance of machine learning classifier. *International Seminar on Machine Learning, Optimization, and Data Science (ISMODE)*.

Engineering Education Program. (2020, December 11). Introduction to random forest in machine learning. *Section*. https://www.section.io/engineering-education/introduction-to-random-forest-in-machine-learning/

Geeks for Geeks. (2022). Bagging vs boosting in machine learning. https://www.geeksforgeeks.org/bagging-vs-boosting-in-machine-learning/

Geeks for Geeks. (2023). ML: Handling imbalanced data with SMOTE and near miss algorithm in Python. https://www.geeksforgeeks.org/ml-handling-imbalanced-data-with-smote-and-near-miss-algorithm-in-python/

JavaTpoint. (2021). Cross-validation in machine learning. https://www.javatpoint.com/cross-validation-in-machine-learning#:~:text=Cross%2Dvalidation%20is%20a%20technique,generalizes%20to%20an%20independent%20dataset

Lutins, E. (2017, August 1). Ensemble methods in machine learning: What are they and why use them? *Towards Data Science*. https://towardsdatascience.com/ensemble-methods-in-machine-learning-what-are-they-and-why-use-them-68ec3f9fef5f

Mitchell, Tom. (2017). *Machine learning*. McGraw Hill Education.

Narkhede, S. (2018, June 26). Understanding AUC-ROC curve. *Towards Data Science*. https://towardsdatascience.com/understanding-auc-roc-curve-68b2303cc9c5

Pardoe, I. (2022). *STAT 501: Regression methods*. Pennsylvania State University, Eberly College of Science. https://online.stat.psu.edu/stat501/lesson/15/15.1

Pearl, J., & Russell, S. (2000). *Bayesian networks*. University of California. https://www.cs.ubc.ca/~murphyk/Teaching/CS532c_Fall04/Papers/hbtnn-bn.pdf

Russell, S., & Norvig, P. (2022, August 22). Bayesian networks. Chapter 14 in *Artificial intelligence: A modern approach*. http://aima.eecs.berkeley.edu/slides-pdf/chapter14a.pdf

Sharma, A. (2021, March 31). Logistic regression explained from scratch (visually, mathematically and programmatically). *Towards Data Science*. https://towardsdatascience.com/logistic-regression-explained-from-scratch-visually-mathematically-and-programmatically-eb83520fdf9a

8

Performance Evaluation and Ensemble Methods

8.1 Introduction

After building a predictive classification model, you need to evaluate the performance of the model, that is, how good the model is in predicting the outcome of new test data that has not been used to train the model. In other words, we need to estimate the model prediction *accuracy* and prediction errors using a new test data set. Because we know the actual outcome of observations in the test data set, the performance of the predictive model can be assessed by comparing the predicted outcome values against the known outcome values. Evaluation metrics are used to measure the quality of the classification model. When we build the model, it is crucial to measure how accurately the expected outcome is predicted. There are different evaluation metrics for different sets of machine learning algorithms. For evaluating classification models, we use classification metrics, and for regression models, we use regression metrics. Evaluation metrics help to assess your model's performance, monitor your machine learning system in production, and control the model to fit the business needs. The goal of any classification system is to create and select a model which gives high accuracy on unseen data. It is important to use multiple evaluation metrics to evaluate the model because a model may perform well using one measurement from one evaluation metric while it may perform poorly using another measurement from another evaluation metric (Agrawal, 2022).

8.2 Classification Metrics

8.2.1 Binary Classification

Classification is about predicting the class labels given input data. In binary classification, there are only two possible output classes (i.e., dichotomy). In multi-class classification, more than two possible classes can be present. There are many ways for measuring classification performance (Beheshti, 2022). Accuracy, confusion matrix, log-loss, and area under curve/receiver operator characteristic (AUC-ROC) are some of the most popular metrics. Precision and recall are widely used metrics for classification problems.

We will first describe the confusion matrix, which is an $n \times n$ matrix (where n is the number of labels) used to describe the performance of a classification model on a set of test data for which the true values are known. Each row in the confusion matrix represents an actual class whereas each column represents a predicted class. A confusion matrix for two classes (binary classification) C1 and C2 is shown in Figure 8.1.

Consider, we have a machine learning model classifying passengers as cancer positive and negative. When performing classification predictions, there are four types of outcomes that could occur (Figure 8.2):

True Positive (TP): When you predict an observation belongs to a class and it actually does belong to that class—in this case, a passenger who is classified as cancer positive and is actually positive.

True Negative (TN): When you predict an observation does not belong to a class and it actually does not belong to that class—in this case, a passenger who is classified as not cancer positive (negative) and is actually not cancer positive (negative).

False Positive (FP): When you predict an observation belongs to a class and it actually does not belong to that class—in this case, a passenger who is classified as cancer positive and is actually not cancer positive (negative).

False Negative (FN): When you predict an observation does not belong to a class and it actually does belong to that class—in this case, a passenger who is classified as not cancer positive (negative) and is actually cancer positive.

Now, given the confusion matrix, we will discuss the various evaluation metrics.

Actual Labels ⟶ Predicted Labels	Class C1 (Positive)	Class C2 (Negative)
Class C1 (Positive)	True Positive (TP)	False negative (FN)
Class C2 (Negative)	False Positive (FP)	True Negative (TN)

FIGURE 8.1
Confusion matrix for binary classification.

Actual Labels ⟶ Predicted Labels	Class C1 (Positive)	Class C2 (Negative)
Class C1 (Positive)	True Positive (TP) **Correctly predicted positive Cancer patient as positive**	False negative (FP) **Wrongly predicted – an actual negative Cancer patient as positive**
Class C2 (Negative)	False Positive (FN) **Wrongly predicted – an actual positive Cancer patient as negative**	True Negative (TN) **Correctly predicted negative Cancer patient as negative**

FIGURE 8.2
Confusion matrix—Binary classification example.

8.2.1.1 Accuracy

The first metric is accuracy. Accuracy focuses on true positive and true negative. Accuracy is one metric which gives the fraction of predictions that are correct. Formally, accuracy is defined as given in Equation (8.1).

$$\text{Accuracy} = \frac{\text{Number of correct predictions}}{\text{Total number of predictions}} \tag{8.1}$$

In terms of the confusion matrix, accuracy is defined as given in Figure 8.3.

Example 8.1

Now, considering a patient data set of 1,00,000, let us assume that 10 of the patients actually have cancer. Now let us assume that all patients in the data set are classified as negative for cancer. So the confusion matrix values are as shown in Figure 8.4.

The accuracy in the example given in Figure 8.3 is 99.9%. The objective here is to identify actual cancer patients, and the incorrect labelling of these positive patients as negative is not acceptable; hence in this scenario accuracy is not a good measure.

8.2.1.2 Sensitivity or True Positive Rate

Recall or sensitivity gives the fraction we correctly identified as positive out of all positives (given in Figure 8.5) or in other words indicates how precise we are during prediction.

This measure shows the fraction of the correctly identified positive cases out of all the actual positive cases. In Example 8.1, recall is $0/10 = 0$. In this scenario recall is a good

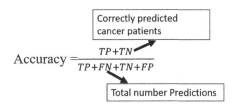

FIGURE 8.3
Accuracy.

	Actual Values	
	Class C1 (Positive)	Class C2 (Negative)
Predicted Class C1 (Positive)	TP =0	FP =0
Values Class C2 (Negative)	FN =10	TN 1,00,000-10= 99,990
Accuracy = 99,900/1,00,000 = 0.999		

FIGURE 8.4
Accuracy calculation.

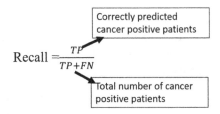

FIGURE 8.5
Recall or sensitivity. A figure shows a Recall measure which gives the fraction we correctly identified as positive out of all positives; in terms of the confusion matrix recall is defined asRecall = TP/TP + FN.

		Actual Values	
		Class C1 (Positive)	Class C2 (Negative)
Predicted Values	Class C1 (Positive)	TP =10	FP =1,00,000-10= 99,990
	Class C2 (Negative)	FN =0	TN =0
	Recall = 10/10 = 1		

(a)

$$\text{Specificity} = \frac{TN}{TN+FP}$$

Correctly predicted cancer negative patients

Total number of cancer negative patients

(b)

FIGURE 8.6
(a) Calculation of recall, (b) specificity.

measure. We normally want to maximize the recall. Now let us assume that all patients in the data set are wrongly classified as positive for cancer. This labelling is bad since it leads to mental agony as well as the cost of investigation. As can be seen from Figure 8.6a, Recall = 1, and this is again not a good measure.

However, this is also not a good measure when measured independently. Recall needs to be measured in coordination with precision. We can also define **specificity** for the negative cases as in Figure 8.6b.

8.2.1.3 Precision

Precision gives the fraction we correctly identified as positive out of all positives that were predicted (given in Figure 8.7) or in other words indicates how good we are at prediction.

Now let us assume again that in Example 8.1 all patients in the data set are wrongly classified as positive for cancer. The calculation of precision in this case is shown in Figure 8.8. For this case we have high recall value and low precision value.

In some cases, we are pretty sure that we want to maximize either recall or precision at the cost of others.

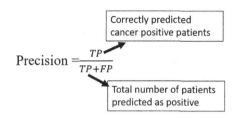

FIGURE 8.7
Precision.

		Actual Values	
		Class C1 (Positive)	Class C2 (Negative)
Predicted Values	Class C1 (Positive)	TP =10	FP =1,00,000-10= 99,990
	Class C2 (Negative)	FN =0	TN =0
	Recall = 10/10 + 99990= 0.0001		

FIGURE 8.8
Calculation of precision.

8.2.1.4 Precision/Recall Trade-off

As we can see, increasing precision reduces recall and vice versa. This is called the precision/recall trade-off as shown in Figure 8.9. Classifier models perform differently for

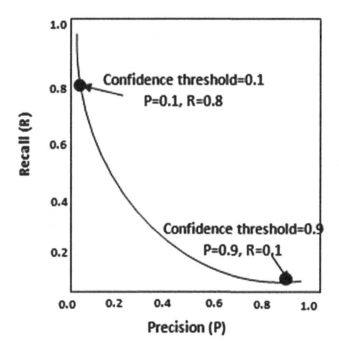

FIGURE 8.9
Precision–recall curve.

different threshold values; that is, positive and negative predictions can be changed by setting the threshold value. We can fix an output probability threshold value for us to label the samples as positive. In order to classify a disease, for example, only if very confident, we increase the threshold, leading to higher precision and lower recall. On the other hand, if we are interested in avoiding missing too many cases of disease, for example, we decrease the threshold, leading to higher recall but lower precision. Precision–recall curves summarize the trade-off between the true positive rate and the positive predictive value for a predictive model using different confidence probability thresholds.

The precision–recall curve shows the trade-off between precision and recall for different thresholds. A high area under the curve represents both high recall and high precision, where high precision relates to a low false positive rate, and high recall relates to a low false negative rate. High scores for both show that the classifier is returning accurate results (high precision), as well as returning a majority of all positive results (high recall).

8.2.1.5 F1 Score

When we want to compare different models with different precision–recall values, we need to combine precision and recall into a single metric to compute the performance. The F1 score is defined as the harmonic mean of precision and recall and is given in Figure 8.10.

Harmonic mean is used because it is not sensitive to extremely large values, unlike simple averages. The F1 score is a better measure to use if we are seeking a balance between precision and recall.

Example 8.2

Let us consider an example where mail can be spam or not spam and classification is used to predict whether the incoming mail is spam or not spam. The corresponding confusion matrix and the classification metrics are shown in Figure 8.11.

8.2.1.6 ROC/AUC Curve

The receiver operator characteristic (ROC) is another common method used for evaluation. It plots out the sensitivity and specificity for every possible decision rule cutoff between 0 and 1 for a model. For classification problems with probability outputs, a threshold can convert probability outputs to classifications. We get the ability to control the confusion matrix, so by changing the threshold, some of the numbers can be changed in the confusion matrix. To find the right threshold we use of the ROC curve. For each possible threshold, the ROC curve plots the false positive rate versus the true positive rate where false positive rate is the fraction of negative instances that are incorrectly classified as positive while true positive rate is the fraction of positive instances that are correctly predicted as positive. Thus the ROC curve, which is a graphical summary of the overall performance of the model, shows the proportion of true positives and false positives at all possible values

$$F1 \text{ Score} = 2 * \frac{Precision * Recall}{Precision + Recall}$$

FIGURE 8.10
F1 score.

Example 8.2		Actual Values		
		Spam	Not Spam	Total
Predicted Values	Spam	TP =37	FP =10	(TP+FP) 47
	Not Spam	FN=8	TN =55	(FN+TN)63
	Total	(TP+FN) 45	(FP+TN) 65	110
Binary Classification – Evaluation Metrics				
Accuracy=(TP+TN)/(TP+FN+FP+TN)		(37+55)/(45+65) = 45.19%		
Recall=TP/(TP+FN)		37/45= 0.82		
Specificity (Not Spam) =TN/(FP+TN)		55/65 =0.85		
Precision =TP/(TP+FP)		37/47=0.79		
F1 Score=2* (Precision * Recall) /(Precision +Recall)		2*(0.82*0.79)/(0.82+0.79) = 0.85		

FIGURE 8.11
Example showing evaluation of binary classification.

of probability cutoff. Figure 8.12a discusses a low threshold of 0.1 and high threshold of 0.9 while Figure 8.12b explains the ROC curve for different values of threshold.

The ROC curve when TPR = 1 and FPR = 0 is the ideal model that does not exist, where positives are classified as positives with zero error. In the strict model when TPR = 0 and FPR = 0, very rarely is something classified as true. The liberal model when TPR = 1 and FPR = 1 classifies every positive as positive but at the cost of many negatives also being classified as positive. For a good model, the ROC curve should rise steeply, indicating that the true positive rate increases faster than the false positive rate as the probability threshold decreases.

One way to compare classifiers is to measure the area under the curve (AUC) for ROC, where AUC summarizes the overall performance of the classifier.

8.2.2 Multi-Class Classification

We have discussed evaluation of binary classifiers. When there are more than two labels available for a classification problem, we have multi-class classification whose performance can be measured in a similar manner as the binary case. Having m classes, the confusion matrix is a table of size $m \times m$, where the element at (i, j) indicates the number of instances of class i but classified as class j. To have good accuracy for a classifier, ideally most diagonal entries should have large values with the rest of entries being close to zero. The confusion matrix may have additional rows or columns to provide total or recognition rates per class. In case of multi-class classification, sometimes one class is important enough to be regarded as positive with all other classes combined together as negative. Thus a large confusion matrix of $m \times m$ can be reduced to a 2×2 matrix.

Let us now discuss the calculation of TP, TN, FP, and FN values for a particular class in a multi-class scenario. Here **TP** is the value in the cell of the matrix when actual and predicted value are the same. **FN** is the sum of values of corresponding rows of the class except the TP value, while **FP** is the sum of values of corresponding column except the TP value. On the other hand, **TN** is the sum of values of all columns and row except the values of that class that we are calculating the values for.

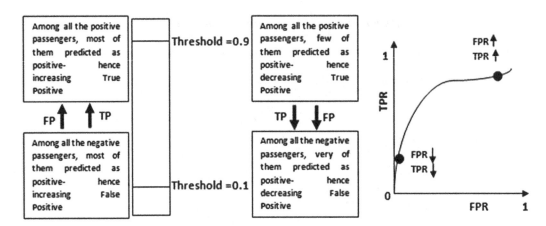

FIGURE 8.12
ROC curve.

Example 8.3

Let us consider an example where a test is carried out to predict the quality of manufactured components. The quality can have four values—Very Good, Good, Fair, and Poor. The corresponding confusion matrix and the classification metrics are shown in Figure 8.13.

Example 8.3		**Actual Values**		
		Very Good	Good	Poor
Predicted Values	Very Good	70	10	5
	Good	5	80	15
	Poor	10	8	20

Multi Classification – Values				
Very Good	TP=70	FN=10+5=15	FP=5+10=15	TN=80+15+8+50= 153
Good	TP=80	FN=5+15=20	FP=10+8=18	TN=70+5+10+50=135
Poor	TP=20	FN=10+8=18	FP=5+15=15	TN=70+10+5+80=165

Multi Classification – Evaluation Metrics				
	Accuracy=(TP+TN)/(TP+FN+FP+TN)	Recall =TP/(TP+FN)	Precision= TP/(TP+FP)	**F1 Score**=2* (Precision * Recall) /(Precision +Recall)
Very Good	88.14%	0.824	0.824	0.824
Good	85.00%	0.800	0.816	0.808
Poor	58.18%	0.526	0.571	0.548

FIGURE 8.13
Example showing evaluation of multi-class classification.

8.3 Cross-Validation in Machine Learning

Cross-validation is a technique to check how the machine learning model generalizes to an independent data set. Here the model efficiency is validated by training the model on the subset of input data and testing on a previously unseen subset of the input data. For validation purposes, we reserve a particular sample of the data set, called the validation data set, which was not part of the training data set, and then test the model on that sample before deployment. A popular cross-validation technique is the k-fold cross-validation, where the input data set is divided into k groups of samples of equal sizes called **folds**. For each learning set, the prediction function uses $k-1$ folds, and the rest of the folds are used for the test set. This approach is less biased than other methods. The first step of k-fold cross-validation is to split the input data set into k groups. Then for each group, one group is taken as the reserve or test data set. The remaining $k-1$ groups are used as the training data set. The training set is used to learn the model, and the performance is evaluated using the reserved test data set.

8.4 Ensemble Methods

Ensemble methods combine several base machine learning models in order to produce one optimal predictive model. **Ensemble learning** is a general meta approach to machine learning that seeks better predictive performance by combining the predictions from multiple models rather than from a single model. The basic idea is to learn a set of classifiers (experts) and to allow them to vote. An ensemble of classifiers combines the individual decisions of a set of classifiers in particular ways to predict the class of new samples (Figure 8.14).

The simplest approach to ensemble classifiers is to generate multiple classifiers which then vote on each test instance, and the class with the majority vote is considered as the class of the new instance. Different classifiers can differ because of different algorithms, different sampling of training data, and different weighting of the training samples or different choice of hyper-parameters of the classification algorithm.

Based on the training strategy and combination method, ensemble approaches can be categorized as follows:

- Parallel training using different data sets: Bagging (bootstrap aggregation) is an example of this category where separate models are trained on overlapping training sets and averaging is used to combine the results. Here instead of learning a single weak classifier, many weak classifiers that are good at different parts of the input space are used. The output will be the weighted vote of each classifier where the weight is determined by the confidence in each classifier.

- Sequential training where the training samples are iteratively reweighted so that the current classifier focuses on hard-to-classify samples of the previous iteration. Boosting is an example of this category.

- Parallel training based on division of labor, where the training set is divided into subsets and each expert is trained on each of the subsets—called a mixture of experts.

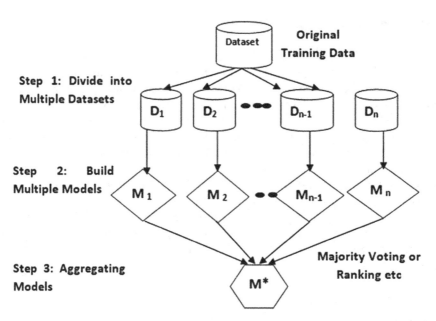

FIGURE 8.14
Concept of ensemble approach.

- Committee approach use multiple base models where each base model covers the complete input space but is trained on slightly different training sets. One method is to manipulate training instances where multiple training sets are created by resembling the original data using some sampling distribution and the classifier is built from each created training set. Examples of this method include bagging and boosting. Another approach is to choose, either randomly or based on domain expertise, subsets of input features to form different data sets and building classifiers from each training set. An example of such an approach is random forest. The predictions of all models are then combined to obtain the output whose accuracy would be better than the base model.

Ensemble methods basically work because they try to handle the variance–bias issues. When the training sets used by the ensemble method are completely independent, variance is reduced without affecting bias (as in bagging) since sensitivity to individual points is reduced. For simple models, averaging of models can reduce bias substantially (as in boosting). We will now discuss three major types of ensemble methods, namely bagging, boosting, and stacking.

8.4.1 Types of Ensemble Methods

8.4.1.1 Bagging

Bagging, is the short form for bootstrap aggregating, and is mainly applied in classification and regression. Bagging is a technique for reducing generalization error by combining several models, often using the same type of model with different data sets. The concept is that several models are trained separately and then all the models are combined on the output for test samples, and the assumption is that different models will not make the

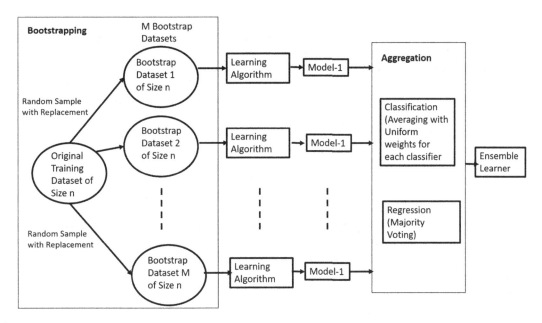

FIGURE 8.15
Bagging (bootstrap aggregation) ensemble learning.

same error. This method is also called model averaging. Bagging consists of two steps, namely bootstrapping and aggregation (Figure 8.15).

- **Bootstrapping** is a sampling with replacement technique where samples are derived from the whole population using a replacement procedure. Suppose the original data set consists of n samples. The bootstrap resampling takes random samples from the original data set with replacement. Randomness is required to obtain different training data sets for different rounds of resampling. Replacement is required to create training sets of equal size n, the same size as the original data set, and helps make the selection procedure randomized. Each bootstrap sample is drawn with replacement, so each one contains some duplicates of training data points. The differences in the bootstrap data sets result in different models. The more bootstraps, the better, since bagging approximates the Bayesian posterior mean. The base learning algorithm is then applied on each bootstrap data set to obtain the classifiers.

- **Aggregation** in bagging is done to incorporate all possible outcomes of the prediction and randomize the outcome. During regression, the base learners are aggregated by taking the average of all learners where each model is given uniform weight. The aggregation can also be carried out through majority voting, normally carried out for classification. Without aggregation, predictions will not be accurate since outcomes of all classifiers are not taken into consideration.

Bagging is advantageous since weak base learners are combined to form a single strong learner that is more stable than single learners. Bagging is most effective when using unstable data sets, nonlinear models where a small change in the data set can cause a significant change in the model. Bagging reduces variance by voting/averaging, thus reducing the overall expected error. The reduction of variance using this method increases accuracy, reducing the overfitting issue associated with many predictive models. One limitation of bagging is that it is computationally expensive.

Random forest is an ensemble machine learning algorithm specifically designed for decision tree models and widely used for classification and regression. A random forest algorithm consists of many decision trees. The "forest" generated by the random forest algorithm is trained through bagging or bootstrap aggregating. The random forest classifier is an extension to bagging which uses *decorrelated* trees. When using bagging for decision trees, the resampling of training data alone is not sufficient. In addition, the features or attributes used in each split are restricted. In other words, we introduce two sources of randomness, that is, bagging and random input vectors. In bagging, each tree is grown using a bootstrap sample of training data, and in addition, in the random vector method, at each node of the decision tree the best split is chosen from a random sample of m attributes instead of choosing from the full set of p attributes (Figure 8.16).

In case a very strong predictor exists in the data set along with a number of other moderately strong predictors using all attributes, then in the collection of bagged trees created using bootstrap data sets, most or all of them will use the very strong predictor for the first split and hence all bagged trees will look similar. Hence all the predictions from the bagged trees will be highly correlated. Averaging these highly correlated quantities does not lead to a large variance reduction, but the random forest using a random input vector decorrelates the bagged trees, leading to further reduction in variance. A random forest eradicates the limitations of a decision tree algorithm. It reduces the overfitting of data sets and increases precision, resulting in a highly accurate classifier which runs efficiently on large data sets. In addition, random forest provides an experimental method of detecting variable interactions.

Boosting is an ensemble technique that learns from mistakes of a previous predictor to make better predictions in the future. It is an iterative procedure that generates a series of base learners that complement each other. This method essentially tackles

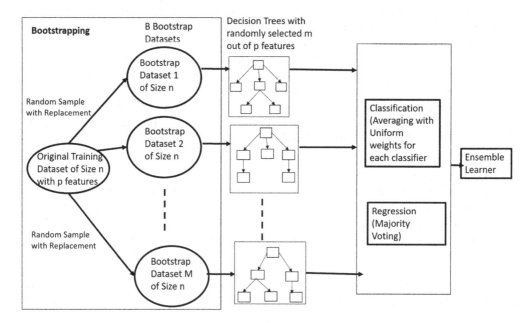

FIGURE 8.16
Random forest.

the mistakes of the previous learner by adaptively changing the distribution of the training data by focusing on previously misclassified samples. In other words, boosting works by arranging weak learners in a sequence, such that weak learners learn from the next learner in the sequence to create better predictive models. In boosting, weights given to samples may change at the end of each iteration, where weights will be increased for samples that are wrongly classified and weights will be decreased for samples that are correctly classified. In each iteration, the training set is sampled considering the weights of each sample. Then learning is carried out on the sampled training set, and then the learned model is applied on the whole training set. Now the performance of the learner on each sample is determined and the weights adjusted according to whether the sample is correctly or wrongly classified. Finally, the decisions of base learners obtained in the different iterations are combined. Boosting uses an intelligent aggregation process where the base learners are aggregated using weighted voting. The learners which have better performance are given larger weightage.

AdaBoost (adaptive boosting) is a popular implementation of boosting. Adaboost helps us to combine multiple weak classifiers into a single strong classifier. The weak learners in AdaBoost are decision trees with a single split, called decision stumps. AdaBoost works by putting more weight on difficult-to-classify instances and less on those already handled well. AdaBoost algorithms can be used for both classification and regression problems. AdaBoost modifies basic boosting in two ways: first, instead of a random sample of the training data, a weighted sample is used to focus on the most difficult examples (samples that are misclassified are given larger weights); and second, instead of combining classifiers with equal voting, weighted voting is used based on performance of the learning model (Figure 8.17). Initially all the samples N of the first iteration are given equal weightage. The misclassification rate or error of the learners is calculated as given in Equation (8.2):

$$\text{Misclassification rate or error} = \frac{(\text{correct} - N)}{N} \qquad (8.2)$$

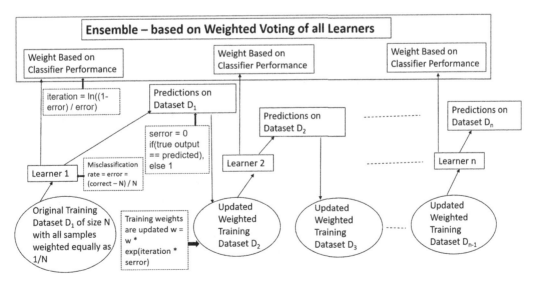

FIGURE 8.17
AdaBoost procedure.

where N is the total number of samples, and *correct* is the number of samples correctly predicted. An iteration value is calculated for the trained model which provides a weighting for any predictions that the model makes. The iteration value for a trained model is calculated as given in Equation (8.3):

$$\text{Iteration} = \ln\left(\frac{1 - \text{error}}{\text{error}}\right) \tag{8.3}$$

The updating of the weight of one training instance (w) is carried out as given in Equation (8.4):

$$w = w * \exp(\text{iteration} * \text{serror}) \tag{8.4}$$

where w is the weight for a specific training instance, *exp()* is the Euler's number raised to a power, *iteration* is the misclassification rate for the weak classifier, and *serror* is the error the weak classifier made predicting the output variable for the training instance, evaluated as given in Equation (8.5).

$$\text{serror} = f(x) = \begin{cases} 0, \text{if trueoutput} == \text{predicted} \\ \qquad 1, \text{otherwise} \end{cases} \tag{8.5}$$

where *trueoutput* is the output variable for the training instance and *predicted* is the prediction from the weak learner.

8.4.1.2 Comparison of Bagging and Boosting

Table 8.1 gives a comparison of the two important ensemble methods, namely bagging and boosting.

TABLE 8.1

Comparison between Bagging and Boosting

	Bagging	Boosting
1.	Combining predictions from multiple similar models	Combining predictions that belong to the different types of models
2.	Resamples data points	The distribution of data is changed by reweighting data points
3.	The objective is to reduce variance, not bias	Objective is to reduce bias while keeping variance small
4.	Each model is built independently	New models are influenced by the performance of previously built models
5.	Weight of each learner model is the same	Learner models are weighted according to their accuracy
6.	Base classifiers are trained in parallel	Base classifiers are trained sequentially
7.	Example: The random forest model	Example: AdaBoost algorithm

8.4.1.3 Stacking

Stacking, also called stacked generalization, involves fitting many different models on the same data and using another model to learn how to best combine the predictions. Stacking has been successfully implemented in regression, density estimations, distance learning, and classifications.

Stacking uses the concept that a learning problem can be attacked with different types of models which are capable of learning some part of the problem, but not the whole space of the problem. The multiple different learners are used to build different intermediate predictions, and a new model learns from these intermediate predictions.

The training data is split into k-folds, and the base model is fitted on the $k - 1$ parts and predictions are made for the kth part. We repeat the same for each part of the training data. The base model is then fitted on the whole training data set to calculate its performance on the test set. These steps are repeated for each of the base models. Predictions from the training set are used as features for the second level model, and this model is used to make a prediction on the test set.

8.5 Handling Missing and Imbalanced Data

The real-world data often has a lot of missing values. The cause of missing values can be data corruption or failure to record data. The handling of missing data is important during the cleaning of the data set as many machine learning algorithms do not support missing values (Dharmasaputro et al. 2021). One simple method of handling missing values is to delete the rows or columns having null values, but this method results in loss of information and works well when the percentage of missing values is negligible. If the columns of the data set have numeric continuous values, the imputation method can be used where the missing values can be replaced by the mean or median or mode of the remaining values in the column. This method prevents loss of information to a certain extent, and use of these approximations is a statistical technique to handle missing values, but the technique does not consider the covariance between features of the data set. If the columns of the data set are categorical columns (string or numerical), then the missing values can be imputed with the most frequent category. If the number of missing values is very large, then it can be replaced with a new category.

Machine learning often has to deal with imbalanced data distribution, where the samples from one of the classes are much higher or lower than the other classes. As machine learning algorithms increase accuracy by attempting to reduce error, class distribution is not taken into consideration. This issue persists in machine learning applications such as fraud detection, anomaly detection, facial recognition, and so on. Most machine learning techniques have a bias toward the majority class and tend to ignore the minority class. They tend only to predict the majority class, resulting in major misclassification of the minority class in comparison with the majority class. There are two widely used algorithms for handling imbalanced class distribution. The first method is **SMOTE (synthetic minority oversampling technique)**, an oversampling method which attempts to solve the imbalance problem by randomly increasing minority class samples by replicating them.

SMOTE synthesizes new minority instances between existing minority instances by linear interpolation. These synthetic training records are generated by randomly selecting one or more of the k-nearest neighbors for each example in the minority class. After the oversampling, the data set is reconstructed, and classification algorithms are applied using this reconstructed balanced data set.

The other method to handle imbalanced class distribution is the **NearMiss algorithm**, an undersampling technique which attempts to balance class distribution by eliminating majority class samples. The method first finds the distances between all instances of the majority class and the instances of the minority class. Then, n instances of the majority class that have the smallest distances to those in the minority class are selected. If there are k instances in the minority class, the nearest method will result in removing $k \times n$ instances of the majority class. After the under sampling of the majority class, class balance is achieved.

8.6 Summary

- Discussed the confusion matrix in detail.
- Explained the various evaluation metrics used for evaluating quality of the binary classification model with illustrative examples.
- Discussed how a confusion matrix can be used for multi-class classification evaluation.
- Discussed the basic concepts of ensemble learning.
- Explained the handling of missing and imbalanced data.

8.7 Points to Ponder

- Accuracy is not always a good evaluation measure for classification.
- It is important to understand the precision–recall trade-off to evaluate a classification model.
- The ROC/AUC curve can be used to evaluate the overall performance of the classification model.
- Ensemble methods basically work because they try to handle the variance–bias issues.
- Bagging works by resampling data points.
- The objective of boosting is to reduce bias while keeping variance small.
- Oversampling and under sampling are both used to handle imbalanced data.

E.8 Exercises

E.8.1 Suggested Activities

E.8.1.1 Implement any three classification algorithms using a standard data set from the UCI machine learning repository. Now evaluate the performance of the three models using different evaluation metrics. Give your comments.

E.8.1.2 Take any free imbalanced data set available and use SMOTE and the NearMiss algorithm to tackle the same. Evaluate the performance of classification of the data with and without balancing.

Self-Assessment Questions

E.8.2 Multiple Choice Questions

Give answers with justification for correct and wrong choices.

E.8.2.1 In the confusion matrix
  i Each row represents an actual class whereas each column represents a predicted class.
  ii Each row represents recall, and each column represents precision.
  iii Each row gives true values, and each column gives false values.

E.8.2.2 False positive (FP) is
  i When you predict an observation does not belong to a class and it actually does belong to that class.
  ii When you predict an observation belongs to a class and it actually does not belong to that class.
  iii When you predict an observation does not belong to a class and it actually does not belong to that class.

E.8.2.3 Specificity is defined as
  i Correctly predicted cases out of total number of predicted cases
  ii Correctly predicted positive cases out of total number of predicted positive cases
  iii Correctly predicted negative cases out of total number of negative cases

E.8.2.4 Bagging is
  i Combining predictions from multiple different models weighted the same
  ii Combining predictions from multiple similar models weighted differently
  iii Combining predictions from multiple similar models weighted the same

E.8.2.5 Each bootstrap data set in bagging is obtained by
  i Taking random samples from the original data set with replacement
  ii Taking random samples from the original data set without replacement
  iii Taking samples from the remaining data set without replacement

E.8.2.6   In random forest,
  i   Each tree is grown using a bootstrap sample of training data, and in addi-
      tion at each node of the decision tree the best split is chosen from the full set
      of attributes
  ii Each tree is grown using a bootstrap sample of training data, and in addi-
      tion, in the random vector method, at each node of the decision tree the best
      split is chosen from a random sample of attributes chosen randomly from
      the full set of attributes
  iii Each tree is grown using a subsample of training data, and in addition, in
      the random vector method, at each node of the decision tree the best split is
      chosen from a random sample of attributes chosen randomly from the full
      set of attributes

E.8.2.7   In AdaBoost algorithms,
  i   A weighted sample is used to focus on the most difficult examples and
      weighted voting is used based on performance of the learning model
  ii A weighted sample is used to focus on most easy examples and equal voting
      is used
  iii A weighted sample is used to focus on most difficult examples and equal
      voting is used

E.8.2.8   The random forest model is an example of
  i   Boosting
  ii Stacking
  iii Bagging

E.8.2.9   Stacked generalization
  i   Involves fitting the same models on slightly different data and using an-
      other model to learn how to best combine the predictions
  ii Involves fitting many different models on the same data and using another
      model to learn how to best combine the predictions
  iii Involves fitting many different models on the same data and voting to com-
      bine the predictions

E.8.2.10   If the columns of the data set have numeric continuous values, the imputation
           method can be used where the missing values
  i   Can be replaced by the mean or median or mode of the remaining values in
      the column
  ii Can be replaced by duplicating the remaining values in the column
  iii Can be replaced by removing the column

E.8.2.11   SMOTE is an
  i   Under sampling method which attempts to solve the imbalance problem by
      randomly decreasing the majority class by removing samples at random
  ii Oversampling method which attempts to solve the imbalance problem by
      randomly increasing the minority class by synthesizing samples by linear
      interpolation
  iii Oversampling method which attempts to solve the imbalance problem by
      randomly increasing the minority class by duplicating samples

E.8.2.12 The NearMiss algorithm an under-sampling technique where
- i Instances of the minority class that have the smallest distances to those in the majority class are selected and removed
- ii Instances of the minority class that have the smallest distances to those in the majority class are selected and added
- iii Instances of the majority class that have the smallest distances to those in the minority class are selected and removed

E.8.3 Match the Columns

No		Match	
E.8.3.1	The fraction correctly identified as positive out of all positives that were predicted	A	True negative (TN)
E.8.3.2	Sequential training where the training samples are iteratively reweighted so that the current classifier focuses on hard-to-classify samples of the previous iteration	B	ROC curve plots
E.8.3.3	Parallel training using different data sets	C	F1 score
E.8.3.4	An extension to bagging which uses decorrelated trees	D	SMOTE
E.8.3.5	When you predict an observation does not belong to a class and it actually does not belong to that class	E	Precision
E.8.3.6	Randomly increasing minority class samples by replicating them	F	Stacking
E.8.3.7	The false positive rate versus the true positive rate	G	NearMiss algorithm
E.8.3.8	Uses the concept that a learning problem can be attacked with different types of models which are capable of learning some part of the problem but not the whole space of the problem.	H	Random forest classifier
E.8.3.9	Eliminating majority class samples	I	Bootstrap aggregation
E.8.3.10	defined as the harmonic mean of precision and recall	J	Boosting

E.8.4 Short Questions

E.8.4.1 Discuss the confusion matrix for binary classification in detail.

E.8.4.2 Differentiate between the recall and precision evaluation measures.

E.8.4.3 Discuss the ROC curve in detail.

E.8.4.4 Discuss the confusion matrix for four-class classification in detail.

E.8.4.5 What is k-fold cross validation? Discuss.

E.8.4.6 Explain the categorization of ensemble methods based on training strategy and combination methods.

E.8.4.7 What are the questions that a machine learning system making decisions or recommendations needs to give explanations for to the different stakeholders?

E.8.4.8 Discuss the bagging method in detail.

E.8.4.9 Differentiate between bagging and boosting ensemble methods.

E.8.4.10 Why is it important to handle missing data and imbalanced data sets? How are these issues handled?

References

Agrawal, S. K. (2022, December 2). Metrics to evaluate your classification model to take the right decisions. *Analytics Vidhya*. https://www.analyticsvidhya.com/blog/2021/07/metrics-to-evaluate-your-classification-model-to-take-the-right-decisions/

Beheshti, N. (2022, February 10). Guide to confusion matrices & classification performance metrics: Accuracy, precision, recall, & F1 score. *Towards Data Science*. https://towardsdatascience.com/guide-to-confusion-matrices-classification-performance-metrics-a0ebfc08408e

Dharmasaputro, A. A., Fauzan, N. M., et al. (2021). Handling missing and imbalanced data to improve generalization performance of machine learning classifier. *International Seminar on Machine Learning, Optimization, and Data Science (ISMODE)*.

Re, Matteo, & Valentini, Giorgio. (2012). Ensemble methods: A review. In *Advances in machine learning and data mining for astronomy* (pp. 563–594). Chapman & Hall.

9

Unsupervised Learning

9.1 Introduction to Unsupervised Learning

Unsupervised learning refers to the use of algorithms to identify hidden underlying patterns in data sets containing data points that are neither classified nor labelled. The algorithms classify, label, and/or group the data points contained within the data sets without having any external guidance, that is, without the need for human intervention in performing that task—in other words, the data have no associated target attribute. Unsupervised learning will group unsorted information according to similarities and differences between data points even though there are no categories provided. Thus unsupervised learning identifies patterns or the intrinsic structures within the training data sets and categorizes the input objects based on the patterns that the system itself identifies by analysing and extracting useful information or features from them. The ability of unsupervised learning to discover similarities and differences in information makes it an ideal solution for applications such as exploratory data analysis, segmentation, and pattern recognition. First, the raw data will be interpreted to find the hidden patterns from the data, and then suitable algorithms such as k-means clustering are applied, which divide the data objects into groups according to the similarities and difference between the objects.

The goals of unsupervised learning include building a model and extracting useful representations of the data, such as clustering of data into groups, carrying out density estimation, learning to draw samples from a distribution, learning to denoise data from a distribution, and finding a manifold that the data lies near. Unsupervised learning is used for many tasks including data compression, outlier detection, clustering, as a preprocessing step to make other learning tasks easier, and as a theory of human learning and perception

9.1.1 Importance of Unsupervised Learning

Unsupervised learning is helpful for finding useful insights from the data. Unsupervised learning is similar to how humans learn to think by their own experiences, which makes it closer to real AI. Unsupervised learning works on unlabeled and uncategorized data, which makes unsupervised learning more important, as in the real world, we do not always have input data with the corresponding output, and hence to solve such cases, we need unsupervised learning. It is often easier to obtain unlabeled data from a laboratory, instrument, or computer than it is to get labelled data, which can require human intervention and is costly, and hence is used for more complex tasks as compared to supervised learning.

DOI: 10.1201/9781003290100-9

9.1.2 Challenges of Unsupervised Learning

While unsupervised learning has many benefits, some challenges can occur when it allows machine learning models to execute without any human intervention. Some of these challenges can include computational complexity due to a high volume of training data. Unsupervised learning is intrinsically more difficult than supervised learning as it does not have corresponding output and generally requires longer training times. As input data is not labelled, and algorithms do not know the exact output in advance, there is higher risk of inaccurate results. Human intervention is often necessary to validate output variables. Another challenge is the lack of transparency of the basis on which data was clustered.

9.2 Applications of Unsupervised Learning

Unsupervised learning provides an exploratory path to view data, allowing businesses to identify patterns in large volumes of data more quickly when compared to manual observation. Unsupervised learning, for example, identifies subgroups of breast cancer patients grouped by their gene expression measurements, groups of shoppers characterized by their browsing and purchase histories, or movies grouped by the ratings assigned by movie viewers, categorization of articles on the same story from various online news outlets, visual perception tasks, anomaly detection, and so on.

9.3 Supervised Learning Versus Unsupervised Learning

Table 9.1 gives the difference between supervised and unsupervised learning.

TABLE 9.1

Supervised Learning Versus Unsupervised Learning

Supervised Learning	Unsupervised Learning
Uses feature tagged and labelled data	Uses feature tagged data
Finds a mapping between the input and associated target attributes	Finds the underlying structure of data set by grouping data according to similarities
Used when what is required is known	Used when what is required is not known
Applicable in classification and regression problems	Applicable in clustering and association problems
Human intervention to label the data appropriately results in accuracy	Accuracy cannot be measured in a similar way
Generally objective with a simple goal such as prediction of a response	More subjective as there is no simple goal
Labelled data sets reduce computational complexity as large training sets are not needed	No reliance on domain expertise for time-consuming and costly labelling of data

9.4 Unsupervised Learning Approaches

Clustering, association mining, and dimensionality reduction are three important unsupervised techniques. Clustering algorithms are used to process raw, unclassified data objects into groups represented by structures or patterns in the information. Clustering algorithms can be categorized into a few types, specifically exclusive, overlapping, hierarchical, and probabilistic.

Association is a rule-based machine learning to discover the probability of the co-occurrence of items in a collection, for example, finding out which products were purchased together.

While more data generally yields more accurate results, it can also impact the performance of machine learning algorithms (e.g., overfitting), and moreover visualization of data sets becomes difficult. Dimensionality reduction is a technique used when the number of features, or dimensions, in a given data set is too high. It reduces the number of data inputs to a manageable size while also preserving the integrity of the data set as much as possible. It is commonly used in the preprocessing data stage.

In the rest of this chapter, we will discuss the different approaches of unsupervised learning.

9.5 Clustering

Clustering is the most important **unsupervised learning** approach associated with machine learning. It can be viewed as a method for **data exploration**, which essentially means looking for patterns or structures in the data space that may be of interest in a collection of unlabeled data. Now let us look at a simplistic definition of clustering. Clustering is an unsupervised learning task where no classes are associated with data instances a priori as in the case of supervised learning. Clustering organizes data instances into groups based on their similarity. In other words, the data is partitioned into groups (clusters) that satisfy the constraints that a cluster has points that are similar and different clusters have points that are dissimilar.

Clustering is often considered synonymously with unsupervised learning, but other unsupervised methods include association rule mining and dimensionality reduction. Clustering groups instances based on similarity, or similar interests or similarity of usage.

A set of data instances or samples can be grouped differently based on different criteria or features; in other words clustering is subjective. Figure 9.1 shows a set of seven people. They have been grouped into three clusters based on whether they are school employees, whether they belong to a family, or based on the gender. Therefore, choosing the attributes or features based on which clustering is to be carried out is an important aspect of clustering just as it was for classification. In general, clustering algorithms need to make the inter-cluster distance maximum and intra-cluster distance minimum.

9.5.1 Clusters—Distance Viewpoint

When we are given a set of instances or examples represented as a set of points, we group the points into some number of clusters based on a concept of distance such that members

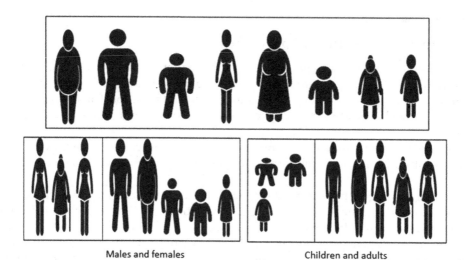

Males and females   Children and adults

FIGURE 9.1
Grouping of people based on different criteria.

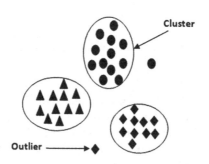

FIGURE 9.2
Clusters and outlier.

of a cluster are close to each other when compared to members of other clusters. Figure 9.2 shows a data set that has three natural clusters where the data points group together based on the distance. An outlier is a data point that is isolated from all other data points.

9.5.2 Applications of Clustering

In the context of machine learning, clustering is one of the functions that have many interesting applications. Some of the applications of clustering are as follows:

- Group related documents for browsing or webpages based on their content and links
- Group genes and proteins based on similarity of structure and/or functionality
- Group stocks with similar price fluctuations
- Cluster news articles to help in better presentation of news

- Group people with similar sizes to design small, medium, and large T-shirts
- Segment customers according to their similarities for targeted marketing
- Document clustering based on content similarities to create a topic hierarchy
- Cluster images based on their visual content
- Cluster groups of users based on their access patterns on webpages or searchers based on their search behavior

9.6 Similarity Measures

As we have already discussed, clustering is the grouping together of "similar" data. Choosing an appropriate (dis)similarity measure is a critical step in clustering. A similarity measure is often described as the inverse of the distance function; that is, the less the distance, the more the similarity. There are many distance functions for the different types of data such as numeric data, nominal data, and so on. Distance measures can also be defined specifically for different applications.

9.6.1 Distance Functions for Numeric Attributes

In general in the case of numeric attributes distance is denoted as $\text{dist}(x_i, x_j)$, where x_i and x_j are data points which can be vectors. The most commonly used distance functions in this context are Euclidean distance and Manhattan (city block) distance. These two distance functions are special cases of Minkowski distance. The different distances used for numeric attributes have been given in Chapter 6.

9.6.2 Distance Functions for Binary Attributes

Attributes that are associated with only two values are called binary attributes. In the case of binary attributes normally a confusion matrix is used where the ith and jth data points are represented as vectors x_i and x_j (Figure 9.3). Distance functions or measures are defined using a confusion matrix.

In Figure 9.3 a corresponds to the number of attributes with the value of 0 for both data points x_i and x_j, b corresponds to 0 for x_i and 1 for x_j, c corresponds to 1 for x_i and 0 for x_j, while d corresponds to the number of attributes with the value of 1 for both data points x_i and x_j.

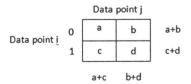

FIGURE 9.3
Confusion matrix.

The confusion matrix can be used if both states (0 and 1) have equal importance and carry the same weights. Then the distance function is the proportion of mismatches of their value (Equation 9.1):

$$\text{dist}(x_i, x_j) = (b+c)/(a+b+c+d) \tag{9.1}$$

However, sometimes the binary attributes are asymmetric where one of the states is more important than the other. We assume that state 1 represents the important state, in which case the Jaccard measure using the confusion matrix can be defined as follows (Equation 9.2):

$$\text{JDist}(x_i, x_j) = (b+c)/(a+b+c) \tag{9.2}$$

For text documents, normally we use cosine similarity, which is a similarity measure, not a distance measure. Cosine similarity is a measure of similarity between two vectors obtained by measuring the cosine of the angle between them (Figure 9.4). The similarity between any two given documents d_j and d_k, represented as vectors is given as (Equation 9.3):

$$\text{sim}(d_j, d_k) = \frac{\bar{d}_j \cdot \bar{d}_k}{|\bar{d}_j||\bar{d}_k|} = \frac{\sum_{i=1}^{n} w_{i,j} w_{i,k}}{\sqrt{\sum_{i=1}^{n} w_{i,j}^2} \sqrt{\sum_{i=1}^{n} w_{i,k}^2}} \tag{9.3}$$

In this case w_i is a weight probably based on the frequency of words in the documents.

The result of the cosine function is equal to 1 when the angle is 0, and it is less than 1 when the angle is of any other value. As the angle between the vectors decreases, the cosine value approaches 1, that is, the two vectors are closer, and the similarity between the documents increases.

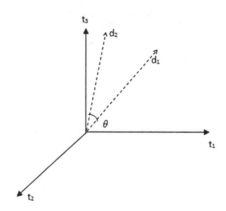

FIGURE 9.4
The cosine angle between vectors.

9.7 Methods of Clustering

The basic method of clustering is the hierarchical method, which is of two types, agglomerative and divisive. Agglomerative clustering is a bottom-up method where initially we assume that each data point is by itself a cluster. Then we repeatedly combine the two nearest clusters into one. On the other hand, divisive clustering is a top=down procedure where we start with one cluster and recursively split the clusters until no more division is possible. We normally carry out point assignment where we maintain a set of clusters and allocate points to the nearest cluster.

9.7.1 Hierarchical Clustering

In the hierarchical clustering approach, we carry out partitioning of the data set in a sequential manner. The approach creates partitions one layer at a time by grouping objects into a tree of clusters (Figure 9.5). In this context there is no need to know the number of clusters in advance. In general, the distance matrix is used as the clustering criteria.

9.7.2 Types of Hierarchical Clustering

Hierarchical clustering methods can be further classified as either agglomerative or divisive, depending on whether the hierarchical decomposition is formed in a bottom-up (merging) or top-down (splitting) fashion. As we have discussed, the hierarchical approach sequentially partitions the data points and constructs a tree of clusters. The following are two sequential clustering strategies for constructing the tree of clusters. The important issues in both cases are cluster distance to be considered and the termination condition to be used.

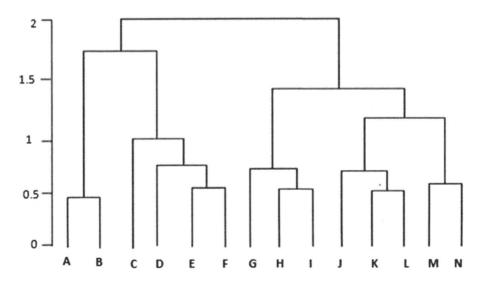

FIGURE 9.5
Hierarchical clustering.

9.7.2.1 Agglomerative Clustering

In agglomerative clustering initially each data point forms its own (atomic) cluster and hence follows the bottom-up strategy. We then merge these atomic clusters into larger and larger clusters based on some distance metric. The algorithm terminates when all the data points are in a single cluster, or merging is continued until certain termination conditions are satisfied. Most hierarchical clustering methods belong to this category. Agglomerative clustering on the data set {*a, b, c, d, e*} is shown in Figure 9.6.

9.7.2.2 Divisive Clustering

Divisive clustering is a top-down strategy which does the reverse of agglomerative hierarchical clustering, where initially all data points together form a single cluster. It subdivides the clusters into smaller and smaller pieces until it satisfies certain termination conditions, such as a desired number of clusters or the diameter of each cluster is within a certain threshold (Figure 9.6).

9.7.3 Hierarchical Clustering: The Algorithm

Hierarchical clustering takes as input a set of points. It then creates a tree or dendogram in which the points are leaves and the internal nodes club similar points together. The method initially places all points in separate clusters. Then as long as there is more than one cluster, the closest pair of clusters is merged.

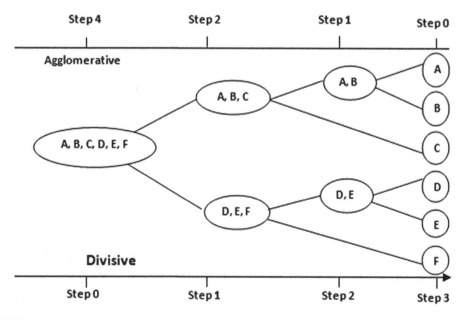

FIGURE 9.6
Agglomerative and divisive hierarchical clustering.

9.7.3.1 Hierarchical Clustering: Merging Clusters

Now an important criterion for merging clusters is the cluster distance. There are three different ways in which this cluster distance can be defined.

Cluster Distance Measures	Pictorial Representation
Single link: Distance between two clusters is the distance between the closest points in the clusters (Figure 9.7a) for single link. This method is also called neighbor joining. The cluster distance $d(C_i, C_j)$ between the clusters C_i and C_j in the case of single link is given as the minimum distance between the data points x_{ip} and x_{jq} in the two clusters (Equation 9.4). $$d(C_i, C_j) = \min\{d(x_{ip}, x_{jq})\} \quad (9.4)$$	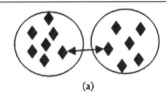 (a) **FIGURE 9.7a**
Average link: Distance between two clusters is the distance between the cluster centroids (Figure 9.7b) for average link. The cluster distance $d(C_i, C_j)$ between the clusters C_i and C_j in the case of single link is given as the average distance between the data points x_{ip} and x_{jq} in the two clusters (Equation 9.5). $$d(C_i, C_j) = \text{avg}\{d(x_{ip}, x_{jq})\} \quad (9.5)$$	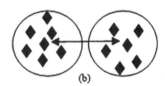 (b) **FIGURE 9.7b**
Complete link: Distance between two clusters is the distance between the farthest pair of points (Figure 9.7c) for complete link. The cluster distance $d(C_i, C_j)$ between the clusters C_i and C_j in the case of single link is given as minimum distance between the data points x_{ip} and x_{jq} in the two clusters (Equation 9.6). $$d(C_i, C_j) = \max\{d(x_{ip}, x_{jq})\} \quad (9.6)$$	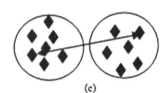 (c) **FIGURE 9.7c**

Example 9.1

Hierarchical Clustering. Given a data set of five objects characterized by a single feature, assume that there are two clusters: C1: {a, b} and C2: {c, d, e}. Assume that we are given the distance matrix (Figure 9.8). Calculate three cluster distances between C1 and C2.

	a	b	c	d	e
a	0	1	2	3	4
b	1	0	3	2	5
c	2	3	0	1	2
d	3	2	1	0	1
e	4	5	2	1	0

FIGURE 9.8
Distance matrix.

Single link:

$$\text{dist}(C1,C2) = \min\{d(a,c),d(a,d),d(a,e),d(b,c),d(b,d),d(b,e)\} = \min\{2,3,4,3,2,5\} = 2$$

Complete link:

$$\text{dist}(C1,C2) = \max\{d(a,c),d(a,d),d(a,e),d(b,c),d(b,d),d(b,e)\} = \min\{2,3,4,3,2,5\} = 5$$

Average link:

$$\text{dist}(C1,C2) = \frac{d(a,c)+d(a,d)+d(a,e)+d(b,c)+d(b,d)+d(b,e)}{6}$$

$$= \frac{2+3+4+3+2+5}{6} = \frac{19}{6} = 3.2$$

9.8 Agglomerative Algorithm

The agglomerative algorithm is a type of hierarchical clustering algorithm that can be carried out in three steps:

1. Convert object attributes to distance matrix.
2. Set each object as a cluster (thus if we have *N* objects, we will have *N* clusters at the beginning).
3. Repeat until number of cluster is one (or known number of clusters).
   o Merge two closest clusters.
   o Update distance matrix.

Example 9.2

Agglomerative Algorithm. We will now illustrate the agglomerative algorithm using an example. Let us assume that we have six data points (A, B, C, D, E, and F). The data points, the initial data matrix, and the distance matrix are shown in Figure 9.9a. In the first iteration, from the distance matrix we find that the data points C and F are the closest with minimum Euclidean distance (1), and hence we merge them to form the cluster (C, F) (Figure 9.9a) and update the distance matrix accordingly (Figure 9.9b). In the second iteration, in the updated matrix, we find that the data points D and E are the closest with minimum Euclidean distance (1), and hence we merge them to form the cluster (D, E) (Figure 9.10c). Similarly, we continue till we get the final result shown in Figure 9.9f.

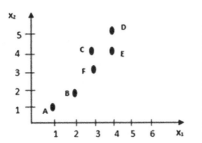

Data Matrix

	X_1	X_2
A	1	1
B	2	2
C	3	4
D	4	5
E	4	4
F	3	3

Distance Matrix

	A	B	C	D	E	F
A	0	1.414	3.60	5	4.24	2.828
B	1.414	0	2.236	3.6	2.828	2.828
C	3.60	2.236	0	1.414	1.414	1
D	5	3.60	1.414	0	1	2.236
E	4.24	2.828	1.414	1	0	1.414
F	2.828	2.828	1	2.236	1.414	0

$d_{AB} = \sqrt{(1-2)^2 + (1-2)^2} = \sqrt{(-1)^2 + (-1)^2} = \sqrt{2} = 1.414$

$d_{AF} = \sqrt{(1-3)^2 + (1-3)^2} = \sqrt{(-2)^2 + (-2)^2} = \sqrt{8} = 2.828$

Euclidean Distance

(a)

Iteration 1- Merging two closed clusters

	A	B	C	D	E	F
A	0	1.414	3.60	5	4.24	2.828
B	1.414	0	2.236	3.6	2.828	2.828
C	3.60	2.236	0	1.414	1.414	1
D	5	3.60	1.414	0	1	2.236
E	4.24	2.828	1.414	1	0	1.414
F	2.828	2.828	1	2.236	1.414	0

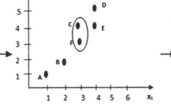

	A	B	C,F	D	E
A	0	1.414	2.828	5	2.828
B	1.414	0	2.236	3.6	2.828
C,F	2.828	2.236	0	1.414	1.414
D	5	3.60	1.414	0	1
E	4.24	2.828	1.414	1	0

$d(C,F) \rightarrow A = \text{Min} \{d(C, A), d(F, A)\} = \text{Min} \{3.60, 2.828\} = 2.828$

$d(C,F) \rightarrow B = \text{Min} \{d(C, B), d(F, B)\} = \text{Min} \{2.236, 2.828\} = 2.236$

$d(C,F) \rightarrow D = \text{Min} \{d(C, D), d(F, D)\} = \text{Min} \{1.414, 2.236\} = 1.414$

$d(C,F) \rightarrow E = \text{Min} \{d(C, E), d(F, E)\} = \text{Min} \{1.414, 1.414\} = 1.414$

(b)

	A	B	C,F	D	E
A	0	1.414	2.828	5	2.828
B	1.414	0	2.236	3.6	2.828
C,F	2.828	2.236	0	1.414	1.414
D	5	3.60	1.414	0	1
E	4.24	2.828	1.414	1	0

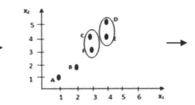

	A	B	C,F	D,E
A	0	1.414	2.828	4.24
B	1.414	0	2.236	2.828
C,F	2.828	2.236	0	1.414
D,E	4.24	2.828	1.414	0

Iteration 2- Merging two closed clusters

$d(D,E) \rightarrow A = \text{Min} \{d(D, A), d(E, A)\} = \text{Min} \{5, 4.24\} = 4.24$

$d(D,E) \rightarrow B = \text{Min} \{d(D, B), d(E, B)\} = \text{Min} \{3.60, 2.828\} = 2.828$

$d(D,E) \rightarrow C,F = \text{Min} \{d(D, (C, F), d(E, (C, F))\} = \text{Min} \{1.414, 1.414\} = 1.414$

(c)

FIGURE 9.9
Example of agglomerative clustering.

(Continued)

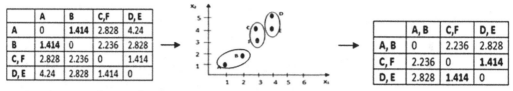

	A	B	C,F	D,E
A	0	1.414	2.828	4.24
B	1.414	0	2.236	2.828
C,F	2.828	2.236	0	1.414
D,E	4.24	2.828	1.414	0

Iteration 3- Merging two closed clusters

	A,B	C,F	D,E
A,B	0	2.236	2.828
C,F	2.236	0	1.414
D,E	2.828	1.414	0

$$d(A,B) \rightarrow (C,F) = \text{Min}\{d(A,(C,F)), d(B,(C,F))\} = \text{Min}\{2.828, 2.236\} = 2.236$$
$$d(A,B) \rightarrow (D,E) = \text{Min}\{d(A,(D,E)), d(B,(D,E))\} = \text{Min}\{4.24, 2.828\} = 2.828$$

(d)

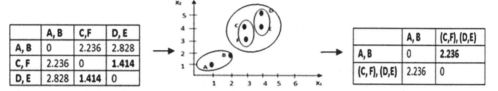

	A,B	C,F	D,E
A,B	0	2.236	2.828
C,F	2.236	0	1.414
D,E	2.828	1.414	0

Iteration 4- Merging two closed clusters

	A,B	(C,F), (D,E)
A,B	0	2.236
(C,F), (D,E)	2.236	0

$$d((C,F),(D,E)) \rightarrow (A,B) = \text{min}\{d((C,F),(A,B)), d((D,E),(A,B))\} = \text{min}\{2.236, 2.828\} = 2.236$$

(e)

Iteration 5- Final result (meeting termination condition)

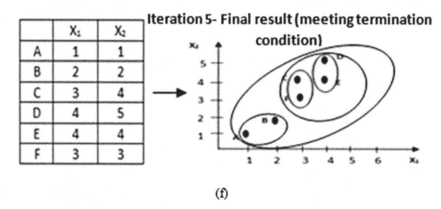

	X_1	X_2
A	1	1
B	2	2
C	3	4
D	4	5
E	4	4
F	3	3

(f)

FIGURE 9.9 (CONTINUED)
Example of agglomerative clustering.

9.9 Issues Associated with Hierarchical Clustering

As we have already seen, the key operation associated with hierarchical clustering is repeatedly combining the two nearest clusters. As you merge clusters, how do you represent the "location" of each cluster to tell which pair of clusters is closest? One solution is the **Euclidean case** where each cluster is associated with a **centroid** which is the average of its data points.

However, in the non-Euclidean case, we define a clusteroid to represent a cluster of data points. The clusteroid is defined as the data point closest to other points. The concept of closeness can be defined in various ways, such as smallest maximum distance to other points, smallest average distance, or smallest sum of squares of distances to other points. The centroid is the average of all (data) points in the cluster. This means the centroid is an "artificial" point. However, the clusteroid is an existing (data) point that is "closest" to all other points in the cluster.

When we are dealing with Euclidean space, we generally measure cluster distances or nearness of clusters by determining the distances between centroids of the clusters. In the non-Euclidean case the defined clusteroids are treated as centroids to find inter-cluster distances.

Another issue is the stopping criteria for combining clusters. Normally we can stop when we have k clusters. Another approach is to stop when there is a sudden jump in the cohesion value or the cohesion value falls below a threshold.

9.10 Partitional Algorithm

In the previous section we discussed hierarchical clustering where new clusters are found iteratively using previously determined clusters. In this section, we will be discussing another type of clustering called partitional clustering where we discover all the clusters at the same time. The k-means algorithm, an example of partitional clustering, is a popular clustering algorithm. In partitional clustering, the data points are divided into a finite number of **partitions**, which are disjoint subsets of the set of data points, that is, each data point is assigned to exactly one subset. This type of clustering algorithm can be viewed as a problem of iteratively relocating data points between clusters until an optimal partition of the data points has been obtained.

In the basic algorithm the data points are partitioned into k clusters, and the partitioning criterion is optimized using methods such as minimizing the squared error. In the case of the basic iterative algorithm of k-means or k-medoids, both of which belong to the partitional clustering category, the convergence is local and the globally optimal solution is not always guaranteed. The number of data points in any data set is finite, and the number of distinct partitions is also finite. It is possible to tackle the problem of local minima by using exhaustive search methods.

9.11 k-Means Clustering

As the case with any partitional algorithm, basically the k-means algorithm is an iterative algorithm which divides the given data set into k disjoint groups. As already discussed, k-means is the most widely used clustering technique. This partitional method uses prototypes for representing the cluster. The **k-means** algorithm is a heuristic method where the centroid of the cluster represents the cluster and the algorithm converges when the centroids of the clusters do not change. Some of the common applications of k-means clustering are data mining, optical character recognition, biometrics, diagnostic systems, military applications, document clustering, and so on.

9.11.1 Steps of *k*-Means

Initialize *k* values of centroids.

The following two steps are repeated until the data points do not change partitions and there is no change in the centroid.

- Partition the data points according to the current centroids. The similarity between each data point and each centroid is determined, and the data points are moved to the partition to which it is most similar.
- The new centroid of the data points in each partition is then calculated.

Initially the cluster centroids are chosen at random as we are talking about an unsupervised learning technique where we are not provided with the labelled samples. Even after the first round using these randomly chosen centroids, the complete set of data points is partitioned all at once. After the next round, the centroids have moved since the data points have been used to calculate the new centroids. The process is repeated, and the centroids are relocated until convergence occurs when no data point changes partitions.

Example 9.3

k-Means Clustering. The numerical example that follows can be used to understand the *k*-means algorithm. Suppose we have four types of medicines, and each has two attributes, pH and weight index (Figure 9.10). Our goal is to group these objects into $k = 2$ groups of medicines.

Figure 9.11a shows the random selection of the initial centroids as centroid 1 = (1,1) for cluster 1 and centroid 2 = (2,1) for cluster 2. We illustrate with data point B and calculate the distance of C with each of the randomly selected centroids (also sometimes called as seed points). We find that C is closer to centroid 2, and we assign B to that cluster. Now Figure 9.11b shows the assignment of each data point to one of the clusters. In our example only one data point is assigned to cluster 1, so its centroid does not change. However, cluster 2 has three data points associated with it, and the new centroid c_2 now becomes (3, 3.33). Now we compute the new assignments as shown in Figure 9.11c. Figure 9.11c shows the new values of centroid 1 and centroid 2. Figure 9.11c shows the results after convergence.

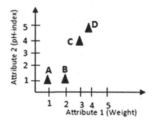

Medicine	Weight	pH-index
A	1	1
B	2	1
C	4	5
D	3	4

FIGURE 9.10
Mapping of the data points into the data space.

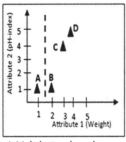

Initial clusters based on
considered centroids

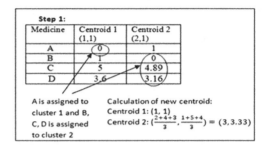

A is assigned to
cluster 1 and B,
C, D is assigned
to cluster 2

Calculation of new centroid:
Centroid 1: $(1, 1)$
Centroid 2: $(\frac{2+4+3}{3}, \frac{1+5+4}{3}) = (3, 3.33)$

(a)

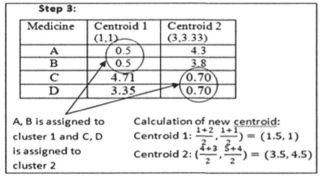

A, B is assigned to
cluster 1 and C, D
is assigned to
cluster 2

Calculation of new centroid:
Centroid 1: $(\frac{1+2}{2}, \frac{1+1}{2}) = (1.5, 1)$
Centroid 2: $(\frac{4+3}{2}, \frac{5+4}{2}) = (3.5, 4.5)$

(b)

Step 3:

Medicine	Centroid 1 (1,1)	Centroid 2 (3,3.33)
A	0.5	4.3
B	0.5	3.8
C	4.71	0.70
D	3.35	0.70

A, B is assigned to
cluster 1 and C, D
is assigned to
cluster 2

Calculation of new centroid:
Centroid 1: $(\frac{1+2}{2}, \frac{1+1}{2}) = (1.5, 1)$
Centroid 2: $(\frac{4+3}{2}, \frac{5+4}{2}) = (3.5, 4.5)$

No change in centroid points

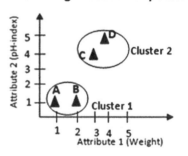

(c)

FIGURE 9.11
The iterations for the example in Figure 9.10.

9.11.2 Issues Associated with the *k*-Means Algorithm

Though *k*-means is considered as an important clustering algorithm, we will now discuss certain issues associated with this algorithm. The first question we need to address is to choose the correct value of *k*, that is, how many partitions we should have. One way of selecting *k* is to first try different values of *k* where the average of distances to the centroid changes rapidly until the right value of *k* when the changes are slow. Another issue associated with *k*-means clustering is the initial choice of the *k*-centroids. We have explained that these initial centroids can be chosen at random, but this may not lead to fast convergence. Therefore, this initial cluster problem needs to be addressed. One method is to use hierarchical clustering to determine the initial centroids. Another approach is to first select more than k initial centroids and then select among these initial centroids which are the most widely separated. Another method is carrying out preprocessing where we can normalize the data and eliminate outliers.

The stopping criteria can be defined in any one of the following ways. We can stop the iteration when there are no or a minimum number of reassignments of data points to different clusters. We can also define the stopping criteria to be when there is no (or minimum) change of centroids, or in terms of error as the minimum decrease in the sum of squared error (SSE), defined in the next section.

9.11.3 Evaluating *k*-Means Clusters

The most common measure is sum of squared error (SSE). This is defined as follows:
For each point, the error is the distance to the nearest cluster (Equation 9.7),

$$\text{SSE} = \sum_{i=1}^{N} \sum_{x \in \text{CL}_i} \text{dist}(x, C_i)^2 \tag{9.7}$$

where CL_i is the ith cluster, C_i is the centroid of cluster CL_i (the mean vector of all the data points in CL_i), and $\text{dist}(x, C_i)$ is the distance between data point x and centroid C_i. Given two clusterings (clustering is the set of clusters formed), we can choose the one with the smallest error. One straightforward way to reduce SSE is to increase N, the number of clusters.

9.11.4 Strengths and Weaknesses of *k*-Means

The major strengths of k-means is the ease of understanding and implementation. k-means is considered a linear time algorithm. It terminates at a local optimum if SSE is used. However, it is complex to find the global optimum, which is one of its weaknesses.

Other weaknesses include that it is only applicable for data where the concept of mean can be defined, the need to specify the value of k, production of different clustering with different initialization (selection of centroids), and its sensitivity to outliers.

9.12 Cluster Validity

Cluster validation is important for comparing clustering algorithms, determining the number of clusters, comparing two clusters, comparing two sets of clusters, and avoiding finding patterns in noise. Good clustering is defined as a clustering where the intra-class similarity is high and the inter-class similarity is low. The quality of clustering is dependent on both the representation of the entities to be clustered and the similarity measure used.

Cluster validation involves evaluation of the clustering using an external index by comparing the clustering results to *ground truth* (externally known results). Evaluation of the

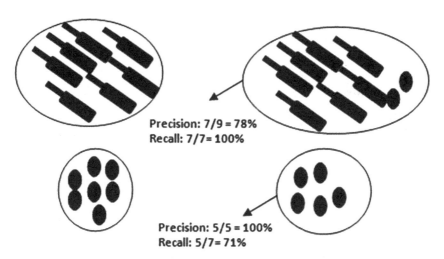

FIGURE 9.12
Precision and recall of clustering.

quality of clusters *without* reference to external information using only the data is called evaluation using internal index.

9.12.1 Comparing with Ground Truth

A simple evaluation of clustering using precision and recall can be determined only if the ground truth is given. Figure 9.12 shows an example where we have a total of 7 bats and 7 balls. The clustering produces two clusters, cluster 1 with 7 bats and 2 balls and cluster 2 with 5 balls only. In this context precision and recall are given in Equations (9.8) and (9.9):

$$\text{Precision} = \frac{\text{the number of items of a particular category obtained in the cluster}}{\text{total number of items in that cluster}} \tag{9.8}$$

$$\text{Recall} = \frac{\text{the number of items of a particular category obtained in the cluster}}{\text{total number of items in that category}} \tag{9.9}$$

Another approach is discussed next where we assume that the data set has N objects. Let G be the set of "ground truth" clusters and C be the set of clusters obtained from the clustering algorithm. There are two $N \times N$ matrices of objects corresponding to G clusters and C clusters. An entry in the G matrix is 1 if the objects of row and column corresponding to that entry belong to the same cluster in C and 0 otherwise. Any pair of data objects falls into one of the following categories: SS, if the entries in both the matrices agree and are 1; DD, if the entries in both the matrices agree and are 0; SD, if the entries in both the matrices disagree with the entry in $C = 1$ and in $G = 0$; and DS, if the entries in both the matrices disagree with the entry in $C = 0$ and in $G = 1$. Two evaluation measures are defined based on these matrices, the Rand index and the Jaccard coefficient (Equations 9.10 and 9.11).

$$\text{Rand} = \frac{|\text{Agree}|}{|\text{Agree}| + |\text{Disagree}|} = \frac{|\text{SS}| + |\text{DD}|}{|\text{SS}| + |\text{SD}| + |\text{DS}| + |\text{DD}|} \tag{9.10}$$

$$\text{Jaccard coefficient} = \frac{|\text{SS}|}{|\text{SS}| + |\text{SD}| + |\text{DS}|} \tag{9.11}$$

9.12.2 Purity Based Measures

Another method used to find the external index is discussed. Figure 9.13 gives the confusion matrix. Let n = the number of data points, K the total number of clusters, L the total number of "ground truth" classes, m_i = the points in cluster i, c_j = the points in class j, n_{ij} = the points in cluster i belonging to class j, and $p_{ij} = n_{ij}/m_i$ = probability of element from cluster i being assigned to class j. Entropy and purity can be measured for a cluster or for a clustering (complete set of clusters). Entropy of a cluster is based on the probability p_{ij} of an element from cluster i being assigned to class j (Equation 9.12).

$$\text{Entropy of a cluster } i : e_i = -\sum_{j=1}^{L} p_{ij} \log p_{ij}. \tag{9.12}$$

Entropy of a clustering is based on average entropy of each cluster as well as the total number of objects in the data set n (Equation 9.13).

$$\text{Entropy of a clustering} : e = \sum_{i=1}^{K} \frac{m_i}{n} e_i \tag{9.13}$$

Purity of a cluster i is the class j for which the probability p_{ij}, that is the probability that an element from cluster i is assigned to class j (Equation 9.14).

$$\text{Purity of a cluster } i : p_i = \max_j p_{ij} \tag{9.14}$$

The purity of the clustering C is given in Equation (9.15):

$$\text{Purity of a clustering} : p(C) = \sum_{i=1}^{K} \frac{m_i}{n} p_i \tag{9.15}$$

Example 9.4

Evaluation of Cluster and Clustering. The preceding evaluation is illustrated using the examples given in Figure 9.14. In Figure 9.14a, the purity of cluster 1, cluster 2, and cluster 3 is calculated. The overall purity of the clustering is the average of the purity of the three clusters and shows a good clustering. Figure 9.14b shows another example for bad clustering.

9.12.3 Internal Measure

As discussed previously, internal measures are used to evaluate the clustering without comparing with external information. There are basically two aspects that are considered,

	Class 1	Class 2	Class 3	
Cluster 1	n_{11}	n_{12}	n_{13}	m_1
Cluster 2	n_{21}	n_{22}	n_{23}	m_2
Cluster 3	n_{31}	n_{32}	n_{33}	m_3
	C_1	C_2	C_3	n

	Class 1	Class 2	Class 3	
Cluster 1	p_{11}	p_{12}	p_{13}	m_1
Cluster 2	p_{21}	p_{22}	p_{23}	m_2
Cluster 3	p_{31}	p_{32}	p_{33}	m_3
	C_1	C_2	C_3	n

FIGURE 9.13
Confusion matrix.

	Class 1	Class 2	Class 3	
Cluster 1	5	10	85	100
Cluster 2	92	7	11	110
Cluster 3	6	86	8	100
	103	103	104	310

Purity: (0.85, 0.83, 0.86) = overall 0.84
Precision: (0.85, 0.83, 0.86) = overall 0.84
Recall: (0.81, 0.89, 0.83) = overall 0.84

(a)

	Class 1	Class 2	Class 3	
Cluster 1	30	30	40	100
Cluster 2	31	50	29	110
Cluster 3	42	23	35	100
	103	103	104	310

Purity: (0.40, 0.45, 0.42) = overall 0.42
Precision: (0.40, 0.45, 0.42) = overall 0.42
Recall: (0.38, 0.48, 0.40) = overall 0.42

(b)

FIGURE 9.14
Good and bad clustering.

namely **cohesion** measures the closeness of the data points in a cluster while **separation** measures the well-separated nature of the data points across clusters.

Cluster cohesion is given by Equation (9.16):

$$WSS = \sum_i \sum_{x \in C_i} (x - m_i)^2 \tag{9.16}$$

Cluster separation is measured as follows (Equation 9.17):

$$BSS = \sum_i |C_i| (m - m_i)^2 \tag{9.17}$$

where $|C_i|$ is the size of cluster i, and m is the centroid of the whole data set.

9.13 Curse of Dimensionality

In any machine learning problem, if the number of observables or features is increased, then it takes more time to compute, more memory to store inputs and intermediate results, and more importantly much more data samples for learning. From a theoretical point of view, increasing the number of features should lead to better performance. However, in practice the opposite is true. This aspect is called the curse of dimensionality and is basically because the number of training examples required increases exponentially as dimensionality increases. This results in the data becoming increasingly sparse in the space it occupies, and this sparsity makes it difficult to achieve statistical significance for many machine learning methods. A number of machine learning methods have at least $O(nd^2)$ complexity where n is the number of samples and d is the dimensionality. If the number of features, that is, dimension d is large, the number of samples n may be too small for accurate parameter estimation.

9.14 Dimensionality Reduction

Some features (dimensions) bear little useful information, which essentially means that we can drop some features. In dimensionality reduction, high-dimensional points are projected to a low-dimensional space while preserving the "essence" of the data and the distances as well as possible. After this projection the learning problems are solved in low dimensions.

If we have d dimensions, we can reduce the dimensionality to $k < d$ by discarding unimportant features or combining several features and then use the resulting k-dimensional data set for the classification learning problem. In dimensionality reduction we strive to find the set of features that are effective. Essentially dimensionality reduction results in reduction of time complexity and space complexity since there will be less computation and less number of parameters. Most machine learning and data mining techniques may not be effective for high-dimensional data since the intrinsic dimension (that is, the actual features that decide the classification) may be small, for example the number of genes actually responsible for a disease may be small, but the data set may contain a large number of other genes as features. The dimension-reduced data can be used for visualizing, exploring, and understanding the data. In addition, cleaning the data will allow simpler models to be built later.

9.15 The Process of Dimensionality Reduction

The process of reducing the number of random variables (features) used to represent the samples under consideration can be carried out by combining, transforming, or selecting features. We have to estimate which features can be removed from the data. Several features can be combined together without loss or even with gain of information (e.g., income of all family members for loan application); however, we need to estimate which features to combine from the data. The basic issues of dimensionality reduction are two-fold, namely how we represent the data and the criteria we use in carrying out the reduction process. Dimensionality can be reduced basically using two methods: feature reduction and feature selection.

9.15.1 Criterion for Reduction

There are many criteria that can be used for dimensionality reduction. These include criteria that are mainly geometric based and those that are information theory based. These criteria need to capture the variation in data since these variations are "signals" or information contained in the data. We need to normalize each variable first and then discover variables or dimensions that are highly correlated or dependent (Figure 9.15). When variables are highly related, they can be combined to form a simpler representation.

9.15.2 Feature Reduction and Feature Selection

As already discussed, there are two approaches to dimensionality reduction, namely feature reduction and feature selection.

In feature reduction all the original features are used; however, the features are linearly or nonlinearly transformed. Here we combine the high-dimensional inputs to a smaller set of features, and then use this transformed data for learning. A simple example is shown in Figure 9.16, where a vector x is transformed to a vector y. Ideally, the new vector y should retain all information from x that is important for learning.

In feature selection only a smaller subset of the original features is selected from a large set of inputs, and this new data is used for learning. Generally, the features are ranked on a defined "interestingness" measure. Then we can select and use $x\%$ of features with top ranking based on feature values.

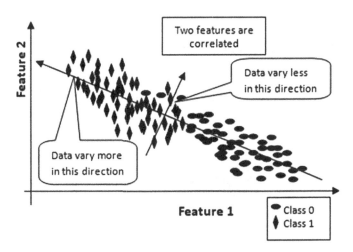

FIGURE 9.15
Dependency of features.

$$x = \begin{bmatrix} x_1 \\ x_2 \\ x_3 \\ x_4 \end{bmatrix} \rightarrow \begin{bmatrix} x_1 + x_2 \\ x_3 + x_4 \end{bmatrix} = y$$

FIGURE 9.16
Feature reduction.

9.16 Dimensionality Reduction with Feature Reduction

Feature reduction refers to the mapping of the original high-dimensional data onto a lower-dimensional space. Criteria for feature reduction can be different based on different problem settings. In an unsupervised setting the criteria could try to minimize the information loss; in a supervised setting it could try to maximize the class discrimination.

Given a set of data points of p variables, we compute the linear transformation (projection; Equation 9.18; Figure 9.17):

$$G \in \mathfrak{R}^{p \times d} : X \in \mathfrak{R}^p \rightarrow y = G^T X \in \mathfrak{R}^d \left(d \ll p \right) \tag{9.18}$$

Applications of feature reduction include face recognition, handwritten digit recognition, text mining, image retrieval, microarray data analysis, and protein classification.

Here we combine the old features x to create a new set of features y based on some optimized function of x as follows (Figure 9.18):

The best $f(x)$ is most likely to be a nonlinear function. Assuming $f(x)$ is a linear mapping, it can be represented by a matrix W as follows (Figure 9.19).

There are basically three approaches for finding optimal transformations, which are as follows:

- **Principle components analysis (PCA)**: Seeks a projection that preserves as much information in the data as possible (in a least-squares sense).

- **Fisher linear discriminant**: Finds projection to a line such that samples from different classes are well separated.

- **Singular value decomposition (SVD)**: Transforms correlated variables into a set of uncorrelated ones.

In the next section we will discuss the first approach, namely PCA.

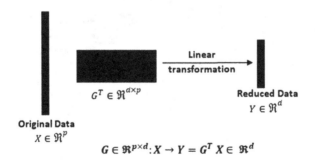

FIGURE 9.17
Feature reduction—linear transformation.

$$X = \begin{bmatrix} X_1 \\ X_2 \\ \vdots \\ X_d \end{bmatrix} \longrightarrow f\left(\begin{bmatrix} X_1 \\ X_2 \\ \vdots \\ X_d \end{bmatrix} \right) = \begin{bmatrix} y_1 \\ \vdots \\ y_k \end{bmatrix} = y \ \ with \ k < d$$

FIGURE 9.18
Optimized function.

$$\begin{bmatrix} X_1 \\ X_2 \\ \vdots \\ \vdots \\ X_d \end{bmatrix} \Rightarrow W \begin{bmatrix} X_1 \\ X_2 \\ \vdots \\ \vdots \\ X_d \end{bmatrix} = \begin{bmatrix} W_{11} & \cdots & W_{1d} \\ \vdots & \ddots & \vdots \\ W_{k1} & \cdots & W_{kd} \end{bmatrix} \begin{bmatrix} X_1 \\ X_2 \\ \vdots \\ \vdots \\ X_d \end{bmatrix} = \begin{bmatrix} y_1 \\ \vdots \\ y_k \end{bmatrix} \text{ with } k < d$$

FIGURE 9.19
Representation of function.

9.16.1 Principle Component Analysis (PCA)

Let us first discuss the basis of PCA, which is to describe the variation in a set of multivariate data in terms of a set of uncorrelated variables. We typically have a data matrix of n observations on p correlated variables $x_1, x_2, \ldots x_p$. PCA looks for a transformation of the x_i into p new variables y_i that are uncorrelated.

Let us project the 2D data to 1D subspace (a line) in such a way that the projection error is minimum. Figure 9.20 shows the cases of two such projections where the right-hand side projection shows small projection error and therefore is a good line to project to. We need to note that the good line to use for projection lies in the direction of largest variance. After the data is projected on the best line, we need to transform the coordinate system to get a 1D representation for vector y (Figure 9.21). Note that new data y has the same variance as old data x in the direction of the green line

9.16.1.1 PCA Methodology

PCA projects the data along the directions where the data varies the most. These directions are determined by the **eigenvectors of the covariance matrix** corresponding to the largest eigenvalues. The magnitude of the eigenvalues corresponds to the variance of the data along the eigenvector directions. Let us assume that d observables are linear combination of $k < d$ vectors. We would like to work with this basis as it has lesser dimension and

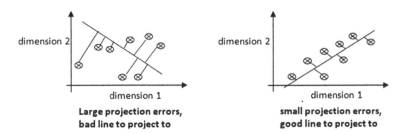

FIGURE 9.20
2D to 1D projection.

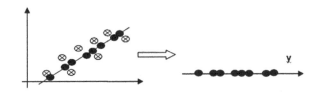

FIGURE 9.21
1D projection of the data.

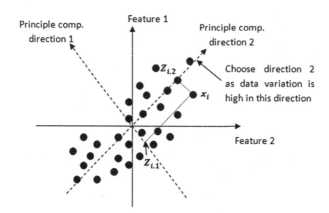

FIGURE 9.22
Direction of principle components.

has all (almost) required information. Using this bias we expect data is uncorrelated, or otherwise we could have reduced it further. We choose the projection that shows the large variance, or otherwise the features bear no information. We choose directions such that the total variance of data will be maximum (Figure 9.22); that is, we choose a projection that maximizes total variance. We choose directions that are orthogonal and try to minimize correlation. When we consider a **d-dimensional feature** space, we need to choose $k < d$ orthogonal directions which maximize total variance. We first calculate d by a d symmetric **covariance matrix** estimated from samples. Then we select the k largest eigenvalue of the covariance matrix and the associated k eigenvector. The larger the eigenvalue, the larger is the variance in the direction of corresponding eigenvector.

Thus PCA can be thought of as finding a new orthogonal basis by rotating the old axis until the directions of maximum variance are found.

PCA was designed for accurate data representation and not for data classification. The primary job of PCA is to preserve as much variance in data as possible. Therefore, only if the direction of maximum variance is important for classification will PCA give good results for classification. Next we will discuss the Fisher linear discriminant approach.

9.16.2 Fisher Linear Discriminant Approach

The main idea of the Fisher linear discriminant approach is finding the projection to a line such that samples from different classes projected on the line are well separated (Figure 9.23).

Suppose we have two classes and d-dimensional samples $X_1,...., X_n$ where $n1$ samples come from the first class and $n2$ samples come from the second class. Consider projection on a line, and let the line direction be given by unit vector V. Scalar $V^t X_i$ is the distance of projection of x_i from the origin. Thus $V^t X_i$ is the projection of X_i into a one-dimensional subspace. Thus the projection of sample X_i onto a line in direction V is given by $V^t X_i$. How do we measure separation between projections of different classes? Let $\widetilde{\mu}_1$ and $\widetilde{\mu}_2$ be the means of projections of classes 1 and 2 (Figure 9.24) and let μ_1 and μ_2 be the means of classes 1 and 2, and $|\widetilde{\mu}_1 - \widetilde{\mu}_2|$ seems like a good measure.

Now let us discuss the goodness of $|\widetilde{\mu}_1 - \widetilde{\mu}_2|$ as a measure of separation. The larger $|\widetilde{\mu}_1 - \widetilde{\mu}_2|$, the better the expected separation. The vertical axes are a better line than the horizontal axes to project to for class separability (Figure 9.36). However, $\hat{\mu}_1 - \hat{\mu}_1| > |\widetilde{\mu}_1 - \widetilde{\mu}_2|$.

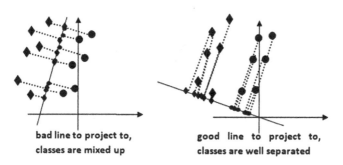

FIGURE 9.23
Bad and good projections.

$$\widetilde{\mu_1} = \frac{1}{n_1} \sum_{x_i \in C_1}^{n_1} V^t X_i = V^t \left(\frac{1}{n_1} \sum_{x_i \in C_1}^{n_1} X_i \right) = V^t \mu_1$$

Similarly, $\widetilde{\mu_2} = V^t \mu_2$

FIGURE 9.24
Means of projections.

The problem with $|\widetilde{\mu_1} - \widetilde{\mu_2}|$ is that it does not consider the variance of the classes. We need to normalize $|\widetilde{\mu_1} - \widetilde{\mu_2}|$ by a factor which is proportional to variance.

Let us consider some samples $Z_1, \ldots, Z_n$. The sample mean is as follows (Equation 9.19):

$$\mu_z = \frac{1}{n} \sum_{i=1}^{n} Z_i \qquad (9.19)$$

Now let us define their **scatter** as (Equation 9.20):

$$S = \sum_{i=1}^{n} (Z_i - \mu_z)^2 \qquad (9.20)$$

Thus scatter is just sample variance multiplied by n. In other words, scatter measures the same concept as variance, the spread of data around the mean, only that scatter is just on a different scale than variance.

9.16.2.1 Fisher Linear Discriminant

The Fisher solution is to find the projection to a line such that samples from different classes projected on the line are well separated, that is, to normalize $|\widetilde{\mu_1} - \widetilde{\mu_2}|$ by scatter.

Let $y_i = V^t X_i$, that is, y_i are the projected samples and the scatter for projected samples of class 1 is as follows (Equation 9.21):

$$\tilde{S}_1^2 = \sum_{y_i \in \text{Class 1}} (y_i - \tilde{\mu}_1)^2 \qquad (9.21)$$

Similarly, the scatter for projected samples of class 2 is Equation (9.22):

$$\tilde{S}_2^2 = \sum_{y_i \in \text{Class 2}} \left(y_i - \tilde{\mu}_2\right)^2 \tag{9.22}$$

We need to normalize by both scatter of class 1 and scatter of class 2. Thus, the Fisher linear discriminant needs to project on a line in the direction v which maximizes $J(V)$ (Figure 9.25). Here $J(V)$ is defined such that we want the projected means to be far from each other and the scatter of each class to be as small as possible; that is, we want the samples of the respective classes to cluster around the projected means. If we find v which makes $J(v)$ large, we are guaranteed that the classes are well separated (Figure 9.26).

9.16.3 Singular Value Decomposition

Now let us discuss the final method of dimensionality reduction, namely singular value decomposition (SVD). *SVD can be viewed as a method for transforming correlated variables into a set of uncorrelated ones that better expose the various relationships among the original data items.* It is a method for identifying and ordering the dimensions along which data points exhibit the most variation. With SVD, it is possible to find the best approximation of the original data points using fewer dimensions. Hence, SVD is used for data reduction. Singular value decomposition factorizes a real or complex matrix. For an $M \times N$ matrix A of rank r, there exists a factorization (singular value decomposition = SVD) as follows (Figure 9.27):

Here the columns of U are orthogonal eigenvectors of AA^T, the columns of V are orthogonal eigenvectors of A^TA, and eigenvalues $\lambda_1 \ldots \lambda_r$ of AA^T are the eigenvalues of A^TA. An illustration of SVD dimensions and sparseness is as given in Figure 9.28.

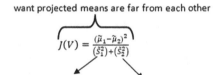

want projected means are far from each other

$$J(V) = \frac{(\tilde{\mu}_1 - \tilde{\mu}_2)^2}{(\tilde{S}_1^2) + (\tilde{S}_2^2)}$$

want scatter in class 1 is as small as possible, i.e. samples of class 1 cluster around the projected mean $\tilde{\mu}_1$

want scatter in class 1 is as small as possible, i.e. samples of class 2 cluster around the projected mean $\tilde{\mu}_2$

FIGURE 9.25
Definition of $J(V)$.

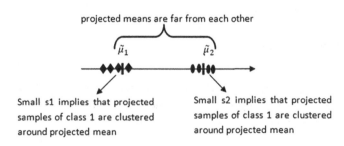

projected means are far from each other

$\tilde{\mu}_1$ $\tilde{\mu}_2$

Small s1 implies that projected samples of class 1 are clustered around projected mean

Small s2 implies that projected samples of class 1 are clustered around projected mean

FIGURE 9.26
Well separated projected samples.

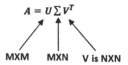

FIGURE 9.27
SVD.

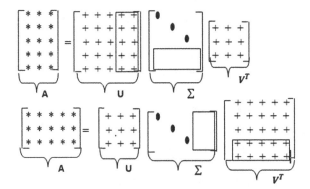

FIGURE 9.28
SVD illustration.

9.17 Association Rule Mining

Another important unsupervised machine learning approach is association rule mining, widely used in data mining. Association rule learning checks for the dependency of one data item on another data item and tries to find some interesting relations or associations among the variables of the data set. It discovers different rules to discover the interesting relations between the variables in the database.

9.17.1 Market-Basket Analysis

Association rule mining was initially associated with market-basket analysis in the context of shelf management of a supermarket. The objective is to identify items that are bought together by sufficiently many customers, and for this purpose the transaction data is processed to find the associations or dependencies among the items that the customers put in shopping baskets to buy. The discovery of such association rules will enable all items that are frequently purchased together to be placed together on the shelves in a supermarket. This model can be described as a general many-to-many mapping or associations between two kinds of things, but we are interested only in the associations between the item side of the mapping.

An example of a market-basket model is shown in Figure 9.29. Here we assume that a large set of **items** are sold in the supermarket. There are also a large set of **baskets** where each basket contains a small subset of items that are bought by one customer in a day.

This model can be used in a number of applications. Examples include the following:

- **Items** = products; **Baskets** = sets of products someone bought in one trip to the store— Predict how typical customers navigate stores; hence items can be arranged accordingly. Another example is Amazon's suggestions where people who bought item X also bought item Y.

- **Baskets** = sentences; **Items** = documents containing those sentences—Items that appear together too often could represent plagiarism. Here the items are not in baskets, but we use a similar concept.

- **Baskets** = patients; **Items** = drugs and side effects. This model has been used to detect combinations of drugs that result in particular side effects. In this case the absence of an item is as important as its presence.

9.17.2 Association Rule Mining—Basic Concepts

Before we describe machine learning algorithms for association rule mining, we need to understand the following related concepts.

- **Itemset** is defined as a collection or representation of a list of one or more items. An example (refer to Figure 9.29) is {Example: {Juice, Sugar, Milk}. A k-itemset is an itemset that contains k items.

- **Support count (σ)** is the frequency of occurrence of an itemset, that is, the number of baskets or transactions that contain the itemset. An example (again refer to Figure 9.29) is where the count of the itemset {Ghee, Sugar, Milk} is 3 and hence support count $\sigma(\{Ghee, Sugar, Milk\}) = 3$.

- **Support** is defined as the fraction of the total transactions that contain the itemset.

An example (again refer to Figure 9.29 where the total count of transactions is 6 and count of itemset {Ghee, Sugar, Milk} is 3 out of a total number of 6 transactions) and hence support of ({Ghee, Sugar, Milk}) = 3/6

- **Confidence** is defined as the likelihood of an item Y occurring given that an item X occurs in a transaction.

- **Frequent itemset** is defined as an itemset whose support is greater than or equal to a minimum threshold value s of the support. In other words, the sets of items

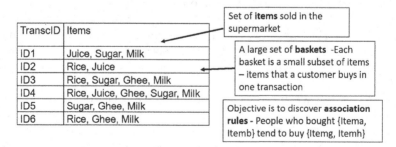

FIGURE 9.29
Example of market-basket model.

TranscID	Items
ID1	Juice, Sugar, Milk
ID2	Rice, Juice, Sugar
ID3	Rice, Sugar, Ghee, Milk
ID4	Rice, Juice, Ghee, Sugar, Milk
ID5	Sugar, Ghee, Milk
ID6	Rice, Ghee, Milk

K of Itemset	Itemsets	Support Count	Frequent Itemset - Minimum support is 50%
1-itemset	{Juice}	3	√
	{Sugar}	5	√
	{Milk}	5	√
	{Rice}	4	√
	{Ghee}	4	√
2-itemset	{Juice, Sugar}	3	√
	{Sugar, Milk}	4	√
	{Juice, Milk}	2	--
	{Rice, Juice}	2	--
	{Rice, Sugar}	3	√
	{Sugar, Ghee}	3	√
	{Ghee, Milk}	4	√
	{Juice, Ghee}	1	--
	{Rice, Ghee}	3	√

Assuming Association Rule is X → Y

Support = Transactions in which X and Y occur/Total number of transactions

Confidence = Transactions in which X and Y occur/Total number of transactions in which X occurs

Sample Association Rules

Let us assume that the association rule requires min support of 50% and confidence of 50%

Sample association rules with support and confidence

Sugar → Milk (support = 66.67%, confidence = 80%)

Milk → Sugar (support = 66.67%, confidence = 80%)

Sugar, Milk → Ghee (support = 50%, confidence= 75%)

Ghee → (Sugar, Milk) (support = 50%, confidence= 75%)

FIGURE 9.30
Example showing association rules.

that appear in at least *s* baskets or transcations are called frequent itemsets. An example of frequent itemsets is explained in Figure 9.30.

- **Association rule** is a pattern that states when X occurs, Y occurs with certain probability and is represented as an implication of the form given in Equation (9.23).

$$X \rightarrow Y, \text{where } X, Y \subset I, \text{and } X \cap Y = \emptyset \qquad (9.23)$$

Let us assume that support itemset X is denoted by X.count, in a particular transaction dataset that contains n transactions.

- **Support of an association rule**: The rule holds with a particular support value *sup* in the transaction data set and is the fraction of transactions that contain both X and Y out of a total number of transactions n.

- **Confidence of an association rule**: The rule holds in the transaction set with confidence *conf* if *conf*% of transactions that contain X also contain Y, that is, *conf* = $\Pr(Y \mid X)$. Confidence measures the frequency of Y occurring in the transactions which contain X.

- **Interest of an association rule**: $X \rightarrow Y$ is the difference between its confidence and the fraction of baskets that contain *j*.

Figure 9.30 shows the example for the preceding concepts where 1-itemsets and 2-itemsets are shown and the corresponding frequent itemsets with minimum threshold of 50% are shown. The figure also shows four sample association rules and their associated support and confidence.

9.17.3 Apriori Algorithm

The Aprori algorithm was described by R. Agrawal and R. Srikant for fast mining of association rules in 1994 and is now one of the basic cornerstones of data mining. The problem to be tackled by the Apriori algorithm is the finding of association rules with support ≥ a given s and confidence ≥ a given c. However, the hard part is finding the frequent itemsets with the fact that if $\{i_1, i_2, ..., i_k\} \rightarrow j$ has high support and confidence, then both $\{i_1, i_2, ..., i_k\}$ and $\{i_1, i_2, ..., i_k, j\}$ will be frequent.

9.17.3.1 Apriori Principle

The following are the principles on which the Apriori algorithm is based:

- All the subsets of an itemset must also be frequent if the itemset itself is frequent.
- If an itemset is not frequent, then all of its supersets cannot be frequent.
- The **anti-monotone** property of support states that the support of an itemset never exceeds the support of its subsets (Equation 9.24), that is,

$$\forall X, Y : (X \subseteq Y) \Rightarrow s(X) \geq s(Y) \tag{9.24}$$

9.17.3.2 The Algorithm

The Apriori algorithm uses a level-based approach where the candidate itemsets and frequent itemsets are generated from 1-itemset to k-itemset until the frequent itemset is empty (Figure 9.31). Let us assume that C_k = candidate itemsets of size k and F_k = frequent itemsets of size k. Initially we generate all candidate 1-itemsets C_1 and then generate frequent 1-itemsets where all candidate itemsets with support < Min_sup are filtered out. The

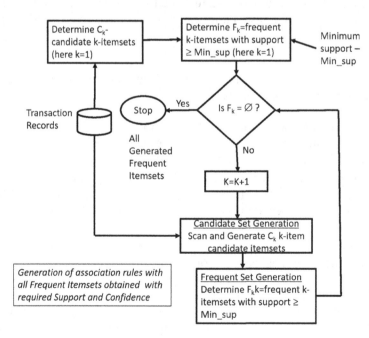

FIGURE 9.31
Apriori algorithm—finding frequent itemsets.

frequent itemset set is then used to generate the next level $K + 1$ candidate dataset. Then the process is repeated until we get an empty frequent itemset.

All the frequent itemsets generated by the Apriori algorithm are then used to generate association rules with given support and confidence.

9.17.3.3 Example of Frequent Itemset Generation Using Apriori Algorithm

The example shown in Figure 9.32 shows four transactions involving five items. C_1 is the 1-itemset obtained after scanning the transactions. After pruning one 1-itemset based on minimum support = 2, we get F_1, the frequent 1-itemset. Using F_1 we generate the C_2 2-itemset and again after pruning we get F_2, the frequent 2-itemset. Finally, we get $C_3 = F_3$, the 3-itemset {Sugar, Egg, Milk}.

9.17.3.4 Improving Apriori's Efficiency

The basic concept of the Apriori algorithm is the use of frequent $(k-1)$ itemsets to generate the candidate k-itemsets by scanning the transaction database and pattern matching to find the counts. The main bottleneck of the algorithm is generation of huge candidate itemsets. Moreover, we need to scan the transaction database $n + 1$ times if n is the size of the largest itemset.

In this context, some of the techniques used to improve the Apriori algorithm include the following:

- Hash-based itemset counting: Here we make use of the fact that if the k-itemset has a hashing bucket count below the threshold, then the itemset cannot be frequent.

- Transaction reduction: We can remove transactions from consideration in the subsequent scans if the previous scan does not contain any frequent k-itemset.

- Partitioning: Any itemset that is frequent in the transaction database must be frequent in at least one of the partitions of the database.

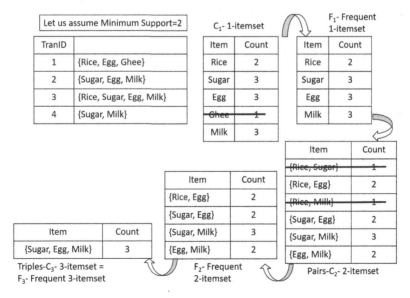

FIGURE 9.32
Example—Apriori algorithm.

9.18 Summary

- Explained the concepts of unsupervised learning and clustering.
- Discussed hierarchical clustering along with different distance measures.
- Explained agglomerative clustering with an illustrative example.
- Discussed the k-means algorithm in detail and illustrated with an example.
- Explained the different aspects of cluster validity and the cluster validation process.
- Explained the curse of dimensionality and the concept of dimensionality reduction.
- Explained in detail the principal component analysis, Fischer discriminant, and singular value decomposition methods of dimensionality reduction.
- Explained the concept of association rule mining and explained the Apriori algorithm.

9.19 Points to Ponder

- Agglomerative clustering is considered to follow the bottom-up strategy.
- Euclidean distance and Manhattan distance are considered as special cases of Minkowski distance.
- Centroid and clusteroid concepts are required.
- The k-means algorithm is called a partitional algorithm.
- It is important to select appropriate initial centroids in the case of k-means algorithm.
- Purity based measures are used to evaluate clustering.
- Having a larger number of features does not necessarily result in good learning.
- The anti-monotone property is the basis of the Apriori algorithm.

E.9 Exercises

E.9.1 Suggested Activities

E.9.1.1 Design a business application where the aim is to target existing customers with specialized advertisement and provide discounts for them. Design appropriate features for the clustering.

E.9.1.2 Suggest a method to group learners for at least five educational purposes. Explain the features used for the different purposes.

E.9.1.3 Give two applications of the market-basket model not given in this chapter.

Self-Assessment Questions

E.9.2 Multiple Choice Questions

Give answers with justification for correct and wrong choices:

E.9.2.1 In unsupervised learning, data points have
    i Associated target attribute
    ii No associated target attribute
    iii No data points

E.9.2.2 Unsupervised learning is helpful for
    i Finding useful insights from the data
    ii Prediction
    iii Finding insights about a problem

E.9.2.3 One of the challenges of unsupervised learning is
    i Finding hidden structure
    ii Need for target attributes
    iii Lack of transparency

E.9.2.4 In clustering, data is partitioned into groups that satisfy constraints that
    i Points in the same cluster should be dissimilar and points in different clusters should be similar
    ii Points in the same cluster should be similar and points in different clusters should be dissimilar.
    iii Points in the same cluster should be similar

E.9.2.5 In Manhattan distance,
    i There is no need for calculation of power and power root functions
    ii There is no need for calculation of the square root of the sum of the squares of the difference between them in each dimension
    iii The difference between the data points in each dimension is weighted

E.9.2.6 For finding similarity between text documents we normally use
    i Manhattan distance
    ii Cosine similarity
    iii Euclidean distance

E.9.2.7 In hierarchical clustering we
    i Carry out partitioning of the data set in a parallel manner
    ii Discover all the clusters at the same time
    iii Carry out partitioning of the data set in a sequential manner

E.9.2.8 Hierarchical clustering takes as input a set of points and creates a tree called _____ in which the points are leaves and the internal nodes reveal the similarity structure of the points.
    i Hierarchical tree
    ii Dendogram
    iii General tree

E.9.2.9 In complete link,
   i   The distance between two clusters is the distance between the farthest pair
       of points
   ii The distance between two clusters is the distance between the cluster cen-
       troids
   iii The distance between two clusters is the distance between the closest
       points in the clusters

E.9.2.10 The curse of dimensionality is the aspect where
   i   The number of training examples required decreases exponentially as
       dimensionality increases
   ii The number of training examples required increases linearly as dimen-
       sionality increases
   iii The number of training examples required increases exponentially as
       dimensionality increases

E.9.2.11 Principal components analysis (PCA)
   i   Seeks a projection that preserves as much information in the data as pos-
       sible (in a least-squares sense).
   ii Finds projection to a line such that samples from different classes are well
       separated
   iii Transforms correlated variables into a set of uncorrelated ones

E.9.2.12 Confidence is defined as
   i   The fraction of the total transactions that contain the itemset
   ii The likelihood of an item Y occurring given that an item X occurs in a
       transaction.
   iii An itemset whose support is greater than or equal to a minimum thresh-
       old value of the support

E.9.3 Match the Columns

No	Match	
E.9.3.1 Unsupervised learning	A	A bottom-up strategy where initially each data point forms its own cluster
E.9.3.2 Clustering	B	the distance between two clusters is the distance between the farthest pair of points
E.9.3.3 Euclidean distance between two data points	C	Finding intrinsic structure in the data set
E.9.3.4 Agglomerative clustering	D	Constructs nested partitions layer by layer by grouping objects into a tree of clusters
E.9.3.5 Hierarchical clustering approach	E	the aspect where inclusion of more features leads to a decrease in performance
E.9.3.6 Hash-based counting	F	No target attribute
E.9.3.7 Complete link	G	Method to improve Apriori algorithm
E.9.3.8 Fisher linear discriminant	H	Seeks a projection that preserves as much information in the data as possible
E.9.3.9 Curse of dimensionality.	I	Find projection to a line such that samples from different classes are well separated
E.9.3.10 Principal components analysis	J	The square root of the sum of the squares of the difference between them in each dimension

E.9.4 Problems

E.9.4.1 For three objects, A: $(1, 0, 1, 1)$, B: $(2, 1, 0, 2)$, and C: $(2, 2, 2, 1)$, store them in a data matrix and use Manhattan, Euclidean, and cosine distances to generate distance matrices, respectively.

E.9.4.2 Use the nearest neighbour clustering algorithm and Euclidean distance to cluster the examples from Exercise E.9.4.2 assuming that the threshold is 4.

E.9.4.3 Use single and complete link agglomerative clustering to group the data in the following distance matrix (Figure E.9.1). Show the dendrograms.

	A	B	C	D
A	0	1	4	5
B		0	2	6
C			0	3
D				0

FIGURE E.9.1

E.9.4.4 Use single-link, complete-link, and average-link agglomerative clustering as well as medoid and centroid to cluster the eight examples of Exercise E.9.4.2. Show the dendrograms.

E.9.4.5 Trace the results of using the Apriori algorithm on the grocery store example with support threshold $s = 33.34\%$ and confidence threshold $c = 60\%$. Show the candidate and frequent itemsets for each database scan. Enumerate all the final frequent itemsets. In addition, indicate the association rules that are generated and highlight the strong ones; sort them by confidence.

Trans ID	Items
T1	Cutlets, Buns, Sauce
T2	Cutlets, Buns
T3	Cutlets, Samosa, Chips
T4	Chips, Samosa
T5	Chips, Sauce
T6	Cutlets, Samosa, Chips

E.9.5 Short Questions

E.9.5.1 How do you think unsupervised learning works? What are the goals of unsupervised learning?

E.9.5.2 Distinguish between supervised and unsupervised learning.

E.9.5.3 What are the main challenges of unsupervised learning?

E.9.5.4 What is Minkowski distance? What are other distances derived from it?

E.9.5.6 What is the difference between agglomerative clustering and divisive clustering?

E.9.5.7 Distinguish between single link, average link, and complete link used to define cluster distance.

E.9.5.8 What is the difference between a centroid and clusteroid?

E.9.5.9   Describe the steps of the *k*-means algorithm.

E.9.5.10   What are the issues associated with the *k*-means algorithm?

E.9.5.11   Describe the soft clustering variation of the *k*-means algorithm.

E.9.5.12   What is good clustering?

E.9.5.13   How are precision and recall defined for clustering?

E.9.5.14   Differentiate between entropy of a cluster and entropy of a clustering.

E.9.5.15   What is the silhouette coefficient? Discuss

E.9.5.16   What is the curse of dimensionality?

E.9.5.17   What is the criterion for dimensionality reduction?

E.9.5.18   What is the difference between feature reduction and feature selection?

E.9.5.19   List the three approaches to finding optimal transformation for dimensionality reduction.

E.9.5.20   What is the concept behind single value decomposition?

E.9.5.21   What are the principles on which the Apriori algorithm is based?

References

Agrawal, R., & Srikant, R. (1994). Fast algorithms for mining association rules in large databases. *Proceedings of 20th Int. Conference on Very Large Databases, Santiago de Chile*, 487–489.

Chouinard, J.-C. (2022, May 5). What is dimension reduction in machine learning (and how it works). https://www.jcchouinard.com/dimension-reduction-in-machine-learning/

Cline, A. K., & Dhillon, I. S. (2006, January). Computation of singular value decomposition. *Handbook of Linear Algebra*, 45-1–45-13. https://www.cs.utexas.edu/users/inderjit/public_papers/HLA_SVD.pdf

Istrail, S. (n.d.). An overview of clustering methods: With applications to bioinformatics. *SlideToDoc*. https://slidetodoc.com/an-overview-of-clustering-methods-with-applications-to/

Jaadi, Z., & Powers, J. (2022, September 26). A step-by-step explanation of principal component analysis (PCA). *BuiltIn*. https://builtin.com/data-science/step-step-explanation-principal-component-analysis

Jin, R. (n.d.). *Cluster validation*. Kent State University. http://www.cs.kent.edu/~jin/DM08/ClusterValidation.pdf

Li, S. (2017, September 24). A gentle introduction on market basket analysis—association rules. *Towards Data Science*. https://towardsdatascience.com/a-gentle-introduction-on-market-basket-analysis-association-rules-fa4b986a40ce

Mathew, R. (2021, January 18). A deep dive into clustering. *Insight*. https://insightimi.wordpress.com/2021/01/18/a-deep-dive-into-clustering/

Shetty, B., & Powers, J. (2022, August 19). What is the curse of dimensionality? *BuiltIn*. https://builtin.com/data-science/curse-dimensionality

Thalles, S. (2019, January 3). An illustrative introduction to Fisher's linear discriminant. https://sthalles.github.io/fisher-linear-discriminant/

Wikipendium. (n.d.). TDT4300: Data warehousing and data mining. https://www.wikipendium.no/TDT4300_Data_Warehousing_and_Data_Mining

10

Sequence Models

10.1 Sequence Models

When the input or output to machine learning models is sequential in nature, these models are called sequence models. Machine learning today needs to deal with text streams, audio clips, video clips, and time-series data, which are all sequence data. In sequence models, data do not have the independently and identically distributed (IID) characteristic since the sequential order of the data imposes some dependency.

10.2 Applications of Sequence Models

A few examples of sequence data that often arise through measurement of time series are as follows:

- Acoustic features at successive time frames in speech recognition
- Sequence of characters in an English sentence
- Parts of speech of successive words
- Machine translation where a sequence of words in one language is translated to the sequence of words of another language.
- Image captioning where the caption of an image is analysed using present action.
- Temperature measurements on successive weeks
- Rainfall measurements on successive days
- Daily values of stock price
- Nucleotide base pairs in a strand of DNA

One example of a sequence model in deep learning is recurrent neural networks (RNNs), which will be discussed later in Chapter 16. However, sequence models in machine learning and their applications will be discussed in this chapter.

10.2.1 Examples of Applications with Sequence Data

Consider the following two natural language processing (NLP) scenarios: Scenario 1 highlights example tasks involving sequential data as input and output, and Scenario 2 highlights tasks involving sequential data as input and symbols as output.

Scenario 1: Sequence-to-sequence—The following Tasks 1–3 in which the input as well the outputs are sequence data.

Task 1

In speech recognition using a sound spectrogram, Figure 10.1 highlights the decomposed sound waves into frequency and amplitude using Fourier transforms.

Task 2

Consider an application of NLP called named entity recognition (NER), which uses the following sequence input:

Input: Jim bought 300 shares of Acme Corp. in 2006

and the following NER sequence is the output:

NER: [Jim]Person bought 300 shares of [Acme Corp.]Organization in [2006] Time

Task 3

Consider a machine translation example: Echte dicke kiste ➔ Awesome sauce, in which the input and outputs are sequence of words.

Scenario 2: Sequence-to-symbol—Let us consider the following Tasks 4 and 5 in which the input is sequence data.

Task 4

Consider the task of predicting sentiment from movie reviews, for example:

Best movie ever ➔ Positive

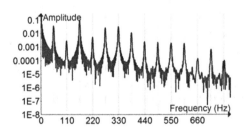

FIGURE 10.1
Sound waves decomposed into frequency and amplitude using Fourier transforms.

Task 5

In a speaker recognition task, given a sound spectrogram which is sequence data, recognising the speaker; for example:

Sound spectrogram → Harry

These examples show that there are different applications of sequence models. Sometimes both the input and output are sequences; in some either the input or the output is a sequence.

10.2.2 Examples of Application Scenario of Sequence Models

1. **Speech recognition**: When an audio clip is given as input to a speech recognition system, we get a corresponding text transcript as output. In this case both the input audio clip and output (text transcript) are sequences of data (Figure 10.2).

2. **Sentiment classification**: In sentiment classification, the input opinions are expressed as a sentence which is essentially a sequence of words, and this sentence needs to be categorized (Figure 10.3).

3. **Video activity recognition**: The video activity recognition model must determine the video clip's activity. A video clip consists of a series of video frames; hence, the input for video activity detection is a series of data (Figure 10.4).

4. **Auto-completion**: Consider the auto-complete issue from the perspective of sequence modelling. Whenever we input a character (l) in this problem, the algorithm attempts to forecast the next possible character based on the previously typed character (Figure 10.5).

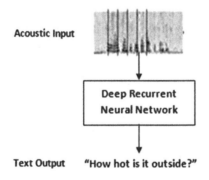

Acoustic Input

Deep Recurrent Neural Network

Text Output   **"How hot is it outside?"**

FIGURE 10.2
Speech recognition.

Review (X)	Rating (Y) (out of 5)
"This movie is excellent! I really loved it because the animation is good!"	😊 😊 😊 😊
"This film is not to my taste, so will watch some another good film"	😊 😊 😊
"Please return my money because this is very atrocious"	😊 😊

FIGURE 10.3
Sentiment classification.

FIGURE 10.4
Video activity recognition.

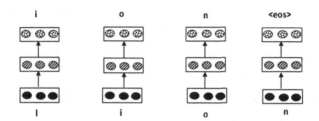

FIGURE 10.5
Auto-completion sequential process.

In other words, the network attempts to anticipate the next character from the potential 26 English alphabets based on the letter "l" that has been entered. Given the previous letters, the neural network would generate a soft max output of size 26 reflecting the likelihood of the following letter. Since the inputs to this network are letters, they must be converted to a one-shot encoded vector of length 26, with the element corresponding to the index of the alphabet set to 1 and the rest set to 0.

5. **Parts of speech tagging**: In parts of speech tagging, we are given a sequence of words and must anticipate the part of speech tag for each word (verb, noun, pronoun, etc.). Again, the outcome depends on both the current and past inputs. If the previous word is an adjective, the likelihood of tagging "girl" as a noun increases (Figure 10.6).

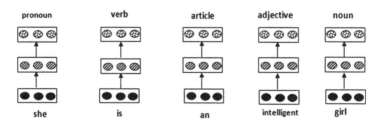

FIGURE 10.6
Parts of speech sequential process.

10.3 Modelling Sequence Learning Problems

In situations involving sequence learning, we are aware that the true output at time step t depends on every input that the model has encountered up to that point. We need to develop an estimate so that the function depends on all of the prior inputs because we don't know the exact relationship (Equation 10.1).

$$y_t = \hat{f}\left(x_1, x_2, \ldots x_n\right) \tag{10.1}$$

The important thing to keep in mind in this situation is that the task remains the same regardless of whether we are predicting the next character or classifying the part of speech of a word. Every time step requires a new input because the function needs to keep track of a larger list of words for lengthier sentences.

In other words, we must define a function with the following properties:

i. Make sure that the output y_t depends on the inputs before it.

ii. Make sure the function can handle a variety of inputs.

iii. The function that is performed at each time step must be the same.

Drawbacks of Sequence Model: The major disadvantage of sequential model is changes can cause confusion and be time consuming. Moreover, the dependence of a current state on all previous states increases the complexity of the model. However, a Markov model restricts the dependence all but the most recent past states.

10.4 Markov Models

Understanding the hidden Markov model requires knowledge about Markov models. First let us discuss the Markov model before we explore hidden Markov models.

In probability theory, stochastic models that represent randomly changing systems have the Markov property defined by a Russian mathematician, Andrey Markov. The Markov property has a memory-less characteristic and states that at any given time, only the current state determines the next subsequent state, and this subsequent state is not dependent on any other state in the past. In terms of probability, when the conditional probability distribution of the future states of a process depends only on the current state and is independent of past states, the stochastic process is said to possess the Markov property. Markov models are based on this Markov property.

In the simplest form, a Markov model assumes that observations are completely independent, that is, like a graph without edges between them as shown in Figure 10.7.

The simplest form can be understood with the following example: To predict whether it rains tomorrow is only based on relative frequency of rainy days. The simplest form ignores the influence of whether it rained the previous day.

FIGURE 10.7
Markov model with independent observations.

The general Markov model for an observation $\{x_n\}$ can be expressed by the product rule which gives the joint distribution of sequence of observations $\{x_1, x_2, ...x_{n-1}\}$ as given in Equation (10.2):

$$P\left(x_1, ..x_N\right) = \prod_{n=1}^{N} p(x_n \mid x_1, ..x_{n-1}) \tag{10.2}$$

10.4.1 Types of Markov Models

Markov models can be broadly classified based on two characteristics of the system, namely whether all states of the system are observable or not and whether the system is autonomous or controlled by external actions that can affect the outcomes. Based on these characteristics, the four types of Markov models are given in Table 10.1.

10.4.2 Markov Chain Model

The Markov chain model is the simplest model of the Markov family. When modelling the state of a system, the Markov model employs a random variable that changes with time. It implies that distribution of a variable is completely dependent on its preceding state distribution.

The **first-order Markov model** is a chain of observations $\{x_n\}$ with a joint distribution for a sequence of n variables as given in Figure 10.8. It is called the **first-order** Markov model because the next state in a sequence depends only on one state—the current state (Equation 10.3).

$$p\left(x_1, ..x_N\right) = p\left(x_1\right) \prod_{n=2}^{N} p(x_n \mid x_{n-1}) \tag{10.3}$$

TABLE 10.1

Four Commonly Used Markov Models

	System State Is Fully Observable	System State Is Partially Observable
System is autonomous	**Markov chain**—show all possible states, and the transition probability of moving from one state to another at a point in time.	**Hidden Markov model**—has some unobservable states. They show states and transition rates and in addition also represent observations and observation likelihoods for each state.
System is controlled	**Markov decision process**—shows all possible states but is controlled by an agent who makes decisions based on reliable information.	**Partially observable Markov decision process**—similar to Markov decision process; however, the agent does not always have reliable information.

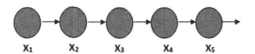

FIGURE 10.8
Markov model with chain of observations.

This can be written as in Equation (10.4):

$$p(x_n|x_1 \ldots x_{n-1}) = p(x_n|x_{n-1}) \qquad (10.4)$$

If the model is used to predict the next observation, the distribution of predictions will only depend on preceding observation and be independent of earlier observations. Stationarity implies conditional distributions $p(x_n|x_{n-1})$ are all equal.

Example: A Markov chain with three states representing the dinner of the day (sandwich, pizza, burger) is given. A transition table with transition probabilities representing the dinner of the next day given the dinner of the current day is also given (Figure 10.9).

From the previous example, let us find out the probability of dinner for the next seven days if it will be "B-B-S-S-B-P-B."

If the given model is $O = \{S3, S3, S3, S1, S1, S3, S2, S3\}$

Then, the probability of the given model O is as follows:

$$P(O\,|\,\text{Model}) = P(S3, S3, S3, S1, S1, S3, S2, S3\,|\,Model)$$
$$= P(S3) \cdot P(S3|S3) \cdot P(S3|S3) \cdot P(S1|S3) \cdot P(S1|S1) \cdot P(S3|S1) \cdot P(S2|S3) \cdot P(S3|S2)$$
$$= \pi_3 \cdot a_{33} \cdot a_{33} \cdot a_{31} \cdot a_{11} \cdot a_{13} \cdot a_{32} \cdot a_{23}$$
$$= 1 \cdot (0.8) \cdot (0.8) \cdot (0.1) \cdot (0.4) \cdot (0.3) \cdot (0.1) \cdot (0.2)$$
$$= 1.536 \times 10^{-4}$$

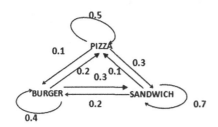

		Tomorrow		
		SANDWICH	PIZZA	BURGER
	SANDWICH	0.7	0.1	0.2
Today	PIZZA	0.1	0.5	0.1
	BURGER	0.3	0.5	0.4

FIGURE 10.9
Markov chain with three states.

Let us consider another example, where we shall apply a Markov model for spoken word production. If the states /k/ /a/ /c/ /h/ represents phonemes, the Markov model for the production of the word "catch" is as shown in Figure 10.10.

The transitions are from /k/ to /a/, /a/ to /c/, /c/ to /h/, and /h/ to a silent state. Although only correct "cat" sound is represented by the model, perhaps other transitions can be introduced, for example /k/ followed by /h/.

In the **second-order Markov model**, each observation is influenced by the previous two observations (Equation 10.5). The conditional distribution of observation x_n depends on the values of two previous observations, x_{n-1} and x_{n-2}, as shown in Figure 10.11.

$$p\left(x_1, \ldots x_n\right) = p\left(x_1\right) p(x_2 \mid x_1) \prod_{n=3}^{N} p(x_n \mid x_{n-1}, x_{n-2}) \tag{10.5}$$

Similarly for the *Mth*-order Markov source, the conditional distribution for a particular variable depends on the previous M variables. The discrete variable with K states in its first order is $p(x_n \mid x_{n-1})$, which needs $K - 1$ parameters for each value of x_{n-1} for each of K states of x_n, giving $K(K-1)$ parameters. The Mth order will need $K^{M-1}(K-1)$ parameters.

Latent variables: While Markov models are tractable, they are severely limited. Introduction of latent variables provides a more general framework and leads to state-space models. When the latent variables are discrete, they are called hidden Markov models, and if they are continuous, then they are linear dynamical systems. Models for sequences are not limited by Markov assumptions of any order but with limited number of parameters. For each observation x_n, we can introduce a latent variable z_n which can be of different type or dimensionality when compared to the observed variable. The latent variables form the Markov chain, resulting in the state-space model.

10.4.3 Hidden Markov Model (HMM)

A Markov chain with partially observable states is called a hidden Markov model, that is, observations about the state of a system are insufficient to determine the state accurately.

HMM is a general way for modeling time-series data. In machine learning applications, HMM is used in almost all speech recognition systems, computational molecular biology, and grouping amino acid sequences into proteins. It is a Bayesian network for representing

FIGURE 10.10
Markov model for spoken word production.

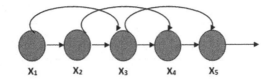

FIGURE 10.11
Second-order Markov model.

probability distributions over sequences of observations. Assumptions of HMM are as follows.

- **Markov assumption**: The state transition depends only on the origin and destination states—that is, it assumes that state at $\mathbf{z}_t$ is dependent only on state z_{t-1} and independent of all prior states (first order).
- **Output-independent assumption**: All observations are dependent only on the state that generated them, not on neighbouring observations.
- Moreover, the observation $\mathbf{x}_t$ at time t was generated by some process whose state $\mathbf{z}_t$ is hidden from the observer.

Consider an example (Figure 10.12), where z represents phoneme sequences, and x are acoustic observations. Graphically HMM can be represented with a state-space model and discrete latent variables as shown in the following Figure 10.12 and the joint distribution has the form as shown in (Equation 10.6).

$$p\left(x_1,\ldots x_N, z_1,\ldots z_n\right) = p\left(z_1\right)\left[\prod_{n=2}^{N} p(z_n \mid z_{n-1})\right]\prod_{n=1}^{N} p(x_n \mid z_n) \tag{10.6}$$

A single time slice in the preceding graphical model corresponds to a mixture distribution with component densities $p(x \mid z)$.

10.4.3.1 Parameters of an HMM

- In hidden Markov models, $S = \{s_1,\ldots, s_n\}$ is a set of states where n is the number of possible states, while $V = \{v_1,\ldots, v_m\}$ is the set of symbols, where m indicates the number of symbols observable in the states.
- **Transition probabilities is a two-dimensional matrix** $A = a_{1,1}, a_{1,2},\ldots, a_{n,n}$ where each $a_{i,j}$ represents the probability of transitioning from state s_i to s_j.
- **Emission probabilities** or the observation symbol distribution probability is a set B of functions of the form $b_i\left(o_t\right)$, which is the probability of observation o_t being emitted or observed by state s_i.
- **Initial state distribution** π is the probability that s_i is a start state.

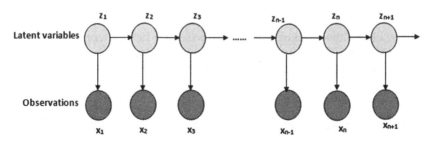

FIGURE 10.12
Graphical model of an HMM.

Therefore, we have two model parameters n, the number of states of the HMM, and m, the number of distinct observation symbols per state. In addition, we have three probability measures: A, the transition probability; B, the emission probability; and π, the initial probability.

10.4.3.2 The Three Problems of HMM

The following are the three problems associated with HMM:

Problem 1 Evaluation

Here given the observation sequence $O = o_1,...,o_T$ and an HMM model,

Q1: How do we compute the probability of a given sequence of observations?
A1: Forward–backward dynamic programming algorithm—the **Baum Welch algorithm**

Problem 2 Decoding

Here, given the observation sequence $O = o_1,...,o_T$ and an HMM model,

Q2: How do we compute the most probable hidden sequence of states, given a sequence of observations?
A2: Viterbi's dynamic programming algorithm

Problem 3 Learning

Here given an observation sequence and set of possible models,

Q3: Which model most closely fits the data? In other words, how are the model parameters—that is, the transition probabilities, emission probabilities, and initial state distribution—adjusted so that the model maximizes the probability of the observation sequence given the model parameters?
A3: The **expectation maximization (EM) heuristic** finds which model most closely fits the data.

10.4.4 Markov Decision Process

Like a Markov chain, the Markov decision process predicts outcomes based only on the current state. However, in the case of the Markov decision process, the decision-making agent may choose take an action associated with the current state that determines the transition of states and may result in the agent getting an award.

10.4.5 Partially Observable Markov Decision Process

A partially observable Markov decision process (POMPD) is a Markov decision process where the states are only partially observable. POMPD models decisions based on a series of partially observable states and decision making agent taking actions based on current state but based on limited observations. POMDPs are used in a variety of applications including the operation of simple agents or robots.

10.4.6 Markov Random Field

The concept of Markov random field (MRF) is that a state is influenced by its neighbors in various directions. It is represented as an undirected connected graph whose nodes are both observed and unobserved random variables having the Markov property. The edges indicate the stochastic dependence between nodes. The distribution of any node depends on the linked neighbor nodes. The joint probability distribution of a MRF is defined over cliques in this undirected graph.

10.5 Data Stream Mining

The process of extracting knowledge structures from continuous data sets is referred to as "data stream mining." A data stream is an ordered sequence of instances that, in many applications of data stream mining, can be read only once or a few numbers of times due to restricted processing and storage resources. In other words, a data stream is a sequence of data that can only be read once. The general process of data stream mining is depicted in Figure 10.13.

Mining data streams presents its own unique set of difficulties, which in turn leads to a wide variety of research problems in this area. When it comes to the requirements of data streams, the development of stream mining algorithms requires significantly more research than standard mining approaches.

10.5.1 Challenges in Data Stream Mining

Mining data streams presents as different from standard mining and has its own unique set of difficulties, which in turn leads to a wide variety of research problems. The various challenges in data stream mining may be broadly classified into the following five categories: uncertainty in arrival rate, heterogeneity in data, significance of interpretations, memory constraints, and volume.

Memory management is a primary difficulty in stream processing due to the fact that the arrival rate of data in many real-world data streams is erratic and varies over the course of time. As a result, the development of approaches for summarising data streams becomes more essential and the need of the hour.

When taking into account the quantity of memory available as well as the massive amount of data that is constantly being added to the system, it is necessary to have a data structure that is as compact as possible in order to store, update, and retrieve the information that has been gathered. In the absence of such a data structure, the effectiveness of the mining algorithm will be significantly reduced. Even if we save the information to discs, the additional I/O operations will cause an increase in the amount of time it takes to process the data. Even though it is impossible to rescan all of the input data, incremental maintenance of the data structure is something that really must take place. In addition, unique strategies for indexing, storage, and querying are necessary in order to manage the continuous flow of data streams, which are always shifting.

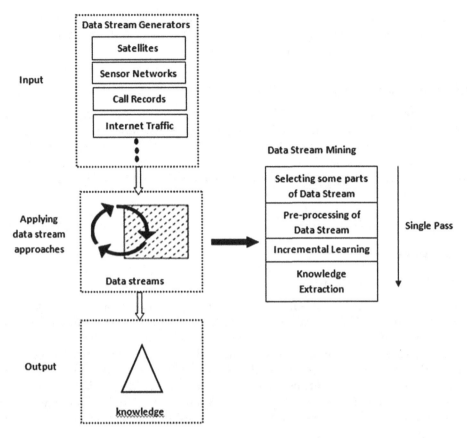

FIGURE 10.13
General process of data stream mining.

When mining data streams, it is important that the data preprocessing step, which is an essential and time-consuming part of the process of discovering new knowledge, be optimized. It is of the utmost importance to develop lightweight preprocessing methods that are capable of ensuring the quality of the mining results.

In order to arrive at reliable estimates when mining data streams, it is essential to take into account the restricted resources that are available, such as memory space and computing power. The accuracy of the results produced by stream data mining algorithms would significantly suffer if those algorithms do not consider these restrictions.

10.6 Learning from Stream Data

With such challenges much research has been conducted for learning from stream data. The following are few of those learning techniques:

1. Tree based learning
2. Adaptive learning

3. Window management models

4. Data stream clustering

10.6.1 Tree Based Learning

An example of a decision tree learning approach which is used for the classification of stream data is the Hoeffding tree (HT) algorithm. At first, it was put to use for monitoring users' click streams on the web and building models to determine which web providers and websites a user was most likely to visit. The average execution takes sublinear amounts of time, and the resulting decision tree is essentially equivalent to those produced by conventional batch learners. It does this by employing Hoeffding trees, which capitalise on the concept that selecting an ideal splitting characteristic may frequently be done with .a relatively small sample size. The Hoeffding bound provides mathematical evidence in support of this concept and is given in Equation (10.7).

$$\varepsilon = \sqrt{\frac{R^2 \ln \frac{1}{\delta}}{2N}} \tag{10.7}$$

In the Hoeffding tree algorithm while choosing a splitting attribute at a node, it uses the Hoeffding bound to find the minimum number (N) of examples required with highest probability. Unlike the majority of other bound equations, the Hoeffding bound is not dependent on the probability distribution. The Hoeffding tree induction algorithm, also called the very fast decision tree (VFDT) algorithm, is explained in the flowchart (Figure 10.14). In this algorithm we start with a tree with a single root node. In order to select a split attribute for a node only sufficient samples are considered. Given a stream of examples, we first select the split for the root, sort incoming examples according to the leaves, pick the best attribute to split, and repeat the procedure till there are no more examples.

The intended probability that the right attribute is selected at every node in the tree is one minus the δ parameter used in the Hoeffding bound. Since the desired probability must be close to one with maximum likelihood of correctness, δ is typically set to a small amount.

10.6.2 Adaptive Learning Using Naïve Bayes

An adaptive technique employing naïve Bayes models, as shown in the following algorithm, operates by the following: (1) monitoring majority class error rate, (2) naïve Bayes judgments at each leaf, and (3) employing naïve Bayes decisions only in circumstances where they have proven to be more accurate in the past. Unlike pure naïve Bayes prediction, the adaptive method introduces a training overhead. Extra time is required with every training example to generate both prediction types and error estimates, and additional storage space is required per leaf to store the estimates (Figure 10.15).

Once an example has reached a leaf, prior to leaf updating, a comparison of the majority class prediction and naïve Bayes prediction with the actual class that the example belongs to is carried out. Counters at the leaf keep track of the total number of mistakes caused by the different procedures. During forecasting, a leaf will use the prediction based on the method that produced fewer errors.

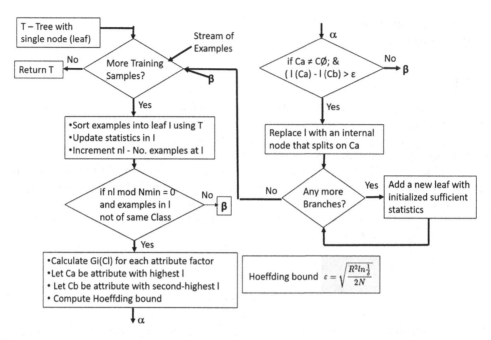

FIGURE 10.14
Hoeffding tree induction or very fast decision tree (VFDT) algorithm.

```
for all training examples do
        Sort example into leaf I using HT
        if majorityClassI != true class of example then
                increment mcErroII
        end if
        if NaiveBayesPredictionI(example) != true class of example then
                increment nbErroII
        end if
        Update sufficient statistics in I
end for
for all examples requiring label prediction do
        Sort example into leaf I using HT
        if nbErroII < mcErroIIthen
                return NaiveBayesPredictionI(example)
        else
                return majorityClassI
        end if
```

FIGURE 10.15
Adaptive learning using naïve Bayes.

10.6.3 Window Management Models

There are two different ways in which mining algorithms use window strategies:

1. The window is embedded externally to the learning algorithm as shown in Figure 10.16. The error rate of the current model is tracked using the window. This error rate should normally keep decreasing or at most stabilise. A change is declared and the model needs to be revised or rebuild with fresh data by the base learning algorithm.

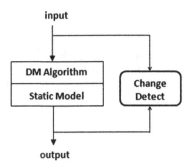

FIGURE 10.16
Windowing strategy—external to the learning algorithm.

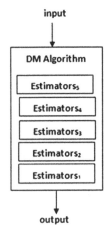

FIGURE 10.17
Windowing strategy—internal to the learning algorithm.

2. In this method, in order for the learning algorithm to maintain and continuously update statistics, the window is embedded internally as shown in Figure 10.17. However, it is the responsibility of the learning algorithm to understand the statistics and act accordingly.

Learning algorithms usually compare statistics of two windows for detecting the change. The methods could use less memory than expected; for example, they might maintain window statistics without keeping all of its constituents. Other different window management strategies are as follows:

- Equal and fixed size sub-windows: In this type comparison is carried out between a nonsliding window of older data and a sliding window of the same size of current data.

- Equal size adjacent sub-windows: Here we compare between two adjacent sliding windows of the same size of recent data.

- Total window against sub-window: In this strategy, the window that contains all the data is compared with a sub-window of data from the beginning. The process extends until the accuracy of the algorithm decreases by a threshold.

10.6.4 Data Stream Clustering

The clustering of continuously arriving data, such as call stream (telephone) records, multimedia content, and financial transactions, is called data stream clustering. Data stream clustering needs to satisfactorily cluster the stream or the sequence of points.

STREAM clustering algorithm: STREAM is a stream data clustering algorithm which achieves a constant factor approximation for the k-median problem in a single pass and using small space. With data stream as input, STREAM solves the k-median problem in a single pass with time $O(n1 + e)$ and space (n) up to a factor $2O(1/e)$, where n is the number of points and $e1/2$.

The STREAM algorithm, as shown in Figure 10.18, performs the clustering in a small space. The small space first divides the data, S, into l partitions, then using k-means it clusters each of the l partitions. Finally, it clusters the centers obtained from each partition.

Algorithm: Small space (S)
    Divide S into l disjoint partitions $X_1,...,X_l$.

  1. For each i,

     1. Find O(k) centers in X_i.
     2. Assign each point in X_i to its closest center.
     3. Assign weight to each center c based on the number of points assigned to it.
     4. Return X' which is the O(lk) centers obtained.

  2. Cluster X' to find k centers.

In step 2 of the technique described previously, we may additionally execute a bi-criteria (a,b) approximation algorithm that produces at most ak medians at a cost of at most b times the optimal k-median solution. Step 3 results in an approximation for the small-space() technique.

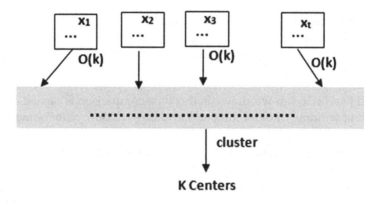

FIGURE 10.18
Small-space algorithm and its representation.

10.7 Applications

10.7.1 Applications of Markov Model

Application in retail domain: If you visit the grocery store once per week, it is quite simple for a computer program to forecast when your shopping trip will take longer. The hidden Markov model determines on which day of the week visits take longer than others, and then uses this knowledge to discover why some trips are taking longer than others for shoppers such as yourself. The recommendation engine is another e-commerce application that employs hidden Markov models. The hidden Markov models attempt to forecast the next thing you will purchase.

Application in travel industry: Using hidden Markov models, airlines are able to forecast how long it will take a passenger to check out of an airport. This allows them to choose when to begin boarding people!

Application in medical domain: Hidden Markov models are utilised in a variety of medical applications that seek to uncover the concealed states of a human body system or organ. For instance, cancer diagnosis can be accomplished by examining specific sequences and calculating the risk they offer to the patient. Hidden Markov models are also used to evaluate biological data such as RNA-Seq, ChIP-Seq, and so on, which aids researchers in comprehending gene regulation. Based on a person's age, weight, height, and body type, doctors can calculate their life expectancy using the hidden Markov model.

Application in marketing domain: When marketers employ a hidden Markov model, they are able to determine at which step of their marketing funnel customers are abandoning their efforts and how to enhance user conversion rates.

10.7.2 Applications of Stream Data Processing

Some applications of **real-time stream processing** include the following

10.7.2.1 Fraud and Anomaly Detection

Using fraud and anomaly detection that is powered by stream processing, one of the major credit card companies in the world was able to lower the amount of money that it writes off due to fraud by an average of $800 million each year. Delays in the processing of credit cards have a negative impact on the shopping experience for both the final consumer and the retailer who is seeking to accept the credit card (and any other customers in line). Historically, credit card companies would wait until after a transaction had been completed before beginning their time-consuming and laborious fraud detection systems. The credit card company runs algorithms to recognize and block fraudulent charges. After detecting fraudulent charges, alerts are triggered for anomalous charges in real time while a card is swiped by a customer.

10.7.2.2 Internet of Things (IoT) Edge Analytics

Stream processing is utilised by companies whose businesses are in the manufacturing, oil and gas, and transportation domains. Many companies that are designing smart cities and smart buildings also utilize stream processing in order to cope up with the data generated by billions of "things." The identification of industrial anomalies that point to issues that need to be solved in order to enhance operations and increase yields is one example of how IoT data analysis may be applied. A manufacturer may be able to notice that a manufacturing line is churning out too many abnormalities while it is occurring with the help of real-time stream processing. This is in contrast to the traditional method of discovering a whole defective batch at the end of the day's shift. By pausing the line for quick repairs, they will be able to realize significant cost savings and avoid significant waste.

10.7.2.3 Customization for Marketing and Advertising

Real-time stream processing enables businesses to provide customers with experiences that are uniquely tailored to the context of their interactions with the brand. This can take the form of a discount for an item that was placed in a basket on a website but was not immediately purchased, a referral to connect with a friend who has just registered on a social media site, or an advertisement for a product that is comparable to the one that you just viewed.

10.8 Summary

- Discussed learning models that deal with stream data like text streams, audio clips, video clips, time-series data, and so on as input and output.
- Outlined various applications of sequence models such as speech recognition, video activity recognition, auto-completion, and so on.
- Explained the Markov model including the Markov chain model, the hidden Markov model, the Markov decision process, partially observable Markov decision process, and Markov random field.
- Outlined the process of data stream mining.
- Described the various learning methods for data stream mining, which are tree based, adaptive, window based, and data clustering.
- Listed the various applications of Markov models and data stream mining.

10.9 Points to Ponder

- In sequence learning, the true output at time step t depends on every input that the model has encountered up to that point, and hence there is a need to find a function that depends on all of the prior inputs.
- Markov property has a memoryless characteristic.
- In the first-order Markov model the next state in a sequence depends only on one state—the current state.
- The assumptions associated with hidden Markov models are the Markov assumption and the output-independent assumption.

- A data stream is an ordered sequence of instances that, in many applications of data stream mining, can be read only once or a few times due to restricted processing and storage resources.

E.10 Exercises

E.10.1 Suggested Activities

E.10.1.1 Use a Markov chain to predict which products will be in a user's next order. Data set to be used: https://www.kaggle.com/competitions/instacart-market-basket-analysis/data

E.10.1.2 Implement the hidden Markov model for named entity recognition using the NER data set: https://www.kaggle.com/datasets/debasisdotcom/name-entity-recognition-ner-dataset

Self-Assessment Questions

E.10.2 Multiple Choice Questions

Give answers with justification for correct and wrong choices.

E.10.2.1 In sequence models, data do not have
   i   Independently and identically distributed (IID) characteristic
   ii Sequential characteristic
   iii Temporal nature

E.10.2.2 When modelling sequence learning problems, we need to make sure that
   i   The function depends on all of the succeeding inputs
   ii The function that is performed at each time step is different
   iii The true output at each time step depends on every input encountered up to that point

E.10.2.3 The Markov property states that at any given time,
   i   The subsequent state is dependent on all states in the past.
   ii Only the current state determines the next subsequent state
   iii Only the subsequent state determines the current state

E.10.2.4 Predicting the price of stock based only on relative frequency of monthly price is an example of a
   i   Markov chain
   ii Markov decision process
   iii Markov model with independence observations

E.10.2.5 All possible states are observed, but the process is controlled by an agent who makes decisions based on reliable information. This is an example of a
    i Markov decision process
    ii Hidden Markov model
    iii Markov chain

E.10.2.6 When discrete latent variables are introduced into Markov models, they are called
    i Latent Markov models
    ii Hidden Markov models
    iii Dynamical systems

E.10.2.7 The output-independent assumption of the hidden Markov model states that
    i All observations are dependent only on the state that generated them
    ii All observations are dependent only neighboring observations
    iii The state transition depends only on the origin and destination states

E.10.2.8 In HMM _____ is the probability of an observation being observed by a state.
    i Transition probability
    ii Initial probability
    iii Emission probability

E.10.2.9 In HMM, the _____ algorithm is used for computing the probability of a given sequence of observations.
    i Viterbi
    ii Baum–Welch
    iii Expectation maximization

E.10.2.10 A state that is influenced by its neighbours in various directions is a concept of
    i Markov random field
    ii Hidden Markov model
    iii Markov decision process

E.10.2.11 The process of extracting knowledge structures from continuous data sets is called
    i Data mining
    ii Deep learning
    iii Data stream mining

E.10.2.12 Hoeffding trees are based on the concept that
    i Selecting an ideal splitting characteristic may require the complete sample set
    ii Selecting an ideal splitting characteristic may frequently be done with a relatively small sample size
    iii Selecting an ideal splitting characteristic is not important

E.10.2.13 Adaptive learning using naïve Bayes for learning from data streams
    i Employs naïve Bayes only when already proven to be more accurate
    ii Always employs the majority class
    iii Always employs naïve Bayes

E.10.2.14 The STREAM algorithm works in a
    i Single pass using small space
    ii Partitioned data context using multiple passes
    iii Single space using large space

E.10.3 Match the Columns

No	Match	
E.10.3.1 Speech recognition	A	Given an observation sequence and set of possible models, finding a model that most closely fits the data
E.10.3.2 Sequence learning	B	Memoryless characteristic
E.10.3.3 Markov model	C	Achieves a constant factor approximation for the k-median problem in a single pass and using small space
E.10.3.4 Markov chain	D	Example of sequence–sequence task
E.10.3.5 Expectation maximization	E	Develop an estimate of the function that depends on all of the prior inputs
E.10.3.6 A data stream	F	Probability of an observation being observed by a state
E.10.3.7 Partially observable Markov decision process	G	Shows all possible states but is controlled by an decision making agent who does not always have reliable information.
E.10.3.8 STREAM algorithm	H	Is an ordered sequence of instances that can be read only once or a few times
E.10.3.9 Hoeffding trees	I	Selecting an ideal splitting characteristic may frequently be done with a relatively small sample size
E.10.3.10 Emission probability	J	Show all possible states, and the transition probability of moving from one state to another at a point in time

E.10.4 Problems

E.10.4.1 Consider the Markov chain with three states, $S = \{1,2,3\}$, that has the following transition matrix P:

$$
\begin{array}{ccc}
0.5 & 0.25 & 0.25 \\
0.33 & 0 & 0.67 \\
0.5 & 0.5 & 0
\end{array}
$$

    a. Draw the state transition diagram.

    b. If we know $P(X_1 = 1) = P(X_1 = 2) = 0.25$, find $P(X_1 = 3, X_2 = 2, X_3 = 1)$.

E.10.4.2 A Markov chain is used to check the status of a machine used in a manufacturing process. Suppose that the possible states for the machine are as follows: idle and awaiting work (I); working on a job/task (W); broken (B); and in repair (R). The machine is monitored at regular intervals (every hour) to determine its status. The transition matrix is as follows:

$$
\begin{matrix}
0.05 & 0.93 & 0.02 & 0 \\
0.10 & 0.86 & 0.04 & 0 \\
0 & 0 & 0.80 & 0.20 \\
0.5 & 0.1 & 0 & 0.4
\end{matrix}
$$

Use the transition matrix to identify the following probabilities about the status of the machine one hour from now:

a. If the machine is idle now, find the probability that the machine is working on a job (i) one hour from now and (ii) three hours from now.

b. If the machine is working on a job now, find the probability that the machine is idle (i) one hour from now and (ii) three hours from now.

c. If the machine is being repaired now, find the probability that the machine is working on a job (i) one hour from now and (ii) three hours from now.

d. If the machine is broken now, find the probability that the machine is being repaired (i) one hour from now and (ii) three hours from now.

E.10.4.3 Assume that a student can be in one of four states: rich (R), average (A), poor (P), or in debt(D). Assume the following transition probabilities:

- If a student is rich, in the next time step the student will be
  Average:0.75, Poor:0.2, In Debt:0.05
- If a student is average, in the next time step the student will be
  Rich: 0.05, Average: 0.2, In Debt:0.45
- If a student is poor, in the next time step the student will be
  Average:0.4, Poor:0.3, In Debt: 0.2
- If a student is in debt, in the next time step the student will be
  Average: 0.15, Poor: 0.3, In Debt:0.55

a. Model the preceding information as a discrete Markov chain, draw the corresponding Markov chain, and obtain the corresponding stochastic matrix.

b. Let us assume that a student starts their studies as average. What will be the probability of them being rich after one, two, and three time steps?

E.10.4.4 Compute the parameters of a HMM model, given the following sequences of pairs (state, emission):
(D,the) (N,wine) (V,ages) (A,alone)
(D,the) (N,wine) (N,waits) (V,last) (N,ages)
(D,some) (N,flies) (V,dove) (P,into) (D,the) (N,wine)
(D,the) (N,dove) (V,flies) (P,for) (D,some) (N,flies)
(D,the) (A,last) (N,dove) (V,waits) (A,alone)

a. Draw the graph of the resulting bigram HMM, and list all nonzero model parameters that we can obtain via MLE from this data.

b. Compute the probability of the following sequence according to the model:

(D,the) (N,dove) (V,waits) (P,for) (DT,some) (A,last) (N,wine)

E.10.5 Short Questions

E.10.5.1   Do sequence models have the independently and identically distributed (IID) characteristic? Justify your answer.

E.10.5.2   Give an example of sequence to symbol application.

E.10.5.3   List five examples of sequence models, justifying your choice.

E.10.5.4   Differentiate between the different types of Markov models.

E.10.5.5   Describe the second-order Markov model with an example.

E.10.5.6   List the various assumptions of HMM.

E.10.5.7   Explain the three problems associated with HMM and name the algorithms that solve the problems.

E.10.5.8   What is data stream mining?

E.10.5.9   Explain in detail the general process of data stream mining.

E.10.5.10   What are the challenges of data stream mining?

E.10.5.11   Discuss in detail the tree based learning method used for data stream mining.

E.10.5.12   Outline two window based methods used for data stream mining.

E.10.5.13   What is data stream clustering?

E.10.5.14   Explain an algorithm used for data stream clustering.

E.10.5.15   Give some typical applications of Markov models.

E.10.5.16   Explain any two applications of real-time stream processing.

11

Reinforcement Learning

11.1 Introduction

The first thought that comes to mind about when we think about the process of learning is how we learn by way of interaction with our environment. This process of learning through interaction results in knowledge about cause and effect, consequence of actions, and so on. Learning through interaction is a foundational idea underlying nearly all theories of learning and intelligence. For example, when a child smiles, it has no explicit trainer, but it does have an explicit connection with its environment. In this chapter we explore a computational model for machines for learning from interaction. This approach is called reinforcement learning (RL), which is more focused on goal-directed learning from interaction than are other approaches to machine learning.

One of the most significant subfields of machine learning is reinforcement learning, in which an agent learns how to behave in an environment by carrying out actions and seeing the effects of those actions. The idea behind reinforcement learning is that an agent will learn from the environment by interacting with it and receiving rewards for performing actions. Humans learn from interaction with the environment using their natural experiences. Reinforcement learning is just a computational approach to learning from action.

Reinforcement learning varies from supervised learning in that the answer key is included with the training data in supervised learning, so the model is trained with the correct answer, whereas in reinforcement learning, there is no answer and the reinforcement agent decides what to do to complete the given task. Without any example data or training data set, it is made to learn by experience.

Example: Consider a question and answering game as an example:

Question—is the environment

Checking the correct answer—is the agent

Various answers—are the state of the environment

Now given the one type of answer, there are only a finite number of answers (actions) that can be made; these are determined by the environment (Figure 11.1).

As shown in the figure, the environment will receive the agent's action as an input and will output the ensuing state and a reward. In the chess example, the environment would restore the state of the chessboard after the agent's move and the opponent's move, and the agent's turn would then resume. The environment will also provide a reward, such as

FIGURE 11.1

Agent, environment, state, and reward in reinforcement learning.

TABLE 11.1

Difference Between Reinforcement Learning and Supervised Learning

Reinforcement Learning (RL)	Supervised Learning
The essence of reinforcement learning is sequential decision making. Simply said, the output is dependent on the state of the current input, whereas the next input is dependent on the outcome of the previous input.	In supervised learning, the choice is determined based on the beginning or initial information.
In reinforcement learning, decisions are dependent, hence sequences of dependent decisions are labelled.	In supervised learning, decisions are independent from one another, hence each decision is labelled.
Chess game is an example for reinforcement learning.	An example for supervised learning is object recognition.

capturing a piece. Table 11.1 lists the differences between reinforcement learning and supervised learning.

Principal aspects of reinforcement learning:

- Input: The input should be a starting state from which the model will begin.
- Output: There are numerous possible outputs because there are numerous solutions to a given problem.
- Training: The training is based on the input. The model returns a state, and the user decides whether to reward or punish the model depending on its output.
- The model continues to learn, and the optimal answer is determined based on the maximum reward.

Types of reinforcement learning: There are two types of reinforcement, positive reinforcement and negative reinforcement.

- Positive reinforcement is when an event that results from a certain behaviour enhances the intensity and frequency of the behaviour. In other words, it influences conduct positively. The benefits of positive reinforcement learning include maximizing the performance, maintaining change over an extended length of time, and an excess of reinforcement can result in an excess of states, which can lower the outcomes.

- Negative reinforcement is described as the strengthening of behaviour due to the elimination or avoidance of a negative condition. The positive aspects of negative reinforcement learning are that it increases conduct, provides resistance to a minimum performance standard, and only gives the bare minimum for acceptable behaviour.

11.2 Action Selection Policies

In this section we shall explore how to decide which action to do based on the relative value of actions. A policy is, therefore, a strategy that an agent uses in pursuit of goals. The policy dictates the actions that the agent takes as a function of the agent's state and the environment. A greedy policy could be defined as always selecting the action with the highest reward. Focusing solely on immediate benefit does not guarantee long-term reward; for example, in chess, choosing a piece for the next move will result in a higher immediate reward but might not be the best move. Using the value function, we must consider the expected reward of future situations.

Maximizing immediate reward is therefore ineffective, and choosing the highest-valued action will cause the model to become stuck in local minima. If the present value function is not optimal and we consistently chose the action with the highest value, then the model may never observe activities that might result in a significantly bigger reward.

For the model to improve its estimation of the value function, it must explore. To optimize the value function, a delicate balance between exploration and exploitation is required. Exploitation refers to selecting the optimal course of action based on the value function (taking what we think is the best move). Exploration refers to executing a random action rather than the one indicated by the value function. This enables us to explore various states by adding randomness and enhancing the performance of the model. Too much exploitation will cause the model to become stuck in local minima, while too much exploration will prevent any convergence.

Without reference to a global reward, there are four fundamental ways to organize action selection. When agents share the same set of activities, we can instantaneously compute all four techniques given subsequently. Here W = weights and Q is the Q-value.

- **Maximize the best happiness**: This is equivalent to $W = Q$ and can be implemented in that form when actions are not shared (or indeed when they *are* shared) (Equation 11.1).

$$\max_{a \in A} \max_{i \in 1,\ldots,n} Q_i(x,a) \tag{11.1}$$

- **Minimize the worst unhappiness**: When actions are not shared, this can be approximated by W-learning (Equation 11.2).

$$\min_{a \in A} \max_{i \in 1,\ldots,n} \left(Q_i(x,a_i) - Q_i(x,a) \right) \tag{11.2}$$

- **Minimize collective unhappiness**: When actions are not shared, this can be approximated by collective W-learning (Equation 11.3).

$$\min_{a \in A} \left[\sum_{i=1}^{n} \left(Q_i\left(x, a_i\right) - Q_i\left(x, a\right) \right) \right] \tag{11.3}$$

- **Maximize collective happiness**: This strategy can only be executed for shared actions. Maximize collective happiness is essentially the same as minimize collective unhappiness. When the actions are not shared it can be approximated by collective W-learning (Equation 11.4).

$$\max_{a \in A} \left[\sum_{i=1}^{n} Q_i\left(x, a\right) \right] \tag{11.4}$$

11.3 Finite Markov Decision Processes

Markov decision processes (MDPs) are mathematical frameworks used to represent an environment in RL that satisfies the Markov property. An MDP consists of a collection of finite environment states S, a set of feasible actions $A(s)$ in each state, a reward function with real-valued rewards $R(s)$, and a transition model $P(s', s \mid a)$. However, environments in the actual world are more likely to lack prior knowledge of environmental dynamics. Model-free RL approaches are useful in such situations.

A Markov decision process is a 4-tuple (S, A, P_a, R_a), where:

S state space—also known as a set of states

A action space—is the set of actions available from state s

P_a probability that action a in state s at time t will lead to state s' at time $t + 1$

R_a is the immediate reward (or expected immediate reward) received after transitioning from state s to state $s's'$, due to action a

The probability for particular values of random variables $s' \in S$ and $r \in R$ occurring at time t, given particular values of the preceding state and action, is given in Equation (11.5):

$$P(s', r \mid a) = \Pr\{S_t = s', R_t = r \mid S_{t-1} = s, A_{t-1} = a\} \tag{11.5}$$

where the function p completely characterizes the dynamics of environment for all s', $s \in S$, $r \in R$, and $a \in A(s)$. $p: S \times R \times S \times A \rightarrow [0, 1]$, indicating the dynamics of the function is an ordinary deterministic function (Equation 11.6).

$$\sum_{s' \in S} \sum_{r \in R} p(s', r \mid s, a) = 1, \text{ for all } s \in S, a \in A(s) \tag{11.6}$$

Therefore only the immediately preceding state–action pair (S_{t-1}, A_{t-1}) decides the probability of each possible value for S_t and R_t. The MDP framework is so flexible and generalized that it can be applied to a variety of problems in many different ways. Time steps, apart from referring to real-time intervals, may also refer to arbitrary decision-making and acting stages. Actions can be like controlling voltages, or high-level decisions. States can be determined by low-level data such as direct sensor readings, or high-level and abstract descriptions of room objects. Some of a state's components may be mental or subjective, depending on past sensations. In other words, actions are any decisions we wish to learn how to make, and states may help us to make those decisions.

Example: A robot arm's pick-and-place motion could be controlled using reinforcement learning. To be able to learn quick and smooth motions, the learning agent needs low-latency information regarding the locations and velocities of the mechanical components in order to have direct control of the motors. In this case, actions may be voltages of the motors at each joint of the robot and states may be the angles and velocities of the joints. +1 may be the reward assigned for every item that is picked up and placed. The "jerkiness" of the motion of the robot may be associated with a modest negative reward.

In a Markov decision process, the objective is to develop a good "policy," which is a function Π. The function Π specifies the action Π (s) which the decision maker will select when in state s. Once a Markov decision process is linked with a policy in this manner, the action for each state is fixed, and the resulting system behaves like a Markov chain. The objective of the optimization is to choose a Π that will maximize some cumulative function of the random rewards. MDPs can have several optimal policies. The Markov property shows the optimal strategy is a function of present state.

11.4 Problem Solving Methods

Problem solving is the process of recognition of a problem, generation of possible options for resolving the issue at hand, and selection of the best of those alternatives.

Design and implementation of an algorithm as a sequence of simple steps that can be followed is the best way to solve a problem. There are various problem solving methods which are discussed in the following subsections:

11.4.1 Dynamic Programming

Dynamic programming (DP) in an optimized recursion. In situations when the same inputs are used multiple times in a recursive solution, DP can be used to improve performance. Keeping track of past solutions to subproblems means we can avoid recomputation in the future. By way of this easy optimization, we reduce the time complexity.

One method that can be used to deal with issues related to self-learning is called dynamic programming. Operations research, economics, and automatic control systems are just some of the many fields that make use of it. Since DP is primarily concerned with artificial intelligence, its primary application is in the realm of machine learning, which is primarily concerned with self-learning in a highly uncertain environment.

In their book titled "Reinforcement Learning: An Introduction," eminent computer science academics Richard Sutton and Andrew Barto provided a simple definition for dynamic programming.

They have defined DP as follows: "Given a Markov decision process representing an environment, dynamic programming refers to a group of methods that can be utilized to derive optimal policies for that environment."

DP assumes that the input model is perfect, that is, aware of all probability parameters and reward functions, in order to create it as a Markov decision process based on its specification (MDP). On this basis, solutions are derived for situations in which a set of action spaces and model states, which are also continuous, are presented. DP identifies the optimal and best policies in the correct model framework. The authors argue that while DP is theoretically conceivable, it can be computationally demanding.

DP is also incredibly useful for huge and continuous-space real-time situations. It delivers insights from complex policy representations via an approximation technique. This necessitates providing an approximation of the vast number of attainable values in DP via value or policy iterations. Sampling enormous amounts of data can have a significant impact on the learning aspect of any algorithm.

The classification of DP algorithms into three subclasses is possible:

1. Value iteration method, which is an iterative method that in general only converges asymptotically to the value function, even if the state space is finite
2. Policy iteration method, which provides a series of stationary policies that are improved over time. The policy iteration method will have the following steps:
   (a) Initialization—Commence with a steady policy
   (b) Policy evaluation—Given the stable policy, determine its expense by solving the linear system of equations.
   (c) Policy improvement by acquiring a new stationary policy that meets a minimum constraint.

   Stop if the policy does not change. Alternatively, continue the steps 2(b) and 2(c).
3. Policy search methodologies.

Let us consider an example for understanding of DP as a solution: Think about a place where a train has to get to the end of a track with N stations along the way that can be skipped. The goal is to return the fewest number of jumps needed to get from the beginning of the track to the end. The train can skip up to K stations at the same time. The necessary condition is that the train must reach the end position but not go past it. If the train goes past the end position, it must start over from the beginning.

A simple way to do this is to call for all the positions that can be reached from the first position. You can figure out how many jumps it takes to get from first to end by figuring out how many jumps it takes to get from first to the positions that lead to end.

$$\text{minJumps}(\text{start},\text{end}) = \min\big(\text{minJumps}(k,\text{end})\big), \text{for all } k \text{ reachable from start}$$

The problem can be seen as a bunch of smaller problems that run into each other. This problem has both an optimal substructure and sub-problems it overlaps, which are both features of dynamic programming. The idea is to just store the answers to sub-problems so we don't have to figure them out again when we need them later. The amount of time needed to do this simple optimization goes from being exponential to being polynomial.

Consider another example—solving for the Fibonacci series. The basic recursion approach and the dynamic programming approach to this problem is as follows (Figure 11.2):

If we write a simple recursive solution for the Fibonacci numbers, it takes exponentially long as shown previously. However, if we optimize it by storing the answers to sub-problems, it takes linear time.

Normal Recursive approach	Dynamic programming approach

int sumofsnumbers(int n)
{
    if(n<=1)
      return n
    return n+sumofsnumbers(n-1);
}
	s[0] = 0;
	s[1]=1;
	for(i=2; i<=n; i++)
	{
	
	    s[i]=s[i]+s[i-1];
	}
	return s[n]

FIGURE 11.2
Recursive versus dynamic programming approach.

It takes up a lot of memory to store the result of each sub-problem's calculation without knowing if that value will be used or not. During execution, the output value is often saved, but it is never used in the next sub-problem.

11.4.2 Monte Carlo Methods

John Neumann and Ulam Stanislaw created the Monte Carlo (MC) method to improve decision making in uncertain conditions. It was named after the famous casino town of Monte Carlo, Monaco, because the element of chance is central to the modelling technique, which is comparable to a game of roulette.

At its abstract level, Monte Carlo Simulation is a method of estimating the value of an unknown quantity with the help of inferential statistics. A Monte Carlo approach is any technique that solves a problem by generating acceptable random numbers and observing the proportion of those numbers that adhere to a particular property or properties.

The only requirement for Monte Carlo methods is experience—samples of state, action, and reward sequences both actual and simulated interactions with an environment. Learning from actual experience is remarkable since it does not necessitate prior understanding of the environment's dynamics yet can achieve optimal behaviour. Any agent involving a Monte Carlo approach will interact with its environment and gather samples for learning. This is the same as drawing samples from the probability distributions $P(s, a, s')$ and $R. (s, a)$. MC estimation is trial-based learning, that is, an MDP can learn through trial-and-error and repeated attempts.

Each attempt in this learning process is referred to as an episode. In the learning process all episodes must conclude. That is, the MDP should attain its final condition. As is the case with the Bellman optimality equation, values for each state are only updated based on the final reward G_t and not on estimates of neighboring states. Because MC only learns from complete episodes, it is only suitable for what we refer to as episodic MDP.

The state value formula is Equation (11.7):

$$V(S_t) \leftarrow V(S_t) + \propto \left[G_t - V(S_t) \right] \tag{11.7}$$

where,

- $V(S_t)$ is the state value, which can be initialized randomly or with a certain strategy
- G_t is the final reward and calculated as in Equation (11.8):

$$G_t = R_{t+1} + \gamma R_{t+2} + \ldots + \gamma^{T-1} R_T \tag{11.8}$$

- T is the termination time
- γ is a parameter like learning rate which influences the convergence

11.4.2.1 *Monte Carlo Reinforcement Learning*

Without prior knowledge of MDP transitions, the Monte Carlo approach for reinforcement learning acquires knowledge directly from experience episodes. Here, the return or reward is the random component. Monte Carlo learning has two important steps, similar to dynamic programming: policy evaluation for finding the value function for a given random policy and a policy improvement step to find the optimum policy.

Step 1—Policy Evaluation: The objective of policy evaluation is to learn the value function $V(S_t)$ from episodes of experience under a policy p_i. Every episode will have states and rewards. By definition, the return is the sum of future rewards.

However, a state might appear one or more times in an episode. Hence while computing state value $V(S_t)$ we will have to adopt different approaches. Sometimes we need to just update the state value rather than computing afresh. There are three basic approaches to compute $V(S_t)$ which are described as follows:

Method 1: First time approach

Method 2: Each time approach

Method 3: Incremental approach

Method 1: The first time approach as shown subsequently is followed for each episode, only the first time that the agent arrives at S counts with the policy.

1. Initialize the policy and state–value function.
2. Generate an episode using the current policy.
   i. Save and track the states encountered through that episode.
3. Choose a state saved in step 2.i.
   i. Create a list and add the return received posterior to the first occurrence of state to this list.
   ii. Calculate the average of all returns.
   iii. Assign $V(S_t)$ = computed average.
4. Repeat step 3.
5. Repeat steps 2–4 until real state s value is reached.

> The first time state s appears: $N(S) \leftarrow N(S) + 1$
> Total rewards update: $S(S) \leftarrow S(S) + G_t$
> State s value: $V(s) = S(s)/N(s)$
> When $N(s) \rightarrow \infty$, $V(s) \rightarrow v_\pi(s)$ so try as many episodes as you can to get as close as possible to the real state s value.

Method 2: Each time the following approach (the only difference between method 1 and method 2 is step 3.i) is used with policy for each episode, every time that the agent arrives at S counts.

1. Initialize the policy and state–value function.
2. Generate an episode using the current policy.
   i. Save and track the states encountered through that episode.

3. Choose a state saved in step 2.i.

    i. Create a list and add the return received posterior to every occurrence of this state to this list.

    ii. Calculate the average of all returns.

    iii. Assign $V(S_t)$ = computed average.

4. Repeat step 3.

5. Repeat steps 2–4 until real state s value is reached.

Method 3: In an incremental approach, for each state S_t in the episode, there is a reward G_t. The average value of the state $V(S_t)$ is calculated by the following formula for every time S_t appears (Equations 11.9 and 11.10):

$$N(s) \leftarrow N(s) + 1 \tag{11.9}$$

$$V(S_t) \leftarrow V(S_t) + \frac{1}{N(S_t)}\left[G_t - V(S_t)\right] \tag{11.10}$$

In nonstationary problems, it can be useful to track a running mean, that is, forget old episodes (Equation 11.11):

$$V(S_t) \leftarrow V(S_t) + \alpha\left(G_t - V(S_t)\right) \tag{11.11}$$

By this approach the progress happening in each episode can be easily understood by converting the mean return into an incremental update. Hence the mean can be updated with each episode easily.

Step 2—Policy improvement: The policy is improved by making it greedy in relation to the current value function. A greedy policy model is not required in this instance, because of the presence of an action-value function. A greedy policy (like the one mentioned previously) will always favor a certain action if most actions are not explored properly. There are two solutions for this.

11.4.2.2 *Finding the Optimal Policy Using Monte Carlo*

In dynamic programming, the policy improvement by the model of the environment is as shown in the following equation, which determines the optimal policy by searching actions that maximize the sum of rewards (Equation 11.12):

$$\pi'(s) = \operatorname*{argmax}_a \sum_{s'.r} p(s',r \mid s,a)\left[r + \gamma v_\pi(s')\right] \tag{11.12}$$

The policy is improved by making it greedy in relation to the current value function. A greedy policy model is not required in this instance because of the presence of an action-value function (Equation 11.13).

$$\pi(s) = \operatorname*{argmax}_a q(s,a) \tag{11.13}$$

A greedy policy, as given in the preceding equation, will always favour a certain action if the majority of actions are not thoroughly studied. There are two possible Monte Carlo learning approaches for the situation explained previously.

11.4.2.3 Monte Carlo with Fresh Exploration

In this procedure, all state–action pairs have a probability greater than zero of being the initial pair. This will ensure that each episode will place the agent to a new condition, allowing for greater environmental exploration.

11.4.2.4 Monte Carlo with Continual Exploration

In a few situations there may be an environment with a single starting point which may require continual exploration. In this approach all the actions are attempted with $1 - epsilon$ (nonzero) probability. An action that maximizes the action value function is selected, and an action is selected at random with probability epsilon.

The Monte Carlo approach to reinforcement learning can update only after a complete episode. This is an important drawback since it does not fully utilize the MDP learning task. This drawback is overcome by the temporal difference (TD) method, which utilizes the MDP structure to the fullest extent. In the following subsection we shall discuss the temporal difference learning approach.

11.4.3 Temporal Difference Learning

The temporal difference learning approach is a combination of deep programming and MC. The temporal difference (TD) method uses the observed reward R_{t+1} at time $t + 1$ and calculates the temporal difference target $R_{t+1}+V(S_{t+1})$, updating $V(S_t)$ with TD error. That is, the TD method only needs to wait until the next time step. By replacing G_t in the MC approach given in Equation (11.11) with an estimated return $R_{t+1}+V(S_{t+1})$, the TD action value equation will look as shown in Equation (11.14):

$$V\left(S_t\right) \leftarrow V\left(S_t\right) + \alpha\left[R_{t+1} + \gamma V\left(S_{t+1}\right) - V\left(S_t\right)\right] \tag{11.14}$$

where, $R_{t+1}+V(S_{t+1})$ is called the TD target value and $R_{t+1}+V(S_{t+1})-V(S_t)$ is called the TD error. While the MC strategy employs exact G_t for updating, the TD approach estimates value using the Bellman optimality equation and then updates the estimated value with the goal value.

Different forms of temporal difference approaches like Q-learning, SARSA, and deep Q-networks are discussed in the following subsections.

11.4.3.1 Q-learning

Q-learning is a type of reinforcement learning which uses action values or expected rewards for an action taken in a particular condition, called Q-values, with which the behavior of agent will be improved iteratively (Figure 11.3). It is also called "model free" since it handles problems with stochastic transitions and rewards without any adaptations, that is, it does not require a model of the environment. Q-learning provides an optimal policy for

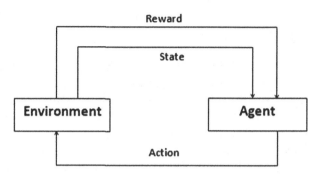

FIGURE 11.3
Components of Q-learning.

any finite MDP by maximizing the anticipated value of the total reward across all successive steps, beginning with the present state. $Q(S, A)$ estimates how well an action A works at the state S. $Q(S, A)$ will be estimated using TD-Update.

Q-learning is a reinforcement learning policy that will find the next best action, given a current state. It chooses this action at random and aims to maximize the reward. The purpose of the model is to determine the optimal course of action given the current situation.

The model aims to find the next best action in the context of the current state. The objective is to maximize the reward, for which the model chooses the action randomly or apply its own rules, thus deviating from the given policy. This means that the necessity of a policy is not mandatory.

There are three important parameters considered in Q-learning: transition function (T), reward function (R), and value function (V). Q-learning is preferred to obtain an optimal solution from a series of actions and states following value iteration, since the maximum values for unknown parameters cannot be identified. In other words, q-values are computed in place of iterations of maximum value. Below is a typical formula (Equation 11.15):

$$Q_{k+1}(s,a) = s'T(s,a,s')\left[R(s,a,s') + \max_{a'} Q(s',a')\right]$$
(11.15)

where $Q_{k+1}(s,a)$ is the iterated function with states s and action a by considering the summation values of parameters T and R along with a discount factor. The apostrophes denote an update function is incorporated all along the process.

The preceding equation is the foundation for Q-learning. In addition to an optimal policy for the RL outcomes, the update function in the parameters also incorporates an optimal policy. For issues with a highly unpredictable environment, the equation can be adjusted to include even RL notions like exploration and exploitation.

In a typical MDP, the T and R parameters are unknown, and Q-learning is best suited for such applications where knowledge of T and R are not known.

Example: Advertisement recommendation systems use Q-learning. Normal advertisement recommendations are based on past purchases or websites visited. You'll get brand recommendations if you buy a TV. The advertisement suggestion system is optimized by using Q-learning to recommend frequently bought products. Reward is assigned depending on the number of user clicks on the product suggested.

Q-learning algorithm: The step involved in Q-learning is shown in the flowchart shown in Figure 11.4. The steps are explained as follows:

1. **Initialization**: Q is initialized to an arbitrary fixed value. Then, at each time t, the agent selects an action a_t, observes a reward r_t, enters a new state s_{t+1} depending on the previous state s_t and the selected action, and the Q is finally updated. The crux of the Q-learning algorithm is a Bellman equation given in Figure 11.5.

   The state's value and the importance of whether to consider it or not is determined by the preceding Bellman equation. An agent uses the equation to decide its next state using various factors like Q value, learning rate, reward, discounted rate, and maximum expected future reward. The learning rate of the model estimates the speed.

2. **Finding the best solution**: As the algorithm executes, the agent will pass by various solutions and will take multiple paths. The best among these solutions is determined by using a table called the Q-table which will be used for storing the findings. The steps used for constructing a Q-table are as follows:

   Step 1: Create an initial Q-table where the values of all states and rewards are set to 0.

   Step 2: Select an action and carry it out. Update the table's values.

   Step 3: Obtain the reward's value and compute the Q-value using the Bellman equation.

   Step 4: Repeat until the table is full or an episode concludes.

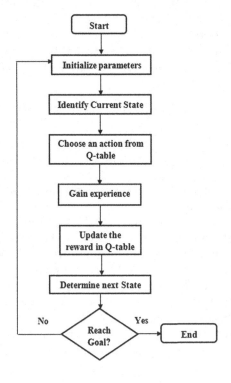

FIGURE 11.4
Flow diagram of Q-learning.

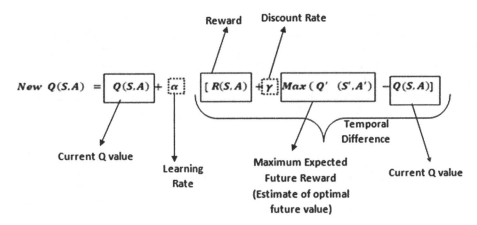

FIGURE 11.5
Bellman equation.

Until the state s_{t+1} is a terminal or final state, the algorithmic episode will continue. Nonepisodic tasks may be used for further learning by the algorithm. If the discount factor is less than 1, even if the problem contains infinite loops, the action values are finite. The $Q(s_f, a)$ is never changed for all final states s_f; it is always set to the reward value r seen for state s_f. $Q(s_f, a)$ can typically be assumed as zero.

Figure 11.5 shows the components of the Bellman equation, namely current Q value, learning rate, reward, discount rate, and maximum expected future reward. The variables in the Bellman equation that greatly influences the outcome are as follows:

1. Learning rate or step size (α): The factor that decides to what extent newly obtained information overrides old information is the learning rate or step size. A factor of 0 indicates that the agent learns exclusively from prior knowledge while a factor of 1 indicates that the agent considers only the most recently acquired information. Normally, α is set to a value of 0.1.

2. Discount factor (γ): The factor that decides the importance of rewards in the distant future relative to rewards in the immediate future is the discount factor γ. When $\gamma = 0$, the learning agent will be concerned only about rewards in the immediate future. In other words, this factor is a way to scale down the rewards as the learning proceeds.

3. Initial conditions (Q_0): Forecasting behavior of an agent will be good if the agent is capable of resetting its initial conditions without assuming any random initial condition (AIC).

However, the major drawback is that only discrete action and state spaces are supported by the typical Q-learning technique (using a Q table). Due to the curse of dimensionality, discretization of these values results in ineffective learning.

11.4.3.2 State–Action–Reward–State–Action (SARSA)

Another method used by reinforcement learning for learning a MDP policy is state–action–reward–state–action (SARSA). The original name of this method was modified connectionist Q-learning" (MCQ-L), later renamed as SARSA by Rich Sutton.

As the name indicates, the function for updating the Q-value is determined by the present state S, of the agent. The sequence that occurs is as follows: agent chooses an action A and subsequent reward R for choosing A; agent enters the state S' after taking that action A, and finally the next action A' that the agent chooses in its new state (Figure 11.6). This sequence is represented as a quintuple $<s_t, a_t, r_t, s_{t+1}, a_{t+1}>$ and hence the name SARSA.

Table 11.2 gives the differences between SARSA and Q-learning approaches. SARSA is an on-policy learning algorithm since it updates the policy based on actions taken. The SARSA algorithm is shown in Figure 11.7.

The policy is updated based on action taken when SARSA agent interacts with the environment. As per the algorithm given previously, first all parameters are initialized to zero. Then for each state S in an episode an action a is chosen using policy derived from Q (ε-greedy). Execute the chosen action a and observe the reward R and the corresponding new

FIGURE 11.6
SARSA representation.

TABLE 11.2

Differences Between SARSA and Q-Learning

SARSA	Q-Learning
Chooses an action following the same current policy and updates its Q-values	Chooses the greedy action and follows an optimal policy, that is, the action that gives the maximum Q-value for the state.
Follows on-policy approach	Follows the off policy approach
The current state–action pair and the next state–action pair are used for calculating time difference	When passing the reward from the next state to the current state, the maximum possible reward of the new state is taken, ignoring policy used

Algorithm: SARSA for estimating Q
1. Initialize Q(s0,a0); for all s ε S, a ε A(s), arbitrarily, and Q(terminal-state)=0
2. for each episode:
    2.1   Initialize S0
    2.2   Choose a and s using policy derived from Q (e.g., ε-greedy)
    2.3   Repeat (for each step of episode)
        2.3.1 Take action a, observe R, s'
        2.3.2 Choose a' from s' using policy derived from Q (e.g., ε-greedy)
        2.3.3 $Q_{new}(s_t, a_t) \leftarrow Q(s_t, a_t) + \alpha [R_t + \gamma Q(s_{t+1}, a_{t+1}) - Q(s_t, a_t)]$
              $s \leftarrow s'; a \leftarrow a'$
        Until S is terminal_state

FIGURE 11.7
SARSA algorithm.

state s'. Then choose the subsequent action a' for the new state s'. The Q value for a state–action is updated by an error, adjusted by the learning rate α as given in Equation (11.15).

$$Q^{\text{new}}\left(s_t,a_t\right) \leftarrow Q\left(s_t,a_t\right) + \propto \left[r_t + \gamma Q\left(s_{t+1},a_{t+1}\right) - Q\left(s_t,a_t\right)\right] \tag{11.15}$$

where Q values represent the potential reward obtained in the next time step for doing action a in state s, in addition to the discounted future reward gained from the next state–activity observation.

The parameters α, γ and the initial conditions $Q(S_0, a_0)$ greatly influence the Q value and determine the outcomes. SARSA implicitly assumes a low (infinite) initial value, also known as "optimistic initial conditions." The first time an action is taken the reward is used to set the value of Q. This allows immediate learning in the case of fixed deterministic rewards.

11.4.3.3 Deep Q-Networks (DQN)

Google DeepMind patented "deep reinforcement learning" or "deep Q-learning," an application of Q-learning to deep learning in 2014 that can play Atari 2600 games at expert human levels.

Deep neural networks are considered to be the best solution for handling high-dimensional continuous states in Q-tables. Deep neural networks can extract complicated characteristics automatically (as will be discussed in detail in succeeding chapters).

Deep Q-Network is a type of algorithm which is a combination of deep learning and reinforcement learning. This integrated approach helps DQN to directly learn strategies from high-dimensional raw data. In fact, DQN has increased the scope of reinforcement learning and its application domains by combining convolutional neural network (CNN) with Q-Learning. CNN's input is the original visual data (as the state), and its output is the value evaluation corresponding to each action (Q value).

In deep Q-learning, the Q-value function is approximated using a neural network. As input, the state is provided, and as output, the Q-values of all feasible actions are computed. The contrast between Q-learning and deep Q-learning is beautifully exemplified subsequently. The input states are mapped to Q-value–action pairs by the neural network rather than mapping a state–action pair to a Q (Figure 11.8).

In deep Q-Learning, the neural network maps input states to (action, Q-value) pairs. The steps involved in the deep Q-network learning algorithm are summarized as gfollows (Figure 11.9):

1. Initialize the primary and secondary neural networks.

2. Using the epsilon–greedy exploration strategy, select a course of action.

3. Using the Bellman equation, revise the network's weights.

   Step 1: Initialize the networks. Deep Q-learning uses two neural networks, the main network and target network, in the learning process. The two networks have the same architecture but use different weights. The weights from the main network are copied to the target network in each of the N steps. Usage of two networks results in improved stability and effective learning. The design of two neural networks is as follows (Figure 11.9):

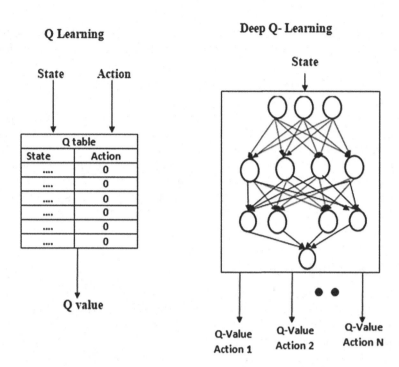

FIGURE 11.8
Q-learning Versus Deep Q-learning.

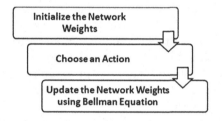

FIGURE 11.9
Steps in deep Q-learning.

i.   Target or prediction network: The target network's input is the current state, the first sample element s. Each action's output is q. Each output's q value determines the agent's next state. This network's parameters are always updatable.

ii. Q-network or evaluation network: The following state, s', in the sample sequence is the input to the main network. Each action's Q value (Q_{next}) is output. The Bellman equation determines the target Q value for action a in state s (q target = r + * max (q next)). The evaluation network's output passes via the Bellman equation, and the target q value is used as the prediction network's label.

In DQL, the agent remembers all of its past interactions and then takes the next step that is determined by the Q-output. The Q-value at state S_t is gained by the Q-network. At the same time the target network (neural network) calculates the Q-value for state S_{t+1} (next state). This is done to have a stabilized training. Any abrupt increments in Q-value count are stopped by copying it as training data on each iterated Q-value of the Q-network. This process is as shown in Figure 11.10.

Step 2: Select a course of action using the epsilon–greedy exploration strategy. In the epsilon–greedy exploration strategy, the agent selects a random action with probability epsilon and then exploits the best-known action with probability 1 – epsilon. The output actions of both the networks are mapped to the input states. The projected Q-value of the model is really represented by these output actions. In this instance, the best-known action in that state is the one with the biggest projected Q-value.

Step 3: Using the Bellman equation, revise the network's weights. The agent performs the chosen action and as per the Bellman equation updates the main and target networks. Replay is used by deep Q-learning and is the act of saving and playing back game states such as the state, action, reward, and next state, which is then used for learning by the reinforcement learning algorithm. To increase the performance level of the agent, deep Q-learning uses experience replay to learn in small batches. Experience replay is actually storing the previous experiences to learn.

This learning approach will ensure the avoidance of skewed data set distribution that the neural network will see. Importantly, the agent does not need to train after each step. The neural network is updated with the new temporal difference target using the Bellman equation. The main objective in deep Q-learning is to replicate the temporal difference target operation using neural networks rather than using a Q-table. The following

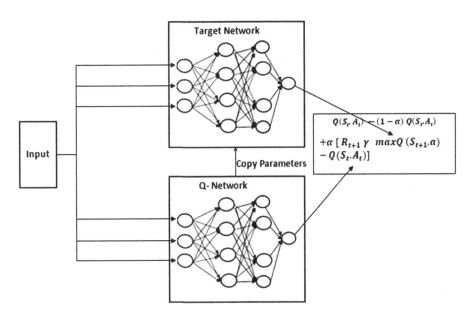

FIGURE 11.10
DQL process.

equation illustrates how the temporal difference target is calculated using the target network rather than the main network (Equation 11.16).

$$Q_{\text{target}} = \left(R_t + \lambda^* \max_a Q\left(S_{t+1}, a\right) \right)$$ (11.16)

The target network uses experience replay for training, and Q-network uses it for calculation of Q-value. The loss is calculated by the squared difference of targeted Q-value and predicted Q-value as per the preceding equation. This is performed only for the training of the Q-network just before the copying of parameters to the target network. The DQN loss expectation can be minimized using stochastic gradient descent. If only the last transition is used, Q-learning is used.

11.5 Asynchronous Reinforcement Learning

Online RL algorithms depend on anticipated data in the present instant. This implies that rewards are contingent on the actions made on the data, and that changes to these algorithms occur in increments. Researchers have endeavored to enhance this procedure by incorporating a stage known as experience replay. However, this has a negative impact on computational resources such as memory and processing capacity, as well as other difficulties such as older RL policy data.

In order to address this issue, asynchronous (separate, parallel computer processes) solutions are developed. In this case, the approach enables numerous agents to act rather than relying on multiple instances in real life. It also facilitates the correlation of input and output data. In the earlier-mentioned paper, the asynchronous technique is applied to common RL algorithms, such as SARSA (state–action–reward–state–action), n-step Q-learning, and actor–critic methods. In addition, the computational advantages of asynchronous approaches are shown by proving that they function on a regular multi-core CPU as opposed to the powerful GPU typically employed in deep learning environments.

11.5.1 Asynchronous Reinforcement Learning Procedure

The actor–learner process is followed for creating an asynchronous RL framework (Figure 11.11). All the available actor–learners are analyzed, and exploration policies are applied on these learners.

The following asynchronous methods have been developed based on the preceding actor–learner procedure:

1. **Asynchronous one-step Q-learning**: In this approach, each thread analyses the gradient at each step of the Q-learning loss by referencing its copy in the computing environment. This reduces the likelihood of overwriting during algorithm upgrades.

2. **Asynchronous one-step SARSA**: In this algorithm the target value for $Q(s, a)$ are derived based on Equation (11.17):

$$r + \gamma Q\left(s', a', \theta^-\right)$$ (11.17)

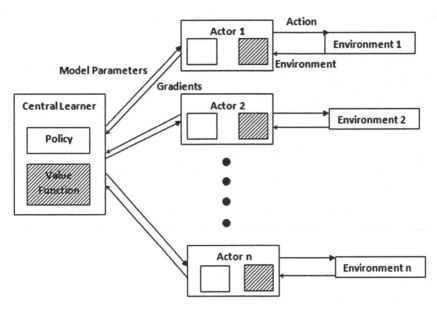

FIGURE 11.11
Asynchronous RL Procedure.

where a' is the action and s' is the state. Except this, it is same as the previous algorithm.

3. **Asynchronous n-step Q-learning:** This algorithm follows a "forward view" algorithm by computing n-step return. It uses the exploration policy for each state–action for a single update and then figures out the gradients for n-step Q-learning updates for each state–action.

4. **Asynchronous advantage actor–critic (A3C):** This algorithm follows the same "forward view" approach as the previous approach; however, it differs in terms of policy.

All these algorithms have proved to exhibit less training time and have been found more stable in terms of performance and learning rates.

11.6 Summary

- Outlined a brief introduction of reinforcement learning.
- Discussed the various action selection policies.
- Explained in detail the concepts of finite Markov decision processes.
- Described the various problem-solving methods such as dynamic programming, Monte Carlo methods, and temporal difference learning.
- Outlined three types of temporal difference learning methods, namely Q-learning, SARSA, and deep Q-networks.
- Gave a brief introduction to asynchronous reinforcement.

11.7 Points to Ponder

- Learning through interaction is a foundational idea underlying nearly all theories of learning and intelligence.
- Reinforcement learning learns how to behave in an environment by carrying out actions and seeing the effects of those actions.
- During reinforcement, the learning environment will receive the agent's action as an input and will output the ensuing state and a reward.
- Maximizing immediate reward is ineffective, and choosing the highest-valued action will cause the model to become stuck in local minima.
- Once a Markov decision process is linked with a policy, the action for each state is fixed, and the resulting system behaves like a Markov chain.
- At an abstract level, Monte Carlo simulation is a method of estimating the value of an unknown quantity with the help of inferential statistics.
- Q-learning uses action values or expected rewards for an action taken in a particular condition, called Q-values, with which the behavior of the agent will be improved iteratively.
- The asynchronous reinforcement learning approach enables numerous agents to act and facilitates the correlation of input and output data.

E.11 Exercises

E.11.1 Suggested Activities

E.11.1.1 Design three example tasks that fit into the reinforcement learning framework, identifying for each its states, actions, and rewards. Make the three examples as different from each other as possible.

E.11.1.2 Model human and animal behaviors as applications of reinforcement learning.

E.11.1.3 What policy would make on-policy and off-policy learning equivalent, specifically if we consider Q-learning and SARSA learning? In other words, what policy used by an agent will make the learning based on Q-learning and SARSA learning the same?

Self-Assessment Questions

E.11.2 Multiple Choice Questions

Give answers with justification for correct and wrong choices.

E.11.2.1 In reinforcement learning,
    i An agent learns how to behave in an environment by carrying out actions and seeing the effects of those actions
    ii An agent learns how to behave by seeing the effects of its actions
    iii An agent learns sees the effects of its actions

E.11.2.2 In reinforcement learning,
    i Decisions are independent from one another, hence each decision is labelled.
    ii Decisions are dependent, hence each decision is labelled.
    iii Decisions are dependent, hence sequences of dependent decisions are labelled.

E.11.2.3 _____ is an example of reinforcement learning.
    i Object recognition
    ii Playing chess
    iii Classification

E.11.2.4 Negative reinforcement is described as
    i Enhancing the intensity and frequency of the behavior due to an event that results from a certain behavior
    ii Strengthening of behavior due to the elimination or avoidance of a negative condition
    iii Weakening of behavior due to the elimination or avoidance of a negative condition

E.11.2.5 The policy dictates the actions that the reinforcement agent takes as a function of the agent's
    i State and the environment
    ii Action
    iii Environment

E.11.2.6 In a Markov decision process, the objective is to develop a good policy, which is a function Π. The function Π specifies
    i The action $\Pi(s)$ which the decision maker will select when in state s.
    ii The action $\Pi(s)$ is not fixed
    iii The reward which the decision maker will select when in state s

E.11.2.7 Given a Markov decision process representing an environment, dynamic programming refers to a group of methods that can be utilized to
    i Select actions
    ii Enhance that environment
    iii Derive optimal policies for that environment

E.11.2.8   At its abstract level, _____ is a method of estimating the value of an unknown
            quantity with the help of inferential statistics.
            i   Dynamic programming
            ii Monte Carlo method
            iii Temporal difference learning

E.11.2.9   In a Monte Carlo procedure with fresh exploration,
            i   There is a single starting point that requires exploration
            ii All state–action pairs have a probability greater than zero of being the ini-
                tial pair
            iii An action that maximizes the action value function is selected and an
                action is selected at random with given probability value.

E.11.2.10   All the following are temporal difference methods except
            i   Monte Carlo method
            ii Q-learning
            iii SARSA

E.11.2.11   SARSA is the abbreviation of
            i   System–Action–Robot–State–Action
            ii Stillberg–Anderson–Reward–State–Action
            iii State–Action–Reward–State–Action

E.11.2.12   The important parameters considered in Q-learning are
            i   Transfer function (T), reward function (R), and value function (V)
            ii Transition function (T), reward function ®, and value function (V)
            iii Transition function (T) and value function (V)

E.11.2.13   Q-learning is a reinforcement learning policy that will find the next best
            action, given
            i   A current state
            ii A current state and the reward
            iii The next state and reward

E.11.2.14   SARSA chooses a(n)
            i   Greedy action that gives the maximum Q-value for the state
            ii Action following the same current policy and updates its Q-values
            iii Action following a random policy and updates its Q-values

E.11.2.15   In deep Q-Learning, the agent remembers
            i   The immediate past interaction and then takes the next step that is deter-
                mined by the Q-output
            ii Only the current interaction and then takes the next step that is determined
                by the Q-output
            iii All of its past interactions and then takes the next step that is determined
                by the Q-output

E.11.3 Match the Columns

No		Match	
E.11.3.1	The variables in the Bellman equation that greatly influences the outcome are	A	Acquires knowledge directly from experience episodes
E.11.3.2	Q-learning	B	A course is selected using the epsilon–greedy exploration strategy
E.11.3.3	Asynchronous one-step Q-learning	C	Initial conditions, learning rate, and discount factor
E.11.3.4	Deep Q-learning	D	In chess choosing a piece for the next move that will result in a higher immediate reward
E.11.3.5	SARSA	E	Is the factor that decides the importance of rewards in the distant future relative to rewards in the immediate future
E.11.3.6	Discount factor	F	Chooses the greedy action and follows an optimal policy
E.11.3.7	Q-values	G	Refers to a group of methods that can be utilized to derive optimal policies for an environment, given a Markov decision process representing that environment
E.11.3.8	Monte Carlo approach for reinforcement learning	H	Expected rewards for an action taken in a particular condition
E.11.3.9	Dynamic programming	I	Each thread analyses the gradient at each step of the Q-learning loss by referencing its copy in the computing environment
E.11.3.10	Greedy policy	J	The original name was modified connectionist Q-learning (MCQ-L)

E.11.4 Short Questions

E.11.4.1   Explain the concept of reinforcement learning.

E.11.4.2   Give some typical applications of reinforcement learning.

E.11.4.3   Compare and contrast reinforcement learning and supervised learning.

E.11.4.4   Compare and contrast positive reinforcement learning and negative reinforcement learning.

E.11.4.5   When agents share the same set of activities, discuss the four techniques used for action selection.

E.11.4.6   Give a detailed description of the finite Markov decision process used for model-free reinforcement learning approaches.

E.11.4.7   Explain the dynamic programming approach to problem solving in the context of Monte Carlo reinforcement learning.

E.11.4.8   Explain the three approaches used by Monte Carlo approaches to calculate value functions.

E.11.4.9   Discuss the Q-learning algorithm in detail.

E.11.4.10   Give the Bellman equation and discuss its use in reinforcement learning.

E.11.4.11   Outline the SARSA algorithm for estimating Q-values.

E.11.4.12   Give a detailed note on deep Q-networks.

E.11.4.13   Explain how the Bellman equation is used to update weights in deep Q-networks.

E.11.4.14   Outline the four asynchronous reinforcement learning methods based on actor–learner procedure.

12

Machine Learning Applications: Approaches

12.1 Introduction

The first step in building machine learning applications is to understand when to use machine learning. Machine learning is not an answer to all types of problems. Generally, machine learning is used when the problem cannot be solved by employing deterministic rule-based solutions. This maybe because it is difficult to identify the rules, when the rules depend on too many factors or may be overlapping. Another situation where you use machine learning is when handling large-scale problems. In essence, good problems for machine learning are those that are difficult to solve using traditional programming. Machine learning needs a different perspective to understanding and thinking about problems. Now rather than using a mathematical basis such as logic, machine learning makes us think in terms of statistics and probability.

Machine learning allows us to effectively identify trends and patterns, allows a maximum amount of automation once the machine learning model is built, and enables continuous improvement in accuracy and efficiency as machine learning algorithms gain experience and are effective in handling multi-dimensional, multi-variety, and dynamic data. However, machine learning also requires massive unbiased, good quality data sets for training, needs time and computational resources, and requires the ability to interpret the results obtained from the machine learning system.

12.2 Machine Learning Life Cycle

Building ML applications is an iterative process that involves a sequence of steps, as shown in Figure 12.1.

Machine learning uses a large amount of available data to train the models so that the organization can take advantage of machine learning algorithms to derive a practical business value. Development of machine learning applications constantly requires tuning parameters, evaluation with new data sets, new algorithms, and so on to enhance the model accuracy.

DOI: 10.1201/9781003290100-12

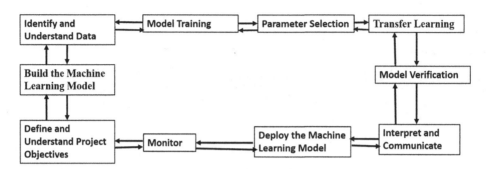

FIGURE 12.1
Machine learning life cycle.

- **Define and understand project objectives**: The first step of the life cycle is to iden-tify an opportunity to tangibly improve operations, increase customer satisfaction, or otherwise create value. We need to frame a machine learning problem in terms of what we want to predict and what kind of input data we have to make those pre-dictions. We need to identify and define the success criteria for the project such as acceptable parameters for accuracy, precision, and confusion matrix values as well the importance of ethical issues such as transparency, explainability, or bias reduc-tion while solving the problem. We also need to understand the constraints under which we operate such as the data storage capacity, whether the prediction needs to be fast as in the case of autonomous driving, or whether the learning needs to be fast.

- **Build the machine learning model**: The choice of the machine learning model depends on the application. A variety of machine learning models are available, such as the supervised models including classification models, regression mod-els, unsupervised models including clustering models, and reinforcement learning models. There is no one solution or one approach that fits all. Some problems are very specific and require a unique approach such as a recommendation system while some other problems are very open and need a trial-and-error approach such as classification and regression. Other factors that help us decide the model are the requirements of the application scenario including the available computational time and training time, size, quality, and nature of data such as linearity, number of parameters, and number of features, and finally accuracy and training time.

- **Identify and understand data**: Depending on the domain of application and the goal of machine learning, data come from applications such as manufacturing com-panies, financial firms, online services and applications, hospitals, social media, and so on, either in the form of historical databases or as open data sets. The next step is to collect and prepare all of the relevant data for use in machine learning. The machine learning process requires large data during the learning stage since the larger the size of data, the better the predictive power. We need to standardize the formats across different data sources, normalize or standardize data into the formatted range, and often enhance and augment data. Sometimes we need to con-sider anonymizing data. Feature selection is dependent on the most discriminative dimensions. Finally, we need to split data into training, test, and validation sets. Sometimes raw data may not reveal all the facts about the targeted label. Feature engineering is a technique to create additional features combining two or more existing features with an arithmetic operation that is more relevant and sensible.

Understanding the type and kind of data plays a key role in deciding which algorithm to use. For this purpose, we need to analyze and visualize the data; carry out preprocessing, profiling, and cleansing of the data; and transform the data to a state for modelling by carrying out feature engineering. Often the number of features and volume of data decides the algorithm to be used. When we have a small number of features but large volume of data, we need to choose low bias/high variance algorithms like KNN, decision trees, or kernel SVM, and when we have a large number of features but less volume of data we need to choose algorithms with high bias/low variance like linear regression, naïve Bayes, or linear SVM. When we have a large number of features as well as large volume of data, we need to carry out dimensionality reduction before applying machine learning.

- **Model training**: This stage is concerned with creating a model from the data given to it. In order to gain insights from your data with machine learning, you must determine your **target** variable, the factor on which you wish to gain deeper understanding. Part of the training data is used to find model parameters such as the coefficients of a polynomial or weights to minimize the error in modelling the given data set. The remaining data are then used to test the model as we need to monitor how well a model generalizes to unseen data. Training and testing are repeatedly carried out to improve the performance of the model. Now, the algorithm will learn the pattern and mapping between the feature and the label. The learning can be linear or nonlinear depending upon the activation function and algorithm. There are a few hyper-parameters that affect the learning as well as training time such as learning rate, regularization, batch size, number of passes (epoch), optimization algorithm, and more.

- **Parameter selection**: This step involves the selection of the parameters associated with the training, called hyper-parameters. These parameters control the effectiveness of the training process and hence, ultimately, the performance of the model.

- **Transfer learning**: Reusing machine learning models across various domains can significantly reduce training time for new domains. The transfer of models across domains is not a direct process but can provide a starting point.

- **Model verification**: Model verification is concerned with determining whether the learned model can be used for the application under consideration. This stage of the machine learning life cycle needs to check whether the model is working properly when treated with novel, hitherto unseen inputs. The confusion matrix values are determined for classification problems. Further fine-tuning of the hyper-parameters is carried out for optimal performance.

- When a model is doing well on the training data but not on the validation data, it is the overfitting scenario. Somehow the model is not generalizing well. The solution for the problem includes regularizing the algorithm, decreasing input features, eliminating the redundant features, and using resampling techniques like k-fold cross-validation. In the underfitting scenario, a model does poorly on both training and validation data sets. The solution to this may include training with more data, evaluating different algorithms or architectures, using more passes, or experimenting with learning rate or optimization algorithm.

- **Interpret and communicate**: One of the most difficult tasks of machine learning projects is explaining a model's outcomes to those without any data science background, particularly in highly regulated industries such as health care. Traditionally, machine learning has been thought of as a "black box" because it is difficult to interpret insights and communicate the value of those insights to stakeholders and regulatory bodies. The more interpretable your model, the easier it will be to meet regulatory requirements and communicate its value to management and other key stakeholders.

- **Deploy the machine learning model**: When we are confident that the machine learning model can work in the real world, it's time to see how it actually operates in the real world, also known as "operationalizing" the model. During the deployment stage of the machine learning life cycle, the machine learning models are integrated for the application to test whether proper functionality of the model is achieved after deployment. The models should be deployed in such a way that they can be used for inference as well as enable regular upgradation. Model deployment often poses a problem because of the coding and data science experience it requires and because the time-to-implementation from the beginning of the cycle using traditional data science methods is prohibitively long.

- **Monitor**: Monitoring ensures proper operation of the model during the complete lifespan and involves management, safety, and updating of the application using the model.

12.3 Choosing a Machine Learning Algorithm for a Problem

First of all, we should understand that no one machine learning algorithm or one approach fits all. There are several factors that decide the choice of a machine learning algorithm. There are some problems that are very specific and require a unique approach, an example being the recommendation system. Some other problems are very open and need a trial-and-error approach. Problems that require supervised learning, classification, and regression are very open. Some of the issues to be considered are the type of answer or prediction you want from your past data, the requirements of your application scenario, and the available computational time and training time. Size, quality, and nature of data such as linearity, number of parameters, and number of features are important, and accuracy, training time, and ease of use are also important in choosing the machine learning model. While many users consider accuracy first, beginners tend to focus on algorithms that they are familiar with. Let us discuss some machine learning algorithms in terms of whether they are suitable for classification and/or regression, their basis, interpretability, the size of data they can handle, and in terms of their accuracy, training time, and prediction time as given in Table 12.1.

TABLE 12.1

Characteristics of Machine Learning Algorithms in Terms of Application

Algorithm	Machine Learning Task	Basis	Interpretability	Data Size	Accuracy	Training Time	Prediction Time
Naïve Bayes	Classification	Probabilistic	Medium	Large	Large	Medium	Low
Logical regression		Parametric	High	Small	Small	Low	Low
Linear regression	Regression		High	Small	Small	Low	Low
Neural networks	Classification/regression		Low	Large	Large	High	Low
Decision tree							
Random forest		Rule based	High	Medium	Medium	High	Low
			Low	Large	Large	High	Medium
K-nearest neighbour		Distance-based	Medium	Medium	Medium	Medium	High
Support vector machine		Nonparametric	Medium	Large	Large	Medium	Low

12.4 Machine Learning and Its Applications

One way to categorize applications of machine learning is to consider applications that are generic and can be used across domains and other applications that are domain oriented. In this chapter we will discuss some generic applications such as natural language processing, computer vision, and anomaly detection and recommendation systems. In the next chapter we will discuss applications of machine learning in specific domains.

12.5 Machine Learning for Natural Language Processing

First let us give a brief review about natural language processing (NLP). The goal of NLP is to make computers understand human language. NLP is considered a difficult problem to tackle since it requires understanding both the individual words and concepts and the way these concepts are connected to deliver the intended message.

In this chapter we will be considering some typical components of NLP and how they are tackled using machine learning. The various components of NLP include morphological analysis, part-of-speech (POS) tagging, syntactic analysis, word sense disambiguation, named-entity recognition, semantic analysis, and discourse analysis. Some typical applications of NLP include information retrieval, text classification, information extraction and summarization, question answering, machine translation, sentiment analysis, and dialogue systems. We will be discussing only some of these components and applications and outline the role of machine learning in tackling them.

- **Text classification**: Text classification is an important component which is based on NLP techniques. Text classification is used to find whether an email is spam or not, the language of the document, whether the document is interesting to a user, for news filtering and organization, information retrieval, and so on. Text categorization can be of two types: single-label text categorization, where exactly one category is assigned to each document, or multi-label text categorization, where a number of categories can be assigned to the same document. A classifier is built for each category C based on the characteristics of a set of documents manually classified under C, and from these characteristics the learner extracts the characteristics that a new unseen document should have in order to be classified under C. Given a set of training documents $d_1, d_2, \ldots d_n$ manually labelled with one of the classes $C_1, C_2, \ldots C_k$, the feature vectors corresponding to each document are obtained and labelled with the corresponding class. These labelled feature vectors are used by the machine learning algorithm to build a classification model. Then when we get a new document d_{new}, its feature vector is built, which is given to the classification model to obtain the predicted class. The strengths of the machine learning approach are that the learning process is domain independent and the inductive process can be repeated if the set of categories changes by replacing the training set. Documents are usually represented as a bag of words in high-dimensional space where we use either all the words after some preprocessing like stop-word removal, or only the most frequent words. In vector space classification, the training set corresponds to a labelled set of points (equivalently, vectors), and the assumptions are that documents in the same class form a contiguous region of space and documents from different classes do not overlap, and learning the classifier is the building of surfaces to delineate classes in the space.

The naïve Bayesian classification, the simplest classification method, treats each document as a "bag of words." The generative model makes the following further assumptions: that words of a document are generated independently of context given the class label and the naïve Bayes independence assumption that the probability of a word is independent of its position in the document. Other supervised classification methods include k-nearest neighbours, decision trees, and support vector machines, all of which require hand-classified training data. Many commercial systems use a mixture of methods.

- **POS tagging**: POS tagging assigns words in a text with a morph syntactic tag, based on the lexical definition and form of the word and the context in which the word occurs. POS tagging is an initial step in many NLP tasks including parsing, text classification, information extraction and retrieval, text to speech systems, and so on. The POS categories are based on morphological properties (affixes they take) as well as distributional properties (the context in which the word occurs).

Example 12.1: POS

The boys have to **play (verb)** on this ground now.
The actors in the **play (noun)** were good.

In this chapter we will discuss the probabilistic learning based sequential approach—the hidden Markov model (HMM) approach to POS tagging. The HMM approach can be trained on an available human annotated corpora like the Penn Treebank. Here we assume an underlying set of **hidden** (unobserved, latent) states in which the model can be (e.g., parts of speech) and probabilistic transitions between states over time (e.g., transition from POS to another POS as sequence is generated). We are given a sentence of n words $w_1...w_n$ (an "observation" or "sequence of observations"); we need to find the best sequence of n tags $t_1...t_n$ that corresponds to this sequence of observations such that $P(t_1...t_n|w_1...w_n)$ is highest. Here we use n-gram models to determine the context in which the word to be tagged occurs. In POS tagging the preceding $N-1$ predicted tags along with the unigram estimate for the current word is used (Figure 12.2).

In HMM tagging the tags corresponds to an HMM state and words correspond to the HMM alphabet symbols in order to find the most likely sequence of tags (states) given the sequence of words (observations). However, we need tag (state) transition probabilities $p(t_i|t_{i-1})$ and word likelihood probabilities (symbol emission probabilities) $p(w_i|t_i)$, which

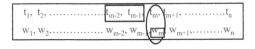

FIGURE 12.2
Sequences of words and tags.

we can determine using the hand tagged corpus, or if there is no tagged corpus then through parameter estimation (Baum–Welch algorithm).

- **Text summarization**: Text summarization can be defined as the process of condensing a document without sacrificing important informational content. Supervised techniques for summarization use features of sentences that make them good candidates for inclusion in the summary for learning. Features used include surface features such as position and length of sentence, content features such as statistics of important content words, and relevant features that exploit inter-sentence relationship such as similarity of the sentence with the title or first sentence in the document. The SVM method is used to find the importance of a sentence based on these features. Sentences are then ranked, and top ranked sentences are included in the summary. Another supervised technique uses topic signatures that are learned using a set of documents preclassified as relevant or nonrelevant for each topic. Topic signatures are then used to find the topic of the text. Sentences are then ranked for selection for summary according to the sum of weights of terms relevant to the topic in the sentence.

  An unsupervised technique such as TextRank and LexRank model the document as a graph and uses an algorithm similar to Google's PageRank algorithm to find top-ranked sentences. Sentences in the text are modelled as vertices of the graph, and two vertices are connected if there exists a similarity relation between them. Here the notion of centrality in social networks is used; that is, a sentence should be highly ranked if it is recommended by many other highly ranked sentences since it is likely to be more informative. After the ranking algorithm is run on the graph, sentences are sorted in reverse order of their score, and the top ranked sentences are selected.

- **Sentiment analysis**: Sentiment analysis is also called opinion extraction, opinion mining, sentiment mining, or subjectivity analysis. With the proliferation of online activity, sentiment analysis has become one of the most important applications of NLP. It is used to review a movie as positive or negative, rate products based on user reviews, find public sentiment such as customer confidence, find opinion of people about a candidate, or predict election results or market trends from sentiment. The first work on sentiment analysis was polarity detection of whether an IMDB movie review is positive or negative. Sentiment classification classifies text based on the overall sentiments expressed and can be carried out at different levels such as document, sentence, or feature based. Sentiment analysis can be formulated as text classification, which analyses the text and tells whether the underlying sentiment is positive, negative, or neutral. A basic machine learning approach to sentiment analysis first carries out tokenization and feature extraction. Classification can be carried out using naïve Bayes, MaxEnt, or SVM methods. SVMs are a widely used machine learning technique for creating feature-vector-based sentiment classifiers which does not assume feature independence but requires annotated training data. Now the features of the text used for sentiment analysis are words (bag of words), n-grams, parts of speech, opinion words (obtained from a dictionary), valence intensifiers (very), and shifters (for negation handling) and syntactic dependency. Features are selected based on frequency, information gain, mutual information, and feature weighting is carried out based on term presence or term frequency, inverse document frequency, and/or term position such as title. The basic idea is based on POS and co-occurrence where frequent nouns or noun phrases are found and then the opinion words associated with them (obtained from a dictionary; for example, for positive *good, clear, interesting* or for negative *bad, dull, boring*) and nouns co-occurring with these opinion words, which can be infrequent. One lexical resource developed for sentiment analysis is SentiWordNet, which attached sentiment-related information with WordNet synsets. Each term has a positive, negative, and objective score summing up to one.

12.6 Recommendation Systems

Recommendation systems are one class of machine learning task which deals with ranking or rating products, users, or in general entities, or in other words predicts the ratings an user might give to a specific entity. The goal of recommendation systems is to create a ranked list of items that caters to the user's interest. Machine learning driven recommendation systems today drive almost every aspect of our life: two-thirds of the movies watched online recommended by Netflix and 35% of items purchased online recommended by Amazon, while news recommendations by Google News generate 38% more click through. In other words, in case the user does not find the product, the product finds you by giving an appropriate search term taken implicitly. The value of recommendation systems is they can help in upselling, cross selling, and even providing new products. The recommender problem can be stated as the estimation of a short list of items that fits a user's interests or in other words the estimation of a utility function that automatically predicts how a user will like an item. This estimation is generally based on features such as past behavior, relations to other users, item similarity, context, and so on.

12.6.1 Basics of Recommendation Systems

Normally a recommendation system is associated with two core aspects, namely a user model that can be described by ratings, preferences, situational context, and so on and items which can be with or without description of item characteristics. The objective is to find the relevance score that can be used for ranking which is then used to generate a ranked list of recommended items. However, note that the relevance can be context dependent and the characteristics of the list such as diversity itself may be important.

The goal of recommendation systems is to serve the right item to a user in a given context to optimize long-term business objectives. It is a discipline that involves large-scale machine learning and statistics. In some scenarios, natural language processing may be used to understand content and recommend topics, "aboutness," entities, breaking news, and so on.

The most important factor affecting recommendation systems are the items that are recommended and can be articles, ads, modules, movies, users, updates, and so on. The next important aspect is the context such as query keywords, pages, mobile, social media, and so on. The next factor is the metric that is used for optimization such as relevance score, click through rate (CTR), revenue, or engagement. Currently, most applications are single-objective, but there can be multi-objective optimization where X can be maximized subject to Y, Z, and so on where objectives may include click rates (CTR), engagement, advertising revenue, diversity, inferring user interest, and constructing user profiles. Another important aspect are the characteristics of the item pool such as size (do we consider all web pages or some n stories) and quality of the pool or lifetime (mostly old items vs. mostly new items). Properties of the context such as whether it is pull based, specified by an explicit user driven query (e.g., keywords, form) or push based, specified by implicit context (e.g., page, user), or hybrid push–pull based. Properties of the feedback on the matches made are also important. These include types and semantics of feedback (such as click or vote), latency (such as available in 5 minutes versus 1 day), or the volume considered. Other factors include the constraints specifying legitimate matches such as business rules, diversity rules, editorial voice, and so on and the available metadata about links between users, items, and so on.

12.6.2 Utility Matrix and Recommendation Systems

Basically, a recommender system can be assumed to consist of two entities, usually users and items. Let us assume we are dealing with m users and n items. Items can vary from books to products, movies, investment choices, future friends, courses in e-learning, and so on. The basis of the recommendation system is a two-dimensional $m \times n$ **utility matrix** or preference matrix which consists of the rating (or preference) for each user–item pair (Figure 12.3). Initially, this matrix may be very sparse because the ratings are available only for a limited number of user–item pairs. In recommendation systems the goal is to fill the empty entries of this utility matrix or in other words estimate a utility function or rating that automatically predicts how a user will like an item.

12.6.3 Issues Associated with Recommendation Systems

12.6.3.1 Construction of Utility Matrix

One of the first issues associated with recommendation systems is the building of the utility matrix. There are two ways in which the ratings for the utility matrix can be collected. The first method is to explicitly ask users to provide binary feedback or to rate items, which however does not work well in practice as users are not likely to respond. The second method is to learn the ratings implicitly based on the users' behavior, for example an action such as purchase indicates high ranking, or through user reviews. However, in case of no action it cannot be assumed that ratings are low. The key issue is that the utility matrix is sparse where most users have not rated most items. It is also possible to extrapolate unknown ratings from known ones where the interest is in discovering high unknown ratings. The methods used for the extrapolation often determine the success of recommendation methods.

	Item1	Item2	....	....	....	Itemn
User1	Rating 1,1					Rating 1,n
User2	Rating 2,1					....
....						....
....						....
....						....
Userm	Rating m,1	....	....	....	....	Rating m,n

FIGURE 12.3
Utility matrix.

12.6.3.2 The Cold Start Problem

Many recommendation systems use historical data about items associated with the user to recommend new items. When a user is using the recommendation system for the first time where they have not yet bought any item, the user is not associated with any history. In this case it is difficult to predict what the user is going to like. This is called the cold start problem. Similarly, when new items are added to the catalogue, it is difficult to obtain the rating for the item, again leading to the cold start problem.

12.6.3.3 Data Sparsity

Similar to the cold start problem, data sparsity occurs when not enough historical data is available. Unlike the cold start problem, this is true about the system as a whole and is not specific to a particular user.

12.6.3.4 Inability to Capture Changing User Behaviour

The customer behaviour of users keeps evolving as their purchase patterns change over time. A good recommendation system must be able to identify these behavioural changes in users' preferences and constantly retrain in real time in order to provide relevant recommendations.

12.6.3.5 Other Issues

One issue is a push attack can occur, where the ratings are pushed up by creating fake users, in which true recommendation is not possible. The more the recommendation algorithm knows about the customer, the more accurate its recommendations will be, but recommendation systems should not invade the privacy of users by employing users' private information to recommend to others. Another issue is that recommendation systems do not provide any explanation of why a particular item is recommended.

12.6.4 Types of Recommendation Algorithms

Basically there are three types of recommendation algorithms (Figure 12.4).

The first type is the popularity based algorithm where the most popular item is recommended. This algorithm is only used as a baseline. Sometimes this algorithm is used to handle the cold start problem where there is not enough data available about either the user or the item. The next type of recommendation algorithm is collaborative filtering, which is based on the similarity of either users or items, or in other words using the user's past behavior to uncover current user preferences. Collaborative filtering can further be classified as memory based and model based. In memory-based methods (either item based or user based), the objective is to discover the missing ratings based on similarities between users or items, respectively. On the other hand, in model-based methods an underlying model is assumed to govern the way users rate.

The other type is the content based recommendation systems which are based on the features or characteristics of the items or the users which are then used to measure similarities between items or users. In other words, items are recommended to customer x similar to previous items rated highly by x. The difference between collaborative filtering and content based recommendation is shown in Figure 12.5.

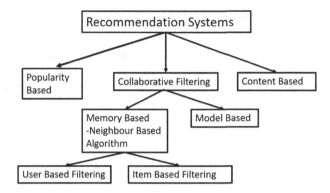

FIGURE 12.4
Classifications of recommendation systems.

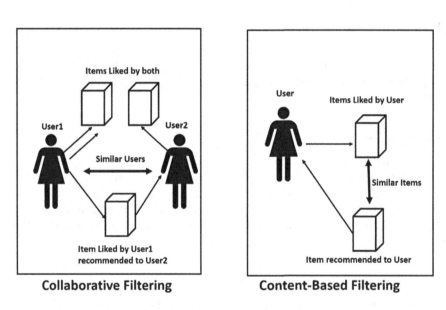

FIGURE 12.5
Collaborative Versus Content-based recommendation.

12.6.5 Collaborative Filtering: Memory Based Methods

In memory based methods (either item based or user based), missing ratings are predicted based on similarities. Explore the social network for raters. Here we aggregate the ratings to compute prediction. The network is explored to find raters in the neighborhood of the target user, and these ratings are aggregated to predict the rating of the target user. Collaborative filtering can offer controllable serendipity (e.g., controlling how many neighbors to use in the recommendation). There are different methods to calculate the "trusted neighborhood" of users. However, these methods do not carry out learning and are rather slow in prediction. Memory based collaborative filtering methods are further categorized as user based collaborative filtering methods and item based collaborative filtering methods. In user based collaborative filtering methods, it is assumed that users having similar previous ratings for items are likely to receive similar ratings for future

	I1	I2	I3	I4
U1	1	3	4	3
U2	1	3	4	?
U3	1	2	2	2
U4	3	4	3	3

(a)

	I1	I2	I3	I4
U1	1	3	4	3
U2	1	3	4	?
U3	1	2	2	2
U4	3	4	3	3

(b)

FIGURE 12.6
Collaborative filtering—memory based: (a) user based, (b) item based.

items (Figure 12.6a). In item based collaborative filtering, future items similar to those that have received similar ratings previously from the user are likely to receive similar ratings (Figure 12.6b).

12.6.5.1 Collaborative Filtering—Neighbor Based Algorithm

Recommendation systems are generally a problem of finding ratings between pairs of item–user pairs. One of the algorithms to discover recommendations is the neighbor based algorithm. Basically, we are creating a user–item matrix, predicting the ratings on items/ users that the active user/item does not know, based on other similar users/items. This technique as already discussed is memory based.

The steps of this algorithm are as follows:

The similarity with current user/item is used to weigh the similarity of all users/items. We need to select a subset of the users/items (neighbors) such as k neighbors as recommenders. We find the k-nearest neighbors (KNN) to the active user/item a, using a similarity function w to measure the distance between each pair of users/items (Equation 12.1):

$$\text{Similarity}(a,i) = w(a,i), i \in K \tag{12.1}$$

1. Next, we predict the rating that user a will give to specific items using the k neighbors ratings for same or similar items.
2. Now we look for the item j with the best predicted rating.

12.6.5.2 User Based Collaborative Filtering

In user based collaborative filtering, the recommendations are based on preferences of the most similar user (users) to the current user. Cosine similarity and Pearson correlation coefficient are commonly used to find similarity between users as shown subsequently. Let us assume that we want to determine the similarity between two users U_i and U_j. Let k be the number of items rated by both U_i and U_j and let $r_{i,k}$ be the observed rating of user i for item k and $r_{j,k}$ the observed rating of user j for item k. Let $r_i\sim$ be user i's mean rating and $r_j\sim$ be user j's mean rating.

Cosine similarity between two users U_i and U_j is given as follows (Equation 12.2):

$$\text{sim}(U_i, U_j) = \cos((U_i, U_j)) = \frac{U_i, U_j}{\|U_i\|\|U_j\|} = \frac{\sum_k r_{i,k} r_{j,k}}{\sqrt{\sum_k r_{i,k}^2} \sqrt{\sum_k r_{j,k}^2}} \tag{12.2}$$

Pearson correlation coefficient between two users U_i and U_j is given as follows (Equation 12.3):

$$\text{sim}(U_i, U_j) = \frac{\sum_k (r_{i,k} - \hat{r}_i)(r_{j,k} - \hat{r}_j)}{\sqrt{\sum_k (r_{i,k} - \hat{r}_i)^2} \sqrt{\sum_k (r_{j,k} - \hat{r}_j)^2}} \qquad (12.3)$$

The next step is to find the predicted rating of user u for item i. Here we use the similarity calculation to predict rating as shown in Figure 12.7.

Example 1:   User Based Collaborative Filtering

Given a user–item matrix of users versus books that they like, shown in Figure 12.8a, we need to calculate the rating of James for the book Dracula assuming a neighborhood of 2. The first step is the calculation of the average rating of each user (Figure 12.8b). Then we calculate the similarity between two users (Figure 12.8c), and finally we calculate the required rating (Figure 12.8d).

12.6.5.3 Item Based Collaborative Filtering

In item based collaborative filtering, in order to find whether a user prefers an item, its similarity to other items already rated by the user is determined. In order to find whether a user will buy item B if they had already bought A, we find the missing rating based on the ratings given to the other items by the user.

The Pearson correlation coefficient is commonly used to find similarity between items as shown subsequently. Let us assume that we want to determine the similarity between item i and item j or the correlation between item i and item j. Let U be the set of users who have rated both item i and item j. Let $R_{u,i}$ be the observed rating of user u for item i and R_j and ~ be item j's mean rating.

Pearson correlation coefficient between two items I and j is given as follows (Equation 12.4):

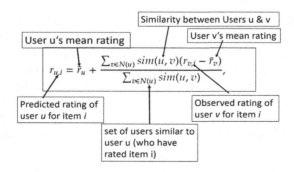

FIGURE 12.7
Calculation of predicted rating—user based collaborative filtering.

	Emma	Dracula	Heidi	Carrie
Jane	3	0	3	2
Mary	5	3	0	1
Alice	0	2	3	1
James	3	?	1	2
John	0	1	2	2

Predict James's rating for Dracula

(a)

1: Calculate average ratings of users

$$\bar{r}_{Jane} = \frac{3+0+3+2}{4} = \frac{8}{4} = 2 \qquad \bar{r}_{Mary} = \frac{5+3+0+1}{4} = \frac{9}{4} = 2.25$$

$$\bar{r}_{Alice} = \frac{0+2+3+1}{4} = \frac{6}{4} = 1.5 \qquad \bar{r}_{James} = \frac{3+1+2}{3} = \frac{6}{3} = 2$$

$$\bar{r}_{John} = \frac{0+1+2+2}{4} = \frac{5}{4} = 1.25$$

(b)

2: Calculate user-user similarity

$$sim(James, Jane) = \frac{3*3+1*3+2*2}{\sqrt{14}\sqrt{22}} = 0.74$$

$$sim(James, Mary) = \frac{3*5+1*0+2*1}{\sqrt{14}\sqrt{26}} = 0.89$$

$$sim(James, Alice) = \frac{3*0+1*3+2*1}{\sqrt{14}\sqrt{10}} = 0.42$$

$$sim(James, John) = \frac{3*0+1*2+2*2}{\sqrt{14}\sqrt{8}} = 0.57$$

(c)

3: Calculate James's rating for Dracula, Assume that neighbourhood size=2

$$\bar{r}_{James, Dracula}$$
$$= \bar{r}_{James} + \frac{sim(James, Mary)(r_{mary,Dracula,} - \bar{r}_{Mary})}{sim(James, Mary) + sim(James, John)} +$$

$$\frac{sim(James, John)(r_{John,Dracula} - \bar{r}_{John})}{sim(James, Mary) + sim(James, John)}$$

$$= 2 + \frac{0.89(3 - 2.25) + 0.57(1 - 2)}{0.89 + 0.57} = 2.067$$

(d)

FIGURE 12.8
Example—prediction of rating of user for an item using user based collaborative filtering.

$$S(i, j) = \mathrm{corr}_{\bar{i}, \bar{j}} = \frac{\sum_{u \in U} (R_{u,i} - \bar{R}_i)(R_{u,j} - \bar{R}_i)}{\sqrt{\sum_{u \in U} (R_{u,i} - \bar{R}_i)^2} \sqrt{\sum_{u \in U} (R_{u,j} - \bar{R}_i)^2}} \qquad (12.4)$$

The next step is to find the predicted rating of user u for item i based on the past ratings for similar items as shown in Figure 12.9.

Example 1: Item-Based Collaborative Filtering

Given a user–item matrix of users versus books that they like, shown in Figure 12.8a, we need to calculate the rating of James for the book *Dracula* assuming a neighborhood of 2. The first step is the calculation of the average rating of each item (Figure 12.10a). Then we calculate the similarity between two items (Figure 12.10b), and finally we calculate the required rating (Figure 12.10c).

12.6.5.4 Advantages and Disadvantages of Collaborative Based Filtering

One important advantage of collaborative filtering is that no domain knowledge is necessary. This method works for any kind of item, and no feature selection is required. Essentially users and items are considered as symbols without any internal structure or characteristics. Another important aspect is that it allows serendipity; that is. collaborative

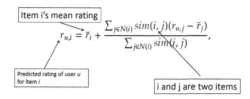

FIGURE 12.9
Calculation of predicted rating—item based collaborative filtering.

1: Calculate average ratings of items

$$\bar{r}_{Emma} = \frac{3+5+0+3+0}{5} = \frac{11}{5} = 2.2 \qquad \bar{r}_{Dracula} = \frac{0+3+2+1}{4} = \frac{6}{4} = 1.5$$

$$\bar{r}_{Heidi} = \frac{3+0+3+1+2}{5} = \frac{9}{5} = 1.8 \qquad \bar{r}_{Carrie} = \frac{2+1+1+2+2}{5} = \frac{8}{5} = 1.6$$

(a)

2: Calculate item-item similarity

$$sim(Dracula, Emma) = \frac{0*3+3*5+2*0+1*0}{\sqrt{14}\sqrt{34}}$$
$$= 0.69$$

$$sim(Dracula, Heidi) = \frac{0*3+3*0+2*3+1*2}{\sqrt{14}\sqrt{22}}$$
$$= 0.46$$

$$sim(Dracula, Carrie)$$
$$= \frac{0*2+3*1+2*1+1*2}{\sqrt{14}\sqrt{10}}$$
$$= 0.60$$

(b)

3: Calculate James's rating for Dracula, Assume that neighbourhood size=2

$$\bar{r}_{James,Dracula}$$
$$= \bar{r}_{Dracula} + \frac{sim(Dracula, Emma)(r_{James,Emma} - \bar{r}_{Emma}}{sim(Dracula, Emma) + sim(Dracula, Carrie)}$$
$$\frac{sim(Dracula, Carrie)(r_{James,Carrie} - \bar{r}_{Carrie})}{sim(Dracula, Emma) + sim(Dracula, Carrie)}$$
$$= 1.5 + \frac{0.69(3 - 2.2) + 0.60(2 - 1.6)}{0.69 + 0.60} = 2.113$$

(c)

FIGURE 12.10
Example—prediction of rating of user for an item using item based collaborative filtering.

filtering can help users discover new items by recommending items because similar users recommended those items.

However, collaborative filtering also has some disadvantages. Collaborative filtering is based on previous ratings and hence cannot recommend items that have previously not been rated or if enough users are not present in the system—called the **cold start problem**. **Sparsity** is another issue, where if the user–item matrix is sparse it is difficult to find users who have rated the same items. In user based collaborative filtering similarity between users is dynamic; precomputing user neighborhood can lead to poor predictions, but in item based collaborative filtering similarity between items is static and enables precomputing of item–item similarity, and prediction requires only a table lookup. Further these systems cannot recommend items to users who have unique tastes since they tend to recommend popular items. Moreover, it is assumed that items are standardized and that prior choices determine current choices without considering contextual knowledge.

12.6.6 Content Based Recommendation

In a content based model, recommendations are based on the content of items and not on the ratings of other users. Machine learning is used to learn a profile of the users' preferences from examples based on description of content based on features. The idea is to recommend items to users that are similar to previous items that were highly rated by the same user. An example is recommendation of movies with the same features such as actor, genre, director, and so on. Now we need to explain what we mean by content of an item. The content can be an explicit attribute of the item such as genre (action/thriller), action (Vijay), or year (2015). The content can also be characterized by textual content where techniques can be used to compute the distance between two textual descriptions or natural language processing can be used to extract features. The content may be in the form of audio or image and then can be extracted from the signal. After the features from the content of the item are extracted, an item profile is created, which is essentially a vector of features. A user profile is created as an weighted average of rated item profiles. Now given the user profile x and an item profile i, the estimate of the rating u of user x for item i is given as in Equation (12.5):

$$u(x,i) = \cos(x,i) = \frac{x \cdot i}{\|x\| \cdot \|i\|} \tag{12.5}$$

12.6.6.1 Advantages and Disadvantages of Content Based Recommendation

The major advantage of content based recommendation is that there is no need of data about other users, which in turn means that there is no cold-start or sparsity problem. Moreover, the model is able to recommend to users with unique tastes and also recommend new and unpopular items. Another important advantage is that recommendations can come with explanations listing content features that resulted in the recommendation can be given.

The major disadvantage is that the content must be amenable to being encoded as meaningful features and user interest must be represented as a learnable function of these features. Another disadvantage is that we are unable to exploit the quality judgements of other users unless we are able to encode these judgements as content features.

12.7 Context Aware Recommendations

Another aspect that affects recommendations is the context, where context is defined as any information that characterizes the situation of an item. Contexts are those variables which may change when the same activity is performed again and again. An example is watching a movie where time, location, or companion may change resulting in change in rating (Figure 12.11).

Context variables are added as dimensions in the feature space in addition to users and items. Here we deal with multidimensional space: User × Item × Contexts —> Ratings where context can be time, location, companion, weather, mood, and so on. The context dimension can be variable, and the context conditions are the values in each dimension where values of time can be binary {weekend, weekday} or tertiary as in companion

User	Movie	Time	Location	Companion	Rating
U1	Master	Weekend	Home	Spouse	4
U2	Master	Weekday	Home	Spouse	5
U3	Master	Weekday	Home	Sister	4
U4	Master	Weekend	Cinema	Child	5
U2	Master	Weekday	Cinema	Sister	?

FIGURE 12.11
Example of context in movie domain.

{spouse, sister, child}. While in traditional recommendation we want a list of movies to see, in context aware recommendation we want a list of recommended movies based on time, location, companion, and so on. In other words, the recommendation needs to adapt to user preferences in dynamic contexts.

12.8 Summary

- Explained the approaches to building machine learning applications.
- Discussed the factors that decide the selection of the machine learning algorithm.
- Outlined the application of machine learning for text classification, POS tagging, text summarization, and sentiment analysis tasks of natural language processing.
- Discussed the underlying concepts of recommendation systems.
- Differentiated between user based and item based collaborative filtering.
- Explained content based recommendation systems.
- Explored the basic concepts of context aware recommendations.

12.9 Points to Ponder

- Machine learning is not an answer to all types of problems.
- Building a machine learning application is an iterative process.
- No one machine learning algorithm fits all types of problems.
- Text classification has many applications.
- Online activity has made sentiment analysis one the most important applications of NLP.
- Recommendation systems can be explained using a utility matrix.
- Cold start is a disadvantage of collaborative filtering.
- In content based recommendation we are not able to exploit the judgements of other users.
- Context aware recommendations add context as features to the user item matrix.

E.12 Exercises

E.12.1 Suggested Activities

Use case

E.12.1.1 Design a recommendation system for a student seeking admission to a university. Use as many contexts as necessary, discussing them in detail. Clearly state any assumptions made. Implement the system using a machine learning technique.

Thinking Exercise

E.12.1.2 Give an everyday example of text classification.

E.12.1.3 Give the use of recommendation systems in the education sector in five different scenarios.

E.12.1.4 Can you give an example user item matrix with five context variables in a finance scenario?

Self-Assessment Questions

E.12.2 Multiple Choice Questions

Give answers with justification for correct and wrong choices.

E.12.2.1 Machine learning allows us to
 i   Solve deterministic problems
 ii Solve rule based problems
 iii Identify trends and patterns

E.12.2.2 We need to frame a machine learning problem in terms of
 i   What we want to predict and what kind of input data we have to make those predictions.
 ii What rules are available to solve the problem
 iii What algorithms are available to solve the problem

E.12.2.3 Feature engineering is a technique
 i   To find new features to suit the problem
 ii To create additional features combining two or more existing features
 iii To delete features that are irrelevant

E.12.2.4 The following are hyper-parameters:
 i   Batch size and epoch
 ii Algorithm and number of parameters
 iii Size of data and labels

E.12.2.5 The basis of *k*-nearest neighbor is
   i Rule based
   ii Distance based
   iii Nonparametric based

E.12.2.6 In document classification, naïve Bayes treats each document as
   i Sentences
   ii Context of words
   iii Bag of words.

E.12.2.7 POS tagging is generally solved using
   i Naïve Bayes
   ii Hidden Markov model
   iii SVM

E.12.2.8 An unsupervised method used to find top ranked sentences for text summarization is
   i Text rank
   ii SVM
   iii *K*-means

E.12.2.9 SentiWordNet attaches sentiment-related information with
   i Dictionary words
   ii WordNet synsets
   iii Bag of words

E.12.2.10 Recommendation systems are the basis of
   i Google search
   ii Text summarization.
   iii Netflix movies search

E.12.2.11 The cold start problem is associated with
   i Content based recommendation
   ii Collaborative filtering
   iii Context based recommendation

E.12.2.12 Similarity between items in collaborative filtering is commonly based on
   i Pearson correlation coefficient
   ii Cosine similarity
   iii TF/IDF

E.12.3 Match the Columns

No		Match	
E.12.3.1	Machine learning process requires large data during the learning stage	A	Classification problems
E.12.3.2	Small number of features but large volume of data	B	Parametric
E.12.3.3	Problems that require supervised learning, classification, and regression	C	Text classification
E.12.3.4	The basis of logistic regression	D	Learning rate, regularization, epochs
E.12.3.5	Confusion matrix values	E	Larger the size of data, the better the predictive power
E.12.3.6	The basis of random forest	F	Rule based
E.12.3.7	Finding whether an email is spam or not	G	Cold start problem
E.12.3.8	In recommendation systems there is no user history	H	Item based filtering
E.12.3.9	Uses similarity between the items and the current item to determine whether a user prefers the item	I	Generally open approach
E.12.3.10	Hyper-parameters that affect the learning	J	Choose low bias/high variance algorithms

E.12.4 Short Questions

E.12.4.1 Discuss briefly the machine learning life cycle.

E.12.4.2 Discuss two problems of your choice and discuss why you would choose a particular machine learning algorithm and why.

E.12.4.3 Can you identify two other natural language processing applications that use machine learning? Discuss how machine learning is used.

E.12.4.4 What are recommendation systems? Give two popular examples.

E.12.4.5 What is a utility matrix? Explain.

E.12.4.6 Discuss some of the issues associated with recommendation systems.

E.12.4.7 Give pictorial representations of collaborative filtering and content based filtering using illustrative examples.

E.12.4.8 Explain the neighbor based algorithm used in collaborative filtering.

E.12.4.9 Give and explain the calculation of predicted rating in user based collaborative filtering.

E.12.4.10 Give and explain the calculation of predicted rating in item based collaborative filtering.

E.12.4.11 Discuss the advantages and disadvantages of collaborative filtering.

E.12.4.12 Compare and contrast user based collaborative filtering and item based collaborative filtering.

E.12.4.13 Compare and contrast collaborative filtering and content based recommendation.

E.12.4.14 Discuss the advantages and disadvantages of content based recommendation.

E.12.4.15 What is context based recommendation? Discuss.

13

Domain Based Machine Learning Applications

13.1 Introduction

Machine learning methodologies are of great practical value in a variety of application domains in realistic situations where it is impractical to manually extract information from the huge amount of data available and hence automatic or semi-automatic techniques are being explored. Machine learning promises to transform our lives and to lead us to a better world, while creating even greater impact for business and society and augmenting human capability, and helping us to go exponentially farther and faster in the understanding of our world. Due to improved algorithms, access to growing and massive data sets, ubiquitous network access, near infinite storage capacity, and exponential computing power, machine learning is at the core of today's technical innovations.

There are many ways in which machine learning tasks can be classified; one such typology of machine learning applications is discussed next (Figure 13.1):

- **Predicting**: Machine learning can forecast or model how trends are likely to develop in the future, thereby enabling systems to predict, recommend, and personalize responses. One such example is Netflix's recommendation algorithm, which analyses users' viewing histories, stated preferences, and other factors to suggest new titles that they might like. Data-intensive applications, such as precision medicine and weather forecasting, stand to benefit from predictive machine learning and are one of the most used types of machine learning for applications.

- **Monitoring**: Machine learning can rapidly and accurately analyse large amounts of data and detect patterns and abnormalities; machine learning is very well suited for monitoring applications, such as detecting credit card fraud, cybersecurity intrusions, early warning signs of illnesses, or important changes in the environment.

- **Discovering**: Machine learning, specifically data mining, can extract valuable insights from large data sets and discover new solutions through simulations. In particular, because machine learning uses dynamic models that learn and adapt from data, it is effective at uncovering abstract patterns and revealing novel insights.

- **Interpreting**: Machine learning can interpret unstructured data—information that is not easily classifiable, such as images, video, audio, and text. For example, AI helps smartphone apps interpret voice instructions to schedule meetings, diagnostic software to analyse X-rays to identify aneurysms, and legal software to rapidly analyse court decisions relevant to a particular case.

DOI: 10.1201/9781003290100-13

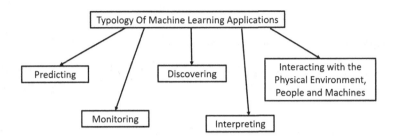

FIGURE 13.1
Typology of machine learning applications.

- **Interacting with the physical environment, people, and machines**: Machine learning can facilitate a diverse range of machine-to-environment interactions that allow autonomous systems to directly engage with the physical environment. For example, autonomous vehicles analyse huge amounts of real-time data from an array of sensors, cameras, GPS systems, and maps to determine a safe and efficient route down a street. Machine learning can interact with systems in a way that they do with other people, since systems can respond to speech, gestures, and even facial expressions. For example, individuals can ask questions of machine learning powered chatbots by having a conversation or beckon a robot to come over with a nod or wave. Machine learning can automatically coordinate complicated machine-to-machine interactions. For example, a control system for a data center can use AI to continuously monitor computing activity, internal temperature, and environmental conditions, and make adjustments to cooling systems to optimize performance while minimizing energy costs.

This typology along with the array of machine learning tasks such as classification, clustering, regression, predictive modelling, ranking problem solving, recognition, forecasting, sequence analysis, anomaly detection, and association discussed in Chapter 1 will help us understand the role of machine learning associated with the applications. We will be discussing various applications in domains such as everyday examples of our daily life, healthcare, education, business, engineering applications, and smart city applications (Figure 13.2).

13.2 Everyday Examples of Machine Learning Applications

An important question is whether machine learning impacts our daily lives, and the answer is an emphatic "yes," where it impacts almost every sphere of our life from the phone we use to our health, entertainment, travel, purchases, and so on. The motivation behind the use of machine learning is to make the applications so effective that we return to them again and again. These technologies have helped companies dramatically increase conversions by targeting audiences with selected, accurate, and relevant digital copy and interesting visuals. Let us consider the example of the phone, where we are connecting with machine learning whether we are aware of it or not. Machine learning based smartphones provide features like virtual reality and enhanced camera features and strive to

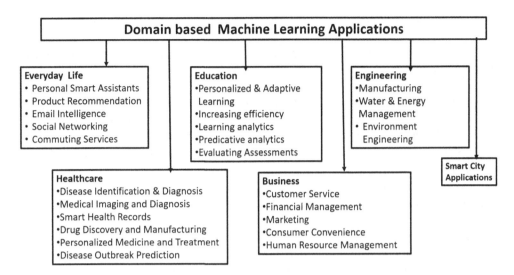

FIGURE 13.2
Domain based machine learning applications.

make a personalized and user-friendly interaction with the phone. Now let us discuss some everyday examples of machine learning which effect the very way we live.

13.2.1 Personal Smart Assistants

Assisting users in performing their tasks is the main goal of personal assistant applications. Now that voice-to-text technology is accurate enough to rely on for basic conversation, it has become the control interface for a new generation of smart personal assistants. Personal smart assistants are designed to discover the user's habits, abilities, preferences, and goals, and to predict the user's actions in advance and perform them without the user's interaction. The assistant is expected to continuously improve its behavior based on previous experiences by deploying a learning mechanism to acquire new information about user behavior. Such a virtual assistant can analyse employee calendars and emails to automatically schedule meetings and adjust calendar appointments and can analyse email text to determine the topic and time of a meeting, determine if there are any conflicts, and automatically schedule calendar appointments.

Personal assistants such as Google assistant, Alexa, Cortana, and Siri help us in finding information using our voice instruction. The first iteration of personal assistants were simpler phone assistants like Siri and Google Now, which could perform internet searches, set reminders, and integrate with your calendar. Amazon expanded upon this model with the announcement of complimentary hardware and software components, and designed Alexa, a machine learning–powered personal assistant. Microsoft has followed suit with Cortana, its own assistant that comes preloaded on Windows computers and Microsoft smartphones. These assistants can help us in various ways just by our voice instructions, such as play music, call someone, open an email, schedule an appointment, create to-do lists, order items online, set reminders, and answer questions (via internet searches). These assistants record our voice instructions, send them over the server on a cloud, and decode them using ML algorithms and act accordingly. Integrated with smart speakers, these personal assistants became a part of your living room, and you could use voice commands to ask natural language questions, order pizza, hail an Uber, and integrate with smart home devices.

The important machine learning components needed by personal smart assistants include the following:

- Speech recognition is needed to convert the voice to text to capture the instructions given by the user. Interpretation of the text using natural language processing is required, and response generation using natural language generation is required.
- Since the personal assistant and the user need to communicate, an important component is the adaptive dialogue management system.
- To achieve personalization, knowledge acquisition using machine learning systems is important.

Two important components of a personal assistant are email management and calendar management components. In email management, pragmatic analysis to determine type of message and folder, email task processing, and response generation are required. In calendar management, semantic analysis to handle domain specific vocabulary and actions, pragmatic analysis for handling appointments and create to-do lists, and task processing and appropriate response generation are needed.

13.2.2 Product Recommendation

This is perhaps the most popular application of machine learning both for the retailers and the consumers. Machine learning has become the latest trend in the retail industry, and retailers have started implementing big data technologies to eliminate the problems involved in data processing. Machine learning algorithms use the data sets to automate the analysis process and help the retailers in achieving their desired growth by exposing customers to similar products that match their taste while using an online shopping portal using different machine learning algorithms that use collated information like website search queries, purchasing behavior, and so on in order to induce the customer to buy their products and services. Product recommendations will get the best product attributes and dynamic information and will also improve customer experience through media and marketing campaigns. Customers can get insights on products they purchased and find similar ones that will make their experience better. Product recommendations can also help in understanding which areas can be improved in terms of composition, product performance, scope, function, and more. This will improve overall product features.

Machine learning is widely used by various e-commerce and entertainment companies such as Amazon and Netflix for product recommendations to the user. Whenever we search for some product on Amazon, then we start getting an advertisement for the same product while internet surfing on the same browser, and when we use Netflix, we find some recommendations for entertainment series, movies, and so on, all carried out with the help of machine learning. Google understands the user interest using various machine learning algorithms and suggests the product as per customer interest. These algorithms automatically learn to combine multiple relevance features from past search patterns and adapt to what is important to the customers. These recommendations for products are displayed as "customers who viewed this item also viewed" and "customers who bought this item also bought," and through personalized recommendations on the home page, bottom of item pages, and through email.

Research has shown that a substantial proportion of sales come from recommendations. The key to online shopping has been personalization; online retailers increase revenue by helping you find and buy the products you are interested in. In the future it is likely that retailers may design your entire online experience individually for you. Some companies have started offering "personalization as a service" to online businesses while others allow businesses to run extensive "A/B tests," where businesses can run multiple versions of their sites simultaneously to determine which results in the most engaged users.

This particular application has resulted in research in the area of recommendation systems where machine learning algorithms are designed to give recommendations based on users and items and handle the cold start problem for first time users.

13.2.3 Email Intelligence

Email intelligence concerns the smart sorting, prioritizing, replying, archiving, and deleting of emails. This is important since in today's world people spend a considerable amount of time on emails. One important component of email intelligence is the spam filter. Simple rules-based filters (i.e., "filter out messages with the words 'online pharmacy' and 'Nigerian prince' that come from unknown addresses") aren't effective against spam, because spammers can quickly update their messages to work around them. Instead, spam filters must continuously *learn* from a variety of signals, such as the words in the message, message metadata (where it's sent from, who sent it, etc.). They must further personalize their results based on your own definition of what constitutes spam—perhaps that daily deals email that you consider spam is a welcome sight in the inboxes of others. Machine learning is used to automatically filter mail as important, normal, and spam. Some of the spam filters used by Gmail are content filter, header filter, general blacklist filter, rules-based filters, and permission filters. Machine learning algorithms such as multi-layer perceptron, decision tree, and naïve Bayes classifier are used for email spam filtering and malware detection.

Another important part of email intelligence is smart email categorization. Gmail categorizes your emails into primary, social, and promotion inboxes, as well as labeling emails as important. Google outlines its machine learning approach and uses manual intervention from users to tune their threshold. Every time you mark an email as important, Gmail learns. Google designed a next-generation email interface called Smart reply which uses machine learning to automatically suggest three different brief (but customized) responses to answer the email.

Machine learning in this application involves monitoring of emails, interpreting them, and using classification and problem solving to handle them.

13.2.4 Social Networking

Mobile usage has been increasing day by day; meanwhile, the usage of mobile applications has also increased. Every application has to maintain some unique features to deliver the personalized content that is being liked by its users. We are living in an information era, where brands have access to a vast customer base, but the problem comes with the customer segmentation, which is basically targeting people with the content they are actually interested in, based on their past activity and demographics. Brands have started implementing big data and machine learning technologies to target specific segments. Now, organizations can convey the message that they understand and are pushing the ads, deals, and offers that appeal to users across different channels. Thus mobile applications have started implementing machine learning to tailor the application according to the needs of every single user. Adding machine learning to develop the mobile application would result in acquiring a new customer base by maintaining the older base strong and stable. Some facilities include customized feeds and content that meets the users' requirements, making searches faster and easier, and fast and protected authentication processes. This would result in improved sales and revenue and driving more customers to your site based on the search made by general people, purchase patterns, site content, and so on. For example, machine learning on Instagram considers your likes and the accounts you follow to determine what posts you are shown on your explore tab. Facebook uses machine learning to understand conversations better and translate posts from different languages automatically. Twitter uses machine learning for fraud detection, removing propaganda, and hateful content and to recommend tweets that users might enjoy, based on what type of tweets they engage with. Machine learning components involved are same as personal smart assistants but now have to deal with the peculiarities of different social networking sites.

13.2.5 Commuting Services

Machine learning has paved a new way in the world of transportation. One important application is the self-driving cars that are capable of handling the driving by letting the driver relax or have leisure time. Driverless cars can identify objects, interpret situations, and make decisions when navigating the roads. Uber uses different machine learning algorithms to make a ride more comfortable and convenient for the customer by deciding the fare for a ride, enabling ridesharing by matching the destinations of different people, minimizing the waiting time once a ride is booked, and optimizing these services by matching you with other passengers to minimize detours. Uber has invented a pricing model called surge pricing by using the machine learning model which can recognize the traffic patterns to charge appropriate fair to a customer.

Another application is platooning autonomous trucks by monitoring each other's speed, proximity, and the road to drive close together to improve efficiency, which can reduce fuel consumption by up to 15% and can also reduce congestion.

GPS technology can provide users with accurate, timely, and detailed information to improve safety. Here machine learning is used by logistics companies to improve operational efficiency, analyse road traffic, and optimize routes. If we want to visit a new place, we take the help of Google Maps, which shows us the correct path with the shortest route and predicts the traffic conditions. It also predicts the traffic conditions such as whether traffic is cleared, slow-moving, or heavily congested with the help of the real-time location of the vehicle from the Google Map app and sensors and average time taken on past days at the same time. Moreover, it takes information from the user and sends back to its database to improve the performance.

Another interesting application is the use of machine learning to reduce commute times. A single trip may involve multiple modes of transportation (i.e., driving to a train station, riding the train to the optimal stop, and then walking or using a ride-share service from that stop to the final destination), in addition to handling unexpected events such as construction, accidents, road or track maintenance, and weather conditions which can constrict traffic flow with little to no prior warning.

Machine learning is used extensively in commuting service applications such as the following:

- Self-driving cars use object detection and object classification algorithms for detecting objects, classifying them, and interpreting what they are.
- Uber leverages predictive modelling in real time by taking into consideration traffic patterns to estimate the supply and demand.
- Uber uses machine learning for automatically detecting the number of lanes and road types behind obstructions on the roads.
- Machine learning also predicts long-term trends with dynamic conditions such as changes in population count and demographics, local economics, and zoning policies.

The applications mentioned previously give some activities where machine learning is used, but every day the type of applications as well as sophistication of the services are increasing.

13.3 Machine Learning in Health Care

With digitalization disrupting every industry, including health care, the ability to capture, share, and deliver data is becoming a high priority. The health care sector is perhaps one of the most prominent that has been transformed by the ability to record and store massive volumes and variety of information. Machine learning, big data, and artificial intelligence (AI) can help address the challenges that vast amounts of data pose by automatically finding patterns and reasoning about the data. Machine learning can help healthcare organizations meet growing medical demands, improve operations, and lower costs. Health care has become the predominant area where machine learning is applied, and it helps in different aspects of health care such as patient care, medical imaging and diagnostics, smart health records, predicting diseases, and handling hospital and healthcare management. Machine learning can help healthcare practitioners detect and treat disease more efficiently and with more precision and personalized care, and it can lead to more effective, holistic care strategies that could improve patient outcomes.

Most challenges in health care, as in any machine learning application, come from handling the data and finding the "right" model. As far as health care is concerned, real-world data sets are messy, incomplete, and come in a variety of formats. Moreover, preprocessing the data often requires clinical knowledge and the right tools. In some cases, many research questions do not actually require machine learning but can be solved using accurate statistical risk prediction models. As we have already discussed, choosing the "right" model is often a trial-and-error process since highly flexible models tend to overfit while simple models make too many assumptions and result in underfitting.

13.3.1 Why Machine Learning for Health Care Now?

Application of machine learning to health care has gained momentum now because of various reasons. The first reason is the large-scale adoption of electronic healthcare records (EHRs) which makes available large volumes of patient data digitally in a prescribed format. The large de-identified data sets of various categories of patients have become available, which include demographics, vital signs, laboratory tests, medications, notes, and so on. In addition, President Obama's initiative to create a one million person research cohort consisting of basic health exam data, clinical data derived from EHRs, healthcare claims, and so on has also helped research in the area. The diversity of digital health data is indeed large and includes laboratory tests, imaging data, clinical notes as text, phone records, social media data, genomics, vital signs, and data from devices, which makes health care a suitable candidate for machine learning. Another fact that has helped in integrating applications of machine learning to health care is the standardization adopted in diagnosis codes (International Classification of Diseases—ICD-9 and ICD-10), laboratory tests (LOINC codes), pharmacy (National Drug Codes—NDCs), and medical concepts (Unified Medical Language System—UMLS), enabling integration of information from different sources. Major advances in machine learning are another factor that has kindled its application to health care. These include the ability to learn with high-dimensional features, and more sophisticated semi-supervised learning, unsupervised learning, and deep learning algorithms. In addition, the democratization of machine learning with the availability of high-quality open source software such as TensorFlow, Theano, Torch, and Python's scikit-learn have all contributed to the widespread adoption of machine learning for health care. The application of machine learning to health care has interested the industry and many machine-learning based health care applications are becoming available such as disease identification and diagnosis, medical imaging and diagnosis, smart health records, drug discovery and manufacturing, personalized medicine and treatment, and disease outbreak prediction.

13.3.2 What Makes Health Care Different?

When we apply machine learning to health care, some aspects are unique. First of all we are dealing with life-or-death situations and hence there is a need for robust, fair, and accountable algorithms and checks and balances need to be built into machine learning deployment. Many health care applications require unsupervised learning where no labelled data is available such as discovering disease subtypes or finding characteristics of people who are likely to be readmitted. Even if labelled data is available, it is not large and hence motivates the use of semi-supervised learning, Sometimes the sample size is very small such as in the case of detection of rare diseases, where we need to learn from data about healthy patients and therefore the specification of the problem is a challenge. In general, there may be missing and imbalanced data or censored labels, and we may need to deal with varying time intervals. Many of the domain's goals are casual in nature and cannot be handled by simple machine learning algorithms. In the case of health care, de-identifying the data is absolutely critical, and there is a need to come up with data sharing agreements for the sensitivity of the data. In addition, there are some specific difficulties in deploying the machine learning systems which include the difficulty of modifying commercial electronic health record software and the difficulty of interoperability of data as available data is often in silos and careful testing and iteration is needed.

13.3.3 Disease Identification and Diagnosis

Machine learning can be used for predicting the occurrence of a disease such as heart attacks, cancer, diabetes, epilepsy, and other prominent diseases. Examples of types of data that could be useful to make an accurate medical diagnosis using machine learning include disease data such as physiological measurements and information about known diseases or symptoms that an individual has experienced, environmental data such as information about an individual's environmental exposures, such as smoking, sunbathing, weather conditions, and so on, and genetic data such as all or key parts of the DNA sequence of an individual. For example, we may have data about the characteristics of previous heart attack patients including biometrics, clinical history, lab test results, comorbidities (diseases occurring with heart disease), drug prescriptions, and so on. Based on these features, it is possible to predict if the given patient can be susceptible to a heart attack and can be advised to take necessary precautions to prevent it. Machine learning can improve the accuracy of diagnosis and prognosis with earlier and more accurate prediction, and risk prediction where the variables which are more associated with the risk of suffering a disease are discovered. New methods are now available for chronic disease risk prediction and visualization that give clinicians a comprehensive view of their patient population, risk levels, and risk factors, along with the estimated effects of potential interventions. Disease diagnosis using machine learning techniques can enhance the quickness of decision making, and it can reduce the rate of false positives.

For example, powered by machine learning, the critical needs of patients and practice administrators are addressed, and ML enables faster and more accurate diagnosis, individualized treatment, and improved outcomes. Supervised learning is used to predict cardiovascular diseases using data on characteristics of previous patients including biometrics, clinical history, lab tests result, comorbidities, and drug prescriptions obtained from electronic health records. Clustering has been used to discover disease subtypes and stages. Risk stratification has been used, for example, for the early detection of diabetes. Here machine learning uses readily available administrative and clinical data to find surrogates for risk factors and then performs risk stratification at the population level with millions of patients.

13.3.4 Medical Imaging and Diagnosis

Diagnostic imaging allows physicians to view the inside of your body to help them find any indications of a health condition. Health images offer a full array of diagnostic imaging services such as MRI scans, MRA scans, CT scans, ultrasound, X-rays, mammography, bone density scans, and so on. Automating detection of relevant findings in pathology, radiology, and so on and other images is an important and probably the most researched topic of machine learning in the area of image processing. Pattern detection approaches have been successfully applied to detect regions of interest in digital pathology slides, X-rays, CT scans, and so on with very efficient, accurate search over subareas of an image and use hierarchy to search at multiple coarse to fine resolutions. Automatic detection of anomalies and patterns is especially valuable when the key to diagnosis is a tiny piece of the patient's health data. Detection is also valuable when key patterns of interest are discovered by integrating information across many patients that might not be visible from a single patient's data. Machine learning has been used to build innovative tools for the automatic, quantitative analysis of 3D radiological images and differentiate between tumors and healthy anatomy using these images and assisted the experts in the field of radiotherapy and surgical planning. Systems are available that enable you to find skin cancer early by taking photos of your skin with your phone and get to a doctor at the right time. Machine learning based medical imaging is also widely used in diagnosing COVID-19 cases and identifying patients who require ventilator support.

13.3.5 Smart Health Records

Maintaining up-to-date health records every day is exhausting as well as time-consuming, and hence machine learning is used to save time, effort, and money. Machine learning is used to enhance the management of health information and health information exchange. The goal is to facilitate access to clinical data, modernize the workflow, and improve the accuracy of health information. Smart charts were developed that are utilized to identify and extract health data from various medical records to aggregate a patient's medical history into one digital profile.

13.3.6 Drug Discovery and Manufacturing

R&D technologies such as next-generation sequencing and precision medicine can help to find therapy of multifaceted health diseases. Machine learning algorithms such as unsupervised learning can identify patterns in data without providing for any predictions. Drug discovery is the process of finding new drugs based on previous data and medical intelligence. Discovering or manufacturing a new drug can be expensive and a long process because there are a number of compounds that are put to the test and only one result can prove to be useful. With the advancements in technology, machine learning can lead to stimulating this process. Machine learning is used to rapidly discover connections between drugs and diseases at a systems level by analysing hundreds of millions of raw human, biological, pharmacological, and clinical data points and find drug candidates and biomarkers predictive of efficacy for diseases. Applied in clinical development, this can lead to improved drug trials and increased success rates, reduce development costs, and bring new-in-class therapeutics to the patients in a time-efficient manner.

Machine learning can consume scientific research data sets, then form and qualify hypotheses and generate novel insights and hence identify novel drug candidates. Machine learning can generate novel insights and predictions about pharmacological properties of drugs and supplements and identify novel biomarkers from biological data, chemical data, and curated databases of approved drugs, and leverage existing data to develop therapies on aging and age-related diseases.

Machine learning helps in screening and repositioning known drugs in unrelated indications at new, lower doses and helps to identify synergistic combinations of repositioned drugs for diseases with high unmet medical needs. It can also synthesize knowledge from multiple biomedical sources and discover potential rare disease indications and subsets of patients who may respond favorably to an existing drug.

Machine learning can search a virtual chemical space, predict binding affinity, and allow filtering for drug-like properties, safety, and synthesizability to speed up drug development with a higher success rate and better targeting of hard-to-drug indications. Machine learning can also be used to integrate clinical trial data with real-world evidence and public data sets to eliminate silos of health information and hence reduce the cost of drug development and improve the time-to-market and likelihood of success for new drugs.

13.3.7 Personalized Medicine and Treatment

Chat bots can help patients self-diagnose or assist doctors in diagnosis where relevant health and triage information based on the symptoms explained by the patient can be provided. However, they explicitly state that they do not provide diagnosis to minimize legal liabilities. Machine learning based audit systems can help minimize prescription errors. Prescriptive analytics are used on patient data to enable accurate real-time case prioritization and triage. There are examples that can precisely and comprehensively foresee the risk of delivering the recommended actions or that can provide patient triaging solutions that scan the incoming cases for multiple clinical findings, determine their priority, and route them to the most appropriate doctor in an available medical network. Another important area is providing personalized medications and care, enabling the best treatment plans according to patient data. reducing cost. and increasing effectiveness of care, where for example machine learning is used to match the patients with the treatments that prove the most effective for them. Another area is patient data analytics, which analyse patient and/or third-party data to discover insights and suggest actions. This provides an opportunity to reduce cost of care, use resources efficiently, and manage population health easily. An example is where all the relevant health care data at a member level is displayed on a dashboard to understand risk and cost, provide tailored programs, and improve patient engagement.

In addition, machine learning can also be used for predicting the occurrence of a disease such as heart attacks. In this case we have data about the characteristics of previous heart attack patients including biometrics, clinical history, lab test results, comorbidities (diseases occurring with heart disease), drug prescriptions, and so on. Based on these features, it is possible to predict if the given patient can be susceptible to a heart attack and can be advised to take necessary precaution to prevent it. By using machine learning for comparing massive amounts of data, including individual patient health data, to the greater population health data, prescriptive analytics can determine what treatments will work best for each patient and deliver on the promise of precision medicine. Machine learning can analyse data from next-gen sequencing, genome editing, chemical genomics, and combinational drug screening to find the most appropriate patients to treat with novel therapeutics and develop precision therapeutics for cancer and rare diseases.

13.3.8 Disease Outbreak Prediction

Machine learning can monitor, predict, model, and slow the spread of disease in a pandemic outbreak. Pandemic outbreaks such as bubonic plague, bird flu, Ebola, and SARS have devastated populations. Globalization and the consequent trade and travel have increased the spread of viruses. Treating outbreaks at this scale and speed is difficult given the unpredictable nature of viruses, which include natural mutations and resistance to existing medicines, and hence time is of the essence; this is where machine learning, which has the potential to monitor, model, predict, and prevent the next global event, becomes important.

By monitoring patient populations and medical data, machine learning can recognize patterns of pharmaceutical intervention to treat historical symptoms. These patterns could forecast an outbreak and identify at-risk locations and the migration of a pending outbreak. These areas can be monitored historically and in real time to model the cause-and-effect relationships that could mitigate the progression of a pandemic and natural path within the population. Machine learning can build causative relationships between travel data and population medical reports to help map out and predict the spread of a disease and then prescribe ways to alter travel routes to help contain or slow the spread of a disease. Machine learning can also be used to help plan more rapid and efficient responses and deploy the right supplies and personnel to the optimal locations at precisely the right time. Machine learning can rapidly learn from large data sets and enable drug development for fighting future pandemics.

All aspects of machine learning including monitoring, analysing, discovering, modelling, and predicting play a role in the application to health care. The availability of public data sets such as MIMIC critical care (https://mimic.physionet.org), multiple myeloma (https://data.mendeley.com/datasets/7wpcv7kp6f/1), Parkinson's disease (https://

archive.ics.uci.edu/ml/datasets/parkinsons), mammography (https://www.bcsc-research.org/data/mammography_dataset), pathology (http://www.i3s.up.pt/digitalpathology/), and diabetic retinopathy (https://www.kaggle.com/c/diabetic-retinopathy-detection/data) as well as many health data sets available at UCI machine learning repository have helped in building effective applications, especially in disease identification, medical imaging, and diagnosis.

13.4 Machine Learning for Education

Machine learning is transforming education by changing all aspects of education such as teaching, learning, and research, especially in the time of the COVID pandemic where educational institutions were forced to adapt to online learning and are now here to stay. Machine learning is expanding the reach and impact of online learning content through localization, transcription, text-to-speech, and most importantly personalization or individualized educational experience. Machine learning techniques are making an indelible mark in the education industry, and the majority of the stakeholders are aware of the changing face of education. Machine learning is beneficial to all stakeholders, the teachers, students, educational institutions, and companies willing to create some kind of product to monetize the educational technology. In the years to come, online training experts expect an even greater increase in the use of machine learning in the education sector, as it can boost both learning and teaching by bringing tremendous benefits to the classroom.

13.4.1 Personalized and Adaptive Learning

Leveraging machine learning applications in education can solve many of the problems regarding the lack of customization. Machine learning truly brings personalization in education to a new level. Machine learning analyses all the data generated by the user and tailors the system to meet the student's expectations and hence ensure that motivation is not lost and retention rates remain high.

Personalization is perhaps the best usage that machine learning provides and could be used to give each student an individualized educational experience. Through this educational model, the students can guide their own learning, going at their own pace and, in some cases, making their own decisions about what to learn. They can choose the subjects they are interested in, the teacher they want to learn from, and what curriculum, standards, and pattern they want to follow. Ideally, in a classroom using personalized learning, students choose what they're interested in, and teachers fit the curriculum and standards to the students' interests.

Machine learning can help in providing customized new class recommendations, personal curriculum modifications, and learning speed adjustments and determining the areas of weakness. Use of machine learning in modern learning management systems (LMSs) can provide every student with a unique, customized experience with access to virtual assistants, easier performance reviews, seamless on-boarding, and various educational plans depending on the student need and experience.

Machine learning analyses a student's performance in real time and modifies teaching methods and the curriculum based on that data. It helps to have a personalized engagement and tries to adapt to the individual to provide a better education. Machine learning suggests learning paths that the student should take. Machine learning in education is creating new hyper-personalized experiences where each student is taken on a customized learning path. A learning path is a series of courses and materials offered to a student based on their previous educational history, knowledge and skills, current progress, preferences, and learning style. Such a high level of customization helps educators dynamically deliver targeted and learner-centric content to their audiences. In other words, by using ML algorithms, you can make your content smarter and more intuitive whether for students or to reskill employees and equip them with the expertise they need for workplace success.

Machine learning in the form of adaptive learning can be used to remediate struggling students or challenge gifted ones. Adaptive learning analyses a student's performance in real time and modifies teaching methods and the curriculum based on that data.

13.4.2 Increasing Efficiency

Machine learning makes the work of teachers and students easier, and that makes them happy and comfortable with education. This also increases involvement and their love towards participation and learning, thus increasing the efficiency of education. Thus, the educators are free to focus on tasks that cannot be achieved by AI and that require a human touch. Machine learning has the potential to make educators more efficient by completing tasks such as classroom management, scheduling, and so on. The tasks delegated to machine learning will be performed automatically and almost instantly. Machine learning has the capability of better content and curriculum organization and management. It helps to bifurcate the work accordingly and understand the potential of everyone. This helps to analyse what work is best suited for the teacher and what works for the student.

Machine learning in education can track learner progress and adjust courses to respond to students' actual needs, thus increasing engagement and delivering high-quality training. Feedback from machine learning algorithms allows instructors to understand learners' potential and interests, identify struggling students, spot skill gaps, and provide extra support to help students overcome learning challenges. Machine learning can determine whether learners are interacting with the course materials, time spent by students on each section, whether the students get stuck or just skim the content, and time the students took to complete the test.

The Georgia Institute of Technology has implemented an automated teaching assistant named Jill, powered by IBM's Watson cognitive computing platform, to help respond to student inquiries for an online course. Jill can analyse and answer student questions, such as where to find course materials, and could help improve retention rates for online courses, which are generally low because students have trouble getting the information they need from professors.

13.4.3 Learning Analytics

Machine learning in the form of learning analytics can help teachers gain insight into data that cannot be gleaned otherwise. Machine learning can analyse content to be provided to students for adaptive learning.

With learning analytics, the teacher can gain insight into data and can perform deep dives into content, interpret it, and then make connections and conclusions. This can positively impact the teaching and learning process. Apart from this, the learning analytics suggests paths the student should take. Students can gain benefits by receiving suggestions concerning materials and other learning methodologies.

Use of machine learning can help to provide all kinds of reports (attendance, academic performance, engagement, certification tracking, trainer/teacher approval, etc.), measuring both quality and quantity of educational materials available, analyzing input data (number of logins, time spent on the platform, students' background, emails, requests, etc.), and visualizing the information flow to determine existing issues and miscommunication sources.

13.4.4 Predicative Analytics

Machine learning in the form of predictive analytics can make conclusions about things that may happen in the future. For instance, using a data set of middle school students' cumulative records, predictive analytics can tell us which ones are more likely to drop out because of academic failure or even their predicated scores on a standardized exam. Predictive analytics in education is all about knowing the mindset and needs of the students. It helps to make conclusions about the things that might happen in the future. With class tests and half-yearly results, it could be understood which students are going to perform well in the exam and which students will have a tough time. This helps the faculty and the parents to get alerts and take appropriate measures. Through this, a student can be helped in a better way and can work on their weak subjects.

13.4.5 Evaluating Assessments

Students often complain about human biases in assessments. Educators, in turn, point to the need for more precise and fairer grading systems. Automated test scoring has been around for a while, but incorporating machine learning in education enables smart assessments that can instantly evaluate multiple formats, including written assignments such as papers, essays, and presentations. Innovative grading tools can evaluate style, structure, and language fluency, analyze narrative depth, and detect plagiarism. Machine learning turns assessment into a matter of a few seconds, ensures accurate measurement of students' academic abilities, and eliminates the chance of human error. Machine learning can be used to grade student assignments and exams more accurately than a human can, though some input from humans is required. But the best results will have higher validity and reliability when a machine does the work as there are higher reliability and low chances of error.

Education software company Turnitin has developed a tool called Revision Assistant that uses machine learning to evaluate students' writing while they draft essays to provide feedback. Revision Assistant evaluates four traits in student writing—language, focus, organization, and evidence—and can detect the use of imprecise language or poor organizational structure to provide both positive feedback and recommendations for improvement. Many high school and college students are familiar with services like Turnitin's popular machine learning based tool used by instructors to analyze students' writing for plagiarism. Machine learning can help detect the plagiarizing of source code by analyzing a variety of stylistic factors that could be unique to each programmer, such as average length of line of code, how much each line was indented, how frequent code comments were, and so on.

13.5 Machine Learning in Business

Machine learning extracts meaningful insights from raw data to quickly solve complex, data-rich business problems and predict complex customer behaviours. It learns from the data iteratively and finds different types of hidden insights without being explicitly programmed to do so. Machine learning in business helps in enhancing business scalability and improving business operations for companies across the globe. Factors such as growing volumes, easy availability of data, cheaper and faster computational processing, and affordable data storage have contributed to the use of machine learning in business. Organizations can now benefit by understanding how businesses can use machine learning and implement the same in their own processes. Experts are of the opinion that machine learning enables businesses to perform tasks on a scale and scope previously impossible to achieve, speeding up the pace of work, reducing errors, and improving accuracy, thereby aiding employees and customers alike. Moreover, innovation-oriented organizations are finding ways to harness machine learning not just to drive efficiencies and improvements but to fuel new business opportunities that can differentiate their companies in the marketplace.

13.5.1 Customer Service

Using machine learning for gathering and analyzing social, historical, and behavioral data enables brands to gain a much more accurate understanding of their customers. Machine learning is used for continuously learning and improving from the data it analyses and is able to anticipate customer behavior. This allows brands to provide highly relevant content, increase sales opportunities, and improve the customer journey.

Machine learning is often used to evaluate customer-service interactions and predict how satisfied a customer is, prompting an intervention if a customer is at risk of leaving a business. Machine learning analyses data such as customer-support ticket text, wait times, and the number of replies it takes to resolve a ticket to estimate customer satisfaction, and it adjusts its predictive models in real time as it learns from more data about tickets and customer ratings. Machine learning will also improve customer trends, aid in improving customer interactions, and extract valuable points. Real-time data will help visually analyse and engage with users on a personal level and help in delivering good support and service for customers and build stronger customer relationships. Machine learning is able to provide digitally connected customers 24/7 online support and help customers with their queries. With predictive analytics and automated phone bot accuracy, it is possible for customers to get smart solutions.

Machine learning based approaches allow customers to have a personalized experience by giving customers the right messages at the right time. Machine learning based chat bots provide customers fast, efficient, and friendly service. Chat bots improves the scope for customers to get the right information as they need it and get consistently better at analyzing that information. Customer support can be a game-changer as it needs to be responsive, consistent, and focused. Chat bots can solve basic queries, reduce touchpoints, streamline interactions, and help with complex issues. Virtual assistants help customers navigate the process and engage them in conversations. AI agents can reduce the hassle of reaching customers online with natural language processing, machine learning, and voice assistant help. Customer engagement often centers on digital content, but machine learning enables the combining of natural language processing to gain better insights into each individual customer experience.

Machine learning based translation uses a combination of crowdsourcing and machine learning to translate businesses' customer-service operations such as web pages, customer service emails and chats, and social-media posts into 14 different languages at a substantially faster rate and reduced cost, making it easier for businesses to reach international audiences. The translated material is then reviewed by human translators for better customer experience.

Machine learning analyses purchase decisions of customers and makes appropriate recommendations to build targeted marketing campaigns that build customer interest. Machine learning understands purchase patterns and performs predictive and prescriptive analysis that will drive engagement and improve opportunities for upselling and cross-selling. Machine learning based tools can make tasks like data cleaning, combining, combing, and rearranging quicker and less expensive. Machine learning can thus influence customer experience by providing voice-enabled customer services like Amazon Echo and Alexa, useful customer insights, streamline customer interactions, data-backed customer and marketing strategies, automated assistance, and personalized content.

13.5.2 Financial Management

Financial monitoring is a typical security use case for machine learning in finance. Machine learning algorithms can be used to enhance network security significantly, to detect any suspicious account behavior such as a large number of micropayments, and flag such money laundering techniques. One of the most successful applications of machine learning is credit card fraud detection. Banks are generally equipped with monitoring systems that are trained on historical payments data. Algorithm training, validation, and back testing are based on vast data sets of credit card transaction data. Machine learning classification algorithms can easily label events as *fraud* versus *non-fraud* to stop fraudulent transactions in real time. Machine learning reduces the number of false rejections, which in turn helps improve the precision of real-time approvals. These models are generally built based on customer behavior on the internet and transaction history.

Machine learning enables advanced **market insights** that allow the creation of automated investment advisors, who identify specific market changes much earlier as compared to traditional investment models. These advisors can also apply traditional data processing techniques to create financial portfolios and solutions such as trading, investments, retirement plans, and so on for their users.

Finance companies use machine learning to reduce repetitive tasks through **intelligent process automation**. Chat bots, paperwork automation, and employee training gamification are examples of machine learning based process automation in the finance industry, which in turn improves customer experience, reduces costs, and scales up their services. In addition, machine learning uses the vast amount of data available to interpret behaviors and enhance customer support systems and solve the customers' unique queries.

Machine learning is also used by **budget management** to offer customers highly specialized and targeted financial advice and guidance. Moreover, machine learning allows customers to track their daily spending and identify their spending patterns and areas where they can save. The massive volume and structural diversity of financial data from mobile communications and social media activity to transactional details and market data make it a big challenge even for financial specialists to process it manually. Machine learning techniques such as data analytics, data mining, and natural language processing enable the management of the massive volume and structural diversity of financial data from mobile communications and social media activity to transactional details and market data, and can bring in process efficiency and extract real intelligence from data for better business productivity. The structured and unstructured data such as customer requests, social media interactions, and various business processes internal to the company can be analyzed to discover trends, assess risk, and help customers make **informed decisions** accurately.

Machine learning can also improve the level of **customer service** in the finance industry where using intelligent chat bots; customers can get all their queries resolved in terms of finding out their monthly expenses, loan eligibility, affordable insurance plan, and much more. Further, use of machine learning in a payment system can analyze accounts and let customers save and grow their money, analyze user behavior, and develop customized offers.

Using machine learning techniques, banks and financial institutions can significantly **lower the risk levels** by analyzing a massive volume of data sources where in addition to credit score, significant volumes of personal information can also be included for risk assessment. Credit card companies can use machine learning to predict at-risk customers and to specifically retain good ones. Based on user demographic data and credit card transaction activity, user behavior can be predicted and used to design offers specifically for these customers. Banking and financial services organizations can be provided with actionable intelligence by machine learning to help them make subsequent decisions. An example of this could be machine learning programs tapping into different data sources for customers applying for loans and assigning risk scores to them. Machine learning uses a predictive, binary classification model to find out the customers at risk and a recommender model to determine best-suited card offers that can help to retain these customers. By analyzing data such as the mobile app usage, web activity, and responses to previous ad campaigns, machine learning algorithms can help to create a robust marketing strategy for finance companies. Unlike the traditional methods which are usually limited to essential information such as credit scores, machine learning can analyze significant volumes of personal information to reduce their risk.

Machine learning in trading is another example of an effective use case in the finance industry. **Algorithmic trading** (AT) has, in fact, become a dominant force in global financial markets. Machine learning models allow trading companies to make better trading decisions by closely monitoring the trade results and news in real time to detect patterns that can enable stock prices to go up or down. Algorithm trading provides increased accuracy and reduced chances of mistakes, allows trades to be executed at the best possible prices, and enables the automatic and simultaneous checking of multiple market conditions.

13.5.3 Marketing

Machine learning enables real-time decision making, that is, the ability to make a decision based on the most recent data that is available, such as data from the current interaction with near-zero latency. Real-time decision making can be used for more effective marketing to customers. One example of real-time decision making is to identify customers that are using ad blockers and provide them with alternative UI components that can continue to engage them. Another is personalized recommendations, which are used to present more relevant content to the customer. By machine learning and real-time decisioning to recognize and understand a customer's intent through the data that they produce in real time, brands are able to present hyper-personalized, relevant content and offers to customers.

Machine learning analyses large amounts of data in a very short amount of time and uses predictive analytics to produce real-time, actionable insights that guide the next interactions between a customer and a brand. This is often referred to as predictive engagement, enabled by machine learning that provides knowledge of when and how to interact with each customer. Machine learning, by providing insights into historical data, can prescribe actions to be taken to facilitate a sale through suggestions for related products and accessories, making the customer experience more relevant to generate a sale, as well as providing the customer with a greater sense of emotional connection with a brand.

13.5.4 Consumer Convenience

Machine learning can be used to facilitate consumer convenience. Machine learning can analyse user-submitted photos of restaurants to identify a restaurant's characteristics, such as the style of food and ambiance, and improve its search results and provide better recommendations. Machine learning can analyse image-based social media sites and identify items in pictures that users like and find out where they can be bought online.

The Google Photos app uses machine learning to recognize the contents of users' photographs and their metadata to automatically sort images by their contents and create albums. The Google Photos algorithms can identify pictures taken in the same environment, recognize and tag landmarks, identify people who appear in multiple photographs, and generate maps of a trip based on the timestamps and geotags of a series of photographs.

13.5.5 Human Resource Management

Integration of machine learning into human resources (HR) practices can help analyze, predict, and diagnose to help HR teams make better decisions regarding **recruitment**. Machine learning can help in the hiring process using the track kept of all resumes and social media activities, the standardized and structured interview process used, and language used in the correspondence to discover whether a particular job website yields more successful hires, owners of certain type of social media are better employers, or certain interviewers are better at identifying the right talent than others. However, some of the patterns and tendencies may turn out to be false positives, and a final decision has to be based on human input. Another area of hiring that is gaining importance is the use of ethical machine learning techniques to ensure that a fair hiring process has been undertaken.

Another important area where machine learning will be extensively used is the **workplace training** department where the need is to create agile and adaptable learning programs that are able to meet the individual needs of employees as well as the impact of such programs on the business. Machine learning can help in personalizing the learning journey based on job role, existing skill sets, development plan and future goals, and proactively addressing any skills gaps that exist.

Using machine learning based real-time analytics, the HR team can understand employees and managers can understand the impact that absences, open shifts, and unplanned schedule changes will have on key performance indicators, allowing them to make more informed decisions that avoid issues before they arise.

Machine learning based chat bots are capable of answering relevant questions such as holiday details, medical benefits, and so on and can be designed to proactively promote benefits to employees they may not yet know about. There is also an opportunity to track employee issues using real-time analytics and then apply sentiment analysis to address these issues. Using machine learning, certain patterns such as responses on employee satisfaction surveys and drops in efficiency can be observed as precursors to employee attrition and their quitting.

13.6 Machine Learning in Engineering Applications

Machine learning impacts many advanced areas of engineering such as generative design, simulation improvements, sensors, and big data design optimization. Many engineering applications require accelerating processing, and increasing efficiency is important, where machine learning can be used to learn patterns in the data created by the chosen model and fine tuning can be carried out quickly to predict outcomes for new conditions. In applications where reliability and safety are important, machine learning can be used to model the probability of different outcomes in a process that cannot easily be predicted due to randomness or noise. Machine learning can tackle complex classification and prediction problems needed in many complex automated engineering applications. Machine learning can take the input of key variables to generate good options and help designers identify which best fits their requirements. Here we look at a few engineering applications such as manufacturing, energy, and environment.

13.6.1 Manufacturing

Machine learning is the core of what are called smart factories. Machine learning helps in harnessing useful data from previously unused data, unlocking insights that were too time-consuming to analyse in the past. Machine learning enables efficient supply chain communication, keeping delays to a minimum as real-time updates and requests are instantly available.

Manufacturers have been successful in including machine learning into the three aspects of the business—operations, production, and post-production. Manufacturers are always keen to adopt technology that improves product quality, reduces time-to-market, and is scalable across their units. Machine learning is helping manufacturers fine-tune product quality and optimize operation. Manufacturers aim to overcome inconsistency in equipment performance and predict maintenance by applying machine learning to flag defects and quality issues before products ship to customers, improve efficiency on the production line, and increase yields by optimizing use of the manufacturing resources.

Machine learning can automatically generate industrial designs based on a designer's specific criteria, such as function, cost, and material, and generate multiple alternative designs that meet the same criteria and provide designers with performance data for each design, alter designs in real time based on designer feedback, and export finalized designs into formats used for fabrication.

By continuously monitoring data (power plant, manufacturing unit operations) and providing them to machine learning based decision support systems, manufacturers can predict the probability of failure. Machine learning based predictive maintenance is an emerging field in industrial applications that helps in determining the condition of in-service equipment to estimate the optimum time of maintenance and saves cost and time on routine or preventive maintenance. Apart from industrial applications, predicting mechanical failure is also beneficial for industries like the airline industry. Airlines need to be extremely efficient in operations, and delays of even a few minutes can result in heavy penalties.Machine learning based analytics can help manufacturers with the prediction of calibration and test results to reduce the testing time while in production. Early prediction from process parameters, descriptive analytics for root-cause analysis, and component failures prediction can avoid unscheduled machine downtimes.

The biggest use case for machine learning is in 3D printing and additive manufacturing and lies in enhancing design and improving the efficiency of the processes. Key challenges that machine learning will help overcome for additive manufacturing will revolve around improving prefabrication printability checks, reducing the complexity involved in the process, and reducing the talent threshold for manufacturing industries. In defect detection, machine learning could be included in 3D modelling programs. These technologies could develop tools that are able to find defects that could make the model nonprintable in a 3D model. A real-time control using machine learning could considerably reduce time and material waste. Machine learning could provide a solution for one of the biggest challenges in additive manufacturing, that is, the need for greater precision and reproducibility in 3D-printed parts, by quickly correcting computer-aided design models and producing parts with improved geometric accuracy, ensuring that the printed parts conform more closely to the design and remain within necessary tolerances.

13.6.2 Water and Energy Management

Predictive machine learning improves water quality analysis and water quality prediction in river and coastal areas and helps to develop a water quality index for lakes, rivers, and estuaries. Integrating with appropriate sensors and the Internet of Things (IOT), machine learning can help to monitor river water quality. Effective forecasting and planning of urban water demand can be achieved using machine learning to analyse data.

Machine learning has been utilized to predict renewable energy availability for weeks in advance by analysing data from weather stations, solar plants, wind farms, and weather satellites and continually refines its models as it receives new data. These machine learning based predictions can help regional power grids better integrate renewable energy sources, as changes in the weather can cause renewable energy production to vary greatly.

Machine learning was used to create highly granular models of a building's energy efficiency and recommend improvements using parameters that influence energy efficiency, such as lighting and ventilation, and learn how to optimize these factors to maximize a building's energy efficiency. Machine learning has also enabled data centers to automatically optimize energy efficiency while responding to factors such as increased usage and changing weather by adjusting equipment performance and cooling systems. Machine learning was also used to learn homeowners' preferences and schedules to optimize home heating and cooling and help save energy costs. Machine learning also helped power companies to quickly evaluate potential locations for wind farms by predicting variations in wind speeds over time.

13.6.3 Environment Engineering

Weather forecasting using meteorological and satellite data uses predictive machine learning. Climate change vulnerability and risk assessment in agriculture, coastal, forest and biodiversity, energy, and water sectors at a cadastral level is an important application of machine learning. Aerosol emission inventory and forecasting is carried out by machine learning using satellite and meteorological data. Machine learning based analytics is used to determine sea level rise estimates in real time with high resolution imagery.

Machine learning was used to analyze satellite imagery of forests over time to detect early warning signs of illegal logging. The system can flag changes such as new roads indicating a new logging operation, as well as learn to identify changes that occur before major cutting to improve its warning system.

Machine learning systems can analyze data about pollution levels to forecast changes to air quality hours in advance. Machine learning is used in the development of an autonomous recycling system that uses a robotic arm and an array of sensors to identify recyclable items in waste and separate them for recycling, removing the need for manual sorting. Machine learning analyses trash on a conveyer belt using 3D scanning, spectrometer analysis, and other methods to determine what a piece of trash is made of, and if it is recyclable, a robotic arm will pick it up and move it to a separate container.

Networked acoustic sensors and machine learning can improve efforts to save threatened species of birds. Networked acoustic sensors collect data about bird calls, and a machine-learning algorithm parses through this audio to identify bird calls of endangered birds and flag when and where they were recorded. This data can help better map the bird's habitat, estimate its population, and guide conservation efforts.

13.7 Smart City Applications

The integration of machine learning based big data analytics and Internet of Things has contributed to cyber-physical smart city applications. Interoperability of smart city data such as city government data, environment data, network and mobility data, city IOT data, community data, transport and GPS data can contribute to increased context awareness with the following categories:

- Physical category data including location, presence , proximity, time, and date
- Environment category including temperature, noise level, humidity, pressure, and air quality
- User centric category including identity, preferences, history, and social interactions
- Resource category including connectivity, bandwidth, nearby networks, and device characteristics

Using and integrating such context aware data, machine learning can provide the following smart city applications:

- Transportation—intelligent multimodal public transportation, intelligent parking, traffic management, fleet tracking, road condition monitoring, and so on.
- Energy—smart metering, smart energy grid, energy storage and load management, smart charging stations, and so on.
- Smart buildings and lighting—building HVAC (heating, ventilation, and air conditioning) and air quality control, environmental and event responsive lighting, security lighting, and so on.
- Health care—emergency response, remote patient diagnostics and monitoring, disease control, smart health records, and so on.

- Economic development and government services—citizen-centric services, e-commerce, intelligent tourism service, smart entertainment service, municipal planning, broadband infrastructure planning, e-government services, access to government records, infrastructure monitoring and resiliency, and so on.
- Public safety—emergency dispatch, real-time incident response, surveillance, authorized subject tracking, and so on.
- Education—eLearning, virtual classrooms, intelligent institution management, intelligent student group services, and so on.
- Water and waste management—water storage and distribution; water quality monitoring; waste water treatment; flood control; waste sensing and collection, sorting, and recycling; waste disposal; and environment controls.

The shared characteristic of all these smart city applications is the availability of huge amounts of different types of data from physical and nonphysical systems at different granularity levels. Machine learning needs to integrate the right data from the right source, at the right level, and at the right time to monitor, analyse, classify, and predict to enable decision making and to in some cases actuate physical systems.

13.8 Summary

In this module, the following topics were discussed:

- Outlined application-based typology of tasks associated with machine learning.
- Explored the different everyday examples where machine learning is used.
- Discussed the different applications of machine learning in health care.
- Explained the areas in education where machine learning is used.
- Outlined the different areas of business where machine learning is utilized.
- Discussed the different applications of machine learning in engineering.
- Explained the role of machine learning in smart city applications.

13.9 Points to Ponder

- Why do you think machine learning applications are suddenly gaining momentum? Discuss.
- Can you think of other areas in which machine learning would be useful such as electoral campaigns, real estate, insurance, and so on?

E.13 Exercises

E.13.1 Suggested Activities

E.13.1.1   By searching the web, find at least five applications of machine learning each in health care and business not mentioned in the chapter and give a suitable objective, features to be used, machine learning task required, and evaluation parameters.

S.No	Healthcare				
	Application	Objective	Features Used	Machine Learning Task	Evaluation Parameter
1.					
2.					
3.					
4.					
5.					
Business					
1.					
2.					
3.					
4.					
5.					

E.13.1.2   Fill the following table with a statement (one or two sentences) on an example to fit the particular machine learning task of the typology discussed in this chapter (do not give examples already mentioned in the chapter):

S.No	Type of Machine Learning Task	Example
1.	Predicting	
2.	Monitoring	
3.	Discovering	
4.	Interpreting	
5.	Interacting with the physical environment	
6.	Interacting with people	
7.	Interacting with machine	

E.13.1.3 Project

1. Design a hospital administration system that uses machine learning to provide efficient and effective services to the management, doctors, and patients. Clearly outline all stakeholders involved and services provided. Implement the system clearly, showing the effect of using machine learning.
2. Design a smart city application with any 10 components that clearly showcase the integration aspects between different sources and types of data. Implement the system clearly, showing the effect of using machine learning.

Self-Assessment Questions

E.13.2 Multiple Choice Questions

Give answers with justification for correct and wrong choices.

E.13.2.1   Early warning signs of illnesses needs
      i   Predicting
      ii   Discovering and monitoring
      iii   Monitoring and predicting

E.13.2.2   Alexa, Cortana, and Siri are examples of
      i   Smartphones
      ii   Personal assistants
      iii   GIS

E.13.2.3   Standardization adopted for medical concepts is
      i   UMLS
      ii   ICD-9 and ICD-10 codes
      iii   LOINC codes

E.13.2.4   _____ is software used to check plagiarism.
      i   Turnitin
      ii   GIS
      iii   Plagdetect

E.13.2.5   Using machine learning to closely monitor the trade results and news in real time to detect patterns and enable stock prices to go up or down is called
      i   Intelligent pricing
      ii   Algorithmic trading
      iii   Predictive trading

E.13.2.6   Meteorological and satellite data uses predictive machine learning for
      i   Water quality testing
      ii   Waste separation
      iii   Weather forecasting

E.13.2.7   Machine learning can improve efforts to save threatened species of birds using
      i   Bird calls
      ii   Networked acoustic sensors
      iii   Satellite data

E.13.3 Questions

E.13.3.1   Outline some more applications of machine learning in engineering applications not discussed in the chapter.

E.13.3.2   Assume you are an edutech company that wants to attract universities to use your system. Outline how you would sell the product, indicating the intelligent components you would provide including facilities to upload legacy data seamlessly.

14

Ethical Aspects of Machine Learning

14.1 Introduction

AI and machine learning applications are permeating the world in applications such as shared economy, driverless cars, personalized health, and improved robots and in fact all situations where we need to learn, predict, prescribe, and make truly data-driven decisions. Harnessed appropriately, AI and machine learning can deliver great benefits and support decision making which is fairer, safer, and more inclusive and informed. However, for machine learning to be effective and acceptable, great care and conscious effort are needed, including confronting and minimizing the risks and misuse of machine learning. Therefore, the amount of influence that AI and machine learning will eventually have is determined by the choices people make while embracing it because of the concerns raised on many fronts due to its potentially disruptive impact. These fears (Figure 14.1) include negative economic and social impact like loss of jobs, loss of privacy and security, potential biases in decision making, human uninterpretable solutions, and failures and lack of control over automated systems and robots.

While the issues of fear are significant, they can be addressed with the right planning, design, and governance. Programmers and businesses need to choose which techniques to apply and for what; within the boundaries set by governments and cultural acceptance, there must be an efficient process to allow one to challenge the use or output of the algorithm, and the entity responsible for designing machine learning algorithms should be identifiable and accountable for the impacts of those algorithms, even if the impacts are unintended.

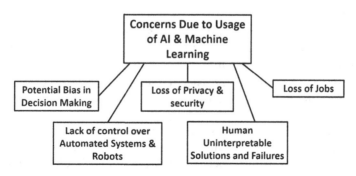

FIGURE 14.1
Concerns related to AI and machine learning.

DOI: 10.1201/9781003290100-14

In today's scenario some of the core principles of AI and machine learning include the generation of benefits for people that are greater than the costs, implementation in ways that minimize any negative outcomes, and compliance with all relevant national and international government obligations, regulations, and laws.

14.2 Machine Learning as a Prediction Model

Use of machine learning has resulted in predictive models being used extensively in the decision-making arena. Decision-making problems such as short listing candidates for interviews, approving loans/credits, deciding insurance premiums, and so on may be used by industries impacting the livelihood of the end users. Hence policy makers, auditors, and end users need these predictive models to take unbiased and fair decisions. Therefore, it is very important for the programmers and business analysts working on machine learning to understand all the intricacies of the biases associated with model prediction.

Considering all these implications, some global companies have come up with their own principles to take care of the social impact of AI and machine learning. For example, AI principles of Google, given by Chief Executive Officer Satya Nadella in 2016 (Sathya Nadella 2016), are as follows:

- **AI should be socially beneficial**: with the likely benefit to people and society substantially exceeding the foreseeable risks and downsides
- **AI should not create or reinforce unfair bias**: avoiding unjust impacts on people, particularly those related to sensitive characteristics such as race, ethnicity, gender, nationality, income, sexual orientation, ability, and political or religious belief
- **AI should be built and tested for safety**: designed to be appropriately cautious and in accordance with best practices in AI safety research, including testing in constrained environments and appropriate monitoring
- **AI should be accountable to people**: providing appropriate opportunities for feedback, relevant explanations, and appeal, and subject to appropriate human direction and control
- **AI should incorporate privacy design principles**: encouraging architectures with privacy safeguards, and providing appropriate transparency and control over the use of data
- **AI development should uphold high standards of scientific excellence**: Technological innovation is rooted in the scientific method, and a commitment to open inquiry, intellectual rigor, integrity, and collaboration should be encouraged.
- **AI should be made available for uses that accord with these principles**: We will work to limit potentially harmful or abusive applications.

The rules specify that scientists need to guard against bias, but at the same time these systems should be transparent so that others can look for bias and undo any harm. From the viewpoint of ethics, the principles specify that AI systems should embrace the concepts of fairness, safety, accountability, and maintenance of privacy. In the next section we will discuss the concepts of ethics.

14.3 Ethics and Ethical Issues

Ethics is a branch of philosophy that involves systematizing, defending, and recommending concepts of right and wrong conduct. Ethics prescribe what humans should do, usually in terms of rights, obligations, benefits to society, fairness, or specific virtues. Ethics is about shared values and societal laws rather than about legal laws. In the context of a team, we need to determine what is a good or right outcome and for whom, whether it is universally good or only for some, whether it is good under certain contexts and not in others, and whether it is good based on some yardsticks but not so good for others. In the context of machine learning, we need to understand the ethical quality of its predictions, the end outcomes drawn out of that, and the impact it has on humans. Being responsible for these ethical issues is an important duty of the developers of machine learning systems.

14.3.1 Examples of Ethical Concerns

Ethically complicated cases of machine learning algorithms include gender-biased results (**discrimination**), resume filtering based on age and sex in human resources industries (**discrimination, fairness**), invisible calculation of credit score (**transparency, accountability**), data brokers (**confidentiality**), Uber taxi price forming (**transparency, fairness**), predictive policing (**discrimination, fairness**), and personal and psychological profiling (**privacy, discrimination, confidentiality**). Some examples that raised ethical concerns are as follows.

During the 1970s and 1980s, St. George's Hospital Medical School in London used a computer program for initial screening of job applicants using information from applicants' forms, which contained no reference to ethnicity. The program was found to unfairly discriminate against female applicants and ethnic minorities (inferred from surnames and place of birth), who were less likely to be selected for interview. This was one of the earliest cases that was raised as an ethical concern.

In 2014, Facebook conducted an experiment where, by manipulating the News Feeds displayed to 689,003 Facebook users, the content that those users posted to Facebook could be affected. More negative News Feeds led to more negative status messages, and vice versa. Researchers condemned this experiment since it breached ethical guidelines for informed content.

In 2016, a data breach at Panamanian law firm Mossack Fonseca is being flagged as the largest ever security concern, where the leaked information allegedly details the ways dozens of high-ranking politicians in more than 40 countries had used offshore companies to hide income and avoid paying taxes, raising ethical concerns. Mossack Fonseca has confirmed news reports saying that the leak stemmed from an email hack where the emails were not encrypted with transport layer security protocols.

In 2018, revelations that Cambridge Analytica, a pro-Trump "psychographic" consulting firm, got hold of detailed personal data of 87 million Facebook users for psychological targeting for digital propaganda. Here the basic ethical issues were about privacy and ethics.

In a recent study at Princeton University, it was shown how the semantics derived automatically from large text/web corpora contained human biases. For example, names associated with whites were found to be significantly easier to associate with pleasant than unpleasant terms, compared to names associated with black people. Therefore, any machine learning model trained on text data, for example for sentiment or opinion mining, has a strong chance of inheriting the prejudices reflected in the human-produced training data.

All these examples show how digital information has been used in an unethical manner. Machine learning based ethical cases in the near future could be associated with autonomous cars, autonomous weapons (will there be meaningful human control?), the Internet of Things (IoT), personalized medicine (use of genomic information), social credit systems (is it based on just credit score?), and so on. Therefore, learning from historical data used for human decision making may lead to these traditional prejudices or biases being propagated and deeply hidden within the machine learning models.

14.4 Ethics and Machine Learning

Now at a time when machine learning systems are having a real, demonstrable impact on society as a whole, ethics has become a very important topic. As already discussed, decision making of numerous aspects of our daily lives is being controlled by machine learning algorithms motivated by speed and efficiency in the decision-making process. However, most machine learning systems are typically developed as black boxes which implies that most of these systems are rarely subject to scrutiny and interpretability, which are usually sacrificed in favour of usability and effectiveness.

The following aspects have to be considered for AI and machine learning systems to be widely acceptable.

- Automated decision making (autonomous systems) will only be acceptable if there is **fairness and transparency**.
- AI and ML systems must work in a **responsible** way which is human-centric and will benefit all humans and not just a few powerful corporations or governments. They must be responsible and should not make our world more imbalanced, unequal, and dangerous.
- The machine learning models should be **transparent**, enabling us to discover if anything went wrong and improve the algorithm with human judgment if needed.

In the following section we discuss some important opinions of ethics in AI and machine learning.

14.4.1 Opinions of Ethics in AI and Machine Learning

"By 2018, 50% of business ethics violations will occur through improper use of big data analytics." —Gartner's 2016 Hype Cycle for Emerging Technologies, STAMFORD, Conn., August 16, 2016

"Nearly 50% of the surveyed developers believe that the humans creating AI should be responsible for considering the ramifications of the technology. Not the bosses. Not the middle managers. The coders." —Mark Wilson, Fast Company on Stack Overflow's Developer Survey Results, 2018 (Fast Company, 2018).

"If machines engage in human communities as autonomous agents, then those agents will be expected to follow the community's social and moral norms. A necessary step in enabling machines to do so is to identify these norms. But whose norms?" —The IEEE Global Initiative on Ethics of Autonomous and Intelligent Systems

"IBM supports transparency and data governance policies that will ensure people understand how an AI system came to a given conclusion or recommendation. Companies must be able to explain what went into their algorithm's recommendations. If they can't, then their systems shouldn't be on the market." —Data Responsibility at IBM, 2017 (IBM, 2017).

"By progressing new ethical frameworks for AI and thinking critically about the quality of our datasets and how humans perceive and work with AI, we can accelerate the [AI] field in a way that will benefit everyone. IBM believes that AI actually holds the keys to mitigating bias out of AI systems—and offers an unprecedented opportunity to shed light on the existing biases we hold as humans." —Bias in AI: How We Build Fair AI Systems and Less-Biased Humans, 2018 (IBM, 2018).

14.5 Fundamental Concepts of Responsible and Ethical Machine Learning

Responsible machine learning describes machine learning that is ethical, inclusive, causes no harm to society, and ensures that the well-being of society is its main objective. In this section we will define some of the concepts associated with ethical machine learning (Figure 14.2). Ethical machine learning is the core of responsible machine learning and ensures that ethical guidelines are always followed. The major components of ethical machine learning are fairness, explainability and interpretability, transparency and accountability, and privacy. Now we define these concepts from the perspective of ethical

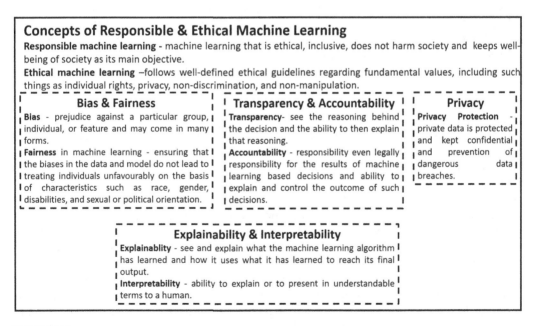

FIGURE 14.2
Concepts of ethical machine learning.

machine learning. **Fairness** in machine learning is about ensuring that the biases in the data and learnt model do not result in systems that treat individuals unfavourably on the basis of characteristics such as, for example, race, gender, disabilities, and sexual or political orientation. Therefore, fairness in machine learning designs algorithms that make fair predictions regardless of the inherent or acquired characteristics.

Explainability is the ability to explain to all stakeholders the various aspects of the machine learning system, including data, algorithm, and output of the machine learning system. On the other hand, **interpretability** is the ability to give and present such explanations in terms that is understandable to humans. **Transparency** is another important aspect of ethical machine learning where the reasoning behind the decision making process is discoverable and understandable. Associated with transparency is **accountability**, which ensures that responsibility is fixed for the decisions taken by machine learning systems and such decisions are explainable and controllable. Further, in case of any harm due to the decisions, there is a fixed legal responsibility. **Privacy protection** is also an important component of ethical machine learning where private data is protected and kept confidential and there is a system in place to prevent dangerous data breaches.

We need some approaches to tackle ethical issues associated with machine learning. One approach is to have strict national regulation or international regulation. We need to decide the ethical position that can be handled technically and legally and the ethical position of the organization.

14.5.1 Current Legislation—General Data Protection Regulation (GDPR)

The current legally binding regulation regarding ethics is called General Data Protection Regulation (GDPR), which a directive or a recommendation. It is based on an expanded definition of personal data including a person's name, location, online identifiers, biometrics, genetic information, and so on. It states that there is a need to notify users of any data breach within 72 hours and a need to maintain records. Companies using EU citizen data are subjected to this regulation, and the fine for noncompliance is 4% of the global revenues. The four cornerstones of GDPR are fairness, explainability, transparency, and privacy.

A legal requirement is that data protection has to be incorporated in the design itself. The GDPR requirements for data protection state that the big data analytics must be fair, with no bias and discrimination. Consumers should be rewarded for data collection, and the processing should be transparent. Consent from users should be clearly given, informed, and specific and can be withdrawn at any time without consequences, and this user consent for data is needed even when used by third parties. There is a right to request for algorithmic explanation. No further processing of data that is incompatible with the original purpose is allowed. Holding to data is not allowed, and one can use only data that is needed to be processed for a specific purpose. Incorrect data must be dismissed. Big data should not represent a general population where the hidden biases in data should be considered in final results, and there should be no discrimination during profiling. Individuals in any case should be allowed to access their own data, and security risks should be specifically addressed during processing. The system should be accountable and the processing carried out with a defined hypothesis.

GDPR is now an important area in AI and machine learning, and its implementation has commenced on May 25, 2018. Now GDPR requirements need to be included into existing machine learning automatic services; that is, they should be GDPR compliant. Finally, however, people and corporations should be convinced that GDPR requirements are beneficial to machine learning services.

14.6 Fairness and Machine Learning

Fair machine learning aims to ensure that decisions guided by algorithms are equitable. Machine learning algorithms must be designed to minimize bias and promote inclusive representation. As humans are inherently vulnerable to biases and are responsible for building AI systems, this human bias tends to be embedded in the systems we design and create. Fairness aware machine learning aims to minimize algorithmic bias through appropriate data collection which is representative of a diverse population and selection of appropriate learning modes.

Fairness in machine learning is often application specific and is associated with unique bias and fairness considerations. Sometimes machine learning systems have to deal with two-sided markets, that is, be fair to both buyers and sellers or to content providers and consumers and so on. Some of the steps that can lead to fair machine learning are employing a diverse pool of talent, using processes and tools to identify bias in data sets as well as the machine learning algorithms, leveraging review and domain expertise, and finally conducting research and employing best practices including analytical techniques and tools. In addition, some of the techniques to ensure fairness include preprocessing through using representative data sets or modifying features or labels, machine learning model training with fairness constraints, carrying out post processing, and finally experimentation and post-deployment.

Machine learning systems should treat everyone fairly and avoid affecting similarly situated groups of people in different ways and hence need to avoid bias and discrimination.

14.7 Bias and Discrimination

As fairness is basically concerned with minimizing bias, let us first discuss bias and the resulting discrimination in the context of ethical machine learning. Machine learning is basically a data driven technology, and therefore any patterns of bias or discrimination that exist in the data and in the dynamics of data can be reproduced and sometimes be amplified by the machine learning systems. Moreover, the features, metrics, and analytical models are decided by the designers of these machine learning systems who may in turn bring their own preconceptions and biases into the systems. Finally, the data samples that are used to train and test algorithmic systems may not be sufficiently representative of the population which they are inferring from, which can again lead to biased and discriminatory outcomes. Finally, bias and discrimination may be caused by insufficient representation of the population characteristics.

14.7.1 Examples of Bias and Dealing with Bias

14.7.1.1 Bias in Face Recognition Systems

Face recognition is a biometric software application capable of uniquely identifying or verifying a person or classifying the type of faces by comparing and analyzing patterns based on the person's facial contours.

Biased AI and machine learning based recognition called for regulation on use of facial recognition after consistently higher error rates were found for darker-skinned and female faces. Bias appears in face recognition systems because of the use of old algorithms, features related to facial features such as color, racial-biased data sets, and due to deep learning classifiers. This bias result in inefficiency of video surveillance systems in public city areas, increased privacy concerns, lower accuracy rate for African American and Asian males and females where innocent black suspects come under police scrutiny, and finally a major lag in mass implementation and acceptance of the technology. This bias can be dealt with by making the training data sets more diverse, using additional operations for detection of faces, and setting more sensitive parameters of the classifier.

14.7.1.2 Gender-Biased Issues in Natural Language Processing

Chat bot user interface (UI) is a hybrid system that interacts with users combining chat, voice, or any other natural language interface with graphical UI elements like buttons, images, menus, videos, and so on. Some applications of chat bots include their usefulness in replacing FAQ sections, in customer service operations, and in automatic emailing for straightforward problems. Chat bots can be designed to deal with ethical issues by filtering political topics of conversation, training with data of diverse topics, and encouraging a diverse set of real users. In addition, the ethical chat bots must be built by a diverse team of developers of both technical and nontechnical background who provide more transparency to the machine learning algorithms used.

14.7.1.3 Credit Score Computation

A credit score is a numeric expression measuring people's or companies' credit-worthiness. Banks use the credit score for decision making for credit applications where the credit score depends on credit history and basically indicates how dependable an individual or a company is. The credit scoring algorithm builds and trains a machine learning model which is then used to assign a score to every credit application. The ethical issues include the protection of personal data that has been collected for credit score calculation and the explainability and transparency of the machine learning algorithm used. There is also the danger of introduction of bias and hence discrimination against ethnic minorities by implicit correlation. All these factors can lead to lack of accuracy, objectivity, and accountability of the credit score computation. These ethical issues can be tackled by using interpretable machine learning algorithms or models, preparation of suitable training data to avoid bias, protection of personal data against breaches through anonymization, training all employees to work with machine learning algorithms and understand issues of bias, and finally auditability of AI algorithms.

14.7.1.4 User Profiling and Personalization

User profiling methods aims to provide a personalized service matching the requirements, preferences, and needs of the user associated with the service delivery. The ethical issues include privacy issues during user data gathering, underrepresentation of minorities, societal bias, construction of bubbles around users, political debates within echo chambers, and the objectivity of search results being impaired due to user profiling and corporate politics. Solving these ethical issues include ensuring transparency of personalization machine learning algorithms; that is, users should know how algorithms work and to have an option to change them; robustness of the machine learning systems against manipulation; and timely reaction to ethically compromised input.

14.7.2 Types of Bias

As we have seen, bias is the root cause of not catering to fairness principles. The two major categories of bias and their differences are shown in Table 14.1.

The distortion in data can be defined along five data properties, namely population biases, behavioral biases, content production biases, linking biases, and temporal biases, as shown in Figure 14.3. Population bias is due to differences in demographics or other user characteristics between a user population represented in a data set and the actual target population. There is a need to tackle population biases, address issues due to oversampling from minority groups, and data augmentation by synthesizing data for minority groups. Behavioral bias is due to differences in user behavior across platforms or contexts, or across users represented in different data sets. Lexical, syntactic, semantic, and

TABLE 14.1

Data Bias and Algorithmic Bias

Description	Data Bias	Algorithmic Bias
Basis	Based on the type of data that is used for building machine learning models	Associated with feature or model selection
Definition	Defined as the systemic distortion in the data that compromises its representativeness	Defined as computer systems that systematically and unfairly discriminate against certain individuals or groups of individuals in favor of others which in turn leads to discrimination and unfairness
Stage of machine learning system	Directly associated with data sampling and has to be dealt with by the designer of the machine learning system Partly dependent on the type of machine learning task undertaken For example, gender discrimination in general is illegal, while gender specific medical diagnosis is desirable	Unintentionally introduced during the development and testing stage; results in a vicious cycle of bias For example—a company with only 8% women employees. The hiring algorithm trained only on current data, based on current employee success, scores women candidates lower, and so the company again ends up hiring fewer women.
Causes	• Label bias, where the attribute that is observed sometimes wrongly becomes data, for instance, arrests not crimes • Subgroup validity where the predictive power of features can vary across subgroup • Representativeness where the training data is not representative of the population due to skewed samples, sample size disparity, or limitation of selected features • Statistical patterns that apply to the majority might be invalid within a minority group	• use data without our knowledge • can be based on incorrect or misleading knowledge about us • Not accountable to individual citizens • Built by specialists who do what they are told without asking questions

structural differences in the contents generated by users can cause content production bias. Linking bias is due to the differences in the attributes of networks obtained from user connections, interactions, or activity while temporal bias is due to the differences in populations and behaviors over time where different demographics can exhibit different growth rates across and within social platforms.

14.7.3 Data Bias and the Data Analysis Pipeline

Data bias can be introduced at any stage of the data analysis pipeline as shown in Figure 14.4.

Bias can be introduced at the data source due to platform differences and algorithms, due to community norms, or by organizations and automated agents. The bias can be

Population Biases Differences in demographics or other user characteristics between a user population represented in a dataset and the actual target population leading to some target groups being under-represented.	**Behavioural Biases** Due to differences in user behavior across platforms or contexts, or across users represented in different datasets. May be due to functional issues -platform functionality cultural elements and social contexts may be reflected in social datasets

Content Production Biases Lexical, syntactic, semantic, and structural differences in the contents generated by users. Community norms and societal biases influence observed behavior and causes variation in content across online and offline communities and contexts	**Linking Biases** Due to the differences in the attributes of the networks obtained from user connections, interactions, or activity. Online social networks interaction depends on external factors such as geography, distance and dynamics of offline relations.	**Temporal Biases** Due to the differences in populations and behaviors over time different demographics can exhibit different growth rates across and within social platforms. Features can change over time and introducing or modifying features can impact usage patterns.

FIGURE 14.3
Distortions of data based on data properties.

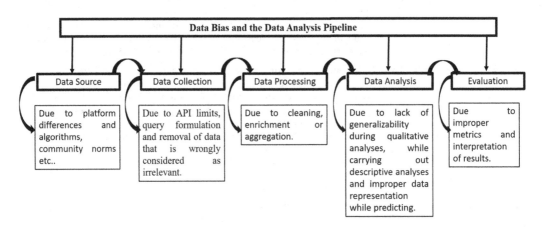

FIGURE 14.4
Data bias and the data analysis pipeline.

introduced during data collection due to API limits, query formulation, and removal of data that is wrongly considered as irrelevant. The bias can also be introduced at the data processing stage due to cleaning, enrichment, or aggregation. Data analysis itself can add on to the bias due to lack of generalizability during qualitative analyses, confusing measurements while carrying out descriptive analyses, and improper data representation while predicting. Even evaluation can introduce bias due to improper metrics and interpretation of results.

14.8 Fairness Testing

It is important to understand how one could go about determining the extent to which the model is biased and hence unfair. One of the most common approaches is to determine the relative significance or importance of input values (related to features) on the model's prediction or output. Determining the relative significance of input values would help ascertain the fact that the models are not overly dependent on the protected attributes or bias-related features such as race, gender, color, religion, national origin, marital status, sexual orientation, education background, source of income, and so on. Other techniques include auditing data analysis, ML modeling pipeline, and so on.

14.8.1 Fairness and Evaluation Metrics

Some of the most common evaluation metrics used in machine learning are based on the confusion matrix of true and false positives and true and false negatives. When we take fairness into consideration, we have to evaluate for inclusion which entails acceptable trade-offs. Considering the example of medical diagnosis, false positives may be better than false negatives. In this case, a false positive indicating disease being present when it is not may be better since this does not result in a serious problem. However, a false negative indicating disease is not present may lead to serious repercussions. Considering the example of job resume filtering, false negatives might be better than false positives. In this case, false negative indicate that a person is not identified, which may lead to loss of a possible employee. However, a false positive indicating that a person is suitable and wrongly identified for a job and employed may result in loss to the company.

H2O, Microsoft's Interpret ML, Azure Interpretability, Microsoft Fair Learn tools, IBM's Open Scale and Fairness 360 tools, and Google's What-if tool are some of the frameworks and tools available for bias detection and bias mitigation. The H20 tool allows interpretability at training time while Microsoft's tools allow explaining machine learning models for data globally or locally. During training the tools require model and training data. These tools can incorporate many measures of fairness and can be easily integrated into existing machine learning systems. The IBM Open Scale tool provides the AI operations team with a toolkit that allows for monitoring and re-evaluating machine learning models after deployment for fairness and accuracy. IBM Fairness 360 consists of data sets and a toolbox that can handle over 30 fairness metrics and over 9 bias mitigation algorithms during preprocessing, the training process itself, and post-processing. The goal of Google's What-if tool is to allow code-free probing of machine learning models and feature perturbations or what-if scenarios including counterfactual example analysis.

14.9 Case Study: LinkedIn Representative Talent Search

LinkedIn attempts to adopt diversity by design in talent solutions. One of the important components of the solution is talent search using representative ranking. The first step is measuring and achieving representativeness where the ideal solution is inspired by "equal opportunity" is that the top ranked results should follow a desired distribution on gender, age, and other such attributes. In other words, the distribution should be same as the underlying talent pool defined by measures such skewness and divergence.

First we need to understand the measures for bias evaluation for the recommendation and search system. Skewness or Skew@k is used and is defined as the ratio of the proportion of candidates having a given attribute value among the top k ranked results to the corresponding desired proportion. A negative $Skew_{ai}$ @k corresponds to a lesser than desired representation of candidates with the desired value in the top k results, while a positive $Skew_{ai}$ @k corresponds to favouring such candidates.

Then we need to ensure that within the attribute of interest we have the desired proportions. These desired proportions are computed based on the proportions of the values of the attribute (e.g., gender, gender–age combination) selected from among the set of qualified candidates. Here qualified candidates indicate the set of candidates that match a search query criterion. These desired proportions may also be based on legal mandate or voluntary commitment. Thus, we would like the ranked list of candidates to satisfy the following two desirable properties.

- Ensure that disproportionate advantage is not given to any specific attribute value, since this could cause disadvantage to other attribute values
- Guarantee there is a minimum representation for an attribute value—this property is more important to ensure fairness.

The fairness-aware re-ranking algorithm for fair recruitment starts with partitioning the set of potential candidates into different buckets for each attribute value. Then the candidates in each bucket are ranked according to the scores assigned by the machine-learned model used. Then the ranked lists are merged so that the representation requirements are balanced and the highest scored candidates are selected. The algorithm was validated and found that that over 95% of all searches are gender representative compared to the qualified population of the search.

14.10 Explainability

In general, people who cannot explain their reasoning cannot be trusted. The same applies even more to machine learning systems, especially when crucial decision-making process should be made explainable in terms that people can understand. This explainability is key for users interacting with machine learning systems specifically to understand the system's conclusions and recommendations. As a starting point the users must always be aware that they are interacting with the machine learning system.

Explainability is needed to build public confidence in disruptive technology, to promote safer practices, and to facilitate broader societal adoption. Explanations given should be actionable, and there should be a balance between explanations and model secrecy. The explanations should be given for failure modes also. There need to be explanations across the machine learning cycle, and they should be focused on both the model developer as well as the end user. In the case of health care, they need to explain why x was classified at risk for colon cancer, or in the case of finance, why y was denied a mortgage loan. There are some application-specific challenges in giving explanations, for example contextual; explanations are necessary for conversational systems, and in some cases there needs to be a gradation of explanations. Even when in certain cases the users cannot be provided with the full decision-making process, the level of transparency should be clearly defined. Explainable machine learning systems bring in transparency. This transparency results in improvement of the machine learning system itself by discovering mismatched objectives, multi-objective trade-offs, and learning about the causality associated with the system.

Definition: Explainable machine learning is defined as systems with the ability to explain their rationale for decisions, characterize the strengths and weaknesses of their decision-making process, and convey an understanding of how they will behave in the future. An open issue is who the explanations are for: advanced mathematicians or engineers, or employees and customers? Much of the machine learning employed today automates more traditional statistical methods, which are more easily explained than neural net based decisions used for image recognition or self-driving cars. There are basically two ways in which explanations can be generated, namely model specific techniques, which essentially deal with the inner working of the algorithm or the model to interpret the results, and model agnostic techniques, which deal with analyzing the features and their relationships with the output.

There are two notable efforts to create explanations, namely DARPA-XAI and Local Interpretable Model-Agnostic Explanations (LIME). The Defense Advanced Research Projects Agency (DARPA) launched the Explainable Artificial Intelligence (XAI) program to identify approaches that will give the systems the ability to give explanations. LIME is a technique developed at the University of Washington that helps explain predictions in an interpretable and faithful manner.

Let us consider an example the classification problem of machine learning. As shown in Figure 14.5, the current systems use the features learnt by the machine learning model to classify the newly unseen image as an elephant. However, an explainable machine

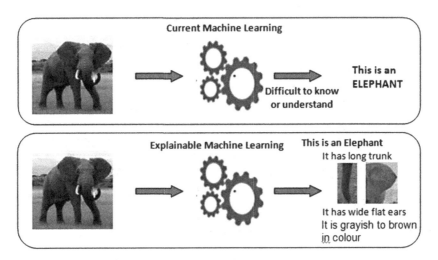

FIGURE 14.5
Example—explainable machine learning.

learning system needs to classify the image as an elephant and in addition indicate the reasons for doing so, in this case that it has a long trunk, wide flat ears, and is generally gray or grayish brown in color, and where possible also show the parts of the image based on which the classification was carried out. However, explanations are not always easy, because for examples where the features learnt are not present, the system is unable to give an explanation.

14.10.1 Handling Black Box Machine Learning

Good machine learning design should not sacrifice transparency since black box machine learning is not ethical machine learning. There need to be explanations across the machine learning cycle, and these should be focused on both the model developer as well as the end user. In a black box machine learning system, the inputs and operations are not visible to the user or another interested party. As shown in Figure 14.6, there are a number of questions that a machine learning system making decisions or recommendations that affect human life needs to answer or give explanations about.

Explainable machine learning can be described as a system that gives explanations for all the decisions that it makes as shown in Figure 14.7. The algorithm used incorporates components for each step of the algorithm, and while it makes decisions, the system also takes care to answer questions about why, why not, and the reason for success or failure. Moreover, the system allows feedback from the user to enhance explainability. This design therefore makes the user trust the system.

Example: Drive PX, NVIDIA's self-driving car platform, was designed to "teach" itself to drive, but the way it did so was not entirely clear. To improve the system, NVIDIA engineers prioritized opening the black box and developed a way to get a Drive PX vehicle to explain its driving style visually. The platform does so by displaying a video of a recently

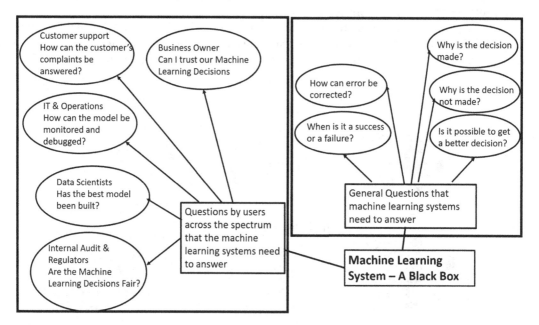

FIGURE 14.6
Questions to black box machine learning system.

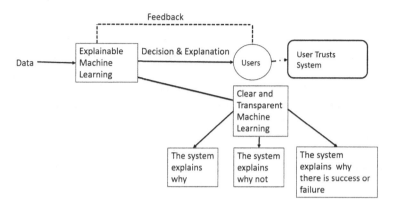

FIGURE 14.7
The flow diagram of an explainable system.

driven streetscape, over which it then highlights areas to which the algorithm gave the most weight during navigation.

14.10.2 Achieving Explainable Machine Learning

First of all, the machine learning system should allow questions to be asked about why the system is doing what it is doing in a continuous manner through a clear and transparent user interface. Decision-making processes must be reviewable, especially if the machine learning system is working with highly sensitive personal data like personally identifiable information, protected health information, and/or biometric data. When the machine learning system is assisting users with making any highly sensitive decisions, the users must be provided with sufficient explanation of recommendations, the data used, and the reasoning behind the recommendations. Finally, the machine learning teams should maintain access to the decision processes and be amenable to verification of those decision processes. Some of the aspects that the team building an explainable machine learning system should consider are as follows:

- To incorporate explainability into the system without affecting the user experience or sacrificing the effectiveness of the task at hand
- To decide the components that need to be hidden from the users due to security concerns and the method to be used to explain this issue to the users
- To decide the components of the decision-making process that can be expressed to the user in an easily palatable and explainable manner

There are basically two approaches to achieve explainability. The first one is to explain a given machine learning model in a post hoc fashion. In this approach, individual prediction explanation can be given in terms of input features, influential examples, concepts, local decision rules, and so on. On the other hand, global prediction explanations can be given for the entire model in terms of partial dependence plots, global feature importance, global decision rules, and so on. In the second approach, the model used itself is interpretable. Such models include logistic regression, decision trees, decision lists and sets, and generalized additive models (GAMs).

14.10.2.1 Attribution Methods

One post hoc individual method to give an explanation is the attribution approach. Here we assign the model prediction on an input to the features of the input. Such examples include attributing the prediction of an object recognition network to its pixels, a text sentiment network to individual words, or a lending model to its features. This useful approach is a minimal formulation of the reason for the prediction. Application of attributions include debugging model predictions like attributing an image misclassification to the pixels responsible for it, analyzing model robustness by for example crafting adversarial examples using weaknesses brought out by attributions, and so on.

There are different attribution methods such as ablations, gradient based methods, score backpropagation based methods, and Shapley value based methods. Ablation methods essentially drop each feature and attribute the corresponding change in prediction to that feature. The disadvantages of ablation methods is that they give rise to unrealistic inputs, give improper accounting of interactive features, and are computationally expensive, specifically if the number of features is large. Gradient based methods attribute a feature to the feature value times gradient where this gradient captures sensitivity of output with respect to the feature. The score backpropagation based methods used for neural network models redistribute the prediction score through the neurons in the network to explain the effect of the weights.

The Shapley value is a concept in game theory used to fairly determine the contribution in terms of both gains and costs of each player in a coalition or a cooperative game determined. The Shapley value applies primarily in situations when the contributions of each actor are unequal, but each player works in cooperation with each other to obtain the gain or payoff. Similarly, a prediction can be explained by assuming that each feature value of the instance is a "player" in a game where the prediction is the pay-out, where Shapley values tell us how to fairly distribute the total gain among the features based on their contribution. In other words, the Shapley value for a feature is a specific weighted aggregation of its marginal over all possible subsets of other features. In the explainability context, players are the features in the input, gain is the model prediction (output), and feature attributions are the Shapley values of this game. However, Shapley values require the gain to be defined for all subsets of features.

The attribution methods can be evaluated by having humans review attributions and/or comparing them to (human provided) ground truth on "feature importance." This evaluation helps in assessing if the attributions are human-intelligible and in addition increases trust in the system; however, the attributions may appear incorrect because the model reasons in a different manner. Another method of evaluation of attributions is the perturbation method, where the perturbation of the top-k features by attribution is carried out and the change in prediction is observed. If the change in prediction is higher, it indicates that the method is good. In the axiomatic justification method, a list of desirable criteria (axioms) for an attribution method is listed and we must be able to establish a uniqueness result that this is the only method that satisfies these criteria. However, attribution does not explain feature interactions, the training examples that influence the prediction (training agnostic), or the global properties of the model.

14.10.2.2 Other Methods for Explainability

Other types of post hoc individual prediction explanation methods include example based explanations where representatives of all the training data are used as prototypes; however, some data instances may not be well represented by the set of prototypes. Another method is determining the influence functions by tracing a model's prediction through the learning algorithm and discovering the training points that are responsible for a given prediction.

Global prediction explanation methods include a partial dependence plot showing the marginal effect that one or two features have on the predicted outcome of a machine learning model and the permutations method, where the importance of a feature is the increase in the prediction error of the model after we permuted the feature's values, which breaks the relationship between the feature and the true outcome.

In addition, machine learning models can provide responsible metadata about data sets, fact sheets, and model cards. Datasheets for data sets (Gebru et al., 2018) provides for every data set, model, or pretrained API that documents the creation, intended uses, limitations, maintenance, legal and ethical considerations, and other features of the data sets. Another important metadata is the factsheets whose data focuses on the final service provided such as the intended use of the service output, the algorithms or techniques this service implement, the data sets the service was tested on, the details of the testing methodology, and the test results.

Responsible metadata also includes model cards which provide basic information about the model including owner, date, version, type, algorithms, parameters, fairness constraints, resources used, license, and so on; the intended users of the system; and factors such as demographic groups, environmental conditions, technical attributes, and so on. Additional data include metrics such as model performance measures and decision thresholds, and evaluation data such as the data sets used for quantitative analysis and ethical considerations. These model cards help the developer to investigate the model and provide information for others to understand the system.

14.10.3 Example: LinkedIn's Approach to Explainability

As already discussed in the previous section on fairness, here we discuss the approach of LinkedIn for recruiter searches for candidates where candidates are filtered using some criteria and then ranked in multiple levels using machine learning models. In their approach to bring in explainability, LinkedIn uses feature importance. Feature digressions, which essentially analyse the change in impactfullness of a feature, are considered important. New features are introduced in bulk, and effective and active features are identified over different time periods of 3 hours, 6 hours, 12 hours, and 24 hours. The next issue is the necessity of keeping all such features. It is also important to separate whether a new feature, a new labeling strategy, a new data source, or a difference in the ordering of the features caused improvement in the results. However, this feature dependent approach gives only a global view, not a case-by-case view.

One method used by LinkedIn, the generalized linear mixed model, utilized a large number of parameters where for a specific recruiter or contract the weights can be summed up. The method is inherently explainable, where the contribution of a feature is "weight × feature value" and can also be explained in a case-by-case manner. Tensor flow models based on integrated gradients were also used for the recruiter problem. Here every query creates its own feature values for the same candidate including query match features, time-based features, recruiter affinity, and candidate affinity features. Therefore, a candidate could be scored differently by each query. This model explains potentially very complex models on a case-by-case analysis of user queries, such as whether a candidate is a better match for a particular position, and shows the ads and other materials accordingly. In general, a global view is not supported, though costly aggregate contributions can be computed.

14.11 Transparency

Let us first understand the subtle difference between two related terms *explainability* and *transparency* in the context of machine learning. As already discussed, explainability is associated with the concept of explanation, as being an interface between humans and the machine learning based decision maker. On the other hand, a transparent machine learning model is understandable on its own. Designers and implementers of machine learning systems must make the affected stakeholders understand the cause and manner in which a model performed in a particular way in a specific context. Increasing transparency can benefit different stakeholders: the end users can better understand the reason why certain results are being generated; developers can more easily debug, tune, and optimize machine learning models; and project managers can better comprehend the technical details of the project.

Most machine learning systems are based on discovering patterns, and unusual changes in the patterns make the system vulnerable; hence we need transparency. When the machine learning systems make critical decisions, such as detecting cancer, allocating loans, and so on, understanding the algorithmic reasoning becomes crucial. In some cases, transparency is necessary for legal reasons.

14.11.1 Issues of Transparency and Their Mitigation

Although from an ethical point of view, transparent machine learning is desirable, it can also become proportionally easier to hack. Narrative explanations may be hacked, and perturbation approaches can be deceived to make algorithmic behaviors biased. Machine learning transparency may make possible privacy violations where unauthorized third parties can ascertain a particular individual's data record and enable hackers to unlock considerable amounts of privacy-sensitive data.

Sometimes, entire machine learning algorithms and training data sets can get stolen through their APIs and other features. Similarly, transparency will also make it possible to partially or entirely reconstruct training data sets, which is an attack known as model inversion. Moreover, complete transparency about the working of machine learning algorithms will accidently disclose technical vulnerabilities and make them vulnerable to attacks designed either to obtain the inferences from live operational data or to inject bogus data into training workflows. Another issue of such transparent systems is protection of proprietary algorithms since the entire algorithms can be known by simply looking at their explanations. Finally, transparent algorithms are harder to design, and transparency is currently applied on less sophisticated algorithms.

In order to mitigate technical risks of algorithmic transparency, the following strategies need to be followed. Firms should control access to model outputs and should monitor to prevent data abuse. Controlled amounts of perturbations can be added into the data used to train transparent machine learning models to make it difficult for adversarial hackers. Intermediary layers can be inserted between the final transparent machine learning models and the raw data, making it difficult for an unauthorized third party to recover the full training data from the explanations generated against final models.

14.12 Privacy

First of all, let us discuss the right to privacy, stated by the United Nations Universal Declaration of Human Rights as "No one shall be subjected to arbitrary interference with [their] privacy, family, home or correspondence, nor to attacks upon [their] honor and reputation." It is also described as "the right of a person to be free from intrusion or publicity concerning matters of a personal nature" by Merriam-Webster and "The right not to have one's personal matters disclosed or publicized; the right to be left alone" by Nolo's Plain-English Law Dictionary.

Threats to privacy are posed by machine learning systems through design and development processes and as a result of deployment. The structuring and processing of data is the core of any machine learning system; such systems will frequently involve the utilisation of personal data. This data is sometimes captured and extracted without gaining the proper consent of the data subject or is handled in a way that reveals personal information. On the deployment side, most machine learning systems target, profile, or nudge data subjects without their knowledge or consent, infringing upon their ability to lead a private life.

The question now arises that, while we get the value and convenience of machine learning systems that operate by collecting, linking, and analyzing data, can we at the same time avoid the harms that can occur due to such data about us being collected, linked, analyzed, and propagated? There is a need to define reasonable agreeable rules that can ensure trade-offs, knowing that people generally have different privacy boundaries.

14.12.1 Data Privacy

Data privacy is the right to have some control over how your personal information is collected and used. Privacy is perhaps the most significant consumer protection issue or even citizen protection issue in the global information economy. Data privacy is defined as the use and governance of personal data and is different from data security, which is defined as the protection of data from malicious attacks and the exploitation of stolen data for profit. In other words, security is the confidentiality, integrity, and availability of data, while privacy is the appropriate use of the information of the user. Although security is necessary, it is not sufficient for addressing privacy.

14.12.2 Privacy Attacks

Attackers are able infer whether a particular member performed an action, for example clicking on an article or an ad, and are also able to use auxiliary knowledge such as knowledge of attributes associated with the target member (say, obtained from this member's LinkedIn profile) or knowledge of all other members that performed similar actions (say, by creating fake accounts). Therefore, rigorous techniques are needed to preserve member privacy.

Some of the possible privacy attacks can be classified as follows:

Targeting: The attacker matched the target having LinkedIn members over a minimum targeting threshold. For example, the attacker could carry out identification through search logs. In another case, AOL Research publishes anonymized search logs of 650,000 users. The attacker was able to get the identity of a particular person through the AOL records of the person's web searches.

Demographic breakdown: The attacker was able to identify a particular company by identifying whether the person clicks on the ad or not. A real case, *Facebook v. Korolova*, was where the context was micro targeted ads and the attacker was able to instrument ad campaigns to identify individual users through inference from impressions and inference from click attacks.

Require minimum reporting threshold: Here the attacker could create fake profiles, for example, if threshold is 10, the attacker created 9 fake profiles that all click to their advantage.

Rounding mechanism: Here the attacker got around a reporting increment of 10 by using incremental counts over time to infer individuals' actions.

De-anonymizing web browsing data with social networks: Here web browsing history was unique for each person, where each person has distinctive social network links appearing in one's feed and users are likely to visit links in their feed with higher probability than a random user. Attacks gave the attacker individual high-dimensional browsing data.

14.12.3 Privacy-Preserving Techniques

In order to avoid data privacy violation, given a data set with sensitive personal information, we need to compute and release functions of the data set appropriately while protecting individual privacy. Privacy can be maintained by privacy-preserving model training, robust against adversarial membership inference attacks. In addition, for privacy of highly sensitive data, the model training and analytics have to be carried out using secure enclaves, homomorphic encryption, federated learning or device learning, and design of privacy-preserving mechanisms for data marketplaces.

Anonymizing data is therefore important, where techniques are used to maintain the statistical characteristics of the data while at the same time reducing the risk of revealing personal data. Techniques used to protect highly sensitive data, such as an individual user's medical condition in a medical research data set, or being able to track an individual user's locations in an advertising data set, include data anonymization such as masking or replacing sensitive customer information in a data set, generalizing data through bucketing a distinguishing value such as age or satisfaction scores into less distinct ranges, and perturbing data, where random noise is inserted into data such as dates to prevent joining with another data set.

More advanced techniques include **differential privacy**, which offer formal guarantees that no individual user's data will affect the output of the overall model. Differential privacy involves publicly sharing information about a data set by describing the patterns of groups within the data set while withholding information about individuals in the data set. A combination of machine learning and differential privacy can be used to further enhance individual user privacy. These methods also increase flexibility with the ability to generate new data sets of any size, and they offer formal mathematical guarantees around privacy. The objective is to create both synthetic and differentially private synthetic data sets of the same size and distribution as the original data.

Federated learning can also be used in a privacy-preserving environment. Federated learning is decentralized learning that works with a network of devices capable of training themselves without a centralized server. In a machine learning context, the machine learning algorithm is implemented in a decentralized collaborative learning manner wherein the algorithm is executed on multiple local data sets stored at isolated data sources (i.e., local nodes) such as smartphones, tablet, PCs, and wearable devices without the need for collecting and processing the training data at a centralized data server. The results of the training (i.e., parameters) are alone exchanged at a certain frequency. The natural advantage of federated learning is the ability to ensure data privacy because personal data is stored and processed locally, and only model parameters are exchanged. In addition, the processes of parameter updates and aggregation between local nodes and a central coordination server are strengthened by differential policy-based privacy-preserving and cryptography techniques, which enhance data security and privacy.

Another approach to privacy preservation is the use of **trusted execution environments** (TEEs), which are CPU-encrypted isolated private enclaves inside the memory, which essentially protect data in use at the hardware level. Hardware enclaves enable computation over confidential data, providing strong isolation from other applications, the operating system, as well as the host, and unauthorized entities cannot remove this confidential data, modify it, or add more data to it. The contents of an enclave remain invisible and inaccessible to external parties, protected against outsider and insider threats, thus ensuring data integrity, code integrity, and data confidentiality.

Homomorphic encryption is another method used to transfer data in a secure and private manner. Homomorphic encryption differs from typical encryption methods in that it allows computation to be performed directly on encrypted data without requiring access to a secret key. The result of such a computation remains in encrypted form and can at a later point be revealed by the owner of the secret key. Hence homomorphic encryption can be used for privacy-preserving outsourced storage and computation.

14.13 Summary

- Explored ethical issues in general and ethical aspects of machine learning in particular.
- Discussed fairness in machine learning and the role of bias in fair machine learning.
- Used case studies to illustrate fairness in machine learning.
- Discussed the basic concepts of explainability in machine learning.
- Explained transparency and privacy issues of machine learning.

14.14 Points to Ponder

- The influence of machine learning is determined by the ethical choices people make while embracing it.
- Ethical predictive models are important in decision-making applications such as short listing candidates for interviews or deciding insurance premiums.
- Personal and psychological profiling affects ethical principles of privacy, discrimination, and confidentiality.
- Interpretability is the ability to explain in terms understandable to a human being.

- GDPR is a legally binding regulation regarding ethics.
- Fair machine learning aims to ensure that decisions guided by algorithms are equitable.
- Data bias is the systematic distortion in the data that compromises its representativeness.
- Black box machine learning is not ethical machine learning.
- Gender bias is sometimes unethical and sometimes desirable.

E.14 Exercises

E.14.1 Suggested Activities

E.14.1.1 If ethical aspects were not taken care of, how do you think it will impact you when using some applications in everyday life?

E.14.1.2 Give two examples how lack of privacy can impact you based on two applications you are currently using.

E.14.1.3 Can you think of new examples of bias in machine learning based applications in health care, banking, or customer care?

E.14.1.4 Taking a business scenario where machine learning based services are provided (at least three), discuss ethical issues of fairness, explainability, and privacy that will be concerns.

E.14.1.5 Assume you have to design a machine learning solution to select the best student for merit cum means scholarship. Discuss how you will introduce explanations at each and every step of the solution, including the algorithm used.

E.14.1.6 Case Study: University administration system. Design a fairness solution to tackle three examples of bias that can affect a machine learning based university administration system

Self-Assessment Questions

E.14.2 Multiple Choice Questions

Give answers with justification for correct and wrong choices.

E.14.2.1 This is not an ethical concern due to usage of AI and machine learning:
    i Loss of jobs
    ii Potential bias in decision making
    iii Ineffectiveness of machine learning solution.

E.14.2.2 Ethics in general is not about
    i Legal laws
    ii Aspects of right and wrong
    iii Societal laws

E.14.2.3 Resume filtering based on age and sex in HR industries requires
    i Transparency and accountability
    ii Discrimination and fairness
    iii Confidentiality

E.14.2.4 Researchers condemned Facebook for analysing news feeds since
    i Ethical guidelines for informed content were breached
    ii It followed discriminatory procedures
    iii Data was not encrypted

E.14.2.5 _____ is legislation for data protection.
    i DPFR
    ii GDPR
    iii EMLS

E.14.2.6 A harm that is caused because a system does not work as well for one person as it does for another, even if no opportunities, resources, or information are extended or withheld, is called
    i Ethical harm
    ii Allocation harm
    iii Quality-of-service harm

E.14.2.7 Fairness deals with
    i Minimizing bias
    ii Maximizing bias
    iii Equalizing bias

E.14.2.8 When the attribute that is observed sometimes wrongly becomes data, it is called
    i Label bias
    ii Representativeness bias
    iii Subgroup validity bias

E.14.2.9 The law that states that the more unusual or inconsistent the result, the more likely it is an error is called
    i Murphy's law
    ii Bernoulli's law
    iii Twyman's law

E.14.2.10 Testing specifically carried out close to launching of the product to search for rare but extreme harms is called
    i Ecologically valid testing
    ii Adversarial testing
    iii Targeted testing

E.14.2.11 Including candidates possessing disjoint protected attribute values with a proportion as close as possible to the desirable proportion is carried out in
    i Fairness-aware ranking
    ii Quick testing
    iii Comprehensive testing

E.14.2.12 Two notable efforts to create explanations are
    i   H2O and LIME
    ii DARPA-XAI and LIME
    iii DARPA-XAI and Shirley cards

E.14.2.13 The attribution method is a
    i   Global prediction explanation method
    ii Fairness method to remove bias
    iii Post hoc method to give an explanation

E.14.2.14 Shapley value based methods are based on the concept of
    i   Network theory
    ii Game theory
    iii Probability

E.14.2.15 Simulatable, decomposable, and algorithmic are types of
    i   Levels of transparent models
    ii Levels of fairness models
    iii Levels of privacy models

E.14.2.16 Publicly sharing information about a data set by describing the patterns of groups within the data set while withholding information about individuals is called
    i   Different policy
    ii Secret policy
    iii Differential policy

E.14.2.17 The ability to partially or entirely reconstruct training data is called
    i   Model creation
    ii Model reconstruction
    iii Model inversion

E.14.3 Match the Columns

No		Match	
E.14.3.1	Programmers and business analysts working on machine learning based decision making	**A**	Cambridge Analytica
E.14.3.2	Providing appropriate opportunities for feedback, explanations, and appeal, and subject to appropriate human direction and control	**B**	General Data Protection Regulation
E.14.3.3	Uber taxi price forming	**C**	Data bias
E.14.3.4	Got hold of detailed personal data on millions of Facebook users for psychological targeting for digital propaganda	**D**	Skewness
E.14.3.5	Nearly 50% of the surveyed developers believe that the humans creating AI should be responsible for considering the ramifications of the technology—not the bosses or the middle managers, but the coders.	**E**	Bias

No		Match	
E.14.3.6	Fairness, explainability, transparency, and privacy are the four cornerstones	F	Transparency, fairness
E.14.3.7	Machine learning model issue caused due to lack of sufficient features and related data sets used for training the models	G	Microsoft
E.14.3.8	Systemic distortion in the data that compromises its representativeness	H	Accountability
E.14.3.9	Fairlearn tool	I	Mark Wilson, Fast Company on Stack Overflow's Developer Survey Results, 2018
E.14.3.10	_____ is defined as the ratio of the proportion of candidates having a given attribute value among the top k ranked results to the corresponding desired proportion	J	Understand biases in model prediction

E.14.4 Short Questions

E.14.4.1 Compare and contrast the following in the context of ethical machine learning:
    i Bias and fairness
    ii Explainability and interpretability
    iii Trust and transparency
    iv Privacy and security

E.14.4.2 Discuss fairness-aware ranking algorithms.

E.14.4.3 Explain how the fairness issue is tackled by Google Assistant.

E.14.4.4 What is data bias? Give an example from the education domain.

E.14.4.5 Discuss two examples where true negatives and true positives are acceptable.

E.14.4.6 Differentiate between model specific techniques and model agnostic techniques of generating explanations.

E.14.4.7 Discuss explainable machine learning in the context of a classification system.

E.14.4.8 What are the questions that a machine learning system making decisions or recommendations needs to give explanations to the different stakeholders?

E.14.4.9 Explain the different attribution methods used for giving explanations

E.14.4.10 Discuss the methods that are followed to mitigate algorithmic transparency.

E.14.4.11 What is data privacy? Discuss.

E.14.4.12 Discuss any two possible privacy attacks.

E.14.4.13 What is the role of anonymizing data in privacy preservation?

E.14.4.14 Explain differential policy in detail.

E.14.4.15 Discuss how trusted execution environments (TEEs) are used for privacy preservation.

E.14.4.16 What is homomorphic encryption?

References

Fast Company. (2018, March 15). What developers really think about bias. https://www.fastcompany.com/90164226/what-developers-really-think-about-ai-and-bias

Gebru, T., et al. (2018). Datasheets for datasets. *Proceedings of the 5th Workshop on Fairness, Accountability, and Transparency in Machine Learning*, Stockholm, Sweden. PMLR, 80.

IBM. (2017, October 10). Data responsibility @IBM. https://www.ibm.com/policy/dataresponsibility-at-ibm/

IBM. (2018, February 1). Bias in AI: How we build fair AI systems and less-biased humans. https://www.ibm.com/policy/bias-in-ai/

Nadella, S. (2016, June 28). The partnership of the future. *Slate*. https://slate.com/technology/2016/06/microsoft-ceo-satya-nadella-humans-and-a-i-can-work-together-to-solve-societys-challenges.html

15

Introduction to Deep Learning and Convolutional Neural Networks

15.1 Introduction

Deep learning is a subset of machine learning, which is based on learning and improving on its own by examining computer algorithms. Deep learning works based on artificial neural networks (ANNs), which are designed to imitate how humans think and learn. In the past, neural networks had limitations pertaining to computing power and hence to complexity also. However, in the recent past, larger, more sophisticated neural networks, allowing computers to observe, learn, and react to complex situations faster than humans, evolved due to advancements in big data analytics. Deep learning finds applications in aided image classification, language translation, and speech recognition, predominately used to solve any pattern recognition problem and without human intervention.

Deep neural networks (DNNs) are driven by ANNs, comprising many layers, where each layer can perform complex operations such as representation and abstraction that make sense of images, sound, text, and so on. Now DNNs are considered the fastest-growing field in machine learning, deep learning represents a truly disruptive digital technology, and it is being used by increasingly more companies to create new business models.

15.2 Example of Deep Learning at Work

Let's say the goal is to have a neural network recognize photos that contain a dog. All dogs don't look exactly alike—consider a rottweiler and a poodle, for instance. Furthermore, photos show dogs at different angles and with varying amounts of light and shadow. So, a training set of images must be compiled, including many examples of dog faces which any person would label as "dog," and pictures of objects that aren't dogs, labeled (as one might expect), "not dog." The images fed into the neural network are converted into data. These data move through the network, and various nodes assign weights to different elements. The final output layer compiles the seemingly disconnected information—furry, has a snout, has four legs, and so on—and delivers the output: dog.

Now, this answer received from the neural network will be compared to the human-generated label. If there is a match, then the output is confirmed. If not, the neural network notes the error and adjusts the weightings. The neural network tries to improve its

DOI: 10.1201/9781003290100-15

TABLE 15.1

Evolution of Deep Learning

1943	For the first time a computational model based on the brain's neural connections using mathematics and threshold magic was created by Walter Pitts and Warren McCulloch.
1950	Alan Turing proposed the "learning machine" which marked the beginning of machine learning.
1958	A pattern recognition algorithm based on a two-layer neural network using simple addition and subtraction was proposed by Frank Rosenblatt.
1959	IBM computerised a computer learning program proposed by Arthur Samuel to play the game of checkers.
1960	The basics of a continuous backpropagation model was proposed by Henry J. Kelley.
1962	Stuart Dreyfus developed a simpler version of a backpropagation model based only on the chain rule.
1965	Neural network models with polynomial equations as activation functions were proposed by Alexey Grigoryevich Ivakhnenko and Valentin Grigor'evich Lapa.
1970	Research in deep learning and artificial intelligence was limited due to lack of funding.
1979	Neocognitron, a hierarchical, multilayered artificial neural network used for handwriting recognition and other pattern recognition problems, was developed by Kunihiko Fukushima.
1985	The term "deep learning" gained popularity because of the use of a many-layered neural network that could be pretrained one layer at a time demonstrated by Hinton and Rumelhart Williams.
1989	Combining convolutional neural networks with backpropagation to read handwritten digits was developed by Yann LeCun at Bell Labs.
1985–1990	Research in neural networks and deep learning was limited for the second time due to lack of funding.
1999	The next significant advancement was the adoption of GPU processing for deep learning.
2000	The vanishing gradient problem appeared for gradient learning methods where "features" learned at lower layers were not being learned by the upper layers, because no learning signal reached these layers.
2009	Launch of ImageNet, an assembled free database of more than 14 million labeled images by Fei-Fei Li, at Stanford.
2011	AlexNet, a convolutional neural network using rectified linear units, won several international competitions during 2011 and 2012.
2012	In its "cat experiment" Google Brain using unsupervised learning, a convolutional neural net given unlabeled data needed to find recurring patterns.
2014	Ian Goodfellow proposed a generative adversarial neural network (GAN) in which two networks compete against each other in a game.
2016	AlphaGo, a neural network based computer program, mastered the complex game Go and beat a professional Go player.

dog-recognition skills by repeatedly adjusting its weights over and over again. This training technique is called supervised learning, which occurs even when the neural networks are not explicitly told what "makes" a dog. They must recognize patterns in data over time and learn on their own.

15.3 Evolution of Deep Learning

After learning what deep learning is, and understanding the principles of its working, let's go a little back and see the rise of deep learning. The evolution of deep learning is given in Table 15.1.

15.4 Deep Learning in Action

Aside from your favorite music streaming service suggesting tunes you might enjoy, how is deep learning impacting people's lives? As it turns out, deep learning is finding its way into applications of all sizes. Anyone using Facebook cannot help but notice that the social platform commonly identifies and tags your friends when you upload new photos. Digital assistants like Siri, Cortana, Alexa, and Google Now use deep learning for natural language processing and speech recognition. Skype translates spoken conversations in real time. Many email platforms have become adept at identifying spam messages before they even reach the inbox. PayPal has implemented deep learning to prevent fraudulent payments. Apps like CamFind allow users to take a picture of any object and, using mobile visual search technology, discover what the object is.

Google, in particular, is leveraging deep learning to deliver solutions. Google Deepmind's AlphaGo computer program recently defeated standing champions at the game of Go. DeepMind's WaveNet can generate speech mimicking human voice that sounds more natural than speech systems presently on the market. Google Translate is using deep learning and image recognition to translate voice and written languages. Google Planet can identify where any photo was taken. Google developed the deep learning software database Tensorflow to help produce AI applications.

Deep learning is only in its infancy and, in the decades to come, will transform society. Self-driving cars are being tested worldwide; the complex layer of neural networks is being trained to determine objects to avoid, recognize traffic lights, and know when to adjust speed. Neural networks are becoming adept at forecasting everything from stock prices to the weather. Consider the value of digital assistants who can recommend when to sell shares or when to evacuate ahead of a hurricane. Deep learning applications will even save lives as they develop the ability to design evidence-based treatment plans for medical patients and help detect cancers early.

Now, as you have clearly understood what deep learning is and want to step up in this cutting-edge technology, you must know the career prospects.

15.4.1 Applications

1. **Automatic text generation**: A corpus of text is learned, and from this model new text is generated, word by word or character by character. Then this model is capable of learning how to spell, punctuate, and form sentences, or it may even capture the style.

2. **Health care**: Helps in diagnosing various diseases and treating them.

3. **Automatic machine translation**: Certain words, sentences, or phrases in one language are transformed into another language (deep learning is achieving top results in the areas of text and images).

4. **Image recognition**: Recognizes and identifies peoples and objects in images as well as to understand content and context. This area is already being used in gaming, retail, tourism, and so on.

5. **Predicting earthquakes**: Teaches a computer to perform viscoelastic computations, which are used in predicting earthquakes.

TABLE 15.2

Comparison Between Machine Learning and Deep Learning

Machine Learning	Deep Learning
Works on small amount of data set for accuracy	Works on large data sets.
Dependent on low-end machine	Heavily dependent on high-end machine
Divides the tasks into subtasks, solves them individually and finally combines the results	Solves problem end to end
Takes less time to train	Takes longer time to train
Testing time may increase	Less time to test the data

15.4.2 Differences Between Machine Learning and Deep Learning

Knowing the differences between machine learning and deep learning techniques is very important and Table 15.2 shows the comparison between machine learning and deep learning techniques.

Understanding the mathematics behind neural networks and deep learning becomes essential to know how and why they work.

15.5 Neural Networks

Neural networks are networks of interconnected neurons, for example interconnection of neurons in human brains. Artificial neural networks are highly connected to other neurons and perform computations by combining signals from other neurons. Outputs of these computations may be transmitted to one or more other neurons. The neurons are connected together in a specific way to perform a particular task.

A neural network is a function. It consists basically of (1) neurons, which pass input values through functions and output the result, and (2) weights, which carry values (real-number) between neurons. Neurons can be categorized into layers: (1) input layer, (2) hidden layer, and (3) output layer.

15.5.1 Basic Components of Biological Neurons

The human nervous system can be divided into three stages as shown in Figure 15.1.

a **Receptors**: Receptors convert stimuli from the external environment into electrical impulses. The best example is the rods and cones of eyes. Pain, touch, hot, and cold receptors of skin are another example for receptors.

b **Neural net**: Neural nets receive information, process it, and make appropriate decisions. The brain is a neural net.

c **Effectors**: Effectors convert electrical impulses generated by the neural net (brain) into responses to the external environment. Examples of effectors are muscles and glands and speech generators.

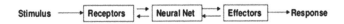

FIGURE 15.1
Stages of human nervous system.

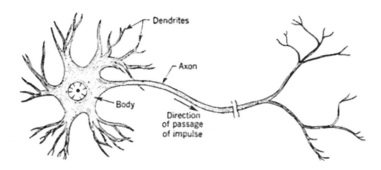

FIGURE 15.2
Basic components of a biological neuron.

The basic components of a biological neuron as given in Figure 15.2 are (1) cell body (soma), which processes the incoming activations and converts them into output activations; (2) the neuron nucleus, which contains the genetic material (DNA); (3) dendrites, which form a fine filamentary bush, each fiber thinner than an axon; (4) the axon, a long, thin cylinder carrying impulses from the soma to other cells; and (5) synapses, the junctions that allow signal transmission between the axons and dendrites.

Computation in biological neurons happens as follows: (1) Incoming signals from synapses are summed up at the soma, and (2) on crossing a threshold, the cell fires, generating an action potential in the axon hillock region.

15.5.1.1 Perceptrons

Perceptrons, invented by Frank Rosenblatt in 1958, are the simplest neural network that consists of n number of inputs, only one neuron, and one output, where n is the number of features of our data set as shown in Figure 15.3. The process of passing the data through the neural network, known as forward propagation, is explained in the following three steps.

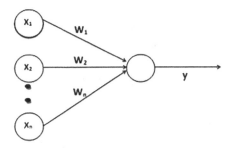

FIGURE 15.3
Single layer perceptron.

Step 1: The input value x_i for each input is multiplied by weights w_i representing the strength or influence of the connection between neurons and summed as given in Equation (15.1). The higher the weights, the higher their influence.

$$\Sigma = (x_1 * w_1) + (x_2 * w_2) + \ldots + (x_n * w_n) \tag{15.1}$$

The row vectors of the inputs and weights are $x = [x_1, x_2, \ldots, x_n]$ and $w = [w_1, w_2, \ldots, w_n]$, respectively, and their dot product gives the summation (Equations 15.2 and 15.3).

$$x.w = (x_1 * w_1) + (x_2 * w_2) + \ldots + (x_n * w_n) \tag{15.2}$$

$$\Sigma = x.w \tag{15.3}$$

Step 2: Bias, also known as the offset, is added to shift the output function (Equation 15.4).

$$y = x.w + b$$
$$y = \begin{cases} 1, if \, \Sigma w_i x_i > threshold \\ 0 \, otherwise \end{cases} \tag{15.4}$$

Step 3: This value will be presented to the activation function where the type of activation function will depend on the need and has a significant impact on the learning speed of the neural network. Here we use the **sigmoid**—also known as a logistic function—as our activation function (Equation 15.5).

$$\hat{y} = \sigma(z) = \frac{1}{1 + e^{-z}} \tag{15.5}$$

where σ denotes the sigmoid activation function, and the output we get after the forward propagation is known as the predicted value $\hat{y}$.

Example: A simple decision via perceptron may be whether you should go to watch amovie this weekend.

The decision variables are:

1. Is there any extra lecture this weekend? (x_1)
2. Does your friend want to go with you? (x_2)
3. Do you have pending assignments due on the weekend? (x_3)

For $b = -8$ and $b = -3$, let's observe the output y as shown in Figure 15.4.

15.5.1.2 Perceptron Training

A perceptron works by taking in some numerical inputs along with what is known as weights and a bias. It then multiplies these inputs with the respective weights (this is known as the weighted sum). These products are then added together along with the bias.

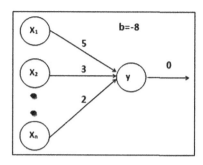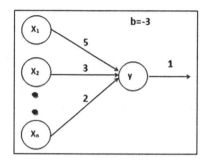

FIGURE 15.4
Sample example.

The activation function takes the weighted sum and the bias as inputs and returns a final output.

A perceptron consists of four parts: input values, weights and a bias, a weighted sum, and an activation function. Let us understand the training using the following algorithm.

Algorithm: Perceptron Training

    Step 1: Absorb bias b as weight.

    Step 2: Start with a random value of weight w_j

    Step 3: Predict for each input x_i:

        If the prediction is correct $\forall x$, then

        Return w

    Step 4: On a mistake for given input x, update as follows:

        • Mistake on positive ($y = 1$), update $w_{j+1} \leftarrow w_j + x$

        • Mistake on negative ($y = 0$), update $w_{j+1} \leftarrow w_j - x$

15.5.2 Activation Functions

An activation function decides whether a neuron should be activated or not. It helps the network to use the useful information and suppress the irrelevant information. An activation function is usually a nonlinear function. If we choose a linear function, then it would be a linear classifier with limited capacity to solve complex problems. Step, sign, sigmoid, tan, and ReLU functions, shown in Figure 15.5, can be activation functions.

- **Sigmoid**

$$\sigma(z) = \frac{1}{1 + \exp(-z)} \tag{15.6}$$

The value of the sigmoid function lies between 0 and 1 ,and the function is continuously differentiable and not symmetric around the origin, but the vanishing gradients problem does occur (Equation 15.6).

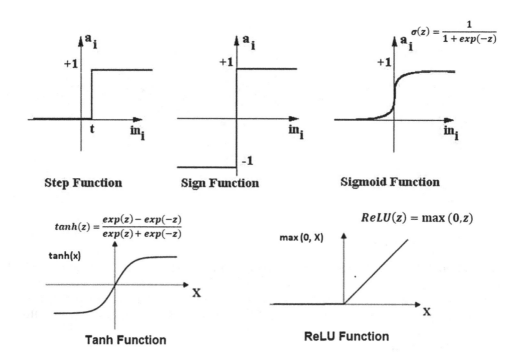

FIGURE 15.5
Activation functions.

- **Tanh**

$$\tanh(z) = \frac{\exp(z) - \exp(-z)}{\exp(z) + \exp(-z)} \tag{15.7}$$

This function is a scaled version of the sigmoid and is symmetric around the origin (Equation 15.7), but the vanishing gradients problem does occur.

- **ReLU**

Also called a piecewise linear function because the rectified function is linear for half of the input domain and nonlinear for the other half.

$$ReLU(z) = \max(0, z) \tag{15.8}$$

This function is trivial to implement, has a sparse representation, and avoids the problem of vanishing gradients (Equation 15.8).

15.6 Learning Algorithm

A neural network with at least one hidden layer can approximate any function and the representation power of the network increases with more hidden units and more hidden layers. The learning algorithm consists of two parts — backpropagation and optimization.

15.6.1 Backpropagation

- A backpropagation algorithm is used to train artificial neural networks; it can update the weights very efficiently.
- It is a computationally efficient approach to compute the derivatives of a complex cost function.
- The goal is to use those derivatives to learn the weight coefficients for parameterizing a multilayer artificial neural network.
- It computes the gradient of a cost function with respect to all the weights in the network, so that the gradient is fed to the gradient descent method, which in turn uses it to update the weights in order to minimize the cost function.

15.6.2 Chain Rule

The simpler version of the backpropagation model is based on chain rules.

Single path: The following Equation (15.9) represents the chain rule of a single path.

$$\frac{\partial z}{\partial x} = \frac{\partial z}{\partial y} \frac{\partial y}{\partial x} \tag{15.9}$$

Figure 15.6 shows the diagrammatic representation of the single path chain rule.

Multiple path: The following Equation (15.10) represents the chain rule of multiple paths.

$$\frac{\partial z}{\partial x} = \frac{\partial z}{\partial y_1} \frac{\partial y_1}{\partial x} + \frac{\partial z}{\partial y_2} \frac{\partial y_2}{\partial x}$$

$$\frac{\partial z}{\partial x} = \sum_{t=1}^{T} \frac{\partial z}{\partial y_t} \frac{\partial y_t}{\partial x} \tag{15.10}$$

Figure 15.7 shows the diagrammatic representation of the multiple path chain rule.

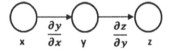

FIGURE 15.6
Diagrammatic representation of single path.

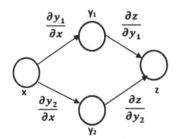

FIGURE 15.7
Diagrammatic representation of multiple paths.

The total error in the network for a single input is given by Equation (15.11).

$$E = \frac{1}{2}\sum_{k=1}^{K}\left(a_k - t_k\right)^2 \tag{15.11}$$

where a_k is the predicted output/activation of a node k, and t_k is the actual output of a node k.

There are two sets of weights in our network as shown in Figure 15.8:

- w_{ij}: from the input to the hidden layer
- w_{jk}: from the hidden to the output layer

To reduce the overall error, the network's weights need to be adjusted as shown in Equation (15.12).

$$\Delta W \quad \alpha \quad -\frac{\partial E}{\partial W} \tag{15.12}$$

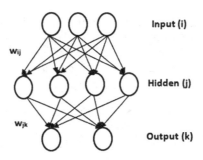

FIGURE 15.8
Sample architecture diagram with weights.

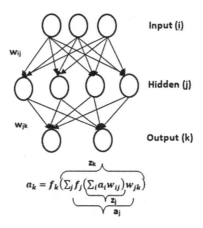

FIGURE 15.9
Backpropagation for outermost layer.

15.6.3 Backpropagation—For Outermost Layer

- Outermost layer parameters directly affect the value of the error function.
- Only one term of the E summation will have a nonzero derivative: the one associated with the particular weight we are considering.

$$\frac{\partial E}{\partial w_{jk}} = \frac{\partial E}{\partial a_k} \frac{\partial a_k}{\partial z_k} \frac{\partial z_k}{\partial w_{jk}} \tag{15.13}$$

Each component of the backpropagation of the outermost layer's equation (Equation 15.13) is derived in the following equations (Equations 15.14–15.17):

$$\frac{\partial E}{\partial a_k} = \frac{\partial}{\partial a_k} \left(\frac{1}{2} \sum_{k \in K} (a_k - t_k)^2 \right) = (a_k - t_k) \tag{15.14}$$

$$\frac{\partial a_k}{\partial z_k} = \frac{\partial}{\partial z_k} \left(f_k(z_k) \right) = f_k'(z_k) \tag{15.15}$$

$$\frac{\partial z_k}{\partial w_{jk}} = \frac{\partial}{\partial w_{jk}} \left(\sum_j a_j w_{jk} \right) = a_j \tag{15.16}$$

For the sigmoid activation function,

$$\frac{\partial z_k}{\partial w_{jk}} = (a_k - t_k) a_k (1 - a_k) a_j) \tag{15.17}$$

15.6.4 Backpropagation—For Hidden Layer

Each component of the backpropagation of the hidden layer's equations is shown and derived in Equations (15.18)–(15.20).

$$\begin{aligned}
\frac{\partial E}{\partial w_{ij}} &= \frac{\partial}{\partial w_{ij}} \left(\frac{1}{2} \sum_{k \in K} (a_k - t_k)^2 \right) \\
&= \sum_{k \in K} (a_k - t_k) \frac{\partial}{\partial w_{ij}} a_k \\
&= \sum_{k \in K} (a_k - t_k) \frac{\partial}{\partial w_{ij}} \left(f_k(z_k) \right) \\
&= \sum_{k \in K} (a_k - t_k) f_k'(z_k) \frac{\partial}{\partial w_{ij}} z_k
\end{aligned} \tag{15.18}$$

$$\frac{\partial z_k}{\partial w_{ij}} = \frac{\partial z_k}{\partial a_j}\frac{\partial a_j}{\partial w_{ij}}$$

$$= \frac{\partial}{\partial a_j}a_jw_{jk}\frac{\partial a_j}{\partial w_{ij}}$$

$$= w_{jk}\frac{\partial a_j}{\partial w_{ij}}$$

$$= w_{jk}\frac{\partial f_j(z_j)}{\partial w_{ij}} \qquad (15.19)$$

$$= w_{jk}f_j'(z_j)\frac{\partial z_j}{\partial w_{ij}}$$

$$= w_{jk}f_j'(z_j)\frac{\partial}{\partial w_{ij}}\left(\sum_i a_iw_{ij}\right)$$

$$= w_{jk}f_j'(z_j)a_i$$

$$\frac{\partial E}{\partial w_{ij}} = \sum_{k\in K}(a_k - t_k)f_k'(z_k)\underbrace{w_{jk}f_j'(z_j)a_i}_{}$$

$$\qquad \qquad \qquad \qquad \qquad \qquad \frac{\partial z_k}{\partial w_{ij}}$$

$$= f_j'(z_j)\,a_i\underbrace{\sum_{k\in K}(a_k - t_k)f_k'(z_k)w_{jk}}_{} \qquad (15.20)$$

$$\qquad \qquad \qquad \qquad \qquad \qquad \delta_k$$

$$= \underbrace{a_if_j'(z_j)\sum_{k\in K}\delta_kw_{jk}}_{}$$

$$= \delta_ja_i$$

$$\qquad \qquad \qquad \delta_j$$

The backpropagation algorithm is used for calculating the gradient of the loss function, which points us in the direction of the value that minimizes the loss function, and using gradient descent iteratively in the direction given by the gradient, we move closer to the minimum value of error. The perceptron uses backpropagation in the following manner.

Step 1: There is a need to estimate the distance between the predicted solution and the desired solution, which is generally defined as a loss function such as mean squared error. In the case of a regression problem using mean squared error as a loss function, the squares of the difference between actual (y_i) and predicted value ($\hat{y}_i$) are as shown in Equation (15.21).

$$MSE_i = (y_i - \hat{y}_i)^2 \qquad (15.21)$$

The average loss function for the entire training data set: the cost function C for the entire data set is the average loss function for all n datapoints and is given in Equation (15.22) as follows.

$$C = MSE = \frac{1}{n}\sum_{i=1}^{n}(y_i - \hat{y}_i)^2 \qquad (15.22)$$

Step 2: In order to find the best weights and bias for our perceptron, we need to know how the cost function changes in relation to weights and bias. This is done with the help of the gradients (rate of change)—how one quantity changes in relation to another quantity. In our case, we need to find the gradient of the cost function with respect to the weights and bias.

The gradient of cost function C with respect to the weight w_i can be calculated using *partial derivation*. Since the cost function is not directly related to the weight w_i, the chain rule can be used as given in Equation (15.23).

$$\frac{\partial C}{\partial w_i} = \frac{\partial C}{\partial \hat{y}} * \frac{\partial \hat{y}}{\partial z} * \frac{\partial z}{\partial w_i}$$

(15.23)

Now we need to find the following three gradients:

$$\frac{\partial C}{\partial \hat{y}} = ? \frac{\partial \hat{y}}{\partial z} = ? \frac{\partial z}{\partial w_1} = ?$$

Let's start with the gradient of the cost function (C) (Equation 15.24) with respect to the predicted value ($\hat{y}$) (Equation 15.24).

$$\frac{\partial C}{\partial \hat{y}} = \frac{\partial}{\partial \hat{y}} \frac{1}{n} \sum_{i=1}^{n} (y_i - \hat{y}_i)^2 = 2 * \frac{1}{n} \sum_{i=1}^{n} (y_i - \hat{y}_i)$$

(15.24)

Let $y = [y_1, y_2, \ldots y_n]$ and $\hat{y} = [\hat{y}_1, \hat{y}_2, \ldots \hat{y}_n]$ be the row vectors of actual and predicted values. Hence the previous equation is simplified as follows (Equation 15.25):

$$\frac{\partial C}{\partial \hat{y}} = \frac{2}{n} \sum (y - \hat{y})$$

(15.25)

Now let's find the gradient of the *predicted value* with respect to z (Equation 15.26). This will be a bit lengthy.

$$\frac{\partial \hat{y}}{\partial z} = \frac{\partial}{\partial z} \sigma(z)$$

$$= \frac{\partial}{\partial z} \left(\frac{1}{1+e^{-z}} \right)$$

$$= \frac{e^{-z}}{\left(1+e^{-z} \right)^2}$$

$$= \frac{1}{\left(1+e^{-z} \right)} * \frac{e^{-z}}{\left(1-e^{-z} \right)}$$

$$= \frac{1}{\left(1+e^{-z} \right)} * \left(1 - \frac{1}{\left(1+e^{-z} \right)} \right)$$

$$= \sigma(z) * (1 - \sigma(z))$$

(15.26)

The gradient of z with respect to the weight w_i is given in Equation (15.27).

$$
\begin{aligned}
\frac{\partial z}{\partial w_i} &= \frac{\partial}{\partial w_i}(z) \\
&= \frac{\partial}{\partial w_i}\left(\sum_{i=1}^{n} x_i w_i + b\right) \\
&= x_i
\end{aligned}
$$
(15.27)

Therefore we get Equation (15.28),

$$
\frac{\partial C}{\partial w_i} = \frac{2}{n}\sum (y-\hat{y})*\sigma(z)*(1-\sigma(z))*x_i
$$
(15.28)

What about bias? Bias is theoretically considered to have an input of constant value 1. Hence (Equation 15.29),

$$
\frac{\partial C}{\partial b} = \frac{2}{n}\sum (y-\hat{y})*\sigma(z)*(1-\sigma(z))
$$
(15.29)

15.7 Multilayered Perceptron

A **multilayered perceptron (MLP)** is one of the most common neural network models used in the field of deep learning. Often referred to as a "vanilla" neural network, an MLP is simpler than the complex models of today's era. However, the techniques it introduced have paved the way for further advanced neural networks.

The MLP is used for a variety of tasks, such as stock analysis, image identification, spam detection, and election voting predictions.

15.7.1 The Basic Structure

A multilayered perceptron consists of interconnected neurons transferring information to each other, much like the human brain. Each neuron is assigned a value. The network can be divided into three main layers as shown in Figure 15.10.

- **Input Layer**: This is the initial layer of the network which takes in an input that will be used to produce an output.
- **Hidden Layer(s)**: The network needs to have at least one hidden layer. The hidden layer(s) perform computations and operations on the input data to produce something meaningful.
- **Output Layer**: The neurons in this layer display a meaningful output.

Connections

The MLP is a **feed forward neural network**, which means that the data is transmitted from the input layer to the output layer in the forward direction.

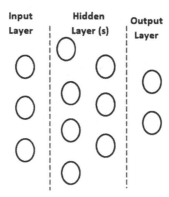

FIGURE 15.10
Multilayer perceptron.

The connections between the layers are assigned **weights** as shown in Figure 15.11. The weight of a connection specifies its importance. This concept is the backbone of an MLP's learning process.

While the inputs take their values from the surroundings, the values of all the other neurons are calculated through a mathematical function involving the weights and values of the layer before it.

For example, the value of the h5 node in figure 15.11 could be (Equation 15.30),

$$h_5 = h_1.w_8 + h_2.w_9h_5 \tag{15.30}$$

15.7.2 Backpropagation

Backpropagation is a technique used to optimize the weights of an MLP using the outputs as inputs.

In a conventional MLP, random weights are assigned to all the connections as shown in Figure 15.12. These random weights propagate values through the network to produce the actual output (Figure 15.13). Naturally, this output would differ from the expected output. The difference between the two values is called the **error**.

Backpropagation refers to the process of sending this error back through the network (Figure 15.14, 15.15), readjusting the weights automatically so that eventually the error between the actual and expected output is minimized (Figure 15.16).

In this way, the output of the current iteration becomes the input and affects the next output. This is repeated until the correct output is produced. The weights at the end of the process would be the ones on which the neural network works correctly (Figure 15.16, 15.17).

15.8 Convolutional Neural Network

Convolutional neural networks are neural networks that are mostly used in image classification, object detection, face recognition, self-driving cars, robotics, neural style transfer, video recognition, recommendation systems, and so on.

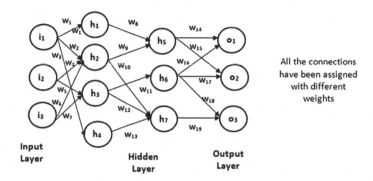

FIGURE 15.11
MLP architecture with weights.

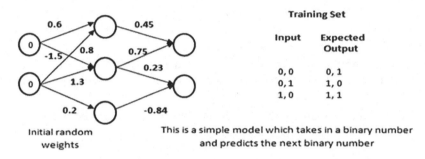

FIGURE 15.12
Simple model for predicting the next binary number.

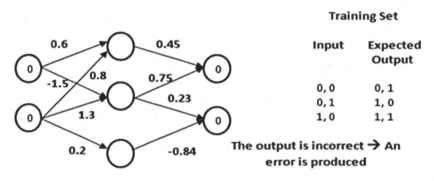

FIGURE 15.13
Iteration 1—training with first input of training set.

CNN classification takes any input image and finds a pattern in the image, processes it, and classifies it in various categories such as car, animal, or bottle. CNN is also used in unsupervised learning for clustering images by similarity. It is a very interesting and complex algorithm, which is driving the future of technology.

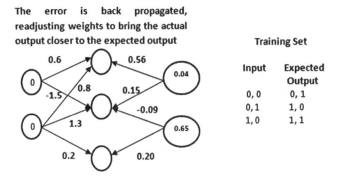

FIGURE 15.14
Backpropagation—adjusting weights from output layer to hidden layer.

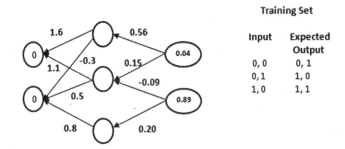

FIGURE 15.15
Back propagation—adjusting weights from hidden layer to input layer.

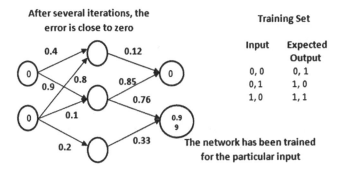

FIGURE 15.16
Training for particular input.

15.8.1 Biological Connection to CNN

When you first heard of the term *convolutional neural networks*, you may have thought of something related to neuroscience or biology, and you would be right. CNNs do take a biological inspiration from the visual cortex. The visual cortex has small regions of cells that are sensitive to specific regions of the visual field.

This idea was expanded upon by a fascinating experiment by Hubel and Wiesel in 1962 where they showed that some individual neuronal cells in the brain responded (or fired) only in the presence of edges of a certain orientation. For example, some neurons fired

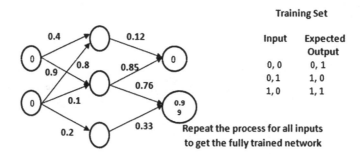

FIGURE 15.17
Generation of final model.

when exposed to vertical edges and some when shown horizontal or diagonal edges. Hubel and Wiesel found out that all of these neurons were organized in a columnar architecture and that together they were able to produce visual perception. This idea of specialized components inside of a system having specific tasks (the neuronal cells in the visual cortex looking for specific characteristics) is one that machines use as well and is the basis behind CNNs.

15.8.2 The Architecture of Convolutional Neural Networks (CNNs)

The term *convolution neural networks* indicates that these are simply neural networks with some mathematical operation (generally matrix multiplication) in between their layers called convolution.

It was proposed by Yann LeCun in 1998. It's one of the most popular uses in image classification. A convolution neural network (Figure 15.18) can broadly be classified into these layers:

Input layers include the following:

1. Convolutional layer
2. Pooling layer (optional)
3. Output layers

Input layers are connected with convolutional layers where the input layer in CNN reshapes the image data represented as a three-dimensional matrix to a single column.

- **Convolutional layer**: The convolutional layer's main objective is to learn or extract all the features of the image which would help in object detection. As we know, the input layer will contain some pixel values with some weight and height; our kernels or filters will convolve around the input layer and give results which will retrieve all the features with fewer dimensions. This is done by convolution filtering, where a window representing the feature of the image is dragged over the input and the convolution product between the feature and each portion of the scanned image is calculated. We finally get a feature map that is an image and a filter giving the features of the image. This layer performs many tasks such as padding, striding, and applying the kernels, and hence this layer is considered as a building block of convolutional neural networks.

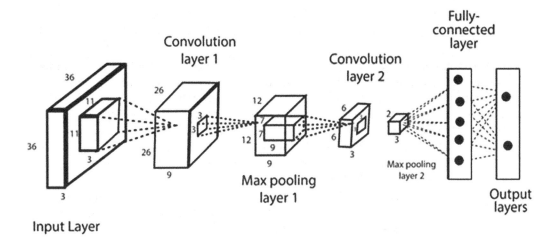

FIGURE 15.18
Convolutional neural network.

- **Pooling layer (optional layer)**: A pooling layer, optionally placed between two layers of convolution, reduces the spatial volume of the input image after convolution while preserving the important characteristics. This layer improves the efficiency and avoids overfitting.

- **Output layer**: The fully connected layer is the last layer of the CNN as is the case of any neural network. This layer applies a linear combination and then possibly an activation function to produce the output. This layer classifies the image and returns as output vector of size N where N is the number of classes of our task and each element of the vector indicates the probability of the input belonging to that particular class.

15.8.3 Convolutional Networks in the History of Deep Learning

A convolutional neural network (CNN) is a particular class of neural networks, used mainly for image analysis. CNN architectures have evolved, giving results that are comparable to those obtained via human execution/intervention. A wide variety of architectures are available and can be applied depending on the task to be carried out.

- **Neocognitron (1980)**: Neocognitron was the originator of CNNs. It introduced the concepts of feature extraction, pooling layers, and using convolution in a neural network with the objective of recognition or classification The configuration of the network is based on human visual perception. It is a hierarchical, multilayered neural network with layers of "S-cells" (simple cells) and "C-cells" (complex cells) arranged alternately and was designed for handwritten (Japanese) character recognition. The process of feature extraction by S-cells and toleration of positional shift by C-cells was alternatively repeated where local features extracted at lower stages were gradually integrated into more global features.

- **LeNet-5 (1989–1998)**: LeNet, largely developed for handwritten digit recognition, was proposed by Yann LeCun and team and was responsible for the term "convolutional neural network." It used 5 x 5 convolution filters with a stride of 1. The pooling (subsampling) layers were 2 x 2 with a stride of 2 and had 60 K parameters.

The ImageNet (a data set) classification challenge started in 2010 and was mainly responsible for the newer architectures of CNN and led to research in machine learning and computer vision models, for image classification, using a common data set. In 2010, a system developed without using neural networks had a winning error rate of 28.2%. In 2011, researchers improved the score from 28.2% to 25.8% error rate. In 2012, Alex Krizhevsky and Geoffrey Hinton introduced a CNN architecture, AlexNet, which reduced the error further to 16.4%, marking a significant improvement in performance.

- **AlexNet (2012)**: AlexNet was the first winner of the ImageNet challenge based on a CNN, and since then every year's challenge has been won by a CNN-based system, significantly outperforming other deep as well as traditional machine learning methods. Here the normalization layer, called the response normalization layer, and a rectified linear unit (ReLU) as an activation function were first introduced.

- **ZFNet (2013)**: In 2013, ZFNet (named after its designers Zeiler and Fergus), similar to AlexNet, with few changes in hyper-parameters was the winner of the ImageNet challenge. The careful selection of hyper-parameters resulted in a significant decrease in error from 16.4% to 11.7%.

- **VGGNet (2014)**: The year 2014 saw the introduction of a new architecture known as the VGGNet by the Visual Geometry Group (at Oxford University). Problems could be solved better with lower error rate on the ImageNet classification challenge by increasing the depth of the network and hence handling nonlinearities in the function. The architecture won the runner-up in the ImageNet challenge in 2014.

- **GoogLeNet (2014)**: In 2014, Google introduced GoogLeNet, where design of deeper networks with the objective of greater efficiency to reduce parameter count, memory usage, and computation was considered. There were 22 layers but without any fully connected (FC) layers, reducing the total number of parameters. GoogLeNet became the ILSVRC-14 classification winner with 6.7% error.

- **ResNet (2015)**: Kaiming He et al. introduced the idea of a residual network, a stack of many "residual blocks" connected to each other through identity (skip) connections in their architecture. Each residual block has two 3×3 convolution layers. The concept of skip connection was also introduced. The network had depths up to 152 layers designed to not compromise the model's generalization power, where the "bottleneck" layer was used to improve efficiency. ResNet won first place in all ImageNet 2015 competitions and is a popular choice for several applications.

15.8.4 Learning in Convolutional Neural Networks

Images are made up of pixels. Each pixel is represented by a number between 0 and 255. Therefore, each image has a digital representation, which is how computers can work with images.

There are five major operations in CNN image detection/classification. These steps are as follows:

1. Image channels
2. Convolution
3. Pooling
4. Flattening
5. Full connection

15.8.4.1 Image Channels

The CNN needs the image to be represented in numerical format where each pixel is mapped to a number between 0 and 255 to represent color. For a black and white image, a 2-dimensional array of size $m \times n$ containing the corresponding pixel value is used. In the case of a colored image, a 3-dimensional array representing the corresponding pixel is used, where the dimensions correspond to the red, blue, and green channels (Figure 15.19).

The image is represented as a 3-dimensional array, with each channel representing red, green, and blue values, respectively, as shown in Figure 15.20.

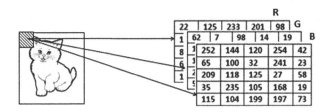

FIGURE 15.19
Representation of image 3D array.

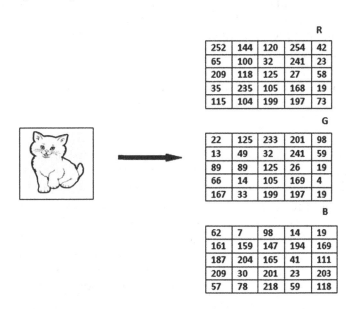

FIGURE 15.20
Representation of 3D image with each channel (red, green, blue).

15.8.4.2 Convolution

A combination of numbers represents the image from which the key features within the image need to be identified for which convolution is used. The convolution operation modifies or convolutes one function to the shape of another, normally used in images to sharpen, smooth, and intensify images for extraction of important features.

Feature Detection

A filter or a kernel is an array that represents the feature to be extracted. This filter is strided over the input array, resulting in a 2-dimensional array that contains the correlation of the image with respect to the applied filter. The output array is referred to as the *feature map*.

The resulting image contains just the edges present in the original input. For example, the filter used in the previous example is of size 3×3 and is applied to the input image of size 5×5. The resulting feature map is of size 3×3. In summary, for an input image of size $n \times n$ and a filter of size $m \times m$, the resulting output is of size $(n - m + 1) \times (n - m + 1)$.

Strided Convolutions

During the process of convolution, you can see how the input array is transformed into a smaller array while still maintaining the spatial correlation between the pixels by applying filters. Here, we discuss an option on how to help compress the size of the input array to a greater extent.

Striding

In the previous section, you saw how the filter is applied to each 3×3 section of the input image. You can see that this window is slid by one column to the right each time, and the end of each row is slid down by one row. In this case, sliding of the filter over the input was done one step at a time. This is referred to as striding. The following example shows the same convolution but strided with two steps.

The filter used in the previous example is of size 3×3 and is applied to the input image of size 5×5 with a stride = 2. The resulting feature map is of size 2×2. In summary, for an input image of size $n \times n$ and a filter of size $m \times m$ with stride = k, the resulting output will be of size $((n - m)/k + 1) \times ((n - m)/k + 1)$

Padding

During convolution, the size of the feature map is reduced drastically when compared to the input. In addition, the filter stride filters the cells in the corners just once, but the cells in the center quite a few times.

To ensure that the size of the feature map retains its original input size and enables equal assessment of all pixels, one or more layers of padding is applied to the original input array. Padding is the process of adding extra layers of zeros to the outer rows and columns of the input array. If we add 1 layer of padding to the input array before a filter is applied, in general, for an input image of size $n \times n$ and a filter of size $m \times m$ with padding = p, the resulting output is of size $(n + 2p - m + 1) \times (n + 2p - m + 1)$.

Applying convolutions over the RGB channels

Convolution over a color image over three channels is next discussed.

For a 5 × 5 image represented over three channels, the 3 × 3 filter is now replicated three times, once for each channel (Figure 15.21). The input image is a 5 × 5 × 3 array, and the filter is a 3 × 3 × 3 array. However, the output map is still a 2D 4 × 4 array. The convolutions on the same pixel through the different channel are added and are collectively represented within each cell.

In general, for an input image of size $n \times n$ and filter of size $m \times m$ over N channels, the image and filters are converted into arrays of sizes $n \times n \times N$ and $m \times m \times N$, respectively, and the feature map produced is of size $(n - m + 1) \times (n - m + 1)$ assuming stride = 1.

Applying convolutions with more than one filter

In the previous section, the output of applying convolution over multiple channels was discussed; however, only one filter was used. In reality, the CNN model needs to use multiple filters at the same time to observe and extract key features. We now discuss thee output when using multiple filters looks like.

In the previous image, you see that applying convolution using three filters (Figure 15.22) over the RGB channels produces three 4 × 4 arrays. Thus, for an input image of size $n \times n$ and filter of size $m \times m$ over N channel and F filters, the feature map produced is of size $(n - m + 1) \times (n - m + 1) \times F$ assuming that stride = 1.

15.8.4.3 Pooling

In order to further reduce the size of the feature map generated from convolution, pooling or subsampling, which helps to further compress the dimensions of the feature map, is used.

Pooling is the process of summarizing the features within a group of cells in the feature map. This summary of cells can be acquired by taking the maximum, minimum, or average within a group of cells. Each of these methods is referred to as min, max, and average pooling, respectively. In CNN, pooling is applied to feature maps that result from each filter if more than one filter is used.

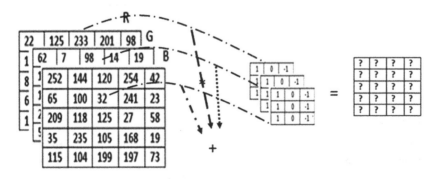

FIGURE 15.21
Applying 3 × 3 filter.

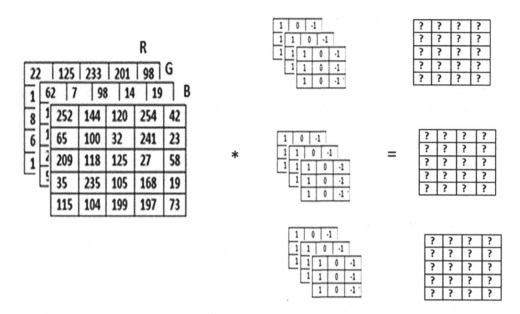

FIGURE 15.22
Applying three filters of size 3 × 3.

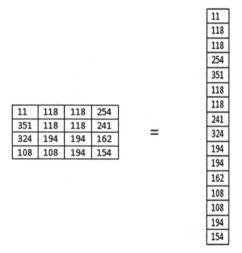

FIGURE 15.23
Flattening.

15.8.4.4 Flattening

We can think of CNN as a sequence of steps that are performed to effectively capture the important aspects of an image before applying ANN on it. In the previous steps, we saw the different transitions that are applied to the original image.

The final step in this process is to make the outcomes of CNN be compatible with an artificial neural network. The inputs to ANN should be in the form of a vector. To support that, flattening is applied (Figure 15.23), which is the step to convert the multidimensional array into an $n \times 1$ vector, as shown previously.

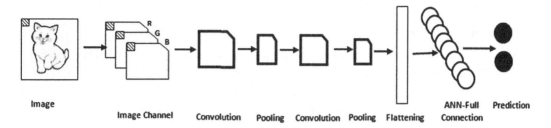

FIGURE 15.24
Overall flow of convolutional neural network.

Note that Figure 15.23 shows flattening applied to just one feature map. However, in CNN, flattening is applied to feature maps that result from each filter.

15.8.4.5 Full Connection: A Simple Convolutional Network

In this final section, we will combine all the steps that were previously discussed to show how the output of the final layer is served as an input to ANN.

Figure 15.24 shows a sample CNN that is built to recognize a cat image. To begin, the original input image is represented using its pixel values over the RGB channel. Convolutions and pooling are then applied to help identify feature mapping and compress the data further.

Note that convolutions and pooling can be applied to CNN many times. The metrics of the model generated depends on finding the right number of times these steps should be repeated.

Once the network is built, then the network is compiled or trained using stochastic gradient descent (SGD). Gradient descent works fine when we have a convex curve. But if we do not have a convex curve, gradient descent fails. Hence, in stochastic gradient descent, a few samples are selected randomly instead of the whole data set for each iteration.

After this, the output is flattened and converted to a single-dimensional vector to make it compatible with ANN. This flattened output is passed through one or more fully connected neural networks. The final layer of this network contains the probability under which the original image is predicted.

15.9 Summary

- Introduced deep learning including its evolution, working, and applications.
- Outlined the basic components of neural networks.
- Discussed perceptrons in detail with an example, activation function used, and the learning algorithm comprising backpropagation and optimization.
- Described briefly multilayered perceptron (MLP) and convolutional neural networks (CNNs) including their components and the use of CNN for image detection or classification.
- Listed some examples of convolutional neural networks.

15.10 Points to Ponder

- Convolutional neural networks are used for computer vision because of their ability to recognize features in raw data.
- Convolutional neural networks can learn features on their own, building up from low-level (edges, circles) to high-level (faces, hands, cars) features.
- Often the features learnt by convolutional neural networks are not human interpretable.
- When using convolutional neural networks, a wild pixel in the image can result in new surprising outputs.

E.15 Exercises

E.15.1 Suggested Activities

E.15.1.1 Use CNN for automatic digit recognition with the MNIST DATABASE, http://yann.lecun.com/exdb/mnist/.

E.15.1.2 In traffic sign classification project we need to identify traffic signs from the image using CNN. You should use the GTSRB dataset: https://www.kaggle.com/datasets/meowmeowmeowmeowmeow/gtsrb-german-traffic-sign.

E.15.1.3 Apply convolutional neural networks (CNNs) for facial expression recognition, and correctly classify each facial image into one of the seven facial emotion categories: anger, disgust, fear, happiness, sadness, surprise, and neutral. Use the Kaggle data set: https://www.kaggle.com/datasets/msambare/fer2013.

Self-Assessment Questions

E.15.2 Multiple Choice Questions

Give answers with justification for correct and wrong choices.

E.15.2.1 Neocognitron was developed by
 i   Kunihiko Fukushima
 ii   Alan Turing
 iii   Bell Yann Lechun

E.15.2.2 Google Brain conducted the "_____" experiment in 2012 for unsupervised learning using a convolutional neural net.
 i   Dog
 ii   Cat
 iii   Lady

E.15.2.3 Effectors convert electrical impulses generated by the neural net (brain) into responses to the external environment. Examples include
  i   Hands
  ii Muscles
  iii Skin

E.15.2.4 Synapses
  i   Form a fine filamentary bush, with each fiber thinner than an axon
  ii Process the incoming activations and converts them into output activations
  iii Are junctions that allow signal transmission between the axons and dendrites

E.15.2.5 On crossing a threshold, the cell fires
  i   Generating an action potential in the axon region
  ii And incoming signals from synapses are summed up at the soma
  iii Due to incoming signals

E.15.2.6 The process of passing the data through the neural network is known as
  i   Inward propagation
  ii Backward propagation
  iii Forward propagation

E.15.2.7 A sigmoid function used as an activation function is also called a
  i   Tanh function
  ii Logistic function
  iii Sign function

E.15.2.8 The _____ method is used to update the weights in order to minimize the cost function.
  i   Gradient
  ii Gradient descent
  iii Weight reduction

E.15.2.9 The _____ algorithm is used for calculating the gradient of the loss function.
  i   Forward propagation
  ii Activation function
  iii Backward propagation

E.15.2.10 The _____ performs computations and operations on the input data to produce something meaningful.
  i   Input layer
  ii Hidden layer
  iii Output layer

E.15.2.11 In the case of a CNN, the convolution is performed on the input data using the
  i   Kernel
  ii Input layer
  iii Pooling

E.15.2.12   The main objective of the convolution layer in CNN is to
     i Apply a fully connected layer to generate the number of classes
    ii Reduce the spatial size of the image
   iii Learn to extract features from the original image

E.15.2.13   The _____ performs many tasks such as padding, striding, and the functioning of kernels.
     i Pooling layer
    ii Convolutional layer
   iii Fully connected layer

E.15.2.14   The first winner of the ImageNet challenge was
     i AlexNet
    ii VGGNet
   iii ZFNet

E.15.2.15   Sliding of the filter over the input done one step at a time is called
     i Padding
    ii Filtering
   iii Striding

E.15.3 Match the Columns

No	Match	
E.15.3.1 Ian Goodfellow	A	Is the process of passing the data through the neural network
E.15.3.2 ImageNet	B	Is the process where a window representing the feature of the image is dragged over the input and the product between the feature and each portion of the scanned image is calculated
E.15.3.3 Rods and cones of eyes, skin	C	The process of readjusting the weights automatically so that eventually, the error between the actual and expected output is minimized
E.15.3.4 Forward propagation	D	Examples of receptors
E.15.3.5 Activation function	E	Reduces the size of the feature map generated from convolution
E.15.3.6 ReLU function	F	Developed for handwritten digit recognition and was responsible for the term "convolutional neural network."
E.15.3.7 Backpropagation	G	Generative adversarial neural network (GAN)
E.15.3.8 Convolution	H	Has a sparse representation and avoids the problem of vanishing gradients
E.15.3.9 Pooling	I	Assembled free database by Fei-Fei Li, at Stanford
E.15.3.10 LeNet-5	J	Helps the network to use the useful information and suppress the irrelevant information

E.15.4 Short Questions

E.15.4.1 What is deep learning? Discuss.

E.15.4.2 Give some typical applications of deep learning.

E.15.4.3 Compare and contrast machine learning and deep learning.

E.15.4.4 Outline the stages of the human nervous system.

E.15.4.5 How is computation carried out in biological neurons?

E.15.4.6 Give a detailed description of the perceptron.

E.15.4.7 How is a perceptron trained?

E.15.4.8 Explain and give three examples of activation functions with illustrations.

E.15.4.9 What is backpropagation? Explain in the context of neural networks.

E.15.4.10 Outline single path and multiple path chain rules.

E.15.4.11 Give details of backpropagation for the hidden as well as output layer of a perceptron.

E.15.4.12 Describe the basic structure of the multilayer perceptron (MLP).

E.15.4.13 Explain in detail how backpropagation readjusts the weights automatically to minimize the error between the actual and expected output using as an example a model to predict the next binary number with appropriate diagrams.

E.15.4.14 Explain the biological connection to convolutional neural networks.

E.15.4.15 Describe the architecture of convolutional neural networks.

E.15.4.16 Explain the evolution of convolutional neural networks in the context of the ImageNet Challenge.

E.15.4.17 Describe the Neocognitron, considered as the originator of convolutional neural networks.

E.15.4.18 How does learning occur in convolutional neural networks? Explain.

E.15.4.19 Explain the terms *padding*, *striding*, and *flattening* in the context of convolutional neural networks.

E.15.4.20 Explain in detail the convolution operation.

16

Other Models of Deep Learning and Applications of Deep Learning

16.1 Recurrent Neural Networks (RNNs)

Recurrent neural networks (RNNs) are a type of neural network in which the output is looped back to input. In general, the input and outputs of traditional neural network (NN) are independent of one another and cannot handle sequential data, can handle only current input, and are not able to remember previous inputs. However, in speech recognition and natural language processing there is a need to understand the sequential characteristics of the data and use the patterns to predict the next possible state. As a result, RNN was developed which can handle sequential data and memorize previous inputs using its memory, for which RNN utilises a hidden layer. The hidden state, which retains some information about a sequence, is the primary and most significant characteristic of RNNs (Figure 16.1).

RNNs have a "memory" that retains all data related to calculations. They execute the same action on all of the inputs or hidden layers to produce the output, using the same settings for each input. In contrast to other neural networks, this minimises the complexity of the parameter set.

Recurrent neural networks solve the issue of variable width inputs, which is a problem with traditional neural networks that arises when dealing with, among other applications, text analysis. This is a problem with photographs as well, of course, but the answer is somewhat different because we can scale and stretch images to fit any size we require at the time. Words do not work like this.

16.1.1 Working of RNN

Let us understand the working of RNN using a sample scenario.

Consider a deeper network that has one input layer, one output layer, and three hidden layers. Normally each hidden layer is associated with its own set of weights and biases, namely ($w1$, $b1$), ($w2$, $b2$), ($w3$, $b3$) (Figure 16.2) for each of the three hidden layers. This in essence means that each of these layers are independent of each other and do not retain information associated with the earlier outputs.

RNN however brings in dependency by using the same weights and biases across all layers, reducing the number of parameters and memorizing previous outputs by feeding each output into the next hidden layer. Therefore these three layers are combined to form a single recurrent layer with the all the hidden layers having the same weights and biases (Figure 16.3).

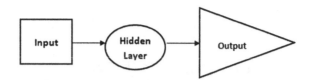

FIGURE 16.1
Recurrent neural network (RNN).

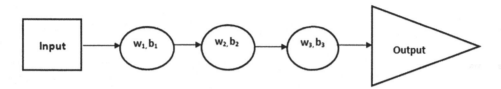

FIGURE 16.2
Deeper recurrent neural network.

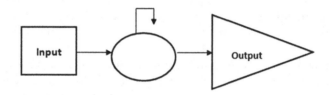

FIGURE 16.3
Combination of three hidden layers.

The following Equation (16.1) determines the current state:

$$h_t = f\left(h_{t-1}, x_t\right) \tag{16.1}$$

where,

- h_t current state
- h_{t-1} previous state
- x_t input state

After applying the activation function (tanh) in Equation (16.1), the current state becomes (Equation 16.2),

$$h_t = \tanh\left(w_{hh}h_{t-1} + w_{xh}x_t\right) \tag{16.2}$$

where,

- $w_{hh} \rightarrow$ weight at recurrent neuron
- $w_{xh} \rightarrow$ weight at input neuron

and the output is determined using Equation (16.3):

$$y_t = w_{hy} h_t \tag{16.3}$$

where,

y_t output

w_{hy} weight at output layer

16.1.2 Training Through RNN

1. The network consists of n input layers having same weight and activation function and is given a single time step of the input.

2. Then, using the current input and the previous state output, the current state is calculated.

3. For the next time step, the current state h_t becomes h_{t-1}.

4. Depending on the problem, one can repeat as many time steps as necessary to join information from all previous states.

5. The final current state is used to calculate the output after all time steps have been completed.

6. Then error is generated which is the difference between the output obtained from the RNN model and the actual target output.

7. This error is then backpropagated and used to update the weights and train the network (RNN).

The main advantage of RNN is that an RNN remembers every piece of information over time. It is only useful in time series prediction because of the ability to remember previous inputs. This is referred to as long short term memory. Recurrent neural networks are also used in conjunction with convolutional layers to increase the effective pixel neighborhood.

However, there are issues with gradient vanishing and exploding in RNN. It is also extremely difficult to train an RNN. Moreover, when using tanh or ReLU as an activation function, it cannot process very long sequences.

In today's world, several machine learning methods are utilized to process the many varieties of data that are available. Sequential data is one of the sorts of data that is most challenging to work with and to forecast. Sequential data is distinct from other types of data in the sense that, whereas all of the characteristics of a normal data set can be considered to be order-independent, this cannot be assumed for a sequential data set. This is one of the ways in which sequential data differs from other types of data. The idea of using recurrent neural networks to process this kind of data came about as a result of the need to do so. The structure of this artificial neural network is unique in comparison to that of other such networks. The recurrent network follows a recurrence relation rather than a feed-forward pass and employs backpropagation through time to learn, whereas other networks "move" in a linear way throughout the feed-forward process or the backpropagation process.

Multiple fixed activation function units make up the recurrent neural network; one of these units is assigned to each time step in the process. A unit's internal state, often known as the concealed state of the unit, can be accessed by the unit. This hidden state is representative of the historical information that the network presently possesses at a certain time step. This hidden state is changed at each time step to signal the change in the network's knowledge about the past, and this update takes place behind the scenes. The hidden state is kept updated by employing the recurrence relation that follows (Equation 16.4).

$$h_t = fW\left(x_t, h_{t-1}\right) \tag{16.4}$$

where
h_t The new hidden state
h_{t-1} The old hidden state
x_t The current input
fW The fixed function with trainable weights

Calculating the new hidden state at each time step requires using the recurrence relation described above. This newly produced hidden state is put to use in the production of yet another newly produced hidden state, and so on (Figure 16.4).

Normally the network starts off in its initial hidden state, which is denoted by h_0 where in most cases this is a vector of zeros. However, it is possible to encode the assumptions concerning the data into the initial hidden state of the network. For example, in order to find out the tenor of a speech delivered by a famous person, the tenor of that person's previous speeches might be encoded into the initial hidden state of the problem. Another approach is to make the initial hidden state a trainable parameter. However, initializing the hidden state vector to zeros is in most cases the best and efficient option.

The following is how each recurrent unit works:

1. Both the current input vector and the previously hidden state vector should be taken as input. The current input and the hidden state are being treated as vectors, and therefore each element of the vector is associated with a dimension that is orthogonal to the other dimensions. This is because each dimension is being treated as a vector. Therefore, the only circumstances in which the product of one element multiplied by another element yields a number that is not zero are those in which both elements are themselves nonzero and both elements belong to the same dimension.

2. Perform element-wise multiplication of the current input vector and hidden state vector by their corresponding weights, producing the associated parameterized vectors. The trainable weight matrix contains the weights that correspond to the various vectors.

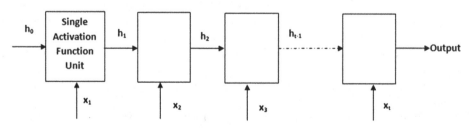

FIGURE 16.4
Basic work-flow of a recurrent neural network.

3. Then the vector addition of the two parameterized vectors is carried out, and in order to construct the new hidden state vector the element-wise hyperbolic tangent is calculated (Figure 16.5).

During recurrent network training (Figure 16.6), the network creates an output at each time step. The network is trained using gradient descent using this output.

The backpropagation that is being employed here is quite analogous to the one that is utilized in a standard artificial neural network, with a few small modifications. These modifications can be identified as follows.

Let the predicted output of the network at any time step be $\bar{y}_t$ and the actual output be y_t. Then the error at each time step is given by (Equation 16.5),

$$E_t = -y_t \log(\bar{y}_t) \tag{16.5}$$

The total error is given by the summation of the errors at all the time steps (Equation 16.6):

$$E = \sum_t E_t$$
$$E = \sum_t -y_t \log(\bar{y}_t) \tag{16.6}$$

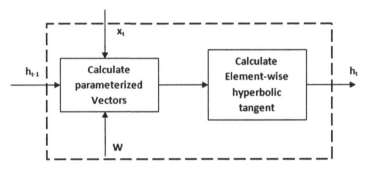

FIGURE 16.5
Working of recurrent unit.

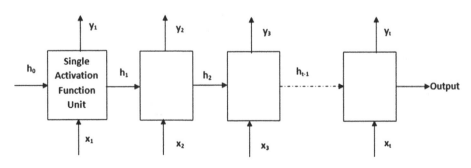

FIGURE 16.6
Recurrent network training.

Similarly, the value $\dfrac{\partial E}{\partial W}$ can be calculated as the summation of gradients at each time step (Equation 16.7).

$$\frac{\partial E}{\partial W} = \sum_t \frac{\partial E_t}{\partial W} \tag{16.7}$$

Using the chain rule of calculus and using the fact that the output at a time step is a function of the current hidden state of the recurrent unit, the following expression arises (Equation 16.8):

$$\frac{\partial E}{\partial W} = \frac{\partial E_t}{\partial \overline{y}_t} \frac{\partial \overline{y}_t}{\partial h_t} \frac{\partial h_t}{\partial h_{t-1}} \frac{\partial h_{t-1}}{\partial h_{t-2}} \cdots \cdots \frac{\partial h_0}{\partial W} \tag{16.8}$$

Take note that the weight matrix W utilised in the preceding calculation is different for the input vector and the hidden state vector. This is done just for the ease of the notation and has nothing to do with the actual meaning of the matrix. Thus the following expression arises (Equation 16.8),

$$\frac{\partial E}{\partial W} = \sum_t \frac{\partial E_t}{\partial \overline{y}_t} \frac{\partial \overline{y}_t}{\partial h_t} \frac{\partial h_t}{\partial h_{t-1}} \frac{\partial h_{t-1}}{\partial h_{t-2}} \cdots \cdots \frac{\partial h_0}{\partial W} \tag{16.9}$$

Therefore, the only difference between backpropagation through time and a standard backpropagation is that the errors at each time step are totaled up to calculate the total error. This is the only difference (Figure 16.7).

In spite of the fact that the fundamental recurrent neural network is reasonably efficient, it is susceptible to a severe difficulty. Backpropagation is a procedure that, when used in deep networks, can result in a number of concerns, including the following:

1. Vanishing gradients results in unstable behaviour and occurs when useful gradient information cannot be propagated from the output back to the previous layers and the gradients may have very small values tending towards zero. This may result in premature convergence to a poor solution.

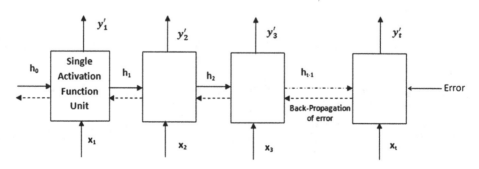

FIGURE 16.7
Backpropagation in RNN.

2. Exploding gradients is a phenomenon that takes place when the gradients keep getting larger during backpropagation, resulting in very large weight updates causing the gradient descent to diverge.

The issue of vanishing gradients may be tackled by using rectified linear units (ReLU) as activation function. The issue of exploding gradients could perhaps be fixed by employing a workaround, which would include imposing a threshold on the gradients that are passed back in time. However, this technique is not considered to be a solution to the issue, and it also has the potential to decrease the effectiveness of the network. Long-short term memory networks and gated recurrent unit networks are the two primary varieties of recurrent neural networks that have been developed in order to address issues of this nature.

16.2 Auto-encoders

One example of how neural networks are typically put to use is in situations that call for supervised learning. It requires training data to be provided, which should include a label for the output. The neural network makes an effort to learn the mapping that exists between the input label and the output label that is provided. What would happen, though, if the input vector itself was used in place of the output label? After then, the network will make an attempt to discover the mapping from the input to itself. This would be the identity function, which is an extremely straightforward mapping. However, if the network is not permitted to merely replicate the input, then the network will be compelled to only record the most important characteristics. This limitation reveals an entirely new realm of applications for neural networks, which was previously unexplored. Dimensionality reduction and particular data compression are among the most important uses. In the beginning, the network is educated using the input that was provided. The network makes an attempt to rebuild the input by using the features that it has collected, and it then provides an output that is a close approximation of the input. During the training process, you will be computing the error and then backpropagating the error. The conventional architecture of an auto-encoder is shaped very similarly to a bottleneck. An auto-encoder can be broken down into its component parts as follows, according to its schematic (Figure 16.8).

16.2.1 Different Types of Auto-encoders

- **De-noising auto-encoder**: This sort of auto-encoder works with an input that has been partially corrupted and learns to recover the original, undistorted image from the training data. As was just pointed out, utilising this technique is an efficient approach to prevent the network from merely replicating the input.
- **Sparse auto-encoder**: This kind of auto-encoder often has more hidden units than the input, but only a few of those hidden units are allowed to be active at the same time. This characteristic of the network is referred to as its sparsity. Controlling the network's sparsity can be accomplished by either manually zeroing the required hidden units, fine-tuning the activation functions, or adding a loss component to the cost function. All three of these methods are described further later in the chapter.

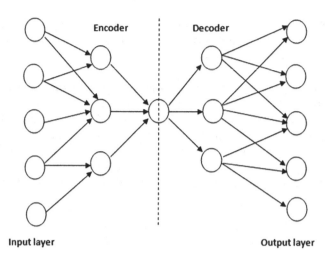

FIGURE 16.8
Components of an auto-encoders.

- **Variational auto-encoder**: This auto-encoder makes strong assumptions about the distribution of latent variables and employs the stochastic gradient variational Bayes estimator during the training process. It makes the assumption that the data was produced by a directed graphical model and attempts to learn an approximation to the value of the conditional property $q_\varnothing(z \mid x)$, where $\varnothing$ and Θ are, respectively, the parameters of the encoder and the decoder.

Let us understand the training of an Auto-encoder for a data compression scenario using the following steps. When doing a data compression technique, the feature of the compression that is most significant is the degree of dependability with which the compressed data can be reconstructed. Because of this need, the structure of the auto-encoder, which is a bottleneck, must be exactly as it is.

1. The first step is to encode the data that was input. The auto-encoder will first attempt to encode the data by making use of the weights and biases that have been initialised (Figure 16.9).
2. The next step is to decode the data that was input. In order to ensure that the encoded data are accurate representations of the original input, the auto-encoder will do a reconstruction of the data using the encoded version (Figure 16.10).
3. Backpropagating the fault is the third step. When the reconstruction is complete, the loss function is computed so that the reliability of the encoding may be evaluated. The error that was generated is then passed backwards (Figure 16.11).

This training process is reiterated multiple times until an acceptable level of reconstruction is reached (Figure 16.12).

After the training phase, the only component of the auto-encoder that is kept is the encoder, which is used to encode data that is comparable to that which was utilised during the training process. The following are the various ways that the network can be constrained:

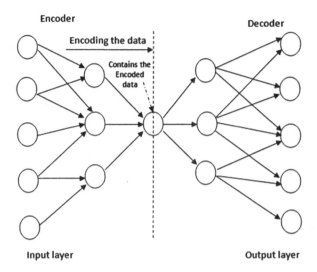

FIGURE 16.9
Step 1—encoding the data.

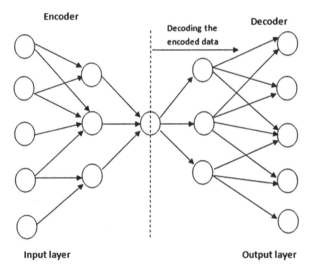

FIGURE 16.10
Step 2—decoding the data.

1. Keep hidden layers small: If the size of each hidden layer is kept as small as feasible, then the network will be forced to pick up only the representative aspects of the data, thereby encoding the data. This can be accomplished by keeping the size of each hidden layer as small as possible.

2. This technique, known as regularisation, involves adding a loss element to the cost function. By doing so, the network is encouraged to train itself in ways other than just duplicating the input.

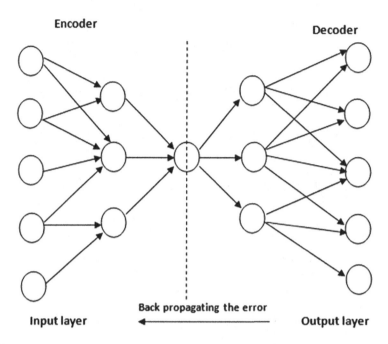

FIGURE 16.11
Step 3—backpropagation of the error.

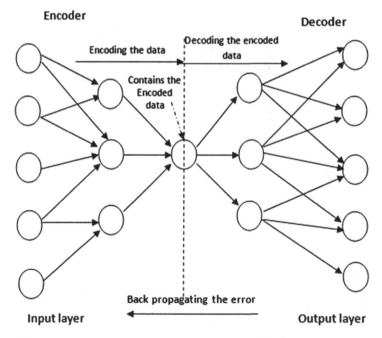

FIGURE 16.12
Iterative training processes.

3. De-noising is a further method of restricting the network in which noise is added to the input and the network is taught how to deny the influence of the noise on the data.

4. Tuning the activation functions: This method involves modifying the activation functions of various nodes so that the majority of the nodes are inactive, effectively reducing the size of the hidden layers. This is accomplished by changing the activation functions of individual nodes.

16.3 Long Short Term Memory Networks

The idea behind the long short term memory network (LSTM) is that it is a recurrent unit that works to "forget" unnecessary material while attempting to "remember" all of the previous information that the network has encountered. In order to accomplish this, many layers of activation functions, often known as "gates," are introduced for a variety of objectives. Each LSTM recurrent unit also keeps track of a vector that is referred to as the internal cell state. This vector provides a conceptual description of the information that was selected to be stored by the LSTM recurrent unit that came before it. A long short term memory network is comprised of four distinct gates, each of which serves a distinct function, as will be detailed subsequently.

1. **Forget gate (*f*):** This gate determines the degree to which the preceding data is forgotten.

2. **Input gate (*i*):** It is responsible for determining the amount of information that will be written into the internal cell state.

3. **Input modulation gate (*g*):** It is frequently thought of as a component of the input gate, and much of the published information on LSTMs either does not mention it or incorrectly assumes that it is contained inside the input gate. It is used to modulate the information that the input gate will write onto the internal state cell by adding nonlinearity to the information and making the information zero-mean. This is done in order to accomplish the purpose of modulating the information. This is done in order to shorten the amount of time required for learning because zero-mean input has a faster convergence. Include this gate in the construction of the LSTM unit even if its actions are less significant than those of the other gates and are frequently regarded as a concept that provides finesse even though this is not the case because it is good practise.

4. **Output gate (*o*):** The function of the output gate (*o*) is to decide what output (next hidden state) should be generated based on the present state of the internal cell.

The fundamental process flow of a long short-term memory network is very comparable to the fundamental process flow of a recurrent neural network; the only difference is that the internal cell state is also transmitted along with the hidden state in the long short-term memory network (Figure 16.13).

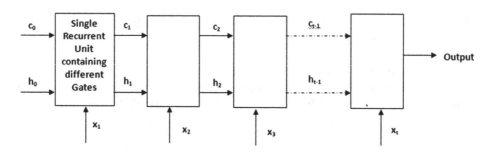

FIGURE 16.13
Process flow of a long short-term memory network.

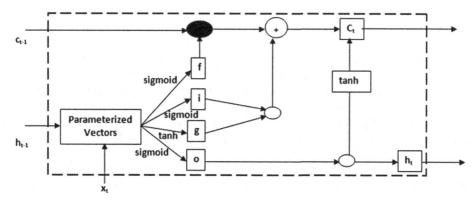

FIGURE 16.14
Working of an LSTM recurrent unit.

The steps involved in the operation of an LSTM unit are given subsequently and as shown in Figure 16.14:

1. The inputs are the current input, the previous hidden state, and the prior internal cell state.
2. Now the values of the four distinct gates are determined as follows:
   - For each gate, element-wise multiplication of the concerned vector with the corresponding weights for each gate is calculated to obtain the parameterized vectors for the current input and the prior concealed state.
   - The corresponding activation function is applied element-wise to the parameterized vectors for each gate. The activation functions to be applied to each gate are described as follows.

3. The current internal cell state is determined by (Equation 16.10)

$$c_t = i \odot g + f \odot c_{t-1}$$

(16.10)

   - first calculating the element-wise multiplication vector of the input gate and the input modulation gate,

- next calculating the element-wise multiplication vector of the forget gate and the previous internal cell state, and
- finally summing the two vectors.

4. The current concealed state is determined by

- first calculating the element-by-element hyperbolic tangent of the current internal cell state vector, and
- next carrying out element-wise multiplication with the output gate.

The circle notation in the figure represents element-wise multiplication. The weight matrix W comprises distinct weights for each gate's current input vector and preceding hidden state.

The LSTM network also generates an output at each time step, which is then used for gradient descent training (Figure 16.15).

Backpropagation methods used by recurrent neural networks and long short-term memory networks are similar but differ in the way mathematical aspects are modelled.

Let y_t be the predicted output at each time step and y_t be the actual output at each time step. Then the error at each time step is given by (Equation 16.11):

$$E_t = -y_t \log\left(\overline{y_t}\right) \tag{16.11}$$

The total error is thus given by the summation of errors at all time steps (Equation 16.12):

$$E = \sum_t E_t$$
$$E = \sum_t -y_t \log\left(\overline{y_t}\right) \tag{16.12}$$

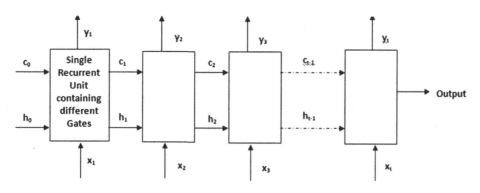

FIGURE 16.15
LSTM network working.

Similarly, the value $\dfrac{\partial E}{\partial W}$ can be calculated as the summation of the gradients at each time step (Equation 16.13).

$$\frac{\partial E}{\partial W} = \sum_t \frac{\partial E_t}{\partial W} \tag{16.13}$$

Using the chain rule and using the fact that $\overline{y}_t$ is a function of h_t and indeed is a function of c_t, the following expression arises (Equation 16.14):

$$\frac{\partial E_t}{\partial W} = \frac{\partial E_t}{\partial \overline{y}_t} \frac{\partial \overline{y}_t}{\partial h_t} \frac{\partial h_t}{\partial c_t} \frac{\partial c_t}{\partial c_{t-1}} \frac{\partial c_{t-1}}{\partial c_{t-2}} \cdots \cdots \frac{\partial c_0}{\partial W} \tag{16.14}$$

Thus the total error gradient is given by the following (Equation 16.15):

$$\frac{\partial E}{\partial W} = \sum_t \frac{\partial E_t}{\partial \overline{y}_t} \frac{\partial \overline{y}_t}{\partial h_t} \frac{\partial h_t}{\partial c_t} \frac{\partial c_t}{\partial c_{t-1}} \frac{\partial c_{t-1}}{\partial c_{t-2}} \cdots \cdots \frac{\partial c_0}{\partial W} \tag{16.15}$$

Note that the gradient equation involves a chain of ∂c_t for an LSTM backpropagation while the gradient equation involves a chain of ∂h_t for a basic recurrent neural network.

16.3.1 How Does LSTM Solve the Problem of Vanishing and Exploring Gradients?

Recall the expression for c_t.

$$c_t = i \odot g + f \odot c_{t-1}$$

The value of the gradients is controlled by the chain of derivatives starting from $\dfrac{\partial c_t}{\partial c_{t-1}}$.
Expanding this value using the expression for c_t (Equation 16.16),

$$\frac{\partial c_t}{\partial c_{t-1}} = \frac{\partial c_t}{\partial f} \frac{\partial f}{\partial h_{t-1}} \frac{\partial h_{t-1}}{\partial c_{t-1}} + \frac{\partial c_t}{\partial i} \frac{\partial i}{\partial h_{t-1}} \frac{\partial h_{t-1}}{\partial c_{t-1}} + \frac{\partial c_t}{\partial g} \frac{\partial g}{\partial h_{t-1}} \frac{\partial h_{t-1}}{\partial c_{t-1}} + \frac{\partial c_t}{\partial c_{t-1}} \tag{16.16}$$

For a simple RNN, the term $\dfrac{\partial c_t}{\partial c_{t-1}}$ begins to take values larger than 1 or less than 1 within the same range after a given duration. This is the underlying source of the problem with vanishing and exploding gradients. The term $\dfrac{\partial c_t}{\partial c_{t-1}}$ in an LSTM can take any positive value at each time step, and hence convergence is not guaranteed. If the gradient begins to converge toward 0, the gate weights can be modified to bring the gradient closer to 1. During the training phase only these weights are adjusted, and hence the network can learn when the gradient can converge to zero and when to retain it.

16.4 Generative Adversarial Networks (GANs)

In June 2014, Ian Goodfellow and his colleagues came up with the concept for a class of machine learning frameworks called generative adversarial networks, or GANs for short.

GAN deploys a learning technique that produces new data which is statistically similar to the input training data. For instance, a GAN that has been trained on images can produce new photographs that, at least to human observers, appear to be superficially legitimate and have many realistic properties. GANs were initially conceived of as a sort of generative model that could be used for unsupervised learning.

The general notion behind a GAN is predicated on the concept of "indirect" training through the discriminator, which is another neural network that can determine how "realistic" the input seems and is also being dynamically updated. That is, during the training, the generator does not minimise the distance with respect to an image; rather, it is trained to deceive the discriminator into thinking that the image is closer than it actually is. Because of this, the model is able to learn in a way that is not supervised. In evolutionary biology, mimicry is analogous to GANs, and both types of networks engage in an evolutionary arms race with one another.

16.4.1 Idea Behind GAN

The general idea behind a GAN is to have two different types of neural networks compete against one another. The first one uses noise as its input and produces samples (and so is called the generator). The second model, which is referred to as the discriminator, is provided with samples from both the generator and the training data, and it is expected to be able to differentiate between the two different data sets. These two networks engage in a never-ending game in which the generator learns to make samples that are more realistic with each iteration, and the discriminator learns to get better and better at separating generated data from actual data with each iteration. Both of these networks are trained at the same time with the expectation that the healthy competition between them will result in the generated samples being virtually indistinguishable from the actual data (Figure 16.16).

Until now, GANs have mostly been used to model natural images. They are presently achieving great results in image creation challenges, generating images that are substantially sharper than those taught with other top generative approaches whose training aims are focused on maximum probability.

Example: Let's say we're attempting to make hand-drawn images that resemble photographs of real people. The objective of the discriminator, when presented with a genuine

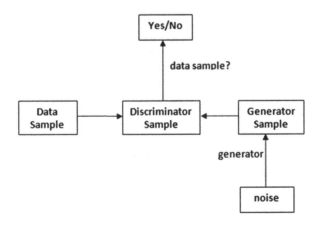

FIGURE 16.16
GAN overview.

photographic image of a real human, is to identify those that are genuine photographs of a real human. The generator generates new synthetic pictures, which are then sent to the discriminator. The purpose of the generator is to produce convincing hand-drawn representations of humans: to deceive without being discovered. The main task of the discriminator is to identify and recognize any images produced by the generator as fraudulent. The steps followed by GAN for the example scenario is summarized in Figure 16.17.

The input to the generator network is a D-dimensional noise vector with random integers, and the output is a synthetic image. This synthetic image along with a set of photographs from the real-world data set acts as an input to the discriminator. The discriminator upon receiving both authentic and counterfeit photographs outputs a number between 0 and 1. This value is a probability value, where 1 indicates authentic and 0 represents counterfeit.

16.4.2 Generative Versus Discriminative Models

While the discriminative network assesses the candidates, the generative network comes up with new potential candidates. The competition will be run according to the distribution of data. Often the discriminative network filters the candidates produced from the original data distribution by the generative network. However, the generative network is responsible for mapping between the latent space and the preferred data distribution. The generative network's training aims to increase the discriminator network's error rate by supplying distinct candidates from the genuine data distribution.

The discriminator uses known training data. During training, it's exposed to instances from the data set until it's accurate enough. The generator learns whether it can fool the discriminator. Most generators are "seeded" using random input from a latent space. The discriminator will next make judgments based on the candidates that were generated by the generator. Both networks undergo their own unique backpropagation techniques so that the generator can produce higher quality samples and the discriminator may become more adept at identifying synthetic samples. When a neural network is being used to generate images, the discriminator is often a convolutional neural network, but the generator is typically a deconvolutional neural network.

Both types of models have their uses, but generative models have one interesting advantage over discriminative models: they have the potential to understand and explain the underlying structure of the input data even when there are no labels to describe it.

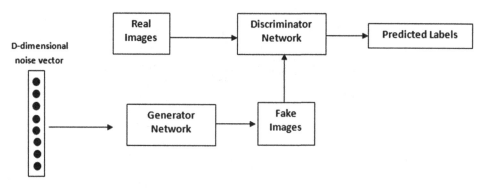

FIGURE 16.17
Working of GAN.

Discriminative models, on the other hand, do not have this capability. Both types of models are useful. When working on data modelling problems in the real world, this is quite desired, as obtaining labelled data can be expensive, at best, and unfeasible, at worst. On the other hand, there is an abundance of unlabeled data, thus this is not a problem.

A mathematical representation of GAN appears as the following game

A GAN game is defined by each probability space (Ω, μ_{ref}).
Types of players—2 nos: generator and discriminator.
$P(\Omega)$—indicates the generator's strategy set
μ_G on (Ω) is the set of all probability measures
$\mu_G : (\Omega) \rightarrow P[0, 1]$ is the discriminator's strategy set which is the set of Markov kernels
where,
$P[0, 1]$—set of probability measures on $[0, 1]$
The objective function for the zero-sum GAN game:
$L(\mu G, \mu D) := \mathbf{E}_{x \sim \mu ref, y \sim \mu D(x)}[\ln y] + \mathbf{E}_{x \sim \mu G, y \sim \mu D(x)}[\ln (1 - y)]$

The objective of the generator is to minimize the objective function, and that of the discriminator is to maximize the objective function.

$$\text{Discriminator output} = \begin{cases} 0, & \text{if input is from or close to generator distribution} \\ 1, & \text{if input from or close to reference distribution} \end{cases}$$

Ultimately the task of the generator is to approach $\mu_G \approx \mu_{ref}$, that is, to match its output in par with the reference distribution.

In discriminator training, keep the generator constant. Train against a static opponent. This enhances the generator's gradient knowledge. Training the discriminator using ground truth data plays a major role for producing a clear gradient by the generator. GAN training is time-consuming, hence the utmost care for training becomes essential.

16.5 Radial Basis Function Neural Network

Radial basis functions are functions that account for a point's distance from the center. RBFs consist of two layers. In the first layer, the input is mapped to all the radial basis functions in the hidden layer. The output is then computed by the output layer. Typically, radial basis function nets are used to simulate data that exhibits any trend or function.

16.5.1 Components of RBNN

The RBNN architecture has an input layer, a hidden layer, and an output layer. The RBNN algorithm can contain no more than one hidden layer at any given time. This hidden layer is referred to as a feature vector in RBNN. The dimension of the feature vector is increased via RBNN (Figure 16.18).

Training the RBNN: The various steps involved in training a RBNN is as shown in Figure 16.19.

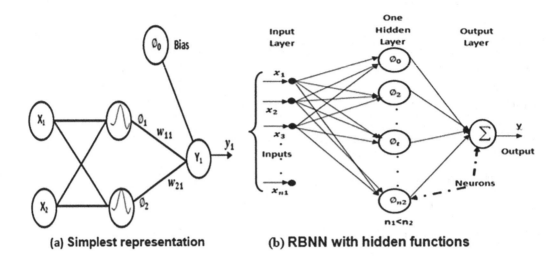

(a) **Simplest representation**   (b) **RBNN with hidden functions**

FIGURE 16.18
Architecture of RBNN.

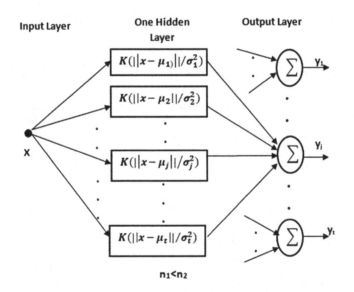

FIGURE 16.19
RBNN training.

1. Initially the hidden layer is trained using backpropagation by fitting a non-linear curve during the training phase.
   - For each of the nodes in the hidden layer, we have to find **t** (receptors) and the variance (σ) (variance—the spread of the radial basis function).
   - In hidden layers, each node represents each transformation basis function or combination of set of functions that satisfy the nonlinear separability criteria.
   - The interpretation of the first training phase is that the **feature vector is projected onto the transformed space**.

2. In the second training phase, the weighting vectors between hidden layers and output layers have to be updated.

Comparison of Radial Basis Neural Network (RBNN) and Multi-Layer Perceptron (MLP)

1. Training in RBNN is faster than in a multilayer Perceptron (MLP); it takes many interactions in MLP.

2. We can easily interpret the meaning or function of each node in the hidden layer of the RBNN. This is difficult in MLP.

3. Parameterization (like the number of nodes in the hidden layer and the number of hidden layers) is difficult in MLP. But this is not found in RBNN.

4. Classification will take more time in RBNN than MLP.

16.6 Multilayer Perceptrons (MLPs)

A multilayer perceptron, sometimes known as an MLP, is a type of feed-forward artificial neural network that is fully connected (ANN). The term *multilayer perceptron* (MLP) is used inconsistently; in some contexts, it refers to any feed-forward artificial neural network (ANN), while in other contexts, it refers more specifically to networks made up of multiple layers of perceptrons (with threshold activation). When they just contain one hidden layer, multilayer perceptrons are sometimes referred to as "vanilla" neural networks.

A minimum of three layers of nodes, namely input, hidden, and output layers, is required for the construction of an MLP. Every node in the network is a neuron that employs a nonlinear activation function, with the exception of the nodes that serve as inputs. Training in MLP is accomplished through the use of a supervised learning method known as backpropagation. In comparison to a linear perceptron, an MLP is distinguished by its nonlinear activation and numerous layers. It is able to differentiate between data that cannot be separated in a linear fashion.

16.6.1 Layers

The MLP is made up of three or more layers of nonlinearly activating nodes, including an input layer, an output layer, and one or more hidden layers. Due to the fact that MLPs are fully connected, each node in one layer connects with a specific weight w_{ij} to every node in the layer that follows it. The pictorial representation of multilayer perceptron learning is shown in Figure 16.20.

As per linear algebra, if a multilayer perceptron has a linear activation function that maps the weighted inputs to the output of each neuron, then any number of layers may be reduced to a two-layer input–output model. In MLPs some neurons use a nonlinear activation function that was intended to simulate the frequency of action potentials, or firing, of real neurons.

The two historically common activation functions are both sigmoids and are described by Equations (16.17) and (16.18).

$$y(v_i) = \tanh(v_i) \tag{16.17}$$

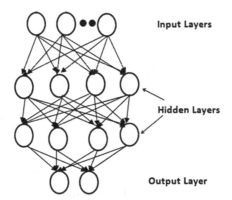

FIGURE 16.20
Multilayer perceptron learning.

and

$$y(v_i) = \left(1 + e^{-v_i}\right)^{-1} \tag{16.18}$$

The rectifier linear unit (ReLU) is one of the most frequently and commonly used activation functions in MLP as it overcomes the numerical problems related to the sigmoids. The first is a hyperbolic tangent that ranges from −1 to 1, while the other is the logistic function, which is similar in shape but ranges from 0 to 1. Here y_i is the output of the ith node (neuron) and v_i is the weighted sum of the input connections. Alternative activation functions have been proposed, including the rectifier and soft plus functions. More specialized activation functions include radial basis functions (used in radial basis networks, another class of supervised neural network models).

16.6.2 Learning in MLP

The perceptron is able to learn by adjusting the connection weights after each piece of data is processed. These adjustments are made based on the degree of mistake in the output in comparison to the result that was anticipated. This is an example of supervised learning, and it is accomplished by backpropagation, which is a generalization of the technique for the linear perceptron that calculates the least mean squares.

We can indicate the degree of error in an output node j in the nth data point (training example) by using Equation (16.19).

$$e_j(n) = d_j(n) - y_j(n) \tag{16.19}$$

where, d is the target value and y is the value that the perceptron produces. After that, the node weights can be modified depending on adjustments that minimize the error in the overall output, which is provided by Equation (16.20):

$$\varepsilon(n) = \frac{1}{2} \sum_j e_j^2(n) \tag{16.20}$$

Using gradient descent, the change in each weight is (Equation 16.21):

$$\Delta w_{ji}(n) = -\eta \frac{\partial \varepsilon(n)}{\partial v_j(n)} y_i(n) \tag{16.21}$$

where y_i is the output of the neuron that came before it and η is the learning rate. The learning rate is chosen to ensure that the weights quickly converge to a response and do not oscillate. Calculating the derivative requires taking into account the variable induced local field v_j, which in turn fluctuates. It is not difficult to demonstrate that this derivative, when applied to an output node, can be simplified to Equation (16.22):

$$-\frac{\partial \varepsilon(n)}{\partial v_j(n)} = e_j(n) \Phi'(v_j(n)) \tag{16.22}$$

where Φ' is the derivative of the activation function that was stated earlier, which does not vary. The analysis is made more challenging by the fact that the change in weights is being applied to a hidden node, yet it is possible to demonstrate that the relevant derivative is (Equation 16.23):

$$-\frac{\partial \varepsilon(n)}{\partial v_j(n)} = \Phi'(v_j(n)) \sum_k -\frac{\partial \varepsilon(n)}{\partial v_k(n)} w_{kj}(n) \tag{16.23}$$

This is dependent on the shift in weights of the kth nodes, which are the ones that constitute the output layer. As a result, in order to modify the weights of the hidden layers, the weights of the output layers must be modified in accordance with the derivative of the activation function. Because of this, the algorithm in question reflects a backpropagation of the activation function.

16.6.3 Applications of MLPs

MLPs are helpful in research because of their capacity to tackle issues in a stochastic manner, which frequently enables approximate solutions to exceedingly difficult problems such as fitness approximation. Because classification is a subset of regression that occurs when the response variable is categorical, multilayer perceptrons (MLPs) are effective classifier algorithms. MLPs are popularly used in diversified applications like speech recognition, image recognition, and software for machine translation.

16.6.3.1 RBNN and MLP

Single perceptron and multilayer perceptron (MLP) are made up of only input and output layers, and hence we can only achieve linear separability with these two types of neural networks (some hidden layers in MLP). For example, the AND and OR functions can be linearly separated; however, the XOR function cannot be linearly separated. In order to obtain a nonlinearity separation, we must have at least one hidden layer. However, RBNN will convert the input signal into a different form, which may then be fed into the network in order to achieve linear separability. Despite this, the RBNN has the same structural make-up as the perceptron (MLP) (Figure 16.21).

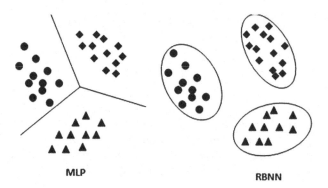

FIGURE 16.21
Functioning—MLP Versus RBNN.

TABLE 16.1

RBNN Versus MLP

S.No		RBNN	MLP
1.	Training time	Faster	Slower—needs many interactions
2.	Interpretation	Easily interpret the meaning / function of each node in hidden layer	Difficult to interpret the meaning / function of each node in hidden layer
3.	Parameterization	Not needed	Difficulty in deciding number of nodes in hidden layer and number of hidden layers)
4.	Time for classification	More time	Less time

16.6.3.2 Comparing RBNN and MLP

Table 16.1 shows the comparison between RBNN and MLP.

16.7 Self-Organizing Maps (SOMs)

A self-organizing map, also known as a self-organizing feature map (SOFM), is an unsupervised machine learning technique. SOM is used to construct a low-dimensional (usually two-dimensional) representation of a higher dimensional data collection while maintaining the topological structure of the data. For instance, a data set that contains p variables that are measured in n observations may be represented as clusters of observations that have values that are comparable for the variables. These clusters might then be represented as a two-dimensional "map" in such a way that observations contained within proximal clusters have values that are more comparable to one another than data contained within distal clusters. Because of this, it could be simpler to view and investigate high-dimensional data.

An SOM is a special kind of artificial neural network that is trained using a process called competitive learning. The SOM was first proposed by the Finnish academic Teuvo Kohonen in the 1980s, it is also frequently referred to as a Kohonen map or a Kohonen network. It is an abstraction built over biological models of neural systems that dates back to 1970.

16.7.1 Architecture SOM

The input layer and the output layer are the two layers that make up SOM. The following is a description of the self-organizing map's architecture (Figure 16.22) with two clusters and n input features for any sample.

16.7.2 Working of SOM

Self-organizing maps operate in two modes: training and mapping. First, training uses input data to build a lower-dimensional representation (the "map space"). Second, mapping classifies input data using the map.

Training aims to represent a p-dimensional input space as a two-dimensional map space. A p-variable input space is p-dimensional. A map space has "nodes" or "neurons" arranged in a hexagonal or rectangular grid. The number of nodes and their placement are determined before data processing and exploration.

Each map node has a "weight" vector that represents its position in the input space. While nodes in the map space stay fixed, training involves moving weight vectors toward the input data (lowering a distance measure like Euclidean distance) without damaging the map space's topology. After training, the map may identify further input space observations by selecting the node with the closest weight vector (smallest distance metric).

Consider an input set with the dimensions (m, n), where m represents the number of training examples and n represents the number of features present in each example. The weights of size (n, C), where C is the number of clusters, are first initialized. The winning vector (the weight vector with the shortest distance from the training example, for example, the Euclidean distance) is then updated after iterating over the input data for each training example. Weight update is decided by the following (Equation 16.25):

$$W_{ij} = W_{ij}(\mathbf{old}) + \alpha(T)(X_{ik} - \mathbf{Old})W_{ij} \tag{16.25}$$

where i stands for the ith feature of the training example, j is the winning vector, α is the learning rate at time t, and k is the kth training example from the input data. The SOM

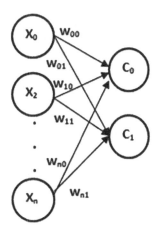

FIGURE 16.22
SOM architecture.

network is trained, and trained weights are utilised to cluster new examples. A new example is included in the collection of successful vectors.

Thus the various steps explained previously are summarized as follows:

1. Initialization of weight
2. For epochs ranging from 1 to N
3. Pick a training instance
4. Determine the winning vector
5. A winning vector update
6. For each training example, repeat steps 3, 4, and 5
7. Creating a test sample cluster

16.7.2.1 An Illustration of the Training of a Self-Organizing Map

The small white disc represents the current training datum, which is taken from the distribution of the training data represented by the blue blob. The SOM nodes are initially placed in the data space at random (seen on the left side of Figure 16.23). The node that is closest to the training datum is chosen (grey shaded concentric circle in first figure). It has been relocated toward the training datum, along with (to a lesser extent) its grid neighbours. The grid usually approximates the data distribution after several rounds (right).

16.7.3 Options for Initialization

For all iterative artificial neural network techniques, including self-organizing maps, choosing beginning weights that are good approximations of the final weights is a well-known difficulty. The initial idea for random weight initiation came from Kohonen. Principal component initialization, in which the initial map weights are selected from the space of the first principal components, has gained popularity more recently since the results can be precisely replicated.

However, it was discovered that the benefits of principle component initialization are not always the case when random initialization and principal component initialization were carefully compared for a one-dimensional map. The shape of the particular data set determines which initialization technique is appropriate. When the principal curve fitting the data set could be univalently and linearly projected on the first principal component, principle component initialization was preferred (for a one-dimensional map) (quasi linear sets). Random initiation, however, fared better for nonlinear data sets.

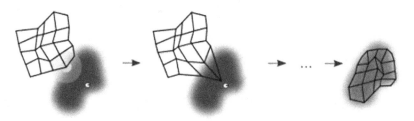

FIGURE 16.23
Illustration of SOM working.

A SOM can be interpreted in many different ways. Similar items frequently fire nearby neurons because in the training phase, the weights of the entire neighbourhood are moved in the same direction. In order to create a semantic map, SOM places similar samples together and dissimilar samples away.

The alternative interpretation is to consider neuronal weights as pointing devices to the input region. They represent a discrete approximation of the training sample distribution. Whereas fewer neurons point when there are few training examples, more neurons point where there are more training samples.

Principal components analysis may be thought of as a nonlinear generalization in the context of SOM (PCA). SOM was not developed at first as an answer to an optimization issue. However, there have been numerous attempts to alter the SOM description and create an optimization problem that yields comparable outcomes.

16.7.3.1 *Drawbacks to Kohonen Maps*

Model preparation takes a long time, and training against slowly changing data is challenging. The model does not grasp how data is formed because it does not create a generative model for the data. When utilizing categorical data, it does not behave well, and when using mixed-type data, it behaves even worse.

16.8 Restricted Boltzmann Machines (RBMs)

The restricted Boltzmann machine, which belongs to the domain of unsupervised learning algorithms, was invented in 1985 by Geoffrey Hinton. RBM is a network of symmetrically connected neuron-like units that generate stochastic decisions.

To ahead understand RBM, we must be aware of Boltzmann machines. A Boltzmann machine is a type of neural network in which each neuron is linked to each and every other neuron in the network. RBM is composed of two layers: the visible layer (v), also known as the input layer, and the concealed layer (h). A layer for output is not present in the Boltzmann machine. Boltzmann machines are a type of neural network that is both random and generative. They are capable of learning internal representations, modelling complex combinatory problems, and solving such problems, provided that they are given enough time. The Boltzmann distribution (Gibbs distribution) of thermodynamics explains the effect of factors such as entropy and temperature on quantum states, and hence these models based on Boltzmann distribution are also referred to as energy-based models (EBMs) (Figure 16.24).

The restricted Boltzmann machine, a variant of the Boltzmann machine, is a stochastic two-layered neural network that belong to a class of energy-based models that may automatically find intrinsic data patterns by reconstructing input. It has two apparent and concealed layers. The visible layer consists of input nodes (nodes that receive input data), while the hidden layer is composed of nodes that extract feature information from the data, and the output at the hidden layer is a weighted sum of the input layers. They have no output nodes and no usual binary output via which patterns are learned, which may seem peculiar. The learning process occurs without the capability that differentiates them. We are just concerned with input nodes and are not concerned with hidden nodes. RBMs automatically record all patterns, parameters, and correlations between data once input is provided.

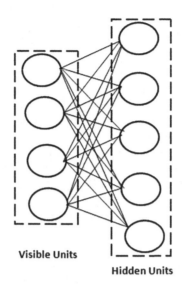

FIGURE 16.24
Restricted Boltzmann machine with three visible units and four hidden units (no bias units).

Important characteristics of the Boltzmann machine are as follows.

1. The structure is recurrent and symmetric.
2. In their learning process, RBMs attempt to link low energy states with high likelihood and vice versa.
3. No intra layer connections exist.
4. It is an unsupervised learning algorithm, meaning it draws conclusions from unlabeled input data.

16.8.1 Working of Restricted Boltzmann Machine

There are two phases in RBM via which the entire RBM process operates:
First phase: The input layer (v) is utilised to activate the hidden layer (h) utilizing the concepts of weights and bias. This method is known as the feed forward pass. In this phase any positive and negative associations between the v and h are discovered.
Second phase: The feed backward pass process is executed in which the input layer (v) is reconstructed to v' using the activated hidden state. Following this, the input is reconstituted by activating the hidden state. Consequently, the inaccuracy (E) is calculated and used to modify the weight ($W_{adjusted}$) as follows (Equations 16.26 and 16.27):

$$E = v' - v \tag{16.26}$$

$$W_{adjusted} = v * E * 0.1 \tag{16.27}$$

where, 0.1 is the learning rate.

After completing all the steps, the pattern responsible for activating the hidden neurons is obtained.

RBM is trained using Gibbs sampling and contrastive divergence. Gibbs sampling is a Markov chain Monte Carlo approach for getting a sequence of observations approximating a defined multivariate probability distribution in statistics when direct sampling is impossible.

If the input is represented by v and the hidden value by h, then the prediction is $p(h \mid v)$. With knowledge of the hidden values, $p(v \mid h)$ is utilised to anticipate the regenerated input values. Suppose this procedure is performed k times, and after k iterations, the initial input value $v\,0$ is transformed into $v\,k$.

Contrastive divergence is an approximation maximum-likelihood learning approach used to approximate the gradient, which is the graphical slope depicting the link between a network's weights and its error. In situations where we cannot directly evaluate a function or set of probabilities, an inference model is used to approximate the algorithm's learning gradient and determine the direction in which to move. In contrastive divergence, updated weights are utilised. After calculating the gradient from the reconstructed input, delta is added to the previous weights to create the new weights.

16.8.2 Advantages and Drawbacks of RBM

RBM benefits are that they are expressive and computationally efficient. Due to connectivity restrictions, this Boltzmann machine is faster. Hidden layer activations can improve the performance of other models.

RBM drawbacks are that in RBM energy gradient function calculation makes training harder and contrastive divergence k is a less-known RBM algorithm than backpropagation. Also weight adjustments are a mentionable drawback of RBM.

16.9 Deep Belief Networks (DBNs)

A deep belief network is a type of DNN which is made of multiple layers of hidden units, in which the layers are well connected but not the hidden units. DBNs were developed to overcome the slow learning, local minima pitfalls in a typical neural network. DBNs were first presented as probabilistic generative models in (Larochelle, Erhan, Courville, Bergstra, & Bengio, 2007) as an alternative to the discriminative character of conventional neural networks.

A DBN is made up of several layers of neural networks, commonly known as Boltzmann machines. Let's examine the example below. Each layer of the restricted Boltzmann machine (RBM) in this interconnects with both the layers before it and the layers after it. It implies that the nodes of a single layer will not be able to communicate horizontally. It is obvious that there can only be one visible layer and one hidden layer for each Boltzmann machine.

A belief network is a directed acyclic graph with stochastic variables. A schematic overview of a deep belief net is as shown in the following diagram (Figure 16.25).

There are two types of problems that can be solved by DBN: (1) the inference problem: determining the states of unobserved variables; and (2) the learning problem: modifying the interactions between variables so that the network is more likely to produce the observed data.

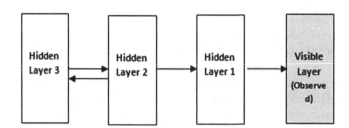

FIGURE 16.25
Schematic overview of a DBN.

16.9.1 Creation of a Deep Belief Network

Each record type includes the restricted Boltzmann machines (RBMs) that compose the layers of the network, the vector representing the size of the layers or the number of classes that are included in the representative data set in the case of classification DBN.

The DBN record merely reflects a model that is comprised of stacked RBMs. Because of this, it is possible to train the top layer to generate class labels corresponding to the input data vector as well as to classify data vectors that have not yet been entered.

Learning a deep belief network (DBN) is made significantly easier by the fact that it is constructed up of RBMs that are taught in an unsupervised fashion. The amount of time spent on RBM training accounts for the vast majority of the total time spent on DBN training.

During the training session the bottom layer is trained first. Then propagation of the data set happens through learned RBM. At last, the newly transformed data set is used as the training data for the next RBM. CDBNs, which stands for convolutional deep belief networks, need the observation labels to be available during the training of the top layer.

The training session continues until the data set has been propagated through the last but one trained RBM. The altered data set is created after this point by concatenating the labels generated so far, and the top-layer associative memory will be trained using the altered dataset.

16.9.2 Benefits and Drawbacks of Deep Belief Networks

16.9.2.1 Benefits

Utilizing hidden layers in a productive manner is easy with DBN (higher performance gain by adding layers compared to multilayer perceptron). DBN has a particular strength in classification resilience (size, position, color, view angle—rotation). The neural network approach developed by DBN can be applied to a variety of different applications and kinds of data. DBN continues to produce the greatest performance results despite the enormous volume of data being processed. DBN's features are routinely gathered, and their settings are fine-tuned to provide the best possible results. DBN avoids time taking procedures.

16.9.2.2 Drawbacks

There are certain hardware requirements for DBN, and DBN demands vast data to conduct better approaches. Because of its intricate data models, DBN requires a significant investment to train. There must be hundreds of different machines. Classifiers are necessary for DBN in order to comprehend the output.

16.9.2.3 Applications of DBN

DBN is widely used for object detection. The DBN is able to identify occurrences of specific classes of things. Image creation is another application for DBN. DBN is also used commonly for image classification. DBN also detects video. It is able to capture motion. DBN is capable of understanding natural language, also known as speech processing, in order to provide a complete description. DBN estimates human poses. DBN is utilised extensively throughout data sets.

16.10 Applications

16.10.1 Deep Learning for Vision

Computer vision is a subfield of machine learning concerned with the interpretation and comprehension of images and videos. It helps computers to view and perform visual tasks similar to human beings. Computer vision models translate visual data into contextful features which allow models to evaluate images and videos. Such interpretations are then used for decision-making tasks. In computer vision, deep learning approaches are delivering on their promise. Computer vision is not "solved," but deep learning is required to solve many difficult challenges in the field at the cutting edge. Let's have a look at three instances to illustrate the results that deep learning may achieve in the field of computer vision:

1. **Automatic object detection**: Object detection is the process of locating and classifying objects in images and video. In object detection, given a snapshot of a scene to a system, it must locate, draw a bounding box around, and classify each object. In this context we'll use a vehicle detection example and understand how to use deep learning to create an object detector. The same steps can be used to create any object detector.

   Step 1: For vehicle detection, first we need a set of labelled training data, which is a collection of photos with the locations and labels of items of interest. Specifically, someone must examine each image or video frame and mark the positions of any things of interest. This method is referred to as ground truth labelling. Labelling the ground truth is frequently the most time-consuming aspect of developing an item detector.

   Step 2: Training the vehicle detector using R-CNN network

   (i) Define a network architecture using any tool/software platform that supports deep learning.

   (ii) Examine parts of an image using R-CNN algorithm.

   Step 3: After training, test the vehicle detector using a few test images to see if the detector is working properly.

   Step 4: Once the vehicle detector is working properly, again test using large set of validation images using various statistical metrics.

Sample deep learning architectures for computer vision:

AlexNet: The AlexNet (2012) is a type of convolutional neural network (CNN). It was created by Alex Krizhevsky, Ilya Sutskever, and Krizhevsky's Ph.D. advisor, Geoffrey Hinton. The AlexNet architecture has five convolution layers and three layers that are fully connected (Figure 16.26).

AlexNet has a structure with two pipelines so that it can use two GPUs during training. Traditional neural networks used sigmoid or Tanh activation functions, but AlexNet uses rectified linear units (ReLU) instead. ReLU is easier to understand and faster to compute, which lets AlexNet train models more quickly. AlexNet is one of the most important papers ever written about computer vision.

GoogleNet: Google researchers came up with the idea for GoogleNet (or Inception V1) in 2014 in a paper called "Going Deeper with Convolutions." GoogleNet was the winner of the ILSVRC 2014 image classification challenge and projected a much lower error rate than previous winner AlexNet (ILSVRC 2012 Winner) (Figure 16.27).

GoogleNet is made up of 22 layers, which are known as inception modules. By using batch normalisation and RMSprop, these inception modules cut down on the number of parameters that GoogleNet has to process. The adaptive learning rate methods are used by the RMSprop algorithm.

2. **Automatic object recognition**: A computer vision technology called object recognition helps identify items in pictures and movies. One of the main results of deep learning and machine learning algorithms is object recognition. The objective is to train a computer to perform something that comes effortlessly to people: grasp what an image conveys. Driverless automobiles use object recognition as a fundamental technology to identify a stop sign (Cireşan et al. 2012) or tell a pedestrian from a lamppost. It is also helpful in many different applications, including robotic vision, industrial inspection, and illness identification in bio imaging.

The use of deep learning algorithms to recognise objects has grown in popularity. Convolutional neural networks are used to automatically learn an object's inborn properties in order to identify that object. For instance, a CNN can study thousands of training images and learn the characteristics that distinguish cats from dogs in order to distinguish between the two species.

When utilising deep learning to accomplish object recognition, there are two methods:

Method 1 —Model construction from scratch: To construct a deep network from scratch, you must collect a sizable labelled data set and design a network architecture that will enable the learning of the features. Although this method can produce amazing results, a lot of training data is needed, and you must configure the CNN's layers and weights.

Method 2 —Making use of a pretrained deep learning model: The majority of deep learning applications employ the transfer learning method, which entails modifying a pretrained model. Starting with an established network like AlexNet or GoogleNet, new data with unforeseen classifications is fed into the system. The model has already been trained on thousands or millions of photos, making this process less time-consuming and perhaps more effective.

Although deep learning is highly accurate, it needs a lot of data to generate reliable predictions.

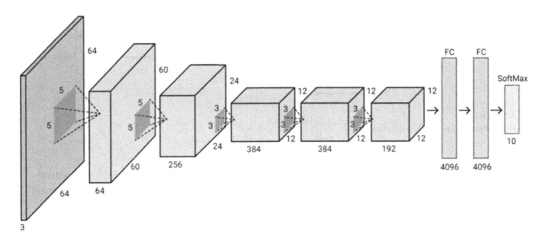

FIGURE 16.26
AlexNet architecture.

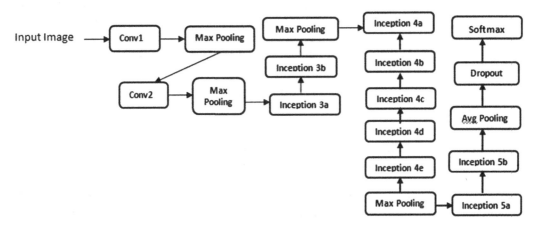

FIGURE 16.27
GoogleNet architecture.

3. **Automatic image and video classification**: Given a photograph of an object or video, image/video classification is the task of classifying the photograph/video into one or more predetermined categories.

Combining a model that has been pretrained for image classification with an LSTM network is shown as an example of how to develop a network for the classification of videos in the following example.

To develop a network based on deep learning for the classification of videos, follow the given steps:

Step 1: Extract features from each frame of a video by utilising a pretrained convolutional neural network, such as GoogleNet, and converting the video into a sequence of feature vectors.

Step 2: Teach an LSTM network to predict the video labels using the sequences as training data.

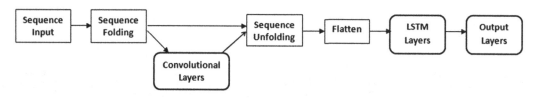

FIGURE 16.28
The structure of the LSTM network.

> **Step 3:** Construct a network as shown in Figure 16.28 that is capable of imme-
> diately classifying videos by integrating layers from the two existing
> networks.

In the previous figure, a sequence input layer is used to input image sequences to the
network. Features are extracted by using convolutional layers to extract features, that is,
to apply the convolutional operations to each frame of the videos. Independently, use a
sequence folding layer followed by the convolutional layers. This will allow you to apply
the convolutional operations to each frame of the videos separately. A sequence unfold-
ing layer in conjunction with a flatten layer is used in order to re-establish the sequence's
original structure and reformat the results as vector sequences. LSTM layers followed by
output layers are used to classify the resulting vector sequences.

16.10.2 Deep Learning for Drug Discovery

Deep learning has made great progress in numerous fields of artificial intelligence research
over the past decade. This technique, which evolved from prior research on artificial neural networks, outperforms other machine learning algorithms in areas such as image and
speech recognition, natural language processing, and others. In recent years, the initial
phase of applications of deep learning in pharmaceutical research has arisen, and its utility has expanded beyond bioactivity predictions to address a variety of difficulties in drug
discovery.

Recently, numerous articles have been published on the use of deep learning in drug
discovery in the following areas of drug research:

1. Application of deep learning in compound representation and activity prediction: Fully connected DNNs are used to build models for compounds which
   are presented by the same number of molecular descriptors. DNN models have
   won the Tox21 challenge on a data set comprising 12 000 compounds for 12 high-
   throughput toxicity analyses. Also a variant of RNN, called UGRNN, was used for
   transforming molecular structures into vectors of the same length as the molecular
   representation and then passes them to a fully connected NN layer to build predictive solubility models that were comparable in accuracy to models built with
   molecular descriptors. The same model was also applied to model drug-induced
   liver injury (DILI). The deep learning models were built based on 475 drugs and
   validated on an external data set of 198 drugs.

   Graph convolution models, which employs NNs, were utilized to automatically generate a molecular description vector, and vector values are learned by
   training NNs. Finally a neural fingerprint encoding information at the molecular

level is learned during the training. Recently, Google researchers rebuilt multiple existing graph convolution methods into a framework known as a message passing neural network (MPNN) and utilised MPNNs to predict quantum chemical characteristics.

Deep learning methods based on other types of molecular representations like SMILES string as the input to LSTM RNNs to build predictive models, and CNN on images of 2D drawings of molecules, were also explored in this field of research.

2. Generation of new chemical structures using deep learning: Another interesting application of deep learning in chemo informatics is the generation of new chemical structures through NNs. A variational auto-encoder (VAE) has been used for the following: (i) to generate chemical structures, (ii) as a molecular descriptor generator coupled with a GAN to generate new structures that were claimed to have promising specific anticancer properties, (iii) to generate novel structures with predicted activity against dopamine receptor type 2.

RNNs also have been very successful to generate novel chemical structures. After training the RNN on a large number of SMILES strings, the RNN method worked surprisingly well for generating new valid SMILES strings that were not included in the training set. Reinforcement learning technology, called deep Q-learning, together with an RNN has been used to generate SMILES with desirable molecular properties. Also a policy-based reinforcement learning approach to tune the pretrained RNNs for generating molecules with given user-defined properties were also attempted in this research.

3. Application of deep learning in biological imaging analysis: Biological imaging and image analysis are used from preclinical R&D to clinical trials in medication discovery. Imaging lets scientists see hosts' (human or animal), organs, tissues, cells, and subcellular components' phenotypes and behaviours. Digital picture analysis reveals underlying biology, disease, and drug activity. Fluorescently labelled or unlabelled microscopic pictures, CT, MRI, PET, tissue pathology imaging, and mass-spectrometry imaging are imaging modalities (MSIs). DL has also found success in biological image analysis, where it outperforms standard classifiers.

For microscopic images, CNNs have been used for segmenting and subtyping individual fluorescently labelled cells, cell tracking, and colony counting. DL identifies tumour areas, leukocytes, and fat tissue. DL is also utilised for histopathology diagnosis beyond picture segmentation.

16.10.3 Deep Learning for Business and Social Network Analytics

In the field of data mining, social network analysis is an important problem. A key part of analysing social networks is encoding network data into low-dimensional representations, called network embeddings, so that the structure of the network and other information can be kept. Network representation learning makes it easier to do things like classify, predict links, find outliers, and group things together. In the past few years, there has been a lot of interest in techniques that are based on deep neural networks, which can be broadly fitted under the following headings:

- **Opinion analysis**: An opinion is a point of view or a statement that may or may not be backed up by facts. Deep learning has been used a lot to sort real and fake content in social media conversations by looking at the semantics of the content.

RNN has been used a lot to model how users interact in social networks by taking text from news and discussions and using temporal properties and influence to model how that text changes over time. Deep learning techniques are used in a framework called DeepInf to find hidden features and analyse social influence. CNN looks at the structure of social networks like Twitter, Open Academic Graph, Digg, and Weibo as well as the features that are unique to each user. In the history of social network research, ontology-based restricted Boltzmann machine (ORBM) models can be used to predict how people will act on online social networks.

- **Sentiment analysis**: A sentiment is a feeling, thought, idea, or opinion that has to do with how a person feels. People's opinions and, as a result, how they feel about a thing or event are affected by social networks in a big way. Text or pictures can both be used to show how someone feels.

  Deep feed forward neural networks, LSTM-RNN, and CNNs are often used to figure out how people feel about trailer comments on YouTube. DL can also be used to analyse how investors feel about stock prices by making use of a model to predict stock prices. Stock market indicators can be analysed using CNN and LSTM for predicting the sentiments of the investors. Many works that combines semantic and emotional features extracted from user generated texts in social media to detect personality using deep learning techniques are attempted in social network analysis research. Other deep learning models like a multiview deep network (MVDN), matrix-interactive attention network (M-IAN), and deep interactive memory network (DIMN) models are used to find interactions of context and target opinion.

- **Text classification**: Capsule network (CapsNet) built using ANN and a gated recurrent unit (GRU) are types of deep learning techniques used for modelling categorised relationships and classifying social text. Other forms of DL based architecture like multitask CNN (mtCNN) and reliable social recommendations using generative adversarial network (RSGAN) frameworks are used for learning from user profiles from social media data. RNN-based deep-learning sentiment analysis (RDSA) algorithm is used for recommendation of nearest spots like streets, shops, hospitals, and so on, which are in the neighbourhood to a user. Also a framework called Friendship using Deep Pairwise Learning (FDPL) based on contextual information and deep pairwise learning based on Bayesian ranking scheme are used for recommending friends based on the geospecific activities of users.

- **Community detection**: An application of social network analysis is community detection. A deep integration representation (DIR) algorithm based on deep joint reconstruction (DJR) has been used to detect events in network communities. A deep multiple network fusion (DMNF) model is used to extract latent structures such as social communities and group the online social network (OSN) data. User roles based on interactions and influences in OSNs are detected using deep RNNs.

- **Anomaly detection**: Anomaly detection in social networks is identifying irregular/malicious behaviour of users/transactions/events/etc. in a social network. Examples for anomalies in social networks can be spams, activities pertaining to terrorist networks, cyber bullying, and so on.

  Deep Friend, used for classification of malicious nodes in an OSN and presented in Wanda and Jie (2021) uses dynamic deep learning. A multitask learning (MTL) framework based on deep neural networks is used for hate speech detection. A deep probabilistic learning method is deployed widely to detect covert networks and fraudsters from fake social network applications. A deep reinforcement-based learning framework is used to generate privacy labels for OSN users.

Various other deep neural frameworks like active learning-based bot detection (DABot) which is a combination of residual network (ResNet), bidirectional gated recurrent unit (BiGRU), and attention mechanism (RGA) models is used for detecting bots from social networks.

- **Fake news detection**: Detection of fake news articles using word embedding techniques and CNNs, reinforcement learning-based ensemble model for rumour tracking (RL-ERT), and ensemble graph convolutional neural network (EGCN) model for rumour detection and tracking are some of the models available in the area of fake news detection. Bidirectional LSTM and a deep learning scheme called RumorSleuth are used for identifying both user stances and veracity of a rumour.

16.11 Summary

- Recurrent neural networks (RNNs) are a type of neural network. They utilise a hidden layer, which retains some information about a sequence. The hidden state is the primary and most significant characteristic of RNNs.
- The long short-term memory network (LSTM) is a type of recurrent neural network. LSTM tries to "forget" unnecessary material while attempting to "remember" all of the previous information that the network has encountered.
- The RBNN architecture has an input, a hidden, and an output layer. A minimum of three layers of nodes are required for the construction of an MLP. Training in MLP is accomplished through the use of a supervised learning method known as backpropagation.
- A self-organizing map (SOM) is an unsupervised machine learning technique. SOM was first proposed by Teuvo Kohonen in the 1980s. It is a special kind of artificial neural network that is trained using a process called competitive learning.
- Deep belief networks (DBNs) are deep layers of random and generative neural networks. DBNs were first presented as probabilistic generative models in 2007 by Larochelle, Erhan, Courville, Bergstra, and Bengio.
- Finally, applications involving various deep learning models have been discussed.

16.12 Points to Ponder

- Hidden state, which retains some information about a sequence, is the most significant characteristic of recurrent neural network (RNN)s.
- Vanishing gradients result in unstable behaviour where the gradients may have very small values tending towards zero.
- In auto encoders, a bottleneck is imposed, which forces a compressed knowledge representation of the original input.

- A long short-term memory network (LSTM) tries to "forget" unnecessary material while still retaining previous information.
- Generative adversarial networks (GAN) were initially conceived of as a sort of generative model that could be used for unsupervised learning.
- While the discriminative network assesses the candidates, the generative network comes up with new potential candidates.
- We can easily interpret the meaning and function of each node in a hidden layer of the radial basis neural network (RBNN).
- A self-organizing map (SOM) is used to construct a low-dimensional representation of a higher dimensional data collection while maintaining the topological structure of the data.
- A restricted Boltzmann machine (RBN) is a network of symmetrically connected neuron-like units that generate stochastic decisions.

E.16 Exercises

E.16.1 Suggested Activities

E.16.1.1   Design and implement a human activity recognition (HAR) using TensorFlow on the Human Activity Recognition Using Smartphones Data Set (https://archive.ics.uci.edu/ml/datasets/human+activity+recognition+using+smartphones) and an LSTM RNN. Here, you need to classify the type of movement among six activity categories, which are walking, walking upstairs, walking downstairs, sitting, standing, and laying. For the input data, you will be using an LSTM on the data to learn (as a cell phone attached on the waist) to recognise the type of activity that the user is doing.

E.16.1.2   Implement an image colorization solution where you color black and white images using GAN. Use the image colorization data set from Kaggle (https://www.kaggle.com/code/shravankumar9892/colorization-dataset/data).

E.16.1.3   Using variation auto encoders, generate fresh data similar to the training data. The MNIST dataset is a good place to start generating numbers: (https://www.kaggle.com/code/ngbolin/mnist-dataset-digit-recognizer/data).

Self-Assessment Questions

E.16.2 Multiple Choice Questions

Give answers with justification for correct and wrong choices.

E.16.2.1   The most significant characteristic of RNNs is
   i   The number of hidden layers
   ii   The hidden state, which retains information about a sequence
   iii   There is no feedback

E.16.2.2   _____ is then backpropagated and used to update the weights.
    i Output
    ii Hidden information
    iii Error

E.16.2.3   The phenomenon that takes place when the gradients keep getting larger, causing the gradient descent to diverge, is called
    i Exploding gradients
    ii Diverging gradients
    iii Vanishing gradients

E.16.2.4   The sort of auto-encoder that works with an input that has been partially corrupted and learns to recover the original, undistorted image from the training data is called a
    i Sparse auto-encoder
    ii De-noising auto-encoder
    iii Variational auto-encoder

E.16.2.5   A variational auto-encoder employs _____ for the training process.
    i Stochastic gradient variational Bayes estimator
    ii Back propagation
    iii Gibbs distribution

E.16.2.6   The gate that is responsible for determining the amount of information that will be written into the internal cell state is
    i Forget gate
    ii Input gate
    iii Input modulation gate

E.16.2.7   Deciding the number of nodes in hidden layer and the number of hidden layers is not required in
    i Convolutional neural networks
    ii Multilayer perceptron
    iii Radial basis neural network

E.16.2.8   Self-organizing maps are also called
    i Radial basis maps
    ii Self-arranging maps
    iii Kohonen maps

E.16.2.9   A neural network in which each neuron is linked to each and every other neuron in the network is called a
    i Radial basis neural network
    ii Restricted Boltzmann machines
    iii Recurrent neural network

E.16.2.10   The inference problem and learning problem are solved by a
    i Deep belief network
    ii Long short-term memory network
    iii Recurrent neural network

E.16.2.11 _____ is a Markov chain Monte Carlo approach for getting a sequence of observations approximating a defined multivariate probability distribution.
  i Gaussian sampling
  ii Gibbs sampling
  iii Boltzmann sampling

E.16.2.12 _____ is an approximation maximum-likelihood learning approach used to approximate the gradient, which is the graphical slope depicting the link between a network's weights and its error.
  i Contrastive divergence
  ii Exploding divergence
  iii Contrastive convergence

E.16.3 Match the Columns

No	Match	
E.16.3.1 Recurrent neural networks	A	Recurrent unit that works to forget unnecessary material while attempting to remember all of the previous information that the network has encountered
E.16.3.2 Multilayer perceptron	B	Used to simulate data that exhibits any trend or function
E.16.3.3 Self-organizing map	C	Find intrinsic data patterns by reconstructing input
E.16.3.4 De-noising auto-encoder	D	Handle sequential data and memorize previous inputs using its memory
E.16.3.5 GoogleNet	E	Produces new data which is statistically similar to the input training data
E.16.3.6 Generative adversarial networks	F	Enables approximate solutions to exceedingly difficult problems such as fitness approximation
E.16.3.7 Deep belief networks	G	Construct a low-dimensional representation of a higher dimensional data collection while maintaining the topological structure of the data
E.16.3.8 Long short-term memory network	H	Works with an input that has been partially corrupted and learns to recover the original, undistorted image from the training data
E.16.3.9 Radial basis function neural network	I	Overcome the slow learning, local minima pitfalls in typical neural networks
E.16.3.10 Restricted Boltzmann machine	J	Image classification with much lower error rate

E.16.4 Short Questions

E.16.4.1 Explain how we say that RNNs have a memory.

E.16.4.2 Give how current state, activation function, and output are defined with respect to RNNs.

E.16.4.3 Discuss some advantages and disadvantages of RNN.

E.16.4.4 Explain the working of each recurrent unit of RNN.

E.16.4.5 Describe the three types of auto-encoders.

E.16.4.6 List the steps of training of an auto-encoder for a data compression scenario.

E.16.4.7   Describe the different ways in which auto-encoders can be constrained.

E.16.4.8   Explain the functions performed by the four gates of a LSTM.

E.16.4.9   Discuss the concept of GANs.

E.16.4.10 Describe the training of RBNN.

E.16.4.11 Compare and contrast RBNN and MLP.

E.16.4.12 Explain the working of SOM.

E.16.4.13 What are the important characteristics of RBM.

E.16.4.14 Discuss some advantages and disadvantages of deep neural networks.

E.16.4.15 Explain in detail how deep learning is used in object detection.

E.16.4.16 Discuss the various areas of drug discovery where deep learning has been used.

E.16.4.17 Outline some applications in social network analysis where deep learning can be used.

References

Cireşan, D., Meier, U., & Schmidhuber, J. (2012, June). Multi-column deep neural networks for image classification. *2012 IEEE Conference on Computer Vision and Pattern Recognition*. New York, NY: Institute of Electrical and Electronics Engineers (IEEE), 3642–3649.

Larochelle, H., Erhan, D., Courville, A., Bergstra, J., & Bengio, Y. (2007, June). An empirical evaluation of deep architectures on problems with many factors of variation. *Proceedings of the 24th International Conference on Machine Learning*, 473–480. https://doi.org/10.1145/1273496.1273556

Wanda, P., & Jie, H. J. (2021). DeepFriend: Finding abnormal nodes in online social networks using dynamic deep learning. *Social Network Analysis and Mining*, 11, 34. https://doi.org/10.1007/s13278-021-00742-2

A1. Solutions

Chapter – 1

Question No.	Answers
E.1.2	
E.1.2.1	iii
E.1.2.2	iii
E.1.2.3	i
E.1.2.4	ii
E.1.3	
E.1.3.1	B
E.1.3.2	A
E.1.3.3	D
E.1.3.4	C

E.1.4

Correct Order

E.1.4.5

E.1.4.9

E.1.4.7

E.1.4.10

E.1.4.1

E.1.4.2

E.1.4.6

E.1.4.8

E.1.4.4

E.1.4.3

Chapter – 2

Question No.	Answer
E.2.2	
E.2.2.1	i
E.2.2.2	iii
E.2.2.3	ii

Question No.	Answer
E.2.2.4	iii
E.2.2.5	i
E.2.2.6	ii
E.2.2.7	i
E.2.3	
E.2.3.1	D
E.2.3.2	J
E.2.3.3	A
E.2.3.4	I
E.2.3.5	B
E.2.3.6	H
E.2.3.7	G
E.2.3.8	E
E.2.3.9	C
E.2.3.10	F

Chapter – 3

Question No.	Answer
E.3.2	
E.3.2.1	ii
E.3.2.2	i
E.3.2.3	i
E.3.2.4	iii
E.3.2.5	ii
E.3.2.6	iii
E.3.2.7	iii
E.3.2.8	i
E.3.2.9	ii
E.3.2.10	i
E.3.2.11	ii
E.3.2.12	i
E.3.2.13	iii
E.3.2.14	ii
E.3.2.15	iii
E.3.2.16	ii
E.3.2.17	ii
E.3.2.18	i
E.3.2.19	iii
E.3.2.20	ii
E.3.2.21	iii
E.3.3	
E.3.3.1	E
E.3.3.2	J

Question No.	Answer
E.3.3.3	D
E.3.3.4	H
E.3.3.5	G
E.3.3.6	B
E.3.3.7	C
E.3.3.8	F
E.3.3.9	A
E.3.3.10	I
E.3.4	
E.3.4.1	7/8
E.3.4.2	9/13
E.3.4.3	5/9
E.3.4.4	0.00379
E.3.4.5	0.56
E.3.4.6	a) 0.016
	b) 0.384
	c) 0.018
	d) 0.582
E.3.4.7	0.144
E.3.4.8	a) 0.5263
	b) 0.4735
E.3.4.9	91.28%
E.3.4.10	0.5556

Chapter – 4

Question No.	Answers
E.4.2	
E.4.2.1	ii
E.4.2.2	iii
E.4.2.3	iii
E.4.2.4	i
E.4.2.5	iii
E.4.2.6	i
E.4.2.7	ii
E.4.2.8	i
E.4.2.9	iii
E.4.2.10	i
E.4.2.11	iii
E.4.2.12	ii
E.4.2.13	iii
E.4.2.14	i
E.4.2.15	ii
E.4.2.16	i

Question No.	Answers
E.4.2.17	iii
E.4.2.18	ii
E.4.2.19	i
E.4.2.20	ii
E.4.3	
E.4.3.1	D
E.4.3.2	J
E.4.3.3	F
E.4.3.4	G
E.4.3.5	A
E.4.3.6	H
E.4.3.7	C
E.4.3.8	I
E.4.3.9	E
E.4.3.10	B

Chapter – 5

Question No.	Answer
E.5.2	
E.5.2.1	i
E.5.2.2	ii
E.5.2.3	iii
E.5.2.4	ii
E.5.2.5	ii
E.5.2.6	iii
E.5.2.7	i
E.5.2.8	iii
E.5.2.9	i
E.5.2.10	ii
E.5.3	
E.5.3.1	I
E.5.3.2	C
E.5.3.3	A
E.5.3.4	E
E.5.3.5	B
E.5.3.6	D
E.5.3.7	J
E.5.3.8	F
E.5.3.9	G
E.5.3.10	H

Chapter – 6

Question No.	Answer
E.6.3	
E.6.3.1	ii
E.6.3.2	i
E.6.3.3	iii
E.6.3.4	ii
E.6.3.5	i
E.6.3.6	iii
E.6.3.7	i
E.6.3.8	ii
E.6.3.9	iii
E.6.3.10	i
E.6.3.11	ii
E.6.3.12	i
E.6.3.13	iii
E.6.3.14	ii
E.6.4	
E.6.4.1	E
E.6.4.2	H
E.6.4.3	J
E.6.4.4	A
E.6.4.5	F
E.6.4.6	G
E.6.4.7	I
E.6.4.8	D
E.6.4.9	C
E.6.4.10	B

Chapter – 7

Question No.	Answers
E.7.2	
E.7.2.1	iii
E.7.2.2	ii
E.7.2.3	i
E.7.2.4	ii
E.7.2.5	iii
E.7.2.6	i
E.7.2.7	iii
E.7.2.8	i

Question No.	Answers
E.7.2.9	ii
E.7.2.10	iii
E.7.2.11	i
E.7.2.12	ii
E.7.2.13	i
E.7.2.14	ii
E.7.2.15	ii
E.7.2.16	ii
E.7.3	
E.7.3.1	D
E.7.3.2	F
E.7.3.3	J
E.7.3.4	G
E.7.3.5	H
E.7.3.6	E
E.7.3.7	A
E.7.3.8	C
E.7.3.9	B
E.7.3.10	I

Chapter – 8

Question No.	Answer
E.8.2	
E.8.2.1	i
E.8.2.2	ii
E.8.2.3	iii
E.8.2.4	iii
E.8.2.5	i
E.8.2.6	ii
E.8.2.7	i
E.8.2.8	iii
E.8.2.9	ii
E.8.2.10	i
E.8.2.11	ii
E.8.2.12	iii
E.8.3	
E.8.3.1	E
E.8.3.2	J
E.8.3.3	I
E.8.3.4	H
E.8.3.5	A
E.8.3.6	D
E.8.3.7	B

Question No.	Answer
E.8.3.8	F
E.8.3.9	G
E.8.3.10	C

Chapter – 9

Question No.	Answer
E.9.2	
E.9.2.1	ii
E.9.2.2	i
E.9.2.3	iii
E.9.2.4	ii
E.9.2.5	i
E.9.2.6	ii
E.9.2.7	iii
E.9.2.8	ii
E.9.2.9	i
E.9.2.10	iii
E.9.2.11	i
E.9.2.12	ii
E.9.3	
E.9.3.1	C
E.9.3.2	F
E.9.3.3	J
E.9.3.4	A
E.9.3.5	D
E.9.3.6	G
E.9.3.7	B
E.9.3.8	I
E.9.3.9	E
E.9.3.10	H

Chapter – 10

Question No.	Answer
E.10.2	
E.10.2.1	i
E.10.2.2	iii
E.10.2.3	ii
E.10.2.4	iii
E.10.2.5	i

Question No.	Answer
E.10.2.6	ii
E.10.2.7	i
E.10.2.8	iii
E.10.2.9	ii
E.10.2.10	i
E.10.2.11	iii
E.10.2.12	ii
E.10.2.13	i
E.10.2.14	i
E.10.3	
E.10.3.1	D
E.10.3.2	E
E.15.3.3	B
E.10.3.4	J
E.10.3.5	A
E.10.3.6	H
E.10.3.7	G
E.10.3.8	C
E.10.3.9	I
E.10.3.10	F

Question No.		Answer			
E.10.4.1	a				
	b	0.083			
E.10.4.2	a				
	b				
	c				
	d				
E.10.4.3	a	0	0.75	0.2	0.05
		0.05	0.2	0.3	0.45
		0.1	0.4	0.3	0.2
		0	0.15	0.3	0.55
	b	5%, 4%, 4.275%			
E.10.4.4	a				
	b				

Chapter – 11

Question No.	Answer
E.11.2	
E.11.2.1	i
E.11.2.2	iii

Question No.	Answer
E.11.2.3	ii
E.11.2.4	ii
E.11.2.5	i
E.11.2.6	i
E.11.2.7	iii
E.11.2.8	ii
E.11.2.9	ii
E.11.2.10	i
E.11.2.11	iii
E.11.2.12	ii
E.11.2.13	i
E.11.2.14	ii
E.11.2.15	iii
E.11.3	
E.11.3.1	C
E.11.3.2	F
E.11.3.3	I
E.11.3.4	B
E.11.3.5	J
E.11.3.6	E
E.11.3.7	H
E.11.3.8	A
E.11.3.9	G
E.11.3.10	D

Chapter – 12

Question No.	Answer
E.12.2	
E.12.2.1	iii
E.12.2.2	i
E.12.2.3	ii
E.12.2.4	i
E.12.2.5	ii
E.12.2.6	iii
E.12.2.7	ii
E.12.2.8	i
E.12.2.9	ii
E.12.2.10	iii
E.12.2.11	ii
E.12.2.12	ii

Question No.	Answer
E.12.3	
E.12.3.1	E
E.12.3.2	J
E.12.3.3	I
E.12.3.4	B
E.12.3.5	A
E.12.3.6	F
E.12.3.7	C
E.12.3.8	G
E.12.3.9	H
E.12.3.10	D

Chapter – 13

Question No.	Answer
E.13.2	
E.13.2.1	iii
E.13.2.2	ii
E.13.2.3	i
E.13.2.4	i
E.13.2.5	ii
E.13.2.6	iii
E.13.2.7	ii

Chapter – 14

Question No.	Answer
E.14.2	
E.14.2.1	iii
E.14.2.2	i
E.14.2.3	ii
E.14.2.4	i
E.14.2.5	ii
E.14.2.6	iii
E.14.2.7	i
E.14.2.8	i
E.14.2.9	iii
E.14.2.10	ii

Question No.	Answer
E.14.2.11	i
E.14.2.12	ii
E.14.2.13	iii
E.14.2.14	ii
E.14.2.15	i
E.14.2.16	iii
E.14.2.17	iii
E.14.3	
E.14.3.1	J
E.14.3.2	H
E.14.3.3	F
E.14.3.4	A
E.14.3.5	I
E.14.3.6	B
E.14.3.7	E
E.14.3.8	C
E.14.3.9	G
E.14.3.10	D

Chapter – 15

Question No.	Answer
E.15.2	
E.15.2.1	i
E.15.2.2	ii
E.15.2.3	ii
E.15.2.4	iii
E.15.2.5	i
E.15.2.6	iii
E.15.2.7	ii
E.15.2.8	ii
E.15.2.9	iii
E.15.2.10	ii
E.15.2.11	i
E.15.2.12	iii
E.15.2.13	ii
E.15.2.14	i
E.15.2.15	iii
E.15.3	
E.15.3.1	G
E.15.3.2	I
E.15.3.3	D
E.15.3.4	A

Question No.	Answer
E.15.3.5	J
E.15.3.6	H
E.15.3.7	C
E.15.3.8	B
E.15.3.9	E
E.15.3.10	F

Chapter – 16

Question No.	Answer
E.16.2	
E.16.2.1	ii
E.16.2.2	iii
E.16.2.3	i
E.16.2.4	ii
E.16.2.5	i
E.16.2.6	iii
E.16.2.7	iii
E.16.2.8	iii
E.16.2.9	ii
E.16.2.10	i
E.16.2.11	ii
E.16.2.12	i
E.16.3	
E.16.3.1	D
E.16.3.2	F
E.16.3.3	G
E.16.3.4	H
E.16.3.5	J
E.16.3.6	E
E.16.3.7	I
E.16.3.8	A
E.16.3.9	B
E.16.3.10	C

Index

Page numbers in **Bold** indicate tables and page numbers in *italics* indicate figures.

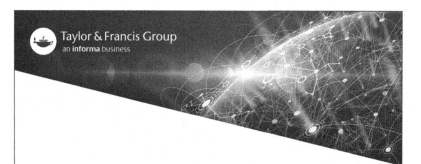

Printed in the United States
by Baker & Taylor Publisher Services